The Witch's Botanical Apothecary
Plants, Potions, and Spells from the English Witch

Copyright © 2024 Pocketbook Company

First Edition

All rights reserved.

Copyright © 2024 Bea St.Clair

All rights reserved.

ISBN: 978-1-916989-07-8

DEDICATION

To Rosy, Isabel, Jess and all the little witches...

"Alone, a witch can stir the winds,
but together we summon the storm"

CONTENTS

	About the Author	5
1	Introduction to Herbal Alchemy	9
2	Setting your Magical Garden	23
3	Essential Tools for the Herbal Alchemist	49
4	Growing Magical Herbs	57
5	My Top 25 Favourite Herbs and Plants	75
6	Creating a Sacred Place	223
7	The Witch's Kitchen	237
8	Silphium	259
9	Witchcraft Essentials	273
10	Potions and Brews	287
11	Introduction to Candles, Smudging and Bath Oils	315
12	Building a Community of Witches	331
13	Making a living as a Witch	337
14	The Apothecary Almanac	343

The information presented in this book is intended for educational and informational purposes only. While it includes details about various herbs, magical spells, and incantations, it does not serve as a substitute for professional advice. The author and publisher strongly recommend consulting with a qualified expert, such as a medical professional, herbalist, or licensed practitioner, before attempting to use any herbs or spells described herein.

All individuals are responsible for their own actions and decisions regarding the use of the information in this book. The author and publisher cannot be held liable for any adverse effects, consequences, or damages resulting from the use or misuse of the information contained in this book. Always exercise caution and conduct thorough research when working with herbs or engaging in magical practices.

By using this book, you acknowledge that you understand these risks and agree to proceed at your own discretion.

About the Author

Hello there, fellow seekers of magic and wisdom! My named is Beatrice (Bea) St. Clair, a dedicated Green Witch with an enduring passion for the mystical properties of herbs and the enchanting world of nature. My journey into witchcraft began in my childhood, amidst the lush landscapes of England, and later flourished within the vibrant, nature-loving community of Portland, USA.

Born and raised in a quaint English village just five minutes' drive, or a leisurely twenty minutes by horse and cart from Chiddingfold in Surrey. Nestled in the rolling countryside, our village is a place where history whispers through the ancient oak trees and standing stones, and every corner holds a touch of enchantment. With its cosy local pubs and a charming village green, it's a haven of tranquillity and tradition.

Our country cottage sits on the site of an old Romano-British garden and vineyard and stands proudly in the middle of the most beautiful English country garden, a haven of magic and tranquillity. By our back door, you'll find upturned wellington boots of every size, ready for the next adventure into the garden. Protective enchantments have kept our home happy and safe for generations. In my country kitchen, you'll find a Golden Retriever lounging in front of the groaning Aga cooker and usually a cat perched on the windowsill, soaking up the sun. Four countertop barrels of tea, each infused with enchantments for Love, Protection, Luck, and Health, sit on the kitchen counter, a testament to our daily magical practices.

This was my parents' house and I miss them dearly, but their strong love and wisdom guide me still. My dad's potting shed is a refuge for me; when I close the door, the familiar musty smells and tools are still there like they have always been, and when I'm in there I know I am wrapped in his love and completely safe. Whatever worries I have I can hear him chuckle in his gravelly voice "don't worry Bee, we'll find a way, we always do!". It may sound strange but when I go for a walk on a Sunday morning, I always start from here and he walks beside me. I sometimes think I get a whiff of his pipe tobacco on the wind.

If the potting shed has the essence of my dad, the kitchen holds the same for my mum. When the window is open, I can sometimes hear her giggling in the garden or talking to the birds, and when I'm cooking and I need guidance for a recipe I only need to look up and she tells me. There are times when the herb I intended to use can't be found no matter how hard I look, yet another stands exactly where the other should be. "yes mum, I'll use that one instead". The garden, the most beautiful I have ever seen, although I am of course, completely biased, is full of magic from the herbs and plants, from the traditions, family, friends, dancing, picnics, children playing, love, and laughter that fill the air. It's a place where the wind swirls the magic around, warmed and sparkling by the sun or sizzling from the light of the moon.

This house and garden has been in our family for as long as we can discover, and so has the magic for hundreds of years. Entering the garden, you can feel the air literally crackle with enchantment if you have a sensitivity to nature or magic. So many people have suddenly stood still, rooted to the spot, the moment they step through the gate as they feel the rush of it swirl around them. Those who recognise what it is look my way and smile, others give a little shiver and then a smile. The garden's power gently nudges you in different directions. It heals, it comforts, it inspires. It's a strong magic palpable to all who visit.

My grandmother, expressive, passionate, forceful I guess you might say, and very, very French if you know what I mean, was a big part of my growing up. She, as a young girl helped her parents as part of the French Resistance and tragically lost them both in a terrible way for a child to see. She has infused our family's practices with resilience and strength. Her *Frenchyness* brought a rich menu of flavours, knowledge, and history to add to our family's magical traditions. She was born in Paris, near the historic Place de Grève, and carried with her the vibrant culture and profound wisdom of French herbalism and magic. The bustling markets and ancient apothecaries of Paris were her training grounds, where she learned to blend the old-world charm with the potent magic of herbs. She met a soldier at the end of the war, my grandfather, who said he could feel her calling him with her spirit before he even first saw her. He picked her up and carried her to safety. She, much younger than he, said she had danced with him before they ever met! Those of you from witchy families will understand that, as we imagine dancing with the man we intend to marry. I will tell you more about them both later in the book, but my granddads mother, my great grandmother, who lived in this house was also a witch, even if she would call it something very different, so it was a marriage of witches' families, which again isn't so unusual.

The French side of our family introduced us to a unique blend of magical and culinary traditions. From delicate pastries infused with protective herbs and flamboyant enchantments to rich stews simmered with healing plants, our family meals have always been a testament to the magical and medicinal properties of food. My grandmother's stories of Paris, filled with the aroma of fresh herbs and the sound of bustling markets, inspired me to incorporate these rich traditions into my own practice.

My true training ground was in Portland, Oregon, where I spent the beginning of my adult life and attended university. I had left England, if I'm honest, wanting nothing more to do with Witchcraft ever again, but it was Portland where I found my own force and really joined my first coven. Portland's lush forests, misty mornings, and vibrant, nature-loving community embraced a quirky confused English girl.

The city's spirit of environmental consciousness and its rich botanical diversity provided the perfect backdrop for me to hone my skills as a witch. It was in here that I learned to see the magic in the mundane, understood it was just as important to connect to people as it is to connect deeply with the earth, and to harness the power of nature in my daily life. I guess I found peace in Portland. It is something a witch, I know now, needs to find for herself. I also made life-long friends.

Life came full circle when I returned to my roots in England, in personally very sad circumstances, to take care of my late parents' affairs. The first morning back I met "the gardener" who my parents had hired to help them whilst I had been away. I walked up to him while he was re-planting some giant Fennell and, only 2 minutes into our conversation, I immediately fell head over heels, hard in love, and got married 6 months later. At first I suspected my mum of conjuring up some magic to keep me here and look after her garden, I wouldn't have put interfering past her, which was why I had fallen out with witchcraft in the first place, but even if it was true and she had found The Gardener and cast a love spell, it has brought me love, passion, children, peace, purpose, and the greatest happiness I could ever imagine. So if her spell was to give all of this to me, I'll take that gift now gratefully and I thank her every day. I wish I had told her so while she was alive. Settling back in my beloved village, I found solace in our family home and its magical garden. Here, surrounded by the familiar sights and sounds of my childhood, I continue to explore and expand my craft.

My journey is enriched by the presence of "The Gardener", who shares my deep love for the environment. Although he does not come from a witchy background he had worked for my parents towards the end of their lives and he knew, or at least suspected, they were either witches or just very odd, or both. His knowledge of local plant names rather than their scientific ones has profoundly influenced our magical practice. I have learnt that using the local name makes all my magic stronger. From the delicate "Lady's Mantle" to the vibrant "Bouncing Bet" and the protective "Thousand Fingers" his understanding of local flora has added a unique dimension to our herbology. His passion for preserving nature and his knowledge of plant lore blend seamlessly with my magical traditions, creating a happy balance between the practical and the mystical. He is so perfect he could have been chosen for me! (Mum!)

Balancing my roles as a part-time journalist for a local paper and a full-time mum to three wonderful children—two daughters and one son—I weave magic into every aspect of my life. Together, we are committed to creating a nurturing and enchanted environment for our family.

I also share my herbal creations with the world, selling herbs, baked goods, potions, and spells, and blogging about my magical experiences, success and monumental failures. I make money from my witchcraft which some find strange, but witches have always had good heads for business. We may not exchange a potion for a rabbit anymore, although actually I have, but through the ages we have provided potions, spells, enchantments, helped some fall in love, kept other safe, all for the coin. My work is a blend of old and new, combining ancient traditions with modern practices to create something I hope is uniquely powerful. "The Witch's Botanical Apothecary" is a tale of my life's journey—a testament to the magic that surrounds us all, waiting to be discovered and harnessed. Join me on this enchanting path and let's explore the transformative power of plants, potions, and spells together. With Love and Magic.

"Wita and frodnes is reccend weoruld, witan we and feorhfruma."

"Wisdom and knowledge govern the world, we must know and cherish them"

Chapter 1: Introduction to Herbal Alchemy

Welcome to the world of Herbal Alchemy, where plants and magic come together in a way that's surprisingly down-to-earth. Now, I know that sounds a bit dramatic but stick with me. Over the years, I've spent more time than I care to admit growing herbs, crafting spells, and brewing up concoctions straight from my garden. It's become a bit of a way of life for me, and in this section, I'll be walking you through why herbal alchemy is so important in modern witchcraft, how it all started, and how it slots into the everyday practices of today's witches.

Herbal alchemy is really at the heart of everything I do. It's not just about grabbing a handful of herbs and calling it magic; it's about building a real connection with the natural world. Each plant I grow feels like it has its own personality, its own story to tell. And when I'm working with them, whether I'm making a potion or putting together a ritual, I'm tapping into that energy. It's like working in partnership with the earth.

There's something deeply grounding about it all. From planting the seeds to watching them grow, and finally harvesting the herbs, the whole process is almost like meditation. It brings me back to basics, reminds me of the cycles we're all a part of. For modern witches, herbal alchemy is a practical way to create change, heal, and grow, both spiritually and literally. It's as much about the journey and the relationship with the plants as it is about the final product.

Using herbs in magic is hardly a new thing. Humans have been at it for as long as we've existed. Our ancestors knew the power of plants, they used them to heal, protect, and influence their surroundings. The idea of turning plants into magical tools isn't some modern invention. It goes back to ancient cultures, right through to medieval Europe where wise women and shamans knew the secrets of the earth. These early practitioners understood each plant's energy and how to use it for a specific purpose. Even during times when this knowledge was persecuted, it was quietly passed down through generations, my own included.

Then came the Middle Ages, and along with it, the alchemists. These were the people who blended early science with the mystical, believing that plants had unique energies that could be transformed with intention. This mix of science and spirituality paved the way for what we now call herbal alchemy.

These days, herbal alchemy is woven into modern witchcraft in all sorts of ways. Witches, whether they're living in a tiny flat in the city or in a countryside cottage, find ways to bring herbs into their magical practices. It's not just about old traditions; today's witches take the knowledge of herbs and mix it with new-age ideas to create a practice that's personal and ever-changing.

From growing and picking herbs to making potions, teas, and spell ingredients, herbal alchemy covers a lot of ground. Some witches, including me, still align their gardening with the phases of the moon or use companion planting to give their herbs an extra boost. And let's not forget how herbs have made their way into self-care. Many witches now make their own herbal teas, bath soaks, and skincare products, blending magic with well-being.

In this book, we're going to dig into all of this. We'll look at where herbal alchemy came from, it's place in botanical apothecary, how it's evolved, and how you can use it in your own life. Whether you're new to it or looking to deepen your practice, you'll learn how to tap into the power of plants in ways that are both magical and practical.

An Overview of Herbal Alchemy: Its Definition and Significance in Modern Witchcraft

Herbal alchemy is such an ancient, beautiful practice. At its core, it's about more than just knowing which plants to grow or what herbs to use in a potion. It's about connecting deeply with nature and learning how to work with plants in a way that honours their magical and medicinal properties. Alchemy, in the old days, was all about transformation, turning base metals into gold, but on a deeper level it's also about personal transformation. When you bring herbs into that mix, it's about unlocking the hidden potential within the plants to heal, protect, and empower.

For me, herbal alchemy isn't just following a recipe; it's about understanding the life cycle of the plant, the energy it absorbs from its surroundings, and how we can tap into that energy. It's building a relationship with nature, where respect, care, and knowledge are key. And honestly, in a world where technology constantly pulls us away from the earth, herbal alchemy feels like a way to reconnect with something real and ancient. It's grounding.

And I've found there's such empowerment in knowing how to grow and use herbs. When I brew chamomile tea to calm my nerves or burn rosemary for protection, I feel like I'm taking control of my own well-being. It's empowering to have this knowledge, to feel that I can rely on what I've grown rather than on something mass-produced. It's about self-sufficiency, confidence, and deep respect for the gifts the earth provides.

The healing side of herbal alchemy is something I hold close. Lavender for anxiety, peppermint for headaches. There's something special about knowing that these remedies come straight from the garden, from the earth itself. It blends practicality and magic in the most natural way.

In today's world, sustainability is more important than ever. By growing my own herbs, I've become more mindful about what I use and how I care for the environment. It feels good knowing that I'm doing my small part for the planet, and it's rewarding to see how the ancient practice of herbal alchemy fits perfectly with living more consciously. There's something so satisfying in that. Plus, I love the idea that by practicing herbal alchemy, I'm keeping alive the traditions of my ancestors, those who relied on plants not just for medicine, but for spiritual and magical purposes too.

When I first started on this path, I'll admit it was a little overwhelming. There was so much to learn, and it felt like I could get lost in all the books, websites, and advice from more experienced practitioners. But what truly guided me? My garden. I learned by watching the plants themselves. Take lavender, for example, one of my favourite plants, but it didn't come easily. It took me seasons of trial and error to figure out how to grow it from seed. But now, lavender is a staple in my spells and remedies, and it holds a special place in my practice because of the patience and persistence it took to nurture it.

And then there's the moon. It's such a powerful force in the world, and in herbal alchemy, it's no different. Planting and harvesting by the phases of the moon has become an essential part of how I work with my herbs. Sometimes people look at me weirdly when I say I plant by the phases of the moon, yet the moon's pull influences everything on our planet from the tides to plant growth, and aligning with that rhythm adds an extra layer of magic to my practice. For instance, seeds represent potential and new beginnings, so planting during the waxing moon feels right when I want to encourage growth or change. I've seen how even the tiniest details, like timing my harvests with the moon's cycle, can make a huge difference in the potency of my herbs. If I haven't convinced you yet, please bear with me; perhaps I will by the end of the book.

Herbal alchemy isn't just something I do in the garden, though, it's woven into my daily life. Every time I make tea or craft a remedy, I'm drawing on the magic of the plants. Chamomile, peppermint, ginger, each cup I brew is a small ritual, a way to connect with the energies of the herbs and use their healing properties. Even something as simple as crafting a lavender syrup to soothe a sore throat feels like a moment of magic.

Crafting potions and remedies has also become a big part of my practice. One of my favourites is a lavender and honey syrup I use to calm both the mind and body. It's such a simple thing, but so effective. And when I work with herbs in spellwork, whether it's rosemary for protection or rose petals for love, it feels like I'm tapping into something far greater than myself. Each herb has its own energy, and learning how to combine them has been a journey of discovery and intuition.

Practicing herbal alchemy has truly transformed my life. It's taught me to slow down, to appreciate the small wonders of the natural world, and to trust in the process of growth, both in the garden and in myself. It's empowered me to take control of my health and well-being, using the earth's gifts to heal and nurture. But more than anything, it's deepened my connection to the magic that's all around us, hidden in every leaf, every root, every flower.

One of the most profound aspects of this practice has been building a relationship with the plants themselves. It's a relationship based on mutual respect. I speak to my plants, yes, I do! I thank them for their gifts, nurture them, and in return, they offer me their energies and healing properties. It's a relationship that feels deeply personal.

I've also found a community of like-minded people through these plants and herbs. Whether it's through gardening groups, witchcraft circles, or just sharing knowledge with a friend who shares my passion, there's a sense of continuity in passing down these traditions. Sharing seeds, swapping spells, exchanging experiences, it all keeps the magic alive.

For me, herbal alchemy is a path that combines the wisdom of the past with the magic of the present. It's about reconnecting with the earth, empowering ourselves, and using the natural world to heal both body and spirit. The journey is one of growth and transformation, and it's a privilege to walk this path and share it with others.

Historical Context: The Evolution of Herbal Magic Through the Ages

Herbal magic is something that has intertwined with human existence for millennia. It's this constant, ancient practice that quietly threads through our history, stretching across different cultures and eras. Even now, as a practicing witch, it feels like there's this unavoidable pull, a need to immerse myself in the study of magical herbs and their lore. I've spent years delving into how this magic has evolved and how it continues to influence us today. And the deeper I go, the more I realise that herbal magic is so much more than just a collection of remedies or spells, it's a reflection of how humans have always interacted with the natural world, drawing on its power for both physical and spiritual needs.

Ancient Civilizations and the Dawn of Herbal Magic

The origins of herbal magic are as ancient as humanity itself. Early humans relied on the natural world for their survival, and through observation and experimentation, they discovered the healing and magical properties of plants. These early practices laid the groundwork for the sophisticated systems of herbal magic that would develop in later civilizations.

The ancient Egyptians were among the first to document their use of herbs for both medicinal and magical purposes. The Ebers Papyrus, dating back to around 1550 BCE, is one of the oldest medical texts and contains a wealth of knowledge on herbal remedies. The Egyptians believed that herbs like myrrh, frankincense, and garlic held powerful magical properties and used them in rituals to invoke the gods and protect against evil spirits. The goddess Isis, associated with magic and healing, was often depicted with herbs, highlighting their significance in Egyptian spirituality.

From there, the Greeks and Romans built on that knowledge, developing extensive systems of herbal use that blended the practical with the mystical. Hippocrates, Theophrastus, and Dioscorides all wrote about the healing power of plants, but there was always an underlying sense that herbs could do more than just heal the body—they could guide the spirit, too. Dioscorides' *De Materia Medica*, for example, became one of the most important works on herbal knowledge for centuries, and it influenced generations of healers and herbalists. The Romans, too, placed a high value on the magic of plants. Pliny the Elder's *Natural History* is full of detailed accounts of how the Romans used herbs in every aspect of their lives, from medicine to magical protection, with the god Mercury often associated with both herbalism and alchemy.

As a practicing witch deeply rooted in the lore and cultivation of magical herbs, I've always been fascinated by how different cultures have developed their own rich traditions of herbal magic. The practices of Traditional Chinese Medicine (TCM) and Ayurveda in India are particularly inspiring, each with a history that spans millennia and a holistic approach that resonates deeply with my own beliefs and practices.

My journey into understanding TCM began with my first introduction to the concept of Qi, the vital life force that flows through all living things. This concept was a revelation to me, as it mirrored my own experiences with the energy of plants. TCM seeks to balance the body's Qi through various practices, including herbal medicine, acupuncture, dietary therapy, and exercises like Tai Chi and Qigong.

The foundational text of TCM, the "Huangdi Neijing" or "The Yellow Emperor's Classic of Medicine," dates back to around 300 BCE. This text is a treasure trove of wisdom, detailing the principles of TCM such as the theory of Yin and Yang, the Five Elements, and the importance of maintaining harmony within the body and with the natural world.

One of the most profound insights I've gained from studying TCM is how herbs are classified according to their energetic properties. Each herb's nature (hot, warm, neutral, cool, or cold), taste (pungent, sweet, sour, bitter, or salty), and the specific organs or meridians they affect are meticulously documented. This classification system helps practitioners, like myself, select the appropriate herbs to restore balance and health.

In TCM, herbs are rarely used in isolation. Instead, they are combined into complex formulas or potions that enhance their synergistic effects. These formulas are tailored to the individual, considering their specific condition, constitution, and the underlying imbalances in their Qi. Some well-known Chinese herbal formulas have become staples in my practice which I discuss with clients, but importantly a key principle of witchcraft is the unwavering belief that true magical power arises from the individual's own judgment and free will. Magic can influence free will, that is true, and a lot of spells seek to do that, but the strongest magic cannot be directed, forced, or persuaded by external influences; it must emanate from a deeply personal decision, rooted in one's own intuition and understanding. This autonomy is sacred, for it ensures that the energy and intent behind any spell or ritual are pure and genuinely aligned with the practitioner's will. Among the many types of witches, a Green Witch exemplifies this principle by imparting the power of knowledge. She teaches that wisdom and insight into nature's secrets should only empower an individual when they choose to embrace and apply this knowledge of their own volition, fostering a deeper, more authentic connection with the earth and its energies.

Over the years, I've cultivated a deep appreciation for the herbs used in TCM, many of which have found a permanent place in my garden and practice which I will talk about in detail later.

The mystical aspect of TCM is beautifully exemplified in Taoist alchemy. Taoist alchemists pursued immortality and spiritual enlightenment through the refinement of both internal and external substances. Taoist alchemists believed that the human body could be transformed into an immortal, enlightened state through the refinement of herbs, minerals, and spiritual practices. This concept of transformation resonates with the alchemical principles I apply in my work, where the goal is not just physical healing but spiritual growth and enlightenment.

The rich tradition of Ayurveda in India parallels that of TCM, offering a holistic approach to health and spirituality. Ayurveda, meaning "the science of life," is based on the concept of the three doshas: Vata, Pitta, and Kapha. These doshas represent different combinations of the five elements (earth, water, fire, air, and ether) and govern various physiological and psychological functions in the body.

My exploration of Ayurveda has been a labour of love. The system's goal is to balance the doshas through diet, lifestyle, and herbal treatments, a holistic approach that aligns closely with my own practices. The texts of Ayurveda, such as the "Charaka Samhita" and the "Sushruta Samhita," are filled with detailed descriptions of herbs and their uses, providing a wealth of knowledge that I draw upon regularly.

Ayurveda uses a wide variety of herbs to treat physical and mental imbalances, enhance vitality, and support spiritual growth.

The spiritual dimension of Ayurvedic herbs is deeply integrated into my practice. Sandalwood, for example, is used in meditation and religious ceremonies to calm the mind and promote spiritual insight. Similarly, incense made from herbs like frankincense and myrrh purifies the air and creates a sacred space for spiritual practices.

Ayurvedic practitioners, known as Vaidyas, take a holistic approach to treatment, considering the patient's physical, mental, and spiritual needs. This comprehensive method of healing emphasises the importance of treating the whole person rather than just the symptoms. By incorporating herbal remedies, dietary recommendations, and lifestyle changes, I, like other Green Witches help clients achieve optimal health and well-being.

The rich traditions of herbal magic in China and India have not only influenced their respective cultures but have also intersected and blended with other traditions over time. The Silk Road, for example, facilitated the exchange of herbs, spices, and medical knowledge between East and West. This cultural exchange enriched the herbal practices of both regions, leading to a more diverse and comprehensive understanding of herbal medicine.

Today, the principles and practices of TCM and Ayurveda are increasingly recognised and integrated into Western medicine. Many healthcare practitioners and Witches, including myself, incorporate these ancient traditions into their treatment plans, offering patients a holistic approach to health that combines the best of both worlds.

Herbal magic has always been a fascinating thread running through human history, evolving alongside us as we've grown and changed. The more I learn, the more I realise how these ancient traditions continue to shape us today. In medieval times, herbal magic wasn't just about remedies for physical ailments; it was about something deeper, a blending of nature's gifts with spiritual wisdom. Back then, wise women, healers, and learned folk were the keepers of this knowledge, using their understanding of herbs to help their communities. They drew on a mix of folklore, early medicine, and even music and dance, blending it all with magical practice.

The Middle Ages saw herbal magic intersect with the growing field of alchemy, where the quest wasn't just to transform base materials into gold but to discover the elixir of life. Alchemists believed that herbs held the key to both physical and spiritual transformation, capable of not only healing the body but also refining the soul. Figures like Paracelsus revolutionised the way we think about herbal magic, suggesting that plants contained both physical and spiritual essences. His ideas laid the groundwork for modern pharmacology but kept that mystical connection alive, showing how herbs could work on multiple levels—physical healing and spiritual enlightenment.

One figure who for me stands out from this period is Hildegard of Bingen, a Benedictine abbess from the 12th century. She was a remarkable woman, deeply spiritual and a keen herbalist. Her works, *Physica* and *Causae et Curae*, are fascinating because they don't just focus on the medicinal properties of plants; they also explore the mystical side of herbalism. Hildegard believed that herbs were divine gifts, imbued with spiritual energy capable of protecting the soul, cleansing negative energies, and bringing people closer to God.

This idea of the physical and spiritual being deeply intertwined resonates with me. I, too, see plants as having their own energy, their own essence, and when we work with them, we tap into something much deeper than just their physical properties.

In her writings, Hildegard explored the idea that illness could be caused by both physical and spiritual imbalances. She believed that herbs could help with both, not just healing the body but also realigning the spirit. For example, she saw fennel as a herb that could clear the mind, aid digestion, and bring spiritual clarity. It's this holistic approach to healing that really resonates with how I practise herbal magic today. There's something timeless in the way Hildegard viewed the world, and her insights still inspire many modern witches and herbalists.

What's amazing about the history of herbal magic is how it has adapted and endured, despite the obstacles. The Renaissance was a time of great intellectual and artistic flourishing, but it also brought intense scrutiny to those who practised herbal magic. The witch trials of the 16th and 17th centuries were a dark period, fuelled by fear, religious fanaticism, and social upheaval. Many women who knew how to use herbs and natural remedies were targeted, accused of witchcraft, and often executed. The *Malleus Maleficarum*, a notorious witch-hunting manual, linked herbal knowledge with diabolical practices, making life incredibly dangerous for those who practised herbalism.

And yet, even in the face of such persecution, the knowledge of herbal magic persisted. It was passed down in secret, from one generation to the next, surviving through the resilience of those who refused to let it be lost. It's a testament to the power of this tradition that it has managed to endure through such tumultuous times.

During the Renaissance, despite the growing dangers, herbalists continued to play a vital role in their communities. Figures like John Gerard and Nicholas Culpeper made huge contributions to keeping herbal knowledge alive. Culpeper, in particular, worked to make this knowledge accessible to everyone, challenging the monopoly of physicians and apothecaries, which is something I really admire. He understood that this wisdom belonged to the people, not just to the elite.

As we moved into the Enlightenment, there was a shift in how herbal magic was perceived. The scientific method began to dominate, and the mystical aspects of herbalism were gradually sidelined in favour of empirical evidence. Advances in botany and chemistry in the 18th and 19th centuries led to a more systematic understanding of plants, with figures like Carl Linnaeus and Joseph Banks playing crucial roles in this transformation. As pharmaceutical companies and modern medicine rose in prominence, folk practices and herbal magic were increasingly marginalised, pushed to the fringes of society. But, even then, herbal knowledge didn't disappear. It continued to survive, passed down in rural areas where modern medicine was limited, keeping these ancient practices alive.

What draws me to herbal magic, and what has always resonated with witches like me, is the sense of autonomy it gives. It's not about telling people what to do; it's about offering knowledge and letting them make their own choices, fostering a deep, authentic connection with the earth and its energies. The Green Witch embodies this principle perfectly, she shares wisdom but respects the individual's free will to use it how they see fit. This respect for personal choice, combined with a deep understanding of nature's magic, is what creates real, meaningful transformation.

For me, this journey into herbal magic has been about more than just learning how to use herbs—it's been about understanding the deep, spiritual connection that we all have to the natural world. Whether I'm studying ancient texts like Hildegard's, tending to the herbs in my garden, or blending magical ingredients for a spell, I feel that connection growing stronger. It's a reminder that the magic of plants is always there, waiting for us to tap into it, to embrace it, and to use it to bring balance and healing into our lives.

Herbal magic has evolved, blended, and adapted through the centuries, but at its core, it remains the same, a powerful, transformative practice that connects us to the earth, to the divine, and to ourselves. Whether we're looking to heal a physical ailment or seeking spiritual enlightenment, the magic of herbs offers a way to restore balance and harmony. And in today's world, where we often feel disconnected and overwhelmed, that connection to nature and to the ancient wisdom of plants feels more important than ever.

The Modern Witch: The 20th Century and the Revival of Herbal Magic

The revival of herbal magic in the 20th century was fuelled by the countercultural movements of the 1960s and 70s. People were looking to reconnect with nature, to explore alternative spiritualities, and out of that came a resurgence in witchcraft and paganism. It's no wonder herbal magic played a central role in these practices, plants, after all, are at the very heart of magic.

What's interesting is how the rise of neo-paganism, particularly Wicca, brought herbal magic back into the spotlight. Pioneers like Gerald Gardner and Doreen Valiente were key figures in this movement. They placed a lot of emphasis on the sacredness of nature and the magical properties of plants, incorporating herbal practices into their teachings. And then you've got books like Scott Cunningham's *Encyclopedia of Magical Herbs*, which became essential reading for modern witches. That book has been such a resource, offering clear, practical guidance on how to work with plants in a magical way. It really helped bridge that gap between ancient herbal knowledge and modern practice.

But it wasn't just about magic. The environmental movement of the late 20th century also encouraged people to return to natural practices. There was a growing awareness of sustainability, of living in balance with the earth, and this resonated deeply with the principles of herbal magic. It's a shift that's still with us today, and it's led to a renewed appreciation for the power of plants, not just in a magical sense, but in terms of health and wellbeing. Books and resources on herbalism and natural healing became more widely available, offering a bridge between traditional knowledge and the latest in modern practices.

Now, herbal magic has become a vibrant, evolving practice. What I love is that we modern witches draw on a rich history of folklore and traditions while integrating new knowledge and techniques. The internet has played such a huge role in this. It's made it easier than ever to access information, allowing practitioners to connect, share resources, and learn from each other across the world. You've got books, online courses, and social media groups, all offering spaces for people to share their experiences and support one another. It's a global community now, and it's amazing to see.

What's also really exciting to me is how herbal medicine is starting to gain more respect within the healthcare world. We're seeing a growing awareness of the value of a holistic approach to health, one that considers the mind, body, and spirit together. Modern herbalists are increasingly working alongside healthcare professionals, offering complementary treatments that blend the best of both worlds, herbal magic and modern medicine.

There's a growing body of research now that backs up the effectiveness of various herbs. For example, St John's Wort has been shown to be as effective as standard antidepressants for mild to moderate depression, but with fewer side effects. And ginger has been proven to help with nausea, especially in chemotherapy patients. These are things we witches have known for years, but it's great to see the medical community starting to recognise the benefits of herbs in a more scientific way.

In my own practice, herbal alchemy allows me to take a deeply personalised approach to health. Each person is unique, and their treatment plan should reflect that. I've found that by combining herbal magic with insights from modern medicine, I can create remedies that support my clients' whole wellbeing. Take insomnia, for example. I like to mix traditional herbs like chamomile, hops and lavender with modern approaches, such as Cognitive Behavioural Therapy for Insomnia (CBT-I). By addressing both the physical and psychological aspects of sleep problems, I can offer more comprehensive support.

Of course, there are challenges when it comes to blending herbal practices with modern medicine. One big issue is that we still need more research to back up the use of herbs. There's a lot of anecdotal evidence, but not always enough high-quality clinical data to convince mainstream healthcare professionals. Plus, there's a knowledge gap, many medical schools don't offer much training in herbal medicine, and not all herbalists are well-versed in modern treatments. But if we can bridge this gap, there's real potential for more effective integrative care.

Looking ahead, I think the future of integrative medicine looks really promising. There's this growing push towards more holistic, patient-centred care, where herbalists and doctors work together to provide comprehensive treatment. We're seeing more research being done on herbal remedies, which is helping to bring them into the mainstream. And with personalised medicine on the rise, we're finding new ways to tailor treatments to each individual's unique needs, blending ancient herbal wisdom with the latest scientific advancements.

Ultimately, the integration of herbal practices with modern medicine is about creating balance. It's about honouring the wisdom of ancient traditions while embracing the advances of modern science. For me, it's such an exciting time to be a part of this movement, because it holds the promise of a more balanced, harmonious, and healthful future for everyone. By weaving the magic of herbs into our everyday lives, we can foster a deeper connection with the earth, with ourselves, and with each other, bringing a bit more magic into the modern world.

CHAPTER 2
Setting Your Magical Garden

"Wæs þū gearu, wīse heorþræden, geleornian frodnesse of niwe dagas, and fremian bēag eorðan."

"Be thou ready, wise hearth-companion, to learn wisdom from new days, and to benefit the ring of the earth."

Chapter 2: Setting your Magical Garden

Choosing the Right Location to Set Up Your Magical Garden

Setting up a magical garden blends the art of herbalism with the spiritual practice of witchcraft. As a practicing herbalist and Green Witch, I've come to understand that selecting the right location for your garden is crucial for the health of your plants and the magical energy of the space. This isn't just about growing herbs; it's about creating a sanctuary where nature, magic, and personal well-being intersect. Let me share some insights and experiences I've gathered over the years about choosing the perfect spot for a magical garden.

Understanding Your Environment

First things first, you need to get to know your environment intimately. This means paying attention to your local climate, soil type, and even the microclimate of your potential garden spaces. Different herbs and magical plants thrive in different climates. For instance, Mediterranean herbs like rosemary, lavender, and thyme love the warmth and sun, while mint and parsley are happier in cooler, shadier spots.

You might want to conduct a soil test to understand its pH level and nutrient content. Most herbs prefer well-drained soil with a neutral to slightly alkaline pH, but some magical plants, like heather and sage, can thrive in more acidic soils. Amending your soil with organic matter can greatly improve its structure and fertility, making it more hospitable for a variety of plants.

Microclimates are another fascinating aspect to consider. These are localized climate conditions that can differ from the general climate of your area due to factors like elevation, proximity to water bodies, and urban structures. For example, a garden on the south side of a building will get more sunlight and be warmer than one on the north side. Spend some time observing your potential garden sites at different times of the day and in different weather conditions to get a feel for these microclimates.

Sunlight and Shade

Understanding the light patterns in my garden has been a game-changer for plant growth. Sunlight is absolutely critical, and most herbs and magical plants need full sun, meaning at least 6-8 hours of direct sunlight each day. But I've learned that some plants, like chamomile and lemon balm, are a bit more forgiving and can tolerate partial shade.

To really get a handle on how sunlight affects my garden, I spend time outside watching where the shadows fall throughout the day and even across different seasons. It's a bit like garden meditation, just sitting there and observing nature's patterns.

In parts of my garden where natural shade is lacking, I've gotten creative. I've added structures like pergolas and trellises, and strategically planted taller plants and trees. These not only create the necessary shade for those plants that need it but also add beautiful layers and depth to the garden's look. It's fun to think about how to create these pockets of shade and sun, accommodating a diverse range of plants and making the garden more dynamic and visually interesting.

Water Access and Drainage

Watering your garden is crucial for keeping plants healthy, but getting the balance just right can be tricky. Too much water and you risk root rot and plant diseases; too little and your plants can dry out. That's why it's so important to have a reliable water source nearby, whether it's a garden hose, a rain barrel, or an irrigation system. Trust me, having easy access to water makes all the difference, especially during those hot, dry spells.

One thing I've learned is to pay close attention to how water drains in different parts of my garden. After a good rain, I'll go out and see where the water pools and where it drains quickly. This helps me figure out which areas might need better drainage solutions. Raised beds have been a lifesaver for me in spots where the drainage isn't great. They let me control the soil quality and drainage much more effectively. Plus, they make the garden more accessible and easier to manage.

Creating these solutions not only helps my plants thrive but also makes my gardening experience more enjoyable. It's all about finding that sweet spot with water and making sure your plants get what they need to grow strong and healthy.

Creating a Sacred Space

A magical garden isn't just a spot to grow plants; it's a sacred space where I connect with nature and practice my craft. For me, finding a location that offers privacy and seclusion is key. It might be a fenced yard, a walled garden, or a hidden corner of my property. Having this private space lets me perform rituals, meditations, and spellwork without interruptions.

I also think about the natural beauty of the location. Are there existing trees, rocks, or water features that can enhance the magical vibe of my garden? Incorporating these natural elements into the garden design makes it feel more immersive and enchanting. I love weaving in sacred geometry too, creating circular garden beds, spiral paths, or arranging plants in patterns that reflect sacred symbols. These designs help boost the energy flow in my garden, turning it into a powerful space for my magical practices.

It's a space where every element has a purpose and contributes to the overall energy and ambiance. This personal touch transforms it into more than just a garden; it's a living, breathing extension of my magical self.

Aromatic and Fragrant Plants

For me, the fragrance of my garden transforms the space into a sensory haven and adds a whole new dimension to my magical practices. I love positioning aromatic plants like lavender, rosemary, and mint near paths, seating areas, and entryways. This way, their delightful scents greet me as I walk through or relax in the garden, instantly lifting my spirits.

These fragrant plants aren't just for smelling, though—they play a big part in my spellwork and rituals. The calming scent of lavender, the invigorating aroma of mint, and the grounding fragrance of rosemary add an olfactory (lovely smelly) layer to my magic that enhances the overall experience.

I've also learned to consider the wind patterns in my area. By placing aromatic plants where the wind will carry their scents through the garden, I can create a more immersive environment. For instance, I've planted lavender on the windward side, so its soothing scent drifts through the space, enhancing the garden's calming ambiance.

One of my cherished rituals involves using light herb seeds to divine the direction of the wind in my garden. Instead of picking grass, I gently cast a handful of these delicate seeds into the air, watching with anticipation as they dance on the breeze. As they float and drift, I utter an incantation to bless the garden: "Seeds of light, winds of grace, spread your scent, and bless this space." This magical act not only reveals the wind's path but also infuses the garden with a sense of enchantment and intention. The seeds will germinate naturally in places to be found.

Every detail, from the fragrant aromas wafting through the air to the whispered words of blessing, creates a sanctuary that is deeply personal and profoundly magical. It is a place where beauty and enchantment converge, a sacred space where I can connect with nature and practice my craft. This harmonious blend of thoughtful gardening and magical ritual makes my garden a true reflection of my inner world, a serene and mystical retreat.

Seasonal Considerations

A magical garden is a year-round endeavour, and planning for all seasons ensures that your garden remains vibrant and productive throughout the year. In colder climates, the angle of the sun changes with the seasons. Consider the position of the sun during winter and ensure that your garden receives enough light. Deciduous trees can provide shade in summer and allow sunlight through in winter when they shed their leaves.

Deciduous trees, which lose their leaves in the autumn or fall, create a unique environment that's perfect for a variety of herbs and plants. When these trees shed their leaves, they allow more sunlight to filter through in the winter and early spring, providing a dynamic growing condition that can benefit many plants.

I love how spring ephemerals like trilliums and bluebells take advantage of the early sunlight before the tree canopy fills in. These plants burst into bloom in early spring, adding beautiful splashes of colour to the garden. They complete their life cycle quickly, making the most of the sunlight before the trees leaf out fully.

Bulbs are another great choice for planting under deciduous trees. Daffodils and tulips are some of my favourites. They pop up early, often while it's still chilly, and bloom beautifully before the canopy thickens. It's always a joy to see those first daffodils heralding the end of winter.

For herbs that prefer partial shade, the dappled light under deciduous trees is just perfect. Mint, for instance, thrives in these conditions. I've found that chervil and sweet woodruff also do really well, providing lush green foliage and useful herbs for my kitchen.

Hostas and ferns are fantastic for these spots too. They love the moist, shaded conditions under the trees. Solomon's seal is another gem, it has lovely arching stems and delicate flowers that add an elegant touch to the garden.

Even some perennial vegetables benefit from the changing light. Ramps, or wild leeks, are a great example. They pop up early in the spring and thrive in the rich, moist soil that deciduous trees help create. Asparagus is another perennial that benefits from the early spring light.

What I find particularly wonderful about gardening around deciduous trees is how they enrich the soil with their fallen leaves, which decompose and provide essential nutrients. The seasonal sunlight they provide supports a diverse range of plants, ensuring that my garden is vibrant and productive throughout the year. Plus, the canopy helps retain soil moisture, which is a boon for many plants that need consistent hydration.

Creating a garden with deciduous trees is like having a natural helper that adjusts the environment with the seasons. It's a beautiful way to blend different plants and create a garden that thrives all year round.

Incorporating a mix of perennial and annual plants is also beneficial. Perennials will provide structure and continuity in your garden, while annuals can be changed each year to add variety and colour. Understanding the life cycles of your plants will help you plan for continuous growth and harvests.

Plan seasonal activities and plantings. Spring might be the time for planting seeds and young plants, summer for harvesting herbs at their peak potency, autumn for gathering roots and preparing the garden for winter, and winter for planning and preparing for the next growing season. Each season brings its own rhythm and tasks, keeping you connected to the natural cycles. We will cover planting in more detail later.

Wildlife and Pollinators

Encouraging wildlife and pollinators in your garden can truly transform it into a vibrant, magical space that brims with life and productivity. I absolutely love the feeling of being surrounded by nature's energy and watching my garden flourish with the help of these tiny, hardworking creatures.

One of the most rewarding aspects of gardening is seeing bees, butterflies, and other pollinators buzzing around. They bring such a sense of vitality and movement. To attract these essential helpers, I include a variety of plants known for their appeal to pollinators. Echinacea, with its striking pink flowers, is a magnet for bees and butterflies. Borage, with its beautiful blue star-shaped flowers, not only attracts pollinators but also adds a touch of whimsy to the garden. Yarrow, with its clusters of tiny flowers, is another excellent choice. Each of these plants plays a vital role in ensuring that pollinators visit and help my garden thrive.

The presence of pollinators is crucial for the health of my garden. They ensure that flowers are pollinated, which leads to the production of fruits and seeds. This natural process is essential for the productivity of the garden. Beyond their practical benefits, pollinators add an enchanting element to the garden, making it a lively and dynamic space.

Beyond pollinators, creating habitats for other beneficial wildlife like birds, frogs, and insects can significantly enhance the ecological balance of the garden. Bird feeders attract a variety of bird species, each bringing its own unique energy and song. I love watching the birds flit around, bringing a sense of movement and life.

Insect hotels are another fantastic addition. These structures provide shelter for beneficial insects like ladybirds (Ladybugs) and solitary bees. They not only support biodiversity but also help with natural pest control. Watching these insects go about their daily activities is both fascinating and rewarding.

Small ponds can attract frogs and other amphibians. These creatures contribute to the ecological balance by preying on pests and adding another layer of diversity to the garden. The gentle croaking of frogs at dusk adds to the garden's magical atmosphere. … and before anyone asks, no, I don't use eye of newt, frogs or wing of bat in any of my magic!

One of the great benefits of encouraging beneficial insects and animals is natural pest control. Ladybirds, spiders, and birds can help keep pest populations in check, reducing the need for chemical interventions. This creates a more harmonious and sustainable garden environment.

Ladybirds are particularly effective at controlling aphid populations. Watching these tiny, vibrant beetles patrol the garden is a delight. Spiders, though often misunderstood, play a crucial role in keeping insect populations balanced. Birds, with their keen eyes and swift movements, can quickly reduce the numbers of harmful insects.

Encouraging these natural predators helps maintain a healthy garden ecosystem. It's a wonderful feeling to know that my garden can thrive without relying on chemical pesticides with nature managing even when I'm not there. This approach not only protects the plants but also safeguards the health of the soil and the wider environment.

Building a Garden for All Seasons

To keep the garden bustling with life throughout the year, it's important to think about how to support wildlife during each season. In the spring and summer, the focus is on providing nectar-rich flowers for pollinators. As autumn approaches, I plant late-blooming flowers like asters and goldenrod to ensure that bees and butterflies have food as they prepare for winter.

During the winter months, providing food and shelter becomes even more critical. I make sure bird feeders are stocked with seeds and suet to help birds survive the colder weather. Creating brush piles or leaving some areas of the garden a bit wild can offer shelter for insects and small mammals.

One of my favourite rituals is to wander through the garden in the early morning with a cup of tea, observing the activities of the various creatures. It's a peaceful time when the garden is just waking up, and the light is soft. I often take a moment to appreciate the intricate web of life that weaves through the plants and flowers.

I also enjoy planting new flowers and watching to see which pollinators they attract. It's like creating a welcoming party for bees and butterflies. Each new plant brings a sense of anticipation and excitement, wondering who will visit it first.

Encouraging wildlife and pollinators in your garden not only enhances the beauty and productivity of the garden but also creates a space filled with life and magic. By planting a variety of flowers, creating habitats, and supporting natural pest control, you can build a garden that is both enchanting and ecologically balanced.

So, take a moment to appreciate the tiny helpers in your garden. Plant a few more flowers for the bees, set up a bird feeder, or build an insect hotel. These small actions can make a big difference, turning your garden into a sanctuary for wildlife and a magical haven for yourself.

Personal Connection and Enjoyment

Your magical garden should be a place where you feel a deep personal connection and enjoyment. Incorporate seating areas where you can relax, meditate, and connect with the energy of your garden. Benches, hammocks, and outdoor cushions can provide comfortable spots to enjoy the beauty and tranquillity of the space.

Add personal touches that reflect your personality and magical practice. This could be statues of deities, crystals, wind chimes, or handmade decorations. Personalising your garden makes it a true extension of yourself and your magic. Consider adding interactive elements like a labyrinth, a fairy garden, or a water feature. These can provide focal points for meditation, play, and ritual work. Engaging with these elements can deepen your connection to the garden and enhance your magical practices.

Long-Term Vision and Adaptability

Creating a magical garden is an ongoing journey that evolves over time. Plan for future growth and changes in your garden. Allow space for plants to mature and spread and be open to redesigning areas as needed. Flexibility and adaptability are key to maintaining a vibrant and thriving garden.

Stay curious and continue learning about plants, gardening techniques, and magical practices. Attend workshops, read books, and connect with other herbalists and witches. Continuous learning keeps your practice dynamic and inspired.

Regularly reflect on your garden's progress and your experiences within it. What worked well? What challenges did you face? Use these reflections to refine your approach and make improvements. Your garden is a living entity, and your relationship with it will deepen as you grow together.

As a Green Witch and herbalist, I have found that the journey of creating a magical garden is as rewarding as the destination. It is a space where nature, magic, and personal well-being converge, offering endless opportunities for growth, healing, and enchantment. Whether you are just starting or are a seasoned gardener, the key is to approach the process with an open heart, a curious mind, and a deep respect for the natural world. May your magical garden flourish and bring you joy, wisdom, and wonder.

Garden Design: Layout Ideas for Both Small and Large Spaces

Creating a magical garden, whether small or large, is a transformative journey. I've learned that the layout of your garden is essential not just for the optimal growth of plants, but also for fostering a space that nurtures your spirit and enhances your magical practices. Let's explore some layout ideas and considerations for designing both small and large garden spaces.

Small Spaces: Maximizing Potential and Creating Intimacy

When working with small spaces, the key is to maximize the potential of every square inch while creating a sense of intimacy and enchantment. Small gardens can be incredibly charming and are often easier to maintain, making them ideal for those new to gardening or with limited time.

One of the best ways to utilise a small space is by thinking vertically. Vertical gardening not only saves ground space but also adds layers and visual interest to your garden. Consider installing trellises, wall-mounted planters, or vertical garden towers. Plants like climbing roses, morning glories, ivy, and herbs such as thyme and rosemary can thrive in vertical setups.

I remember my first small garden in a tiny urban courtyard. The walls were bare and uninspiring, but once I installed a few trellises and hung some planters, it was transformed into a lush, green oasis. The scents of the herbs and flowers mingled in the air, creating a perfect spot for morning meditations and evening rituals.

Containers are perfect for small spaces and courtyards but are equally beautiful on large terraces. They allow you to grow a variety of plants, including those that might not thrive in your native soil. Use pots of different sizes and heights to create a dynamic arrangement. Group plants with similar water and sunlight needs together for easy care. Herbs like basil, parsley, and mint do well in containers, and you can even grow small fruit trees or vegetables in larger pots.

Container gardening became a profound passion of mine during my time in Portland. The limited space of my tiny garden encouraged me to explore the versatility and beauty of growing plants in containers. This approach not only maximized my use of space but also added a unique charm and character to the garden.

One of my favourite elements of container gardening is the use of antique terracotta pots. These pots, with their warm, earthy tones and rustic appeal, bring a timeless beauty to the garden. Terracotta is a breathable material, which helps to regulate moisture levels and keep the roots of the plants healthy. The slight imperfections and weathered patina of antique terracotta pots add a sense of history and character, making each pot a piece of art in itself.

Among my collection, the large terracotta strawberry pots were particularly delightful. These pots, designed with multiple holes, are traditionally used for growing strawberries. However, their design is incredibly versatile and perfect for growing a mixture of herbs and other small plants. I planted basil, thyme, and oregano in some, and strawberries in others. The cascading greenery and vibrant red strawberries peeking out from the holes created a stunning visual effect.

Arranging pots of different sizes and heights allowed me to create a dynamic and visually appealing garden. I grouped plants with similar water and sunlight needs together, which made care and maintenance much easier. The larger pots formed the backbone of the arrangement, while smaller pots added layers and depth. The variety of heights and textures created a sense of movement and flow, making the garden feel more expansive than it actually was.

Another creative use for the terracotta strawberry pots was planting different varieties of lavender. Each hole in the pot housed a different type of lavender, from the delicate English lavender to the more robust French and Spanish varieties. As the lavender grew, it gave the pot a whimsical, hedgehog-like appearance, with tufts of fragrant purple and white flowers poking out from all angles. The combined scent of the different lavenders was intoxicating, filling the garden with a soothing aroma.

In addition to the terracotta pots, I used a variety of colourful pots to add vibrancy to the garden. Bright blues, sunny yellows, and deep reds contrasted beautifully with the green foliage, creating focal points that drew the eye. Arranging these colourful pots in clusters added to the garden's visual appeal, making each section feel like a curated art installation.

Herbs like basil, parsley, and mint thrived in these containers, providing fresh ingredients for the kitchen and a delightful sensory experience in the garden. The versatility of container gardening also allowed me to grow small fruit trees. Dwarf lemon and fig trees have always done so much better than I ever expected in pots, even in climates that you wouldn't expect if you can find little sun traps in the garden. These, nestled in large terracotta pots, added a touch of the exotic and provided delicious fruit.

Container gardening offered several practical benefits. It allowed me to control the soil quality and drainage, which is particularly useful in an urban setting where soil conditions may not be ideal. Containers can be moved around to catch the best light or to create different looks throughout the season. This flexibility made it easy to experiment with plant placements and combinations.

Container gardening continues to be a cherished part of my gardening practice. It offers a way to cultivate a diverse range of plants, create stunning visual displays, and enjoy the beauty and tranquillity of nature, no matter how limited or how large the space. The magic of container gardening is that it turns constraints into opportunities, allowing for a unique and personal expression of the gardener's vision.

Creating Zones:

Even in a small garden, creating distinct zones can make the space feel larger and more functional. Designate areas for different activities, such as a small seating area for relaxation, a corner for potting and planting, and a section for magical workings. Use pathways, stepping stones, or different ground covers to delineate these zones.

My Time in Portland: Small Garden Beauty

When I was living in Portland, I had a tiny garden that became a sanctuary of sorts. Despite its modest size, I found that with thoughtful planning and a bit of creativity, I could transform it into a multifunctional haven. The secret lay in creating distinct zones, each serving a unique purpose and contributing to the overall charm and functionality of the space.

I began by laying a path of mosaic stepping stones that snaked its way through the garden. These stones were a personal project, each one stencilled with vibrant patterns and symbols that held personal significance. The path led to a cozy nook with a bench surrounded by rosemary, lavender, and thyme. This spot quickly became my favourite place for sipping tea and reflecting on the day's work. The heady fragrance of the herbs combined with the gentle rustle of leaves created a serene atmosphere, perfect for unwinding.

The seating area, though small, was designed with comfort and relaxation in mind. I chose a rustic wooden bench that blended seamlessly with the natural surroundings. To enhance the coziness, I added colourful cushions and a small table, just large enough for a teacup and a book. This little corner of the garden was my retreat, where I could escape the hustle and bustle of daily life and immerse myself in nature.

Adjacent to the seating area, I set up a corner dedicated to potting and planting. This zone was equipped with a sturdy potting bench, a collection of terracotta pots, and an array of gardening tools. It was here that I spent many enjoyable hours planting seeds, repotting herbs, and nurturing seedlings. The potting area added a practical dimension to the garden, allowing me to engage in hands-on gardening activities while keeping the space organized and clutter-free.

A small section of the garden was reserved for magical workings. This zone was slightly hidden, offering a sense of privacy and mystery. I placed a small altar made of natural stones and decorated it with crystals, candles, and sacred objects. This area became a focal point for my rituals and meditations, a place where I could connect with the earth and the energies of the garden. The presence of this sacred space added a layer of enchantment to the garden, making it not just a physical retreat but also a spiritual one.

One of the challenges of a small garden is maximizing space. In Portland, I discovered the beauty and efficiency of vertical gardening. I installed trellises along the fence and planted climbing plants like sweet peas, morning glories, and even some beans. These vertical elements not only saved ground space but also added a lush, green backdrop that made the garden feel more expansive. Hanging pots and wall-mounted planters also provided additional space for growing herbs and flowers.

One of the joys of having a garden in Portland was experiencing the changing seasons. In spring, the garden burst into life with colourful blooms and fresh green growth. Summer brought a riot of flowers and the heady fragrance of herbs. Autumn transformed the garden into a tapestry of golds and reds, while winter, though quieter, had its own charm with evergreen foliage and the occasional dusting of snow. Each season added a new layer of beauty and interest, making the garden a dynamic and ever-changing space.

Despite its small size, my garden became a haven for wildlife. Birds, butterflies, and bees were frequent visitors, attracted by the variety of plants and the welcoming environment. I installed a small birdbath and a few bird feeders, which not only provided water and food for the birds but also added to the charm and liveliness of the garden. Watching the wildlife brought an extra dimension of joy and connection to nature.

Reflecting on my time in Portland and my tiny garden, I realized that size truly does not matter when it comes to creating a beautiful and functional outdoor space. The key lies in thoughtful design, personal touches, and a connection to nature. Each zone in the garden had its own character and purpose, contributing to the overall harmony and functionality of the space

The experience of transforming a small garden in Portland taught me valuable lessons about creativity, resourcefulness, and the joy of gardening. By creating distinct zones, embracing vertical gardening, and incorporating personal touches, I was able to turn a tiny outdoor space into a multifunctional haven. This garden, though small in size, was rich in beauty, functionality, and enchantment, proving that with a bit of imagination and effort, any garden can become a cherished retreat.

Mirrors and Reflective Surfaces:

Mirrors and reflective surfaces can create the illusion of more space. Position a mirror on a wall or fence to reflect light and greenery, making the garden appear larger and more open. This trick can also add a magical quality, as if there's a secret garden just beyond reach.

I once used an old, ornate mirror in my small garden, positioning it to reflect a particularly beautiful rose bush. The effect was enchanting, creating a sense of depth and mystery. It also helped to brighten a shady corner, bringing more light to the plants growing there.

In a similar vein, I stumbled across a really old beaten up door in a reclamation yard when I was searching for old terracotta pots. It was arched and the stories it must have been able to tell of people who had once walked through it. I didn't have a doorway to put it in, so I attached it to a wall in the garden giving the appearance there was a secret garden or passageway through this magical door.

Compact Furniture and Accessories:

Choose compact, foldable, or multifunctional furniture to maximize space. A small bistro table and chairs, a foldable bench, or even a hammock can provide comfortable seating without overwhelming the garden. Accessories like lanterns, fairy lights, and small statues can add personality and charm without taking up much space.

In my experience, a simple wooden bench with storage underneath became a valuable addition to my small garden. It provided a place to sit and relax while also storing my gardening tools and supplies, keeping the area tidy and organized.

Large Spaces: Creating Expansive and Enchanting Landscapes

With larger garden spaces, the possibilities are endless. You can create a more expansive and varied landscape, incorporating a wider range of plants, features, and magical elements. However, the challenge lies in ensuring that the garden remains cohesive and manageable.

Garden Rooms:

Creating "rooms" in a large garden can add a touch of magic and whimsy to your outdoor space. Imagine each area with its unique theme and purpose, connected by charming pathways, inviting arches, or secretive hedges. It's like turning your garden into an enchanting journey where each step brings a new delight.

The Herb Garden: My Personal Apothecary

Near my kitchen, I've created a herb garden that's both practical and beautiful. It's my personal apothecary, filled with culinary and medicinal herbs. Think of it as a Hogwarts potion classroom, but with fewer explosions and more delicious smells. There's basil, thyme, rosemary, and sage, all thriving and ready to be plucked for my next culinary adventure. And let's not forget lavender and chamomile, which add a calming touch – perfect for when my culinary adventures don't go as planned.

The herb garden isn't just about practicality; it's a sensory delight. Each time I brush past the herbs, their aromas fill the air, making the whole garden smell like a gourmet kitchen. It's a constant reminder that nature's pantry is just a few steps away.

The Wildflower Meadow: A Pollinator's Paradise

Further along, I have a wildflower meadow that's like a buzzing carnival for bees, butterflies, and other pollinators. Picture a bustling market square, but with flowers instead of food stalls. Echinacea, borage, and yarrow stand tall and proud, attracting all manner of winged visitors. The meadow is a riot of colours and a flurry of activity, like a floral Piccadilly Circus or Times Square at rush hour.

The meadow is my nod to nature's wild beauty. I love wandering through it, watching the bees perform their intricate dance and the butterflies flutter about like confetti at a parade. It's a living, breathing tapestry of life, full of energy and vibrancy.

The Woodland Retreat: My Shady Sanctuary

Nestled in a quieter corner, the woodland area is my shady sanctuary. It's the perfect spot to escape the summer heat, with tall trees providing a cool canopy and the undergrowth lush with ferns and hostas. Imagine a serene forest glade, but with no risk of meeting the big bad wolf.

In this tranquil space, I've set up a hammock and a few benches, ideal for a peaceful nap or a good book. The gentle rustling of leaves and the occasional birdsong create a soothing soundtrack. This area feels like my secret hideaway, a place to relax and recharge away from the hustle and bustle of everyday life.

The Sacred Circle: My Magical Nexus

One of the most special areas in my garden is the sacred circle, a space dedicated to rituals and meditation. It's my magical nexus, where I can connect with the earth and "channel my inner witch". I've arranged stones and plants in a pattern that resonates with me, creating a circle of power and peace.

In the centre stands a small tree, symbolizing growth and life, surrounded by protective herbs like sage, mugwort, and rosemary. This sacred space is where I perform rituals, meditate, and ground myself. It's a place brimming with energy and intention, a testament to the magic of nature.

Pathways and Connections: The Journey Begins

Connecting these garden rooms are pathways lined with stepping stones, arches adorned with climbing roses, and hedges that provide both structure and privacy. Each path invites exploration, leading from one magical space to another. Walking these paths feels like embarking on a grand adventure, where each turn reveals a new surprise, especially for my daughters, whose imaginations runs wild with visions of pixies, fairies, and fairy-tale creatures.

The pathways are crafted from various materials, each chosen to complement the adjoining rooms and enhance the sense of journey and discovery. Gravel crunches satisfyingly underfoot, adding a tactile element that makes each step feel deliberate and grounding. The gentle rustle of bark mulch underfoot adds a rustic touch, connecting us to the earth with every step. These different textures not only provide practical benefits but also engage the senses, making the simple act of walking through the garden a delightful experience.

Arches covered in clematis and honeysuckle mark the entrances to some rooms. The fragrant flowers offer a welcoming embrace, their scents mingling in the air to create a fragrant pathway. Each archway feels like a portal to a different world, sparking the imagination and setting the stage for what lies beyond. My youngest daughter loves to run through these arches, imagining she is entering a new fairy-tale land where magical creatures await.

The pathways twist and turn, creating a sense of mystery and anticipation. Some paths are lined with stepping stones, leading the way like a trail of breadcrumbs. These stones are sometimes spaced irregularly, inviting a playful hop, skip, and jump as we follow the path. Hedges of yew and boxwood provide structure and privacy, creating natural walls that guide us through the garden. These hedges add an element of surprise, as the view is often obscured, making each turn an exciting reveal. I like to watch my daughters playing here with their friends, eyes lighting up with curiosity and excitement as they round each corner, never quite knowing what enchanting scene will unfold next. Usually they are pretending they are on a quest to find hidden treasure or discover a secret fairy grove.

Along these winding paths are various nooks and hidden wonders that spur the imagination. A small stone bench tucked under an overhanging rose arch creates the perfect spot for a fairy to rest. Scattered throughout are little fairy houses nestled at the base of trees, each carefully crafted to add a touch of whimsy and magic. We sometimes leave tiny gifts—like pebbles or flowers—by these houses, believing that the fairies come to collect them at night.

A small, hidden grotto made of stones and moss is another favourite spot. It's a quiet, shaded area that feels secret and secluded, perfect for storytelling and daydreams. We often sit here and make up tales about the woodland creatures and magical beings that might live in our garden. This grotto, with its cool, damp air and the gentle sound of a nearby trickling stream, feels like a sanctuary from the outside world.

In one corner of the garden, we've created a small labyrinth. Unlike a maze with dead ends and wrong turns, a labyrinth has a single winding path that leads to the centre and back out again. Walking this path is a meditative experience, a journey inward that helps clear the mind and connect with the garden's energy.

The pathways and their surrounding flora change with the seasons, adding to the garden's dynamic beauty. In spring, the arches are alive with fresh blooms, and the hedges are vibrant with new growth. Summer brings a riot of colour and fragrance, with roses and honeysuckle in full bloom. Autumn turns the hedges into a tapestry of reds and golds, and the crunch of fallen leaves underfoot adds a new texture to the paths. In winter, the bare branches create a stark, enchanting beauty, and the pathways take on a quiet, contemplative character.

These pathways are more than just connections between garden rooms; they are catalysts for imagination and exploration. As all my children have grown they have had marvellous adventures along these paths, tackled pirates, tigers, hob-goblins, chased and giggled and filled the garden with laughter and wonder. Today apparently a fairy queen has lost her handbag somewhere in the garden!

We do sometimes take a walk through the garden all together gathering flowers to create potions and spells, inspired by the herbs and blooms we find along the way. Other times, we'll all lay on the grass between the stepping stones, looking up at the sky through the archways, daydreaming about the adventures that await.

The pathways in our garden are more than just practical routes; they are the threads that weave together the tapestry of our garden's story. Each walk down these paths is an opportunity to connect with nature, to explore and discover, and to create lasting memories. For my children, these pathways are a magical playground, a place where imagination can run wild and a sense of wonder can flourish.

In crafting these pathways, I like to think that I have created not just a garden, but a living storybook. Each path, each turn, each hidden nook is a chapter in the tale of our garden. It's a place where the magic of nature and the magic of imagination come together, creating a sanctuary that nurtures both body and spirit. If you have a large garden, I encourage you to create your own pathways of discovery. Let them lead you to places of beauty and let them be the setting for your own magical adventures.

Seasonal Magic: A Garden for All Seasons

One of the greatest joys of having a large garden divided into distinct rooms is witnessing its magical transformation through the seasons. Each phase of the year brings unique enchantment and energy, painting the garden with different hues and moods. As a witch, these transformations align beautifully with the Wheel of the Year, enhancing the spiritual and natural connection of my space. Let me take you on a journey through my garden as it changes from the vibrant burst of Ostara to the serene beauty of Yule.

Ostara (Spring Equinox): A Burst of Life

Spring in my garden is a magical time when everything comes alive, celebrating Ostara, the Spring Equinox. The herb garden near the kitchen is one of the first areas to wake up from its winter slumber. Fresh green shoots of basil, thyme, and rosemary emerge, and the air fills with their fragrant promise of culinary delights. Lavender and chamomile begin to bloom, their soft colours adding a gentle touch to the garden. The awakening of the garden parallels the rebirth of the earth, making this a powerful time for planting and renewal rituals.

The wildflower meadow is a riot of colours during Ostara. Echinacea, borage, and yarrow burst into bloom, attracting bees and butterflies. The meadow becomes a buzzing carnival of pollinators, each one contributing to the garden's life cycle. The vibrant blooms create a patchwork of colours, from the deep purples and blues of borage to the sunny yellows of yarrow.

In the woodland retreat, fresh green leaves unfurl on the trees, creating a lush canopy that filters the sunlight. Ferns and hostas emerge from the forest floor, their intricate leaves adding texture and depth. The sacred circle, too, awakens with new energy. The central tree (I'll talk a lot more about this tree later) begins to leaf out, and the surrounding herbs, sage, mugwort, and rosemary, grow more robust, ready to play their part in rituals and meditations celebrating the balance of light and dark.

Litha (Summer Solstice): A Festival of Blooms

As summer arrives and Litha, the Summer Solstice, approaches, the garden transforms into a vibrant festival of blooms and activity. The herb garden is in full swing, with mature plants offering their bounty for cooking and healing. The lavender bushes are now heavy with blossoms, filling the air with their calming scent. Chamomile flowers create a delicate carpet of white and yellow, perfect for making soothing teas.

The wildflower meadow reaches its peak at Litha. It's a living tapestry of colours and textures, with bees and butterflies performing their daily dance among the flowers. The meadow hums with life, and it's a joy to sit and watch the pollinators at work, knowing they are playing a crucial role in the garden's ecosystem. You will know my name is Bea, and my name was chosen by my dad as he stood painting with his easel in the flower meadow.

In the woodland retreat, the trees provide cool, dappled shade, a perfect refuge from the summer heat. The ferns and hostas are lush and green, thriving in the cooler, moist conditions. The hammock in this area becomes my favourite spot for a mid-afternoon nap, swaying gently under the protective canopy of leaves.

The sacred circle feels particularly powerful during Litha. The central tree is full and vibrant, its branches heavy with leaves. The surrounding herbs are at their most potent, and the air is filled with their earthy, grounding scents. It's the perfect time for outdoor rituals and meditations, connecting deeply with the energy of the earth and the warmth of the sun.

Mabon (Autumn Equinox): A Kaleidoscope of Colours

Autumn brings a dramatic change to the garden, turning it into a kaleidoscope of reds, golds, and oranges as we celebrate Mabon, the Autumn Equinox. The herb garden starts to wind down, but there's still plenty to harvest. The last of the basil and thyme are picked, and the rosemary continues to provide its woody, aromatic branches. Lavender and chamomile begin to fade, preparing for their winter rest.

The wildflower meadow transitions to autumn hues. The flowers start to set seed, and the once bright colours soften into earthy tones. This is the time to collect seeds for next year, ensuring the meadow will continue to thrive. The bees and butterflies linger, making the most of the remaining blooms.

In the woodland retreat, the trees put on a spectacular display. The leaves turn brilliant shades of red, gold, and orange, creating a breathtaking canopy. The ground is covered with a colourful carpet of fallen leaves, and the air is crisp and cool. This area becomes a tranquil, reflective space, perfect for quiet walks and contemplation. This is the time of year you'll find me wandering around, usually with by brolly (umbrella) and a dirty pair of wellies (wellington boots).

The sacred circle feels even more powerful during Mabon. The energy shifts towards introspection and renewal as the earth prepares for winter. The herbs in the circle release their final bursts of fragrance, and the central tree begins to shed its leaves, adding to the circle's sense of groundedness and stability.

Yule (Winter Solstice): A Quiet Contemplative Space

Winter transforms the garden into a quiet, contemplative space, perfect for celebrating Yule, the Winter Solstice. The herb garden rests under a blanket of frost, the plants dormant but full of promise for the coming spring. The wildflower meadow lies quiet, the vibrant colours replaced by the stark beauty of seed heads and dried grasses.

In the woodland retreat, the trees stand bare, their intricate branches silhouetted against the winter sky. The ground is covered in a crisp layer of frost or snow, and the air is filled with the quiet stillness of winter. The hammock is put away, replaced by a cozy bench where I can sit and enjoy the serene beauty of the garden.

The sacred circle takes on a stark, powerful beauty in winter. The central tree, now bare, stands as a symbol of resilience and endurance. The surrounding herbs, though dormant, hold the energy of the earth, ready to burst forth when the warmth returns. It's a time for quiet reflection and deep connection with the natural cycles.

A Year-Round Journey

Each season in my garden brings its own unique beauty and energy, making it a place of constant discovery and delight. The changing seasons remind me of the cyclical nature of life and the importance of being present in each moment. Whether it's the vibrant burst of Ostara, the lively festival of Litha, the colourful transformation of Mabon, or the quiet contemplation of Yule, my garden is a sanctuary that nurtures both body and soul.

Through hot summers and snowy winters, the garden evolves and grows, offering new surprises and joys with each passing season. It's a living, breathing testament to the magic of nature and the deep connections that can be forged in a space thoughtfully designed to embrace the natural world.

My Garden Journey

Of course there is great fun in creating these garden rooms. Each space reflects a part of my life and my connection to nature. The herb garden near the kitchen is a testament to the nurturing power of plants and their role in daily life. The wildflower meadow celebrates the untamed beauty of nature and the importance of pollinators. The woodland area is my peaceful retreat, while the sacred circle is my spiritual sanctuary.

These garden rooms are more than just physical spaces; they are expressions of my love for nature and my desire to create a sanctuary that nurtures both body and soul. Each visit to the garden is a journey through different aspects of life, a chance to connect with the earth and its cycles.

Designing a large garden with distinct rooms has transformed it into a place of magic and discovery. It's a living, breathing space that reflects the changing seasons and the deep connections between all living things. Each room tells its own story, inviting exploration and offering moments of beauty, reflection, and wonder.

Encouraging wildlife and creating habitats within these garden rooms adds to their magic, bringing a sense of vitality and movement. The presence of birds, bees, butterflies, and other creatures enhances the garden's atmosphere, making it a truly enchanting place.

If you have a large garden, I encourage you to experiment with creating your own garden rooms. Think about what each space could represent and how it can contribute to the overall magic of your garden. Whether it's a practical herb garden, a vibrant wildflower meadow, a serene woodland retreat, or a sacred circle, each room can become a special part of your garden's story. So, grab your gardening gloves, let your imagination run wild, and start crafting your own magical sanctuary.

Water Features:

Water features can be a stunning addition to a large garden. Ponds, streams, fountains, and waterfalls not only enhance the visual appeal but also create a soothing auditory backdrop. Water features attract wildlife, adding to the garden's biodiversity and creating opportunities for reflection and meditation. I installed a small pond in my large garden, complete with a gentle waterfall. The sound of trickling water was incredibly calming, and the pond quickly became a haven for frogs, dragonflies, and birds. It also provided a focal point for meditation and ritual work, connecting me to the element of water in a profound way.

Sacred Spaces and Altars:

Incorporate sacred spaces and altars throughout your garden. These can be used for meditation, rituals, and offerings. Create a sacred circle with stones or plants, or designate a quiet corner as an altar space. Decorate with meaningful symbols, statues, crystals, and candles to enhance the magical atmosphere.

One of my Favourite parts of my large garden is the sacred circle I created under a canopy of ancient oak trees. I used large stones to mark the circle and planted lavender and sage around the perimeter. In the centre, a simple altar holds candles, crystals, and offerings. This space has become my sanctuary for rituals and connecting with the natural world.

Plant Groupings and Themes:

Group plants by their needs and themes to create cohesive and visually appealing sections. For example, you might have a moon garden with white and silver plants that glow in the moonlight, a medicinal herb garden, or a butterfly garden filled with nectar-rich flowers. Themed plantings can enhance the garden's beauty and its magical and practical functions.

In my large garden, I created a moon garden near the sacred circle. Plants like evening primrose, moonflower, and silver sage created a serene, luminous space that came alive at night. It became a favourite spot for moonlit rituals and quiet contemplation. Themed plantings helped me organize the garden and gave each area a unique identity.

Personal Connection and Enjoyment

Regardless of the size of your garden, it's essential to create a space where you feel a deep personal connection and enjoyment. Incorporate seating areas where you can relax, meditate, and connect with the energy of your garden. Benches, hammocks, and outdoor cushions can provide comfortable spots to enjoy the beauty and tranquillity of the space.

Add personal touches that reflect your personality and magical practice. This could be statues of deities, crystals, wind chimes, or handmade decorations. Personalizing your garden makes it a true extension of yourself and your magic. Consider adding interactive elements like a labyrinth, a fairy garden, or a water feature. These can provide focal points for meditation, play, and ritual work. Engaging with these elements can deepen your connection to the garden and enhance your magical practices.

Creating a magical garden is an ongoing journey that evolves over time. Plan for future growth and changes in your garden. Allow space for plants to mature and spread and be open to redesigning areas as needed. Flexibility and adaptability are key to maintaining a vibrant and thriving garden.

Stay curious and continue learning about plants, gardening techniques, and magical practices. Attend workshops, read books, and connect with other herbalists and witches. Continuous learning keeps your practice dynamic and inspired.

Regularly reflect on your garden's progress and your experiences within it. What worked well? What challenges did you face? Use these reflections to refine your approach and make improvements. Your garden is a living entity, and your relationship with it will deepen as you grow together.

Soil Preparation and Fertility: Ensuring Your Soil is Ready for Planting

The earth beneath our feet is not just a medium for plants to grow in; it is a living, breathing entity teeming with microorganisms, nutrients, and energy. Preparing your soil properly is essential to ensure that your plants not only survive but flourish. So how do you prepare and enhance the fertility of your soil to create a garden that is both productive and magically potent?

Understanding Your Soil

The first step in soil preparation is to get to know your soil intimately. This means observing its texture, structure, and composition. Soil can be sandy, loamy, or clay-based, each with its own set of characteristics. Sandy soil drains quickly and doesn't hold nutrients well, while clay soil retains water and nutrients but can become compacted and difficult for roots to penetrate. Loamy soil, which is a balanced mix of sand, silt, and clay, is generally considered ideal for most plants.

To get a more precise understanding of your soil, I recommend conducting a soil test. This can be done with a home testing kit. A soil test will provide you with valuable information about the pH level and nutrient content of your soil. Most herbs prefer a slightly alkaline to neutral pH, but some plants, like blueberries, prefer more acidic conditions. Knowing your soil's pH will help you make necessary adjustments. If this sounds like a bit of a bore then just think a little bit of preparation now will result in years of success with your herbs, plants, brews, bakes, recipes, potions, and the impact it will have on health, love and protection…. it's exciting!

Once you have a clear understanding of your soil's characteristics, it's time to amend it to improve its structure and fertility. Organic matter is the key to healthy soil. It improves soil texture, enhances water retention in sandy soils, improves drainage in clay soils, and provides essential nutrients as it breaks down.

Composting: One of the best ways to add organic matter to your soil is through composting. Compost is decomposed organic material, rich in nutrients and beneficial microorganisms. I maintain a compost pile in my garden where I add vegetable kitchen scraps, garden waste, and even cardboard. Over time, these materials break down into a dark, crumbly substance that is perfect for enriching your soil. Spread a layer of compost over your garden beds and work it into the top few inches of soil.

Green Manure: Another method I use is planting green manure crops, such as clover or rye, which are grown specifically to be turned back into the soil. These plants help to improve soil structure, prevent erosion, and add organic matter. Once they have grown, they are cut down and turned into the soil, where they decompose and release their nutrients.

Animal Manure: Well-rotted animal manure is another excellent amendment. It's important to use aged manure, as fresh manure can be too strong and may burn plants. Manure adds nitrogen, phosphorus, and potassium to the soil, which are essential nutrients for plant growth. I source manure from local farms, ensuring that it is well-composted before applying it to my garden.

Balancing Soil pH

Adjusting the soil pH to the optimal range for your plants is crucial for nutrient availability. If your soil test indicates that your soil is too acidic, you can raise the pH by adding lime. Conversely, if your soil is too alkaline, sulfur or peat moss can help lower the pH.

For example, I once had a section of my garden where the soil was too acidic for the herbs I wanted to plant. By gradually incorporating lime over the course of a few seasons, I was able to bring the pH to a more neutral level, which greatly improved plant health and growth. Always follow the recommended application rates based on your soil test results to avoid over-correction.

Enhancing Soil Fertility

Beyond amending the soil with organic matter, there are several other practices I follow to enhance soil fertility and ensure my plants have access to the nutrients they need.

Crop Rotation: Rotating crops helps prevent nutrient depletion and reduces the risk of soil-borne diseases. Different plants have different nutrient requirements and pests. By changing the location of plant families each season, I can maintain soil fertility and keep my plants healthy.

Mulching: Mulching is another essential practice. A layer of mulch helps retain soil moisture, suppress weeds, and as it decomposes, adds organic matter to the soil. I use straw, leaves, or grass clippings as mulch, depending on what's available. Mulching not only improves the soil but also creates a more stable environment for plant roots.

Cover Cropping: Cover crops, like green manure, are planted to cover the soil rather than to be harvested. They help prevent erosion, improve soil structure, and add organic matter when they are turned into the soil. I often plant cover crops like oats or buckwheat in the off-season to keep the soil healthy and productive.

Respecting the Soil's Energy

As a Green Witch, I believe that soil holds not only nutrients and microorganisms but also energy. Working with this energy is an integral part of my gardening practice. Before planting, I take time to connect with the soil, often by walking barefoot in the garden, feeling the earth beneath my feet, and meditating on the natural energy flowing through it.

I also perform rituals to honour the soil, such as sprinkling a mixture of salt and water to purify it or burying crystals like quartz to enhance its energy. Planting by the phases of the moon is another practice I follow, aligning my activities with the natural rhythms of the earth and moon to enhance growth and vitality.

Preparing and maintaining fertile soil is an ongoing process that requires attention, patience, and respect for the natural world. It's a labour of love that pays off in the form of healthy, vibrant plants that are not only useful for their medicinal and culinary properties but also for their magical energy.

Over the years, I've come to appreciate the deep connection between healthy soil and the well-being of my garden. It's a reminder that we are stewards of the earth, and our actions have a direct impact on the health of our environment. By nurturing the soil, we are nurturing ourselves and the magical energy that flows through all living things.

Gardening connects us to the cycles of nature, the rhythms of the earth, and the magic that flows through all living things. The tools we use are extensions of our hands and hearts, helping us to nurture and cultivate life. As a Green Witch, I view my garden as a sacred space where I can practice my craft, connect with the natural world, and find solace and inspiration.

The process of preparing the soil, planting seeds, and tending to growing plants is a form of alchemy. We transform raw materials into living, thriving entities that nourish our bodies, minds, and spirits. Each tool I use, from the humble hand trowel to the sacred moon calendar, plays a role in this transformative process. They are not just tools but companions on my journey as an herbalist and witch.

Chapter 3
Essential Tools

"Mid hīerda stæf, se wyrhtan wealdan þā eorðan, mildheortnesse and miht ætsomne."

"With the shepherd's staff, the worker commands the earth, blending gentleness and strength together."

Chapter 3: Essential Tools for the Herbal Alchemist

Essential Tools for the Herbal Alchemist: Basic Gardening Tools for Planting and Maintenance

I've found that having the right tools can make all the difference in the world when it comes to cultivating a thriving magical garden. Gardening is both an art and a science, and the tools you choose can greatly influence the efficiency and enjoyment of your gardening experience. Over the years, I've come to rely on a collection of essential tools that have become indispensable in my practice of herbal alchemy. In this chapter, I'll share my personal experiences and insights on the must-have items for planting and maintenance, which I believe every aspiring herbal alchemist should have.

Starting with the basics, there are certain tools that every gardener, whether seasoned or novice, should have in their toolkit. These foundational tools will help you with the fundamental tasks of planting, weeding, pruning, and maintaining your garden.

A hand trowel is one of the most versatile and essential tools in any gardener's arsenal. It's perfect for digging small holes for planting seeds, bulbs, and seedlings. I find it particularly useful for transplanting young plants from pots to the garden. When choosing a hand trowel, look for one with a sturdy, comfortable handle and a durable blade. Stainless steel or high-carbon steel blades are preferable as they resist rust and can handle tougher soils.

Pruning shears are indispensable for cutting back plants, harvesting herbs, and removing dead or diseased foliage. A good pair of pruning shears will have sharp, durable blades and a comfortable grip. I use mine almost daily during the growing season, whether it's to trim back overgrown branches or to gather fresh herbs for tinctures and teas. For precision tasks, such as cutting delicate stems or shaping small plants, a pair of fine-tip shears can be incredibly helpful.

Protecting your hands while gardening is crucial. Garden gloves not only keep your hands clean but also protect them from thorns, splinters, and blisters. I recommend investing in a good pair of gloves that are both durable and comfortable. There are many types of gloves available, from lightweight options for delicate tasks to heavy-duty versions for more rugged work. Personally, I prefer gloves with reinforced fingertips and a snug fit that allows for dexterity.

A garden fork is essential for turning and aerating soil, breaking up clumps, and mixing in compost or other amendments. It's particularly useful for working in heavy or compacted soils. A sturdy garden fork with strong tines will make these tasks much easier. I often use mine when preparing new garden beds or refreshing existing ones at the start of each season.

Water is life for your plants, and how you deliver it can make a big difference. A watering can with a fine rose (the part that disperses the water) is ideal for delicate seedlings and newly planted herbs. For larger gardens, a hose with an adjustable nozzle can save time and effort. I like to use a gentle spray setting to avoid damaging plants and to ensure even watering. Drip irrigation systems are also an excellent option for conserving water and providing consistent moisture to your plants.

Beyond the basic tools, there are specialized items that can enhance your ability to cultivate and harvest herbs, flowers, and other plants with magical and medicinal properties. These tools help you work with greater precision and care, ensuring that your plants thrive and that you can make the most of their healing and magical qualities.

A harvesting basket is an elegant and practical tool for gathering herbs, flowers, and other plant materials. It allows for airflow, which is important for keeping your harvest fresh as you move through the garden. I have a beautiful woven basket that I use to collect my daily harvests. It's sturdy, with a comfortable handle, and it adds a touch of charm to the process of gathering plants. Some people prefer to use a garden trug or a dedicated harvest bag, which can be equally effective.

The Hori Hori knife is a traditional Japanese gardening tool that combines the functions of a trowel and a knife. It's excellent for digging, weeding, cutting, and even dividing plants. The serrated edge can saw through roots, while the pointed tip is perfect for precise digging. I've found my Hori Hori knife to be incredibly versatile and durable. It's my go-to tool for tasks that require a bit more strength and precision than a hand trowel can provide.

Understanding the condition of your soil is vital for growing healthy plants. A soil testing kit can help you determine the pH level and nutrient content of your soil, allowing you to make informed decisions about amendments and fertilizers. I test my soil at the start of each growing season to ensure it's in the best possible condition for my plants. There are simple kits available that provide basic information, as well as more advanced versions that offer detailed analyses.

A dibber is a pointed tool used to make holes in the soil for seeds, bulbs, and seedlings. It's particularly useful for planting at consistent depths and spacings. Some dibbers come with graduated markings to help you measure the depth accurately. Paired with a planting guide, which can be a simple template or a more elaborate grid system, a dibber helps ensure that your plants have the right amount of space to grow and thrive.

Once you've harvested your herbs, proper drying is essential to preserve their potency and quality. An herb drying rack provides a dedicated space for drying herbs evenly and efficiently. I use a tiered drying rack that allows for good airflow and easy organization. Hanging bundles of herbs in a cool, dark, and dry place is also an effective method. Properly dried herbs can be stored for months and used in teas, tinctures, salves, and other preparations.

Enhancing Your Garden with Magical Tools

In addition to practical gardening tools, incorporating magical tools and practices into your gardening routine can enhance the energy and intention of your space. As a Green Witch, I find that blending practical and magical approaches creates a more harmonious and powerful garden.

Moon Calendar

Planting by the phases of the moon is an ancient practice that aligns gardening activities with the natural rhythms of the earth and moon. A moon calendar helps you keep track of the lunar phases and plan your gardening tasks accordingly. For example, planting seeds during the waxing moon can encourage growth, while harvesting during the waning moon can enhance the potency of your herbs. I find that working with the moon's energy adds a deeper layer of connection to my gardening practice.

Crystals and Stones

Incorporating crystals and stones into your garden can enhance its energy and provide specific benefits to your plants. Clear quartz is a versatile crystal that can amplify energy and intentions. Burying quartz in the soil or placing it around your garden can promote growth and vitality. Other stones, such as rose quartz, amethyst, and green aventurine, can be used to attract love, healing, and abundance. I like to create small crystal grids around my most cherished plants to infuse them with positive energy.

Rituals

Performing rituals to honour the soil and plants is an integral part of my practice as a Green Witch. These rituals are not just ceremonial; they are a way to communicate with the natural world, to show respect for the earth, and to infuse my garden with positive energy. Through these rituals, I feel a deep connection to the rhythms of nature, and they bring a sense of sacredness to my gardening practice.

Creating a Garden Altar

First off, let's talk about creating a garden altar. Picture it: a quiet, cozy corner of your garden where you can escape the chaos of the world and just be one with nature. My altar isn't some grandiose setup with gold-plated statues and ruby-encrusted chalices—though that does sound fun. Instead, it's a small, humble space adorned with items that make me smile and connect with the earth.

Candles are a must-have. I like to use ones that smell like cookies, because who doesn't love cookies? They represent the element of fire and bring a warm, comforting glow to my rituals. Incense is another Favourite. Sometimes, I go for the classic lavender or frankincense, but on days when I need a little extra zing, I burn incense that smells like fresh coffee. Ah, the smell of morning magic!

Symbolic objects are key. I scatter crystals, feathers, and random cool rocks I've collected (because who can resist picking up a shiny rock?). My Favourite is a piece of quartz that looks suspiciously like a chicken nugget. It's fun, it's quirky, and it totally brings good vibes. Seasonal elements like fresh flowers, leaves, or fruits also find their way onto my altar, adding a touch of nature's ever-changing beauty.

Using a Wand or Athame

Next up, the wand or athame. Now, if you're imagining a Harry Potter-esque wand or a dagger straight out of a fantasy novel, you're not too far off. I have a few wands and talk about some of those a bit later in the book. I find different wands call me for different things. The wand I used this morning is an oak branch, ok, more of a twig, I found on a hike and then sanded and polished, complete with some wonky carvings. It's a bit rustic but packed with personality.

The athame, on the other hand, is a sleek, black-handled knife. I use it not for slicing and dicing but for directing energy and setting boundaries. It's a handy tool for drawing sacred symbols in the air or making energetic separations. During rituals, I wave my wand around like a maestro, drawing symbols like the pentagram for protection or spirals for growth. It's a bit like gardening charades, minus the guessing game.

Drawing Sacred Symbols

Speaking of drawing symbols, this part is where the magic really happens. Before planting, I like to purify the soil and space with a salt and water mixture. I sprinkle it around, muttering blessings and sometimes the lyrics to my Favourite songs (because, why not?). Then, using my trusty wand, I draw symbols in the air over my garden beds. It's a bit like interpretive dance for witches, flowing, graceful, and slightly kooky.

Each symbol carries its own energy. The pentagram is like a cosmic security system, keeping negative vibes at bay. Spirals represent growth and transformation, which is perfect for a garden. Circles signify unity and wholeness, bringing everything together. As I draw these symbols, I imagine the energy flowing from my heart, through the wand, and into the earth. It's a meditative, almost zen-like experience, with a dash of whimsy.

Enhancing the Ritual with Elements

To kick things up a notch, I like to incorporate the four elements, earth, air, fire, and water, into my rituals. These elements are the building blocks of nature and can bring balance and harmony to your garden.

Earth: Representing soil is simple. I use stones or crystals on my altar. Burying a crystal like amethyst or clear quartz near a plant's roots can help ground its energy and promote growth. I also keep a bowl of fresh soil on my altar to symbolize fertility and abundance. Sometimes, I'll even put a small fairy figurine in the mix for my children to find.

Air: Air is represented by incense or feathers. Burning incense purifies the space and sends your intentions wafting into the spirit world. Feathers, especially those found naturally (thanks, neighbourhood pigeons!), can be placed on the altar or used to fan the incense smoke over the plants. It's like a fragrant game of tag.

Fire: Fire is all about candles. Lighting a candle at the beginning of a ritual symbolizes the spark of life and the sun's energy. I use different coloured candles depending on my mood and intention, green for growth, white for purity, yellow for clarity. And yes, sometimes they smell like cookies.

Water: Water is for purification and emotional balance. I collect rainwater in a fancy jar (well, as fancy as a repurposed pickle jar can get) and use it in my rituals, believing it holds the energy and power of the storms. Sprinkling this water over the garden adds a layer of sacredness and connects the plants to the cycles of nature.

Seasonal Rituals

Seasonal rituals are another fun and meaningful way to honour the soil and plants. These rituals align with the Wheel of the Year, celebrating solstices, equinoxes, and cross-quarter days. Each season brings its own energy and focus, making every ritual unique and exciting.

Spring: Spring is all about renewal and planting. My spring ritual involves blessing the seeds before planting them. I hold each seed in my hand, channelling my inner plant whisperer, and infuse it with intentions of growth and abundance. It's like giving the seeds a pep talk before they embark on their journey.

Summer: Summer is a time of growth and abundance. During the summer solstice, I honour the sun and its life-giving energy by creating a sun wheel with flowers and herbs. I light a yellow candle and bask in the warmth and light, thanking the sun for nurturing my garden. Sometimes, I even break out into a sun salutation yoga pose, though I'm not very good at it.

Autumn: Autumn is for harvest and reflection. My autumn ritual focuses on gratitude and giving back to the earth. I gather the last of the summer herbs and create an offering of herbs, fruits, and flowers, placing it on the altar. I then bury a portion of this offering in the garden as a way to thank the earth for its bounty. It's a bit like Thanksgiving, but with more dirt and fewer awkward family conversations.

Winter: Winter is a time of rest and introspection. During the winter solstice, I honour the dark and the return of the light by lighting a white candle and meditating on the cycles of nature. I also take this time to plan for the coming year, reflecting on what worked well and what could be improved. It's a quiet, contemplative ritual that brings a sense of peace and renewal.

Personal Connection and Intuition

One of the most important aspects of performing rituals in the garden is to trust your intuition and personal connection to the space. While there are many traditional rituals and tools, your practice should reflect your own beliefs, experiences, and connection to the natural world. I often find that my most powerful rituals come from a place of deep personal intuition and connection, rather than strictly following a prescribed formula.

Listening to the whispers of the plants, feeling the energy of the soil beneath my feet, and allowing my heart to guide my actions are all part of the magical practice. Sometimes, a simple act of gratitude, like whispering thanks to a plant or offering a small token of appreciation, can be as powerful as a formal ritual, at least in my eyes.

Journaling Tools

Keeping a garden journal is a wonderful way to document your gardening experiences, observations, and magical practices. A dedicated notebook or digital journal allows you to record planting dates, weather conditions, successes, and challenges. It's also a space to reflect on your personal connection to the garden and any insights or inspirations you receive. Over time, your journal becomes a valuable resource that helps you learn and grow as a gardener and herbal alchemist.

The essential tools for the herbal alchemist encompass both practical gardening implements and magical items that enhance the energy and intention of your garden. From basic tools like hand trowels and pruning shears to specialized items like Hori Hori knives and herb drying racks, each tool serves a specific purpose in the planting and maintenance of your garden. By incorporating magical tools and practices, you can create a harmonious and powerful space that supports your work as a Green Witch. May your garden flourish with health, beauty, and magic, and may your tools serve you well on your journey of herbal alchemy.

"Sē siþ is hælend, þē lēadð þū in middangeardes bēag."

"The journey is healing, leading you into the circle of the world."

Chapter 4: Growing Magical Herbs

Growing magical herbs is more than just a gardening task; it is a spiritual journey that connects you to the very essence of the earth. I have spent many years cultivating herbs, years of trial and error, having huge successes but also had my fair share of disappointments, but I have learnt from each one.

Seed Starting: The Beginning of Magic

Starting herbs from seeds is like witnessing the birth of magic. Each tiny seed holds the potential to grow into a powerful plant that can be used for healing, protection, or enhancing spells. There is something incredibly satisfying about nurturing a plant from a seed and watching it grow into its full potential.

Choosing the right seeds is the first step in seed starting. Over the years, I've found that sourcing seeds from trusted suppliers, friends, family or fellow witches ensures that the seeds are potent and healthy. I remember the time when I ordered a batch of African Blue Basil seeds from an unknown supplier, and they weren't cheap, only to find that most of them failed to germinate. Lesson learned. Now, I either purchase from reputable sources, exchange seeds with fellow practitioners who understand the importance of quality, or I forage seeds from the wild.

The soil is the foundation of your plant's health. I prepare my seed-starting mix by combining equal parts of peat moss, coconut coir, a little well-rotted leaf compost and sand. This mix is light, well-draining, and provides the perfect environment for seeds to germinate. One spring when I experimented with different soil mixtures. The batch with heavy garden soil resulted in poor germination and weak seedlings. Since then, I've stuck to my trusted seed-starting mix.

Sowing seeds is a delicate process. I fill small pots or seed trays with my soil mix, water it thoroughly, and then plant the seeds according to their specific needs. Some seeds, like chamomile, need light to germinate, so I scatter them on the surface and lightly press them into the soil. Others, like rosemary, need to be covered with a thin layer of soil.

One spring, I decided to teach my oldest daughter how to start basil from seeds. It was a sunny afternoon, and we set up our seed trays on the patio. The tiny basil seeds, resembling specks of dust, proved challenging for her small fingers. We laughed as we fumbled with the seeds, trying to space them evenly and avoid planting them too densely.

I explained the importance of giving each seed enough space to grow. "Too close, and they'll compete for food," I told her. "Too far apart, and we waste space." It was a lesson in patience and precision, skills that gardening teaches so well.

As the days passed, we eagerly checked the trays each morning. To our delight, tiny green shoots began to appear. The joy of seeing those first seedlings emerge is a feeling I never tire of and has become infectious with those around me. Within a few weeks, we had a jungle of basil seedlings. The scent of fresh basil filled the air every time we brushed against them.

Caring for Seedlings: Providing the Right Conditions

Once the seeds are sown, providing the right conditions is crucial for their germination and growth. Seeds need warmth, moisture, and light to sprout and develop into healthy seedlings. Although I occasionally use a seed-starting heat mat to provide consistent warmth, particularly useful in the early spring when the house can be quite chilly, I generally prefer to place my seed trays on a sunny windowsill in my kitchen or potting shed. The natural light and warmth from the sun create an ideal environment for germination. This windowsill approach adds a cozy, homely touch to the process.

There's something enchanting about watching them grow, see them bask in the shifting light throughout the day. I am well aware that without sufficient light, seedlings can become leggy and weak. Yet, there's a special joy in nurturing them in the sunniest spots of my home, where I can keep a close eye on their progress while going about my daily routines.

In the end, it's about finding a balance. Using grow lights to supplement natural sunlight when necessary ensures that my seedlings receive consistent, adequate light. But whenever possible, I let them enjoy the warmth and energy of the sun. This method allows me to blend practical gardening techniques with the joy of experiencing nature's light. The result is a thriving garden that brings both beauty and a profound sense of well-being. Watching the seedlings transform into strong, vibrant plants under the natural light is a reminder of the simple pleasures of gardening and the magical bond it creates between us and the natural world.

Before transplanting seedlings into the garden, they need to be hardened off. This process involves gradually exposing them to outdoor conditions, starting with a few hours of shade and gradually increasing their exposure to sunlight and wind. This toughens them up and reduces transplant shock.

My early attempts at hardening off seedlings were far from successful. I was so eager to get them into the garden that I skipped this step or gave it lip service. The poor plants wilted under the intense sun and wind, and I lost many of them. Now, I take the time to properly harden off my seedlings, ensuring they are strong and resilient.

Propagation: Creating New Life

Propagation is another magical aspect of growing herbs. It involves creating new plants from existing ones, either through cuttings, division, or layering. This method not only saves money but also allows you to multiply your favourite plants and share them with others.

Taking cuttings is my Favourite method of propagation. It feels like performing a miracle, creating new life from a small piece of an existing plant. I often propagate rosemary, sage, and mint using this method.

To take cuttings, I choose a healthy, non-flowering stem and cut it just below a node (where the leaves attach to the stem). I remove the lower leaves, dip the cut end in natural rooting powder, and place it in a pot filled with a mix of perlite and peat moss. Keeping the cuttings moist and in indirect light encourages root development.

Last summer, I decided to propagate a particularly fragrant variety of rosemary. I took several cuttings and placed them in a shaded corner of my garden. Every day, I misted them and whispered words of encouragement. Within a few weeks, they developed roots and were ready to be transplanted into pots. Today, those rosemary plants are thriving, and their scent fills my garden every time I brush against them.

Dividing plants is another effective way to propagate herbs. This method works well for perennials like chives, oregano, and lemon balm. Dividing plants not only creates new plants but also rejuvenates the original plant, encouraging more vigorous growth.

To divide a plant, I carefully dig it up, ensuring I get as much of the root system as possible. I then gently separate the plant into smaller sections, each with its own roots and shoots. Replanting these divisions in well-prepared soil ensures they establish quickly.

We had a lovely clump of chives growing along the side of the greenhouse and was taking over that corner of my garden, so I decided it was time to give it some space. After dividing it into several smaller clumps, I planted them around my garden, but mostly shared with friends. The chives thrived, and now I have a bountiful supply for cooking and magical use and some appreciative friends.

Layering is a propagation method that involves encouraging a stem to develop roots while still attached to the parent plant. This method works well for herbs like thyme and rosemary.

To propagate through layering, I choose a low-growing stem and gently bend it to the ground. I remove the leaves from the section that will be buried and make a small cut in the stem to encourage rooting. I then bury the stem in the soil, securing it with a small rock or garden staple. Keeping the soil moist encourages root development. Once the stem has developed a good root system, I cut it from the parent plant and transplant it.

Planting Plans: Designing Your Magical Garden

Creating a planting plan is like painting a living canvas. It involves selecting the right plants, arranging them in a way that maximizes their growth and magical potential, and ensuring they have the right conditions to thrive.

Choosing the right plants for your magical garden is a fun part of the process but also personal as it blends your intentions with the unique properties and energies of each herb. This selection process is not just about filling your garden with greenery; it's about creating a space that resonates with your spirit and enhances your magical practices.

Each herb carries its own distinct vibrational frequency and magical attributes, making the selection process both exciting and deeply meaningful. When choosing plants, I always consider the specific energies I want to invite into my garden and my life

In my garden, lavender is a cornerstone that I cherish for its calming and protective properties. Its soothing fragrance helps to reduce stress and anxiety, creating a peaceful environment. I often place lavender near entrances to ward off negative energies and invite tranquillity into my home.

Another staple in my garden is rosemary, known for its purifying and healing energies. This incredibly versatile herb serves many purposes; I use it in cleansing rituals, healing spells, and even in my kitchen for its robust flavour. Planting rosemary by the garden gate is an old tradition that is said to protect and bless all who enter.

Sage holds a prominent place as well, valued for its powerful cleansing abilities. Burning sage, or smudging, is a common practice I use to purify spaces, objects, and people. Beyond its cleansing properties, sage also enhances my culinary creations, adding depth and flavour to a variety of dishes.

Then there's thyme, another essential herb that I appreciate for its courage and healing properties. In folklore, thyme is believed to inspire bravery and strength, so I often incorporate it into spellwork aimed at boosting confidence and resilience. It's also a favourite seasoning in my kitchen, perfect for enhancing the taste of many recipes.

Mint is a must-have for its refreshing scent and invigorating properties. Known for its ability to attract positive energy and prosperity, I plant mint near my home to promote abundance and ward off negativity. Its leaves are fantastic for making teas that soothe digestion and refresh the mind.

I also treasure marshmallow root for its soothing and healing qualities. This herb is excellent for creating remedies that calm irritated tissues and skin. I plant it in a damp, shaded spot to replicate its natural habitat, ensuring it thrives in my garden.

Chamomile is another favourite of mine, known for its calming and protective effects. I enjoy making teas from chamomile that promote relaxation and sleep. The delicate, daisy-like flowers also add beauty and serenity to my garden, and they're often used in rituals to attract abundance and peace.

Finally, while it may seem like an unusual choice, asparagus holds a special place in my garden for its resilience and health benefits. As a perennial, it returns year after year, symbolizing endurance and longevity. The spears are a delightful spring treat, packed with nutrients and a reminder of the rewards of patience and care in gardening.

When selecting plants, I strive to create a harmonious blend of herbs that support my magical intentions and provide practical benefits. The layout of the garden is just as important as the selection of plants. I consider the growth habits and companion planting benefits to ensure that each plant thrives.

For instance, lavender and rosemary not only complement each other's growth but also create a visually pleasing and aromatic combination. Mint, being quite invasive, is best planted in containers to prevent it from overtaking other herbs. Sage, thyme, and chamomile can be interspersed throughout the garden, filling gaps and creating a lush, interconnected tapestry of greenery.

Intentional Planting

Intentional planting is at the heart of creating a magical garden. This approach involves selecting and placing each herb with specific intentions in mind, whether it's for protection, healing, love, or prosperity. By carefully considering the magical properties and energies of each plant, you transform your garden from a mere collection of greenery into a living, breathing entity that supports your magical and everyday life.

The concept of intentional planting begins with understanding the power of intention itself. In magical practices, intentions are the focused thoughts and desires that drive the manifestation of your goals. When you plant with intention, you are not just placing a seed in the soil; you are embedding your desires and wishes into the earth, allowing them to grow and flourish alongside the plants. This connection between you and your garden enhances the magical properties of the herbs, making them more potent in your rituals and spells.

Selecting Herbs with Purpose

Each herb carries its own unique energy and magical properties. By selecting herbs with specific purposes, you can tailor your garden to meet your spiritual and practical needs. For instance, lavender is known for its calming and protective qualities. Planting lavender near the entrance of your garden or home creates a barrier against negative energies and promotes peace and tranquillity. The soothing scent of lavender also aids in relaxation and sleep, making it a valuable addition to any magical garden.

Rosemary is another powerful herb, often associated with purification and healing. Its robust and invigorating aroma can cleanse spaces of stagnant energy and promote physical and emotional healing. Planting rosemary near your garden gate or in a prominent spot allows its protective energy to safeguard your home and garden.

Intentional planting also involves considering the practical aspects of gardening, such as companion planting. Companion planting is the practice of placing certain plants near each other to enhance their growth and deter pests. This technique not only supports the health of your garden but also aligns with the principles of harmony and balance central to magical practices.

For instance, planting basil near tomatoes not only improves the flavor of the tomatoes but also helps repel insects that might otherwise damage the plants. Similarly, marigolds can be planted throughout the garden to deter nematodes and other pests, while their bright flowers add a touch of beauty and joy.

One of the most rewarding aspects of intentional planting is the opportunity to infuse your garden with your personal energy. Spend time with your plants, talking to them, and expressing your hopes and desires. This personal connection strengthens the bond between you and your garden, enhancing the magical properties of the herbs.

Incorporate rituals and meditations into your gardening routine. For example, as you plant each herb, visualize the energy and intention you are embedding into the soil. You might say a small blessing or incantation as you plant, reinforcing your desires and focusing your energy.

By approaching your garden with intention, you transform it into a living, breathing entity that supports your magical and everyday life. Each herb is a partner in your spiritual journey, working with you to manifest your goals and desires. This intentional and mindful approach to gardening not only enhances the effectiveness of your magical practices but also brings a deeper sense of connection and fulfilment to your life.

Ultimately, the plants you choose should resonate with you on a personal level. Spend time with each herb, learn about its properties, and feel its energy. This connection will enhance your ability to work with the plants in your magical practices.

As we delve further into the uses of these herbs later, you'll discover the depth of their magical and medicinal qualities. Each herb, whether it's lavender, rosemary, sage, thyme, mint, marshmallow root, chamomile, or asparagus, brings its own unique magic to your garden, creating a space that is both beautiful and powerfully transformative.

Designing the Planting Layout

Designing the layout of your garden involves more than just aesthetics. It's about creating a space where plants can thrive and where you can connect with the natural energies.

When planning my garden, I consider the growth habits and needs of each plant. Taller plants, like fennel and angelica, are placed at the back or centre of the garden to provide structure and height. Low-growing herbs, like thyme and chamomile, are planted along the edges to create a lush, carpet-like effect.

One year, I experimented with an additional spiral herb garden in an area we had just cleared. I created a raised bed in the shape of a spiral, planting herbs with similar water and light requirements together. The spiral design not only looked beautiful but also allowed me to make the most of my garden space.

Planning for the changing seasons is crucial for a thriving garden. Different herbs have different growing seasons, and understanding these cycles ensures that your garden remains productive throughout the year.

In the spring, I focus on planting cool-season herbs like parsley, cilantro, and chervil. These herbs thrive in the mild temperatures and grow quickly, providing an early harvest.

As summer approaches, I plant heat-loving herbs like basil, oregano, and rosemary. These plants thrive in the warm weather and provide abundant harvests throughout the summer months.

In the Autumn of Fall, I plant hardy herbs like sage, thyme, and mint. These herbs can withstand cooler temperatures and provide fresh greens well into the autumn.

Winter is a time of rest for the garden, but it's also an opportunity to plan for the coming year. I use this time to review my planting plans, order seeds, and prepare the soil for the next growing season.

Over the years, my garden has become a reflection of my journey as a Green Witch. Each plant holds a story, a memory, and a piece of my heart.

I mentioned earlier that I have a moon garden filled with white and silver plants that glow in the moonlight. I planted white sage, silver thyme, and moonflowers, creating a serene and magical space that I could enjoy during my nighttime rituals.

Another memorable project was creating a medicinal herb garden. I carefully selected plants with potent healing properties, like echinacea, calendula, and comfrey. This garden became my go-to source for creating herbal remedies and tinctures.

I also have a specific corner of my garden dedicated to pollinator-friendly plants. I planted borage, bee balm, and lavender, attracting bees, butterflies, and other pollinators. Watching these creatures dance among the flowers added an extra layer of magic to my garden.

Growing magical herbs is a rewarding and enriching experience that connects you to the natural world and the cycles of life. Whether you're starting seeds, propagating plants, or designing your garden, each step is an opportunity to infuse your practice with intention and magic.

I find it is good and fun to do a sketch of where I am going to plant my different herbs. Here is an example for planting a bed with Lavender, Rosemary, Sage, Basil, Thyme Chamomile and Mint.

Lavender (Lavandula)

- **Position:** Back row
- **Spacing:** 18-24 inches apart
- **Light:** Full sun
- **Water:** Well-drained soil, moderate water
- **Notes:** Lavender attracts pollinators and repels pests.

Rosemary (Rosmarinus officinalis)

- **Position:** Back row
- **Spacing:** 18-24 inches apart
- **Light:** Full sun
- **Water:** Well-drained soil, drought-tolerant
- **Notes:** Rosemary's aroma deters many garden pests.

Sage (Salvia officinalis)

- **Position:** Middle row
- **Spacing:** 18-24 inches apart
- **Light:** Full sun
- **Water:** Well-drained soil, moderate water
- **Notes:** Sage is a versatile culinary and medicinal herb.

Basil (Ocimum basilicum)

- **Position:** Middle row
- **Spacing:** 12-18 inches apart
- **Light:** Full sun
- **Water:** Moist, well-drained soil
- **Notes:** Basil benefits from being near tomatoes if you have a vegetable garden adjacent.

Thyme (Thymus vulgaris)

- **Position:** Front row
- **Spacing:** 12 inches apart
- **Light:** Full sun
- **Water:** Well-drained soil, moderate water
- **Notes:** Thyme is great for edging and provides excellent ground cover.

Chamomile (Matricaria chamomilla)

- **Position:** Front row
- **Spacing:** 6 inches apart
- **Light:** Full sun to partial shade
- **Water:** Well-drained soil, moderate water
- **Notes:** Chamomile attracts beneficial insects and has soothing properties.

Mint (Mentha)

- **Position:** In a container, middle row
- **Spacing:** 18-24 inches apart (if not in a container)
- **Light:** Full sun to partial shade
- **Water:** Moist, well-drained soil
- **Notes:** Mint spreads rapidly, so contain it to prevent it from overtaking the other herbs

Plant Care: Watering, Weeding, and Feeding Your Plants

My garden is not just a collection of plants but a living, breathing sanctuary of magical energy and herbal allies. Caring for these green companions is a labour of love, sprinkled a touch of the unexpected. Let's dive into the essentials of plant care: watering, weeding, and feeding your plants, and then explore the art of harvesting your precious herbs.

Watering your plants might seem straightforward, but there's a delicate balance to strike. Too much water and you'll drown your plants, too little and they'll wither away. I like to think of watering as a form of communication with my plants. They tell me when they're thirsty, and I, in turn, provide the life-giving elixir they crave.

Every morning, I wander out to my garden with a watering can in hand, feeling like some kind of nature goddess. There's a certain ritualistic charm to the process—gently pouring water at the base of each plant, taking care to avoid wetting the leaves too much. Wet leaves can invite all sorts of pesky diseases, and nobody wants that.

I have a variety of watering tools at my disposal, from a classic metal watering can that makes me feel like I'm in an old English garden, to a hose with a fancy spray nozzle for those hot summer days when everyone, including the plants and the children, needs a good shower. However, my favourite method is using a rain barrel. There's something magical about using water collected from the sky. It's as if the heavens themselves are blessing my garden.

Of course, there are times when I forget to water, usually because I get caught up in some spellwork or, let's be honest, binge-watching shows on Netflix or the BBC. When this happens, I rush out to find my plants looking like they've had a rough night out. A good soaking usually revives them, but I can almost hear their leafy sighs of exasperation.

Weeding is perhaps the least glamorous part of gardening. No one likes to bend over and yank out uninvited plants, but it's a necessary task to keep your garden healthy and vibrant. Weeds are like those annoying guests who show up uninvited, drink all your wine, and never leave.

I approach weeding with a mixture of determination and resolve. I arm myself with my trusty trowel and garden gloves and dive into the task. There's something oddly satisfying about pulling out a weed, roots and all. It's a little victory, a reminder that I'm in control of this space.

There are times, though, when the weeds seem to conspire against me. There is one part of the garden where it always feels like I'm fighting a losing battle. The weeds grow faster than I can pull them, and I started to feel like I was in a scene from a horror movie. That's when I discovered the magic of mulch. A good layer of mulch not only keeps the soil moist but also suppresses those pesky weeds. It's like a cozy blanket for your plants, and who doesn't love a cozy blanket?

Occasionally, I enlist the help of my rather lazy black cat named Dusty. He's not much help with the actual weeding, but he does like to pounce on the piles of pulled weeds, scattering them back across the garden. His antics make the task a bit more bearable, and we always end up having a good laugh.

I do have a couple of old Hoe's that are left around the garden, which I occasionally pick up and just murder a few weeds here and there when I'm in a pottering around mood.

Feeding your plants is like cooking for your family. You want to give them the best so they can grow strong and healthy. I like to use a combination of compost and natural fertilizers to keep my garden thriving. My compost pile is a thing of beauty, a smelly, wriggling mass of organic matter that magically transforms into rich, black gold.

Every few weeks, I'll scatter a layer of compost, dug out from the bottom of the pile, around the base of my plants, giving them a boost of nutrients. I also make my own fertilizer tea, a delightful brew made from compost, water, and a bit of molasses. It smells awful but works wonders. I imagine my plants throwing a little party every time I feed them. The tea is for the plants not me, just to be clear!

I have tried making fish emulsion fertilizer. It seemed like a great idea until I realized I had to ferment fish parts in a bucket for several weeks. The smell was something out of a nightmare and not something I would recommend if you have close neighbours, but my plants loved it. The things we do for our green friends!

Harvesting: Best Practices for Gathering Your Herbs

Harvesting is the reward for all your hard work. It's the moment you get to gather the fruits (or in this case, herbs) of your labour. But it's not just about snipping off leaves and flowers willy-nilly. There's an art to it, and a bit of magic, too.

First and foremost, timing is everything. Harvesting your herbs at the right time ensures they are at their most potent. Early morning is the best time to harvest, just after the dew has dried but before the sun gets too hot. This is when the essential oils in the herbs are at their peak, giving you the most flavour and medicinal benefits. There are some herbs where moonlight harvesting is better, but we'll come to those later.

When I head out to harvest, I bring a basket and a pair of sharp scissors (easier to keep sharp then secateurs). I also bring a bit of gratitude and respect. Harvesting is a sacred act, and I like to take a moment to thank the plants for their gifts. Sometimes I'll say a little blessing or leave an offering, a small crystal or a pinch of tobacco from my pipe. Yes I do smoke a pipe sometimes, not particularly lady like perhaps but my mother smoked a pipe, so did grandma, as did her mother. I blame the DNA.

Different herbs require different harvesting techniques. For leafy herbs like basil and mint, it's best to snip off the stems just above a pair of leaves. This encourages the plant to bush out and produce more leaves. For woody herbs like rosemary and thyme, you'll want to cut the stems back to a point where new growth is visible.

Flowers like chamomile and calendula should be picked when they are fully open but before they start to wilt. These delicate blooms can be carefully pinched off or cut with scissors. And then there are roots, like those of dandelion and burdock, which are best harvested in the Autumn when the plant's energy has returned to the roots.

One summer, I decided to harvest my entire mint pot at once as I had a great idea for using the pot. Big mistake. I ended up with more mint than I knew what to do with. I made mint tea, mint syrup, mint jelly, and even tried my hand at mint pesto. My kitchen smelled like a toothpaste factory for weeks. The lesson? Harvest what you need, when you need it.

Drying and storing your herbs properly is just as important as the harvesting itself. I like to tie the herbs into small bundles and hang them upside down in a dark, well-ventilated space. This method preserves their colour, flavour, and potency. Once they're dry, I store them in glass jars, away from direct sunlight. There's nothing quite like opening a jar of summer-harvested basil in the middle of winter and being transported back to warmer days.

When it comes to harvesting, it's important to approach it with the right mindset. It's not just about taking; it's about giving thanks and acknowledging the cycle of life. I like to make harvesting a special event. Do you dress for the occasion, I do. I'll wear a flowy dress, don a wide-brimmed hat, wear a trusty striped garden apron and carry a woven basket. It's my little nod to the romanticism of gardening.

One of my favourite herbs to harvest is lavender. There's something incredibly soothing about snipping off those fragrant purple spikes. I use lavender in everything from sachets to soaps to tea. Plus, hanging bundles of lavender around the house not only looks beautiful but also helps to keep the air fresh and calming.

Basil is another joy to harvest. I love the way it fills the air with its sweet, peppery scent. I always make sure to leave some leaves behind so the plant can continue to grow. Freshly harvested basil is a treat in the kitchen, whether it's in a Caprese salad, a pesto, or simply scattered over a dish.

When it comes to harvesting, it's important to approach it with the right mindset. It's not just about taking; it's about giving thanks and acknowledging the cycle of life. I like to make harvesting a special event. Do you dress for the occasion, I do. I'll wear a flowy dress, don a wide-brimmed hat, wear a trusty striped garden apron and carry a woven basket. It's my little nod to the romanticism of gardening.

One of my favourite herbs to harvest is lavender. There's something incredibly soothing about snipping off those fragrant purple spikes. I use lavender in everything from sachets to soaps to tea. Plus, hanging bundles of lavender around the house not only looks beautiful but also helps to keep the air fresh and calming.

Basil is another joy to harvest. I love the way it fills the air with its sweet, peppery scent. I always make sure to leave some leaves behind so the plant can continue to grow. Freshly harvested basil is a treat in the kitchen, whether it's in a Caprese salad, a pesto, or simply scattered over a dish. Over the years, I've gathered a wealth of tips and tricks for plant care and harvesting, often through trial.

Watering Wisdom: Plants are like people; they each have their own preferences. Some like to be soaked thoroughly and then left to dry out, while others prefer a little water more frequently. Pay attention to your plants' needs and adjust accordingly. And always, always, turn off the hose before you go to bed. Do you remember in the cartoon 101 Dalmatians, one of my favourites, there's a scene where the dog owners all look like their pets. It's probably a little mean of me but there are so many herbs that look like or remind me of people in my life. It's a fun and meaningful way to deepen my connection with both my plants and the individuals in my life. Here's a whimsical exploration of how various herbs can remind me of the people I know, based on their distinctive qualities and behaviours… or odd looks.

Lavender-Like Laura: Laura is my best friend from college, and she is the epitome of lavender. Whenever I was stressed about exams, Laura would come over with a pot of chamomile tea and a lavender-scented candle. She has this incredible ability to create a peaceful atmosphere, no matter the chaos around her. Her home is a sanctuary of calm, with soft lighting, cozy blankets, and the constant, soothing scent of lavender. Laura's gentle presence and nurturing spirit make her my go-to person when I need to unwind.

Rosemary-Reliable Richard: Richard, my older brother (much older), is the quintessential rosemary. He's always been the leader of our family, organizing get-togethers and taking charge in emergencies. I remember once when our basement flooded, and while the rest of us were panicking, Richard was already knee-deep in water, sorting out the situation with a calm, commanding presence. His confidence and reliability are invigorating, just like the scent of rosemary, and his practical, no-nonsense advice has guided me through many tough times.

Ginger-Georgie: Georgie, my colleague at the paper, red headed and has the charm and zest of Ginger. She's the life of every party, always surprising us with her culinary creations. Georgie's vibrant personality and infectious laughter make even the most mundane workday enjoyable. Her adventurous spirit and ability to find joy in the little things remind me of the sweet and spicy Ginger in my garden.

Sage-Savvy Samantha: Samantha, my brother's wife, mentor, fellow lover of wine and singing outrageously out of key after too much wine, embodies the wisdom and clarity of sage. She has a way of turning complex problems into simple solutions with her thoughtful insights. I often find myself seeking her advice, whether it's about career choices or personal dilemmas. Her stories are filled with life lessons that resonate deeply. Samantha's calm demeanor and vast knowledge make her the sage of my life, providing clarity and wisdom whenever I need it.

Thyme-Tenacious Tom: Tom, my dependable neighbour, is the thyme in my community. Whenever I need help, whether it's moving furniture or watering my plants while I'm away, Tom is always there. He's the first to show up and the last to leave, ensuring everything is taken care of. His reliability and quiet strength are comforting, much like the resilient thyme in my garden. Tom's consistent support and practical nature make him an invaluable friend.

Chamomile-Caring Claire: Claire, my cousin, has the gentle, healing presence of chamomile. As a nurse, she spends her days caring for others, and her empathy and kindness extend beyond her profession. During a particularly tough time in my life, Claire would call me every evening, just to check in and offer a listening ear. Her nurturing spirit and calming presence are as soothing as a cup of chamomile tea, bringing comfort and healing to those around her.

Mint-Merry Michael: Michael, my childhood friend, is the mint of my social circle. He's always full of energy and ready for an adventure. Michael once convinced me to go on a spontaneous road trip, and it turned out to be one of the most memorable experiences of my life. His enthusiasm and zest for life are contagious, making even the simplest activities exciting. Michael's bright personality and invigorating spirit are as refreshing as mint.

Echinacea-Empowered Ethan: Ethan, a friend from the farmers market, is the echinacea among us. Having faced significant challenges in his life, Ethan has emerged stronger and more resilient. His determination and ability to overcome adversity inspire everyone around him. I once witnessed Ethan lead a community project to build a playground, tirelessly working despite numerous setbacks. His strength and tenacity are as robust as the hardy echinacea plant, making him a powerful example of resilience.

Basil: The Sweet and Spicy Charmer: Basil is an easy one, as his name is actually Basil. Over the top vibrant personality, an infectious laugh, and an easy going nature that draws people in. Adventurous in the kitchen, always trying new recipes and inviting friends over for dinner parties. Basil sells my herbs at the local farmers market so being a charmer always helps.

Magical Marigold: Cheery: Marigold, with its bright, sunny flowers, reminds me of my daughter who is always cheerful and optimistic. Always smiling, giggling, an infectious sense of joy.

Saffron: Reminds me of Sophie, a friend I miss and we lost tragically. When the crocuses are out it reminds me to say a little hello.

Who are the herbs in your garden?

While I'm kinda off down a rabbit hole, there was a children's TV programme many years ago called the Herb Garden or The Herbs, which always brings a warm, nostalgic smile to my face when I hear the theme song. Each character in the show was personified as an herb, and I later learned that they were inspired by Nicholas Culpeper's 17th-century herbal book. What a whimsical way to introduce kids to botany! The unique signature songs for each character were a delightful touch, making the herb garden feel like a magical, musical place. I had forgotten all about the show until recently and then it dawned on me that you never know what the influencers on your life really are.

Parsley the Lion was the heart of the show for me. He didn't speak, but his thoughts, voiced by the narrator, were like a window into his gentle, shy personality. I can still hear his signature tune, "I'm a very friendly lion called Parsley…" Parsley's shyness around strangers until he got to know them reminded me so much of my own hesitant early life and it was ok to be shy. Dill the Dog, always hyperactive and getting into trouble, brought so much energy and fun. He was the perfect foil to Parsley's calm demeanour.

And then there was Sage the Owl, the plump and grumpy member of the trio, whose testy signature song still makes me chuckle.

The human characters were just as memorable. Sir Basil, with his deerstalker hat and monocle, was the self-proclaimed "King of The Herbs," though his authority was always humorously undercut by his wife, Lady Rosemary. Lady Rosemary, prim and proper, kept everything in check, especially Sir Basil's bumbling attempts at hunting and fishing. Constable Knapweed's futile efforts at law enforcement in the garden were endlessly amusing, particularly his nonsensical note-taking. And Bayleaf the Gardener, with his West Country accent, was the ever-diligent worker, often at his wit's end due to the antics of the other characters. (hmm perhaps I should call my husband Bayleaf?)

The semi-regulars added even more charm. Aunt Mint, always knitting in her rocking chair, and Mr. Onion, the stern schoolmaster. Tarragon the Dragon, a clumsy little fire-breather who hatched from an egg atop a tarragon plant, was a favourite with his lisped signature song and his knack for making things disappear with his fiery breath.

I remember Belladonna the Witch's appearance vividly. She turned several characters into weeds, only to be thwarted by Dill, who used his namesake herb's properties to ward off witches, hmmm. That episode was a thrilling adventure that had me giggling!

"The Herbs" wasn't just a show; it was a magical world where every character had a unique personality and story, making each episode a new adventure. The simple yet enchanting portrayal of a herbaceous community left an indelible mark on my childhood although I've only just recently realised.

Ok back to the book….

Weeding Wonders: Mulch is your best friend. It helps retain moisture, suppress weeds, and even adds nutrients to the soil as it breaks down. Plus, it makes your garden beds look neat and tidy. And remember, even the most diligent gardener will have a few weeds. Embrace the imperfection.

Feeding Fun: Don't be afraid to experiment with different fertilizers. Whether it's homemade compost, fish emulsion, or a natural store-bought option, find what works best for your plants. And always wear gloves when handling fish emulsion. Trust me on this one.

Harvesting Happiness: When harvesting, use sharp scissors or pruning shears to avoid damaging the plants. Be mindful of the moon phases, as some gardeners believe harvesting during a waxing moon preserves the plant's energy. And most importantly, enjoy the process. Savor the scents, the textures, and the knowledge that you are reaping the rewards of your care and attention.

Gardening is a journey filled with growth, both for the plants and for the gardener. It's about more than just watering, weeding, and harvesting; it's about connecting with nature, learning from your mistakes, and finding joy in the simple act of nurturing life. So, grab your trowel, don your garden gloves, and step into your magical garden with a smile. The plants are waiting for you.

Chapter 5

"Mid eorðan hēafod, gāst wēge, āstīgan on wyrde's sēle."

"With the earth's head, carry the spirit, ascend into the world's soul."

Chapter 5: My Top 25 Magical Herbs & Plants

1	Aloe Vera
2	Apple Blossom
3	Basil
4	Bay Laurel
5	Bee Balm
6	Blackberries
7	Blackthorn
8	Borage
9	Candy Leaf
10	Chamomile
11	Chanterelles
12	Cherry
13	Cowslip
14	Damiana
15	Dittany of Crete
16	Elderberry
17	Hops
18	Horseradish
19	Lavender
20	Mullein and Coltsfoot
21	Pumpkin
22	Romanesco
23	Rowan Berries
25	Silver Birch
25	Sweet Chestnut

The Witch's Botanical Apothecary

Aloe Vera

One of the most profound stories I hold close to my heart, a story my dear grandmother shared with me many times before she passed, revolves around the Aloe vera plant. In her later years she tended to repeat herself quite a bit and tell the same stories from her youth, but the stories were always so captivating no one minded and

you sometimes got extra snippets. My grandmother you see was an incredible woman, full of quiet strength and wisdom, and her stories were always laced with the kind of magic that only comes from living through extraordinary times. She had this way of making everything she talked about seem both real and larger than life, and I adored her for it. Losing her was one of the hardest things I've ever experienced, but the memories and lessons she left me with are things I cherish every day.

One of her most vivid memories, and one she shared with me when I was old enough to understand the weight of it, was from her time during the war. My grandmother grew up in France, and her parents were part of the French Resistance. She was just a young girl then, but even so, she was thrust into a world of secrecy, danger, and resilience. She told me how they lived with the constant fear of discovery, and how every day was a struggle to survive, not just for themselves but for the others they helped.

Medical supplies were a rarity, a precious commodity that could mean the difference between life and death. The British did their best to drop supplies by parachute whenever they could, but those moments were few and far between, and they were always fraught with danger. My grandmother would tell the tale of standing in a freezing field with her parents, waiting in the dead of night, hearts pounding, listening for the faint sound of aircraft propellers overhead. They would signal with lights, hoping desperately that the parachutes would land close enough to retrieve. When they did, the relief was enormous, but the supplies never lasted long. They were rationed out carefully, saved for the most critical moments.

Burns were a common injury among the Resistance fighters. These brave souls worked with explosives, sabotaging enemy supply routes, railway lines, and factories. It was dangerous work, and many of them suffered burns from explosions or mishandled devices. There were no hospitals to go to, few doctors who could be trusted without risking everyone's lives. So, they relied on whatever they had, whatever nature could offer them.

She spoke about a greenhouse and veranda run by a group of nuns on the outskirts of Tarascon-Sur-Rhone, Monastère de la Visitation Sainte Marie. The nuns, despite their own risks, supported the Resistance quietly and faithfully where they could. They cultivated a variety of plants, but it was the Aloe Vera in particular that my grandmother remembered. The nuns tended the plants with care, knowing their medicinal properties and how needed they were at this time.

She would tell me how she and her mother, my great-grandmother, would slip away to the monastère under cover of night. They would be welcomed by the nuns, who would guide them through the dimly lit rows of plants. My grandmother always described the greenhouse as a place where you could smell the calm amidst the chaos, a place where the air was thick with the scent of earth and leaves, and where the gentle whispers of the nuns provided comfort against the backdrop of war.

My grandmother said she sometimes helped the nuns in the greenhouse, learning how to care for the plants, how to coax them into providing the gel that would soothe so many burns and wounds. The nuns, with their quiet dedication, became close allies. My grandmother would always smile mischievously when she talked about how, in that greenhouse, there was no divide between witches and nuns. They were united by their shared mission, to heal, to protect, and to resist the horrors unfolding around them. She'd say, with a twinkle in her eye, that there was far more similarity between witches and nuns than most people would think and there is probably more to that story then I ever found out, but we do have a pipe that is known as Sister Geneviève-Aimée's pipe! Both nun and witch it seems understood the power of nature, the importance of nurturing life, and the necessity of caring for the soul as well as the body.

One night, a young Resistance fighter, almost a boy, arrived at their home, his hands and arms terribly burned from trying to set fire to a German warehouse with petrol. There was no morphine, no proper medical supplies, only the Aloe vera leaves they had collected from the nuns' greenhouse. My great-grandmother mixed the gel with honey, applying it gently to the boy's wounds. My grandmother, still a child herself, watched as her mother and the nuns worked together to ease his pain, their hands moving with practiced care.

Over the next few days, from I understand, the boy's burns began to heal, thanks to the soothing properties of the Aloe vera. My grandmother would visit the greenhouse (and I think the boy!) often during this time, bringing fresh leaves back to her mother. She saw firsthand how the nuns, in their quiet way, fought the war with healing hands and steadfast hearts. They, like her family, risked everything for the sake of others, and in those moments, the distinctions between their worlds blurred. They were simply healers, doing what needed to be done.

That story, like so many others my grandmother shared, taught me the deep connections that can be forged in the most unlikely places. The Aloe Vera plant became more than just a source of physical healing; it was a symbol of the unity between those who cared enough to act. It showed me that even in the darkest of times, people from different walks of life can come together to create something powerful, something that transcends the labels the world tries to impose.

Whenever I tend to my own Aloe Vera plants, I think of those nuns, of my grandmother, and of the quiet strength they all possessed. The plants remind me that healing and nurturing are universal acts, not bound by any one belief or practice. They connect us to something deeper, something that speaks to the core of our humanity. I like to think that, in some way, I'm continuing that legacy, carrying forward the lessons my grandmother and those nuns taught me. And in doing so, I keep her memory alive, knowing that through these simple acts of care, the spirit of those times endures.

Aloe vera, or Aloe barbadensis miller, has been a constant companion in my journey as a Green Witch. Its thick, fleshy leaves hold more than just a soothing gel; they embody ancient wisdom, a connection to nature's healing power, and a bridge between the magical and the mundane. For me, Aloe vera is not just a plant, it's a vital presence in my home, my garden, and my craft.

My relationship with Aloe vera began long before I even knew it had a name. I remember as a child, my grandmother tending to her small collection of potted plants, one of which was an unassuming green succulent that sat on her kitchen windowsill. I recall the day I came running into her kitchen with a scrape on my knee. Instead of reaching for a bandage, she simply washed my knee then plucked a leaf from that very plant, sliced it open, and pressed the cool, sticky gel onto my skin. The relief was instant. That was my first introduction to Aloe vera, and I've carried that memory, and the plant, with me ever since.

As I grew older and deepened my practice as a witch, Aloe vera took on new meanings. Its medicinal properties were well-known to me, but it was the plant's magical attributes that truly captivated my interest. Aloe vera has been revered for thousands of years for its healing powers. The ancient Egyptians called it the "plant of immortality," using it not only for healing but also in the sacred process of embalming. For me, Aloe vera symbolizes the intersection of life and death, health and spiritual protection, making it a powerful ally in my magical practice.

Cultivating Aloe vera is a rewarding experience. The plant thrives in conditions that mimic its native desert environment, full sun, well-drained sandy soil, and minimal water. I grow my Aloe vera in a greenhouse, where it basks in the sunlight filtering through the glass. There's something meditative about tending to it, feeling the warmth of the sun, and knowing that with just a little care, this plant will thrive. It doesn't demand much, which is perhaps why I feel such a kinship with it. Aloe vera teaches me the importance of resilience, of flourishing with what little you have.

Propagation of Aloe vera is straightforward, and I find the process almost ritualistic. I usually propagate Aloe vera by separating the small pups, or offsets, that grow at the base of the parent plant. Gently removing these and planting them in their own pots feels like a small act of magic, creating new life from the old. It's a reminder of the cycles of growth and renewal that are so central to my practice.

In my magical work, Aloe vera is a versatile and potent tool. I use it in spells for protection, healing, and prosperity. The plants are often placed around my home, particularly near doors and windows, to ward off negative energy. The plant's ability to heal physical wounds translates beautifully into its capacity to heal spiritual wounds as well. When I'm crafting a spell for emotional or spiritual healing, I often incorporate Aloe vera gel into the ritual. I'll mix the gel with essential oils and herbs, anointing candles or talismans to amplify the spell's intention. Its soothing energy helps to calm the mind and spirit, creating a safe space for healing to take place.

Aloe vera's medicinal uses are, of course, one of its most well-known attributes. The gel inside its leaves is a powerhouse of soothing and healing properties, particularly for burns, cuts, and skin irritations. I always have a jar of fresh Aloe vera gel in my refrigerator, ready to use whenever needed. It's my go-to remedy for everything from minor burns to insect bites, but also as a hand moisturiser. There's a certain comfort in knowing that, no matter what happens, I can turn to this plant for relief. For harvesting I carefully choose the outermost leaves, thanking the plant for its gift, and then allow the yellow latex to drain out before peeling away the outer skin to reveal the clear, soothing gel inside.

Despite its resilience, Aloe vera isn't entirely free from the challenges that face any plant. It can be prone to pests such as aphids, and while these are relatively easy to manage with natural remedies like neem oil or soapy water, they serve as a reminder that even the most robust plants need care and attention. Overwatering is another common issue, leading to root rot—a problem I learned to avoid the hard way. Aloe vera prefers to dry out completely between waterings, and in my experience, it's better to err on the side of underwatering than overwatering. Maintaining a balance in its care is crucial, and this is another lesson Aloe vera has taught me: balance is key, in gardening as in life.

Container gardening with Aloe vera is an ideal setup, particularly for those who don't have outdoor space. I keep several pots of Aloe vera both in my greenhouse and indoors. The plant doesn't require much space, and its architectural shape adds a touch of green elegance to any room. The pots I use are always well-draining, with a mix of sandy soil that replicates its natural habitat. Seeing these little pots of life scattered around my home gives me a sense of comfort and continuity, knowing that no matter where I am, I have a piece of nature close by.

In terms of culinary uses, Aloe vera is not as common as other herbs, but it does have its place. I've experimented with adding small amounts of Aloe vera gel to smoothies for its health benefits, although I must admit, it's an acquired taste. The gel is packed with vitamins and antioxidants, making it a nutritious addition to beverages. However, it's important to be cautious, as the yellow latex can act as a strong laxative and should be completely drained before consuming the gel. When used correctly, Aloe vera can be a wonderful supplement to a healthy diet, but as with all things, moderation is key.

The history of Aloe vera is as rich and varied as the plant itself. From its use in ancient Egypt to its prominence in traditional medicine across the world, Aloe vera has earned its place as one of the most valuable plants in human history. It's fascinating to think that the same plant I use in my daily life was once considered sacred by civilizations long past. This connection to the ancient world deepens my appreciation for Aloe vera and its enduring relevance in both magic and medicine.

There are several varieties of Aloe, but Aloe barbadensis miller is the one most commonly associated with medicinal and magical uses. I've experimented with growing other types, like Aloe arborescens, which has a more sprawling growth habit and is also used for its healing properties. However, Aloe barbadensis remains my favourite for its versatility and ease of care. Its compact form and prolific growth make it an ideal plant for both beginners and seasoned green witches.

I visited Tarascon-Sur-Rhone, Monastère de la Visitation Sainte Marie with my mum, when I was too young to really know the significance of it. When my children are older I will take them there and tell them about their great grandmother. I would also love to write to any relations of Sister Geneviève-Aimée if we have her name correct, and if we could trace them. I wonder if they knew what a hero she was.

The Witch's Botanical Apothecary

Apple Blossom

Apple blossoms have always held a special place in my heart, both for their delicate beauty and for the powerful magic they bring into my life as a green witch. The moment those pink and white petals start to unfurl in the spring, there's an almost electric energy in the air, a sense of renewal, hope, and the promise of something magical just around the corner. As someone who feels deeply connected to the earth and its rhythms, the apple tree and its blossoms have become central to many of my practices, rituals, and even the way I approach my everyday life.

The history of the apple blossom is as rich as the fruit it heralds. Apples have been cultivated for thousands of years, with origins tracing back to the mountains of Central Asia. Over the centuries, the apple tree spread across Europe, becoming a symbol of fertility, love, and immortality in various cultures. The ancient Celts held the apple tree sacred, associating it with the Otherworld, where its fruit was believed to grant eternal youth and knowledge. Even today, these themes resonate with me, and I find myself drawn to the apple blossom's ability to bridge the gap between the mundane and the magical.

In my garden, apple trees are more than just providers of fruit. They are living, breathing beings with whom I have built a relationship over the years. Cultivating these trees has taught me the patience and attentiveness that comes with nurturing something from its infancy to maturity. I usually propagate apple trees through grafting, a method that allows me to combine the strengths of different varieties. While it's a technique that requires some skill, the results are worth the effort. Watching a grafted tree grow and eventually produce blossoms is a deeply satisfying experience. I also like to start apple trees from seed, although I'm aware that the fruit from these trees may not be true to the parent. There's something magical about planting a seed and waiting to see what nature has in store, even if it's a bit of a gamble.

When the apple trees begin to bloom, I find myself spending more and more time among them. There's something almost intoxicating about the scent of apple blossoms, sweet, but not overpowering, delicate yet persistent. It's during this time that I start gathering the blossoms for my magical practices. Each year, I collect the petals with reverence, careful not to disturb the tree's natural cycle too much. The blossoms are delicate, and I always make sure to leave plenty behind to ensure a good fruiting season. In my practice, I've found that the energy of apple blossoms is most potent when harvested at dawn, just as the first light of the sun touches the petals. There's a purity in that moment, a connection between the earth and the heavens that's almost palpable.

Apple blossoms have a wide range of magical and medicinal uses, and I've incorporated them into many aspects of my life. In love spells, for example, apple blossoms are unparalleled. Their association with Venus, the goddess of love, makes them a perfect ingredient for attracting new love or deepening an existing relationship. I've often used apple blossoms in love sachets, which I carry with me when I feel the need to draw in positive, loving energy. I also create love potions using dried apple blossoms, mixed with rose petals and a touch of honey. This blend, when steeped in wine or tea, has a subtle but powerful effect, enhancing feelings of affection and emotional connection.

Medicinally, apple blossoms are soothing and gentle, much like the fruit they precede. I've found that a tea made from dried apple blossoms is excellent for calming the nerves and easing anxiety. The blossoms have a mild sedative effect, making them a good choice for those nights when sleep seems elusive. I also use apple blossom tea as a facial rinse, especially in the spring when my skin needs a little extra care after the harsh winter months. The blossoms help to tone and refresh the skin, leaving it soft and slightly fragrant.

In terms of pests and diseases, apple trees can be a bit finicky, but with proper care, they thrive. The most common issues I've encountered are aphids, apple scab, and powdery mildew. I've developed a routine over the years that keeps these problems at bay. I spray my trees with a homemade garlic and neem oil mixture, which deters pests naturally. For apple scab, I prune the trees regularly to improve air circulation, which helps prevent the fungal spores from taking hold. Powdery mildew is a bit trickier, but I've found that a weekly spray of diluted milk works wonders. It's all about balance, keeping the trees healthy and strong so they can resist disease on their own.

Maintaining my apple trees requires dedication, but it's a labour of love. Pruning is perhaps the most important task, and I usually do this in late winter or early spring before the buds begin to swell. Pruning helps shape the tree and promotes healthy growth, ensuring that the blossoms and fruit receive ample sunlight. I also mulch around the base of the trees to retain moisture and suppress weeds. Composting is another key aspect of maintenance. I feed my apple trees with composted kitchen scraps and well-rotted manure, which keeps the soil rich and fertile. There's something incredibly rewarding about returning nutrients to the earth, knowing that they'll be transformed into the blossoms and fruit that sustain me.

While apple blossoms are incredibly versatile, there are some warnings to consider. Like all things in nature, apple blossoms should be used with respect and caution. Some people may have allergies to the blossoms, so it's always a good idea to test a small amount first. Also, while apple blossoms are generally safe to consume in small quantities, it's important to remember that apple seeds contain cyanogenic compounds, which can be toxic if ingested in large amounts. I always make sure to remove the seeds when using apples or apple blossoms in culinary or medicinal preparations.

Speaking of culinary uses, apple blossoms have a delicate, sweet flavour that makes them a lovely addition to various dishes. I often sprinkle fresh apple blossoms over salads or use them as a garnish for desserts. They pair beautifully with fruit salads, especially those featuring apples, pears, or strawberries. I've also infused apple blossoms in honey, creating a fragrant and subtly flavoured sweetener that's perfect for drizzling over yogurt or stirring into tea. One of my favourite springtime treats is apple blossom jelly, made by steeping the blossoms in water and then combining the infused liquid with sugar and pectin. The result is a translucent, pale pink jelly that captures the essence of spring in every bite.

When I was in Portland I had a much smaller garden, so I grew apple trees in containers and I then added some in containers when I came back to Surrey, partly because I wanted a reminder of my Portland garden! This is especially useful if you have limited space or poor soil. Dwarf or semi-dwarf varieties are ideal for container gardening, as they don't require as much room to grow. I've found that growing apple trees in containers allows me to move them around to catch the best sunlight or to protect them from harsh weather. The key to successful container gardening with apple trees is ensuring the pot is large enough to accommodate the tree's root system and that it has good drainage. I use a high-quality potting mix and amend it with compost to provide the nutrients the tree needs. Regular watering is crucial, especially during the hot summer months, but I'm careful not to overwater, as apple trees prefer soil that's moist but not waterlogged.

Apple trees come in many varieties, each with its unique characteristics. I've experimented with several over the years, each bringing something different to my garden and my magical practices. One of my favourites is the 'Granny Smith' apple tree, known for its tart green apples and abundant blossoms. The 'Honeycrisp' variety, with its sweet, crisp fruit, also produces beautiful blossoms that I use in love and healing spells. For container gardening, the 'Dwarf Red Delicious' is a perfect choice, offering lovely red blossoms in the spring and sweet fruit in the fall. I've also had success with heirloom varieties like 'Ashmead's Kernel,' which has a rich history and produces fruit with a complex, almost spicy flavour. Each variety has its own energy, and I choose which to work with depending on the intention of my spell or the need at hand.

Beyond their magical and culinary uses, apple blossoms have a place in many other aspects of my life. I use them in crafting, pressing the delicate flowers between the pages of heavy books to preserve them for later use in art projects. They make beautiful additions to handmade greeting cards, bookmarks, or even as decorations in a shadow box. The blossoms can also be dried and added to potpourri or used in sachets to bring their sweet scent indoors long after the trees have finished blooming. I've even used apple blossoms in homemade candles, embedding the dried petals into the wax to create a stunning visual effect that also releases a subtle fragrance when burned.

Basil

The very scent of Basil evokes memories of sunlit gardens, magical workings, and comforting meals shared with loved ones. It's a plant that I've come to rely on not just for its culinary benefits but for its deep-rooted magical properties that weave seamlessly into my life.

Basil, or *Ocimum basilicum*, is a herb steeped in history and tradition. Known as the "King of Herbs," its name is derived from the Greek word "basileus," meaning "king," which hints at the reverence it has commanded for centuries. In ancient times, basil was associated with royalty, sacred rites, and protection. The Romans believed it would bring wealth, while in India, it was seen as a symbol of love and devotion, often used in religious ceremonies. For me, basil is a bridge between the mundane and the mystical, a humble plant with the power to connect the physical and spiritual realms.

I've been cultivating basil for years, and it's one of those plants that, even if I say so myself, never fails to thrive under my care. Some plants I have green fingers for, some I don't, but I must be a Basil whisperer, as I can grow that in abundance. There's something deeply satisfying about nurturing it from seed, watching the tiny green shoots push through the soil, eager to reach the light. I start my basil indoors, in small pots filled with a rich, well-draining potting mix. The seeds are tiny, almost fragile, but they carry within them the promise of abundance. I gently press them into the soil, covering them lightly, and place the pots on a sunny windowsill. Within days, the first sprouts appear, delicate yet determined. It's a reminder of the resilience of life, and I find myself talking to them, encouraging their growth with whispered blessings.

Once the seedlings are strong enough, I transplant them into larger pots or directly into the garden, depending on the season, or if I'm selling them. Basil loves warmth and sunlight, so I always ensure its placed in a spot where it can soak up the sun's rays. I've found that basil grows best in slightly alkaline soil with good drainage. I often mix in some compost to enrich the soil and add a little crushed eggshell to maintain the pH balance. It's a simple act, but one that feels deeply connected to the earth, grounding me in the rhythms of nature.

One of the things I love most about basil is its versatility in magical and medicinal uses. As a green witch, I've come to appreciate its protective qualities. Basil is known to ward off negative energies and can be used in various forms to create a shield around oneself or one's home. I often make basil-infused water, which I use to sprinkle around the perimeter of my property, particularly at the entrances, to keep harmful influences at bay. The ritual is simple yet powerful; as I walk around my home, I chant softly, asking for protection and peace. The scent of basil, released into the air as the water falls, feels like a veil of safety wrapping around my space.

But basil isn't just for magic; its medicinal properties are equally impressive. Known for its anti-inflammatory and antibacterial qualities, basil has been used for centuries to treat a variety of ailments. When I feel a cold coming on, I brew a strong basil tea, sweetened with a touch of honey. The warmth of the tea, combined with basil's natural healing properties, works wonders in soothing a sore throat and easing congestion. I've also used basil as a natural remedy for headaches, chewing on a fresh leaf or massaging basil oil into my temples to relieve tension.

Of course, like any plant, basil has its challenges. Pests such as aphids, whiteflies, and spider mites can be a problem, particularly in warm, humid weather. I've learned to keep a close eye on my plants, checking for signs of infestation. A strong spray of water usually dislodges most pests, but, when necessary, I make a natural insecticidal soap using dish soap and water, sometimes adding a few drops of neem oil for extra potency. Basil is also prone to fungal diseases like downy mildew and fusarium wilt, especially if the soil is too wet or the plants are overcrowded. Good air circulation and careful watering are key to preventing these issues, so I always make sure to plant my basil with enough space to breathe and dry out between waterings.

Maintaining basil is relatively straightforward, but it does require some attention. Regular pruning is essential to keep the plant bushy and prevent it from bolting (going to seed too early). I pinch off the top leaves every couple of weeks, using them in my cooking or drying them for later use. This encourages the plant to produce more leaves and delays flowering, which can cause the leaves to turn bitter. When basil does flower, the blooms are lovely, but I typically remove them to keep the plant focused on leaf production. However, I'll sometimes leave a few flowers to attract bees and other pollinators, who seem to love basil as much as I do.

In the kitchen, basil is a cornerstone of my cooking. Its fresh, peppery flavour adds a burst of brightness to everything from salads to pasta dishes. I particularly love making pesto, blending fresh basil leaves with garlic, pine nuts, Parmesan cheese, and olive oil. There's something magical about the way these simple ingredients come together to create such a rich, vibrant sauce. Pesto is one of those foods that feels like a celebration of summer, and I often make large batches to freeze, ensuring I have a taste of sunshine even in the depths of winter.

Basil also pairs beautifully with tomatoes, another staple in my garden. A simple caprese salad of fresh tomatoes, mozzarella, and basil, drizzled with olive oil and balsamic vinegar, is one of my favourite summer meals. It's a dish that highlights the quality of the ingredients, with basil providing the perfect aromatic counterpoint to the sweet, juicy tomatoes. For me, this dish is more than just food; it's a way of honouring the plants I've nurtured and the earth that sustains us.

One of the most personal connections I have with basil is a story from a few summers ago. My grandmother, who you will have already read a lot about in this book, had always been my inspiration and guide in herbal magic, was nearing the end of her life. She had taught me so much about the power of plants and the importance of respecting nature. In her final days, she asked me to bring her some fresh basil from my garden. She wanted the smell of it around her when her final time came, to be surrounded by its familiar scent. This may sound a bit sad, but smells evoke the greatest memories. I carefully picked the most vibrant leaves and brought them to her. As she held the basil to her nose, her face softened, and a peaceful smile spread across her lips. She told me that basil had always been her favourite herb, not just for its culinary uses but for its protective energy. It was a moment I carry with me every time I tend to my basil plants.

Basil thrives in containers, which makes it perfect for those who, like me, who like their herbs close to the Kitchen. I often grow basil in large terracotta pots on my patio, where it receives plenty of sunlight and warmth. Container gardening allows me to move the plants around as needed, ensuring they always have the best conditions. Plus, having basil close at hand means I can easily snip a few leaves whenever I need them, whether for a spell, a remedy, or a recipe.

There are many varieties of basil, each with its unique characteristics. Sweet basil is the most common, with its classic flavour and bright green leaves. However, I also grow Thai basil, which has a more anise-like flavour, perfect for adding a spicy kick to stir-fries and curries. Then there's purple basil, with its striking dark leaves and slightly more intense flavour, which I love using in salads for a splash of colour. Lemon basil is another favourite, with its citrusy notes adding a refreshing twist to both culinary and magical applications. Each variety brings something special to the table, and I enjoy experimenting with them in different ways.

Beyond the kitchen and the garden, basil has other uses that I've found invaluable. I often make basil-infused oil, which I use in both cooking and skincare. The oil is easy to make – simply steep fresh basil leaves in a good-quality olive oil for a few weeks, then strain. The resulting oil is fragrant and flavourful, perfect for drizzling over salads or using as a base for homemade beauty products. Basil's antibacterial properties make it a great addition to lotions and balms, helping to soothe and heal the skin.

In my practice as a green witch, basil has become a trusted ally, a plant that offers both practical and spiritual support. Its history is rich, its uses varied, and its presence in my life is constant. Whether I'm tending to my garden, crafting a spell, or preparing a meal, basil is always there, a reminder of the connection between nature and magic. And Grandma.

The Witch's Botanical Apothecary

Bay Laurel

Bay Laurel

This unassuming yet powerful plant has been a steadfast companion offering wisdom, protection, and a deep connection to the ancient world. The Bay Laurel has woven itself into the very fabric of my daily rituals and practices, becoming more than just a plant, it's a trusted ally, a protector, and a source of inspiration.

My journey with Bay Laurel began when I first delved into the rich history of this sacred herb. The Bay Laurel has been revered since ancient times, particularly in the Mediterranean, where it was used to crown the victors of athletic contests and warriors returning from battle. The Greeks and Romans believed the plant was sacred to Apollo, the god of prophecy and healing, and thus, it was often associated with wisdom and protection. This historical connection resonated with me deeply, and I found myself drawn to the plant's aura of strength and resilience.

When I decided to grow Bay Laurel, I knew I was bringing a piece of that ancient wisdom into my home. Cultivating Bay Laurel is an act of patience and care, something that feels almost like a ritual in itself. The plant thrives in warm, sunny locations, which makes it ideal for container gardening in my space. I keep mine in a large terracotta pot, where it basks in the sunlight filtering through my kitchen window. Bay Laurel prefers well-drained soil, so I mix in some sand to ensure it doesn't get waterlogged, a lesson I learned the hard way when I overwatered my first plant and it began to droop. Now, I water it sparingly, allowing the soil to dry out between waterings, and the plant rewards me with lush, aromatic leaves.

Propagation of Bay Laurel can be done through seeds or cuttings, though I've found that cuttings are the easiest method. I take cuttings from the plant in the spring, selecting healthy, green stems about six inches long. After removing the lower leaves, I dip the cut end in natural rooting powder (see earlier notes) and place it in a pot of moist soil, covering it with a plastic bag to create a humid environment. With a little patience and care, roots begin to form, and I have a new plant to nurture.

Bay Laurel is not without its challenges, though. Pests like spider mites can sometimes plague the plant, and I've had to be vigilant in keeping these tiny invaders at bay. I've found that a simple spray of neem oil mixed with water works wonders in keeping my Bay Laurel healthy and free of pests. However, it's important not to let the oil build up on the leaves, as it can block the sunlight the plant needs to thrive. I always make sure to wipe down the leaves gently with a damp cloth after a few days to ensure they can breathe and soak up the sun's energy.

The maintenance of Bay Laurel is relatively straightforward once you get the hang of it. It's a hardy plant that doesn't require constant attention, but it does benefit from regular pruning. I trim back the branches to maintain its shape and encourage new growth, which also prevents the plant from becoming too leggy. This pruning ritual has become a meditative practice for me, a time to connect with the plant and express my gratitude for the gifts it provides.

One of the most rewarding aspects of growing Bay Laurel is the way it seamlessly integrates into both my magical and medicinal practices. In magic, Bay Laurel is a potent herb, often used for protection, purification, and divination. I've come to rely on its energy in my rituals, particularly when I need to cleanse my space or create a protective barrier around my home. One of my favourite uses of Bay Laurel is to burn the dried leaves as incense during rituals. The aromatic smoke fills the room with a sense of calm and clarity, purifying the energy and setting the stage for deeper spiritual work.

Bay leaves are also a powerful tool in divination. I've often used them in scrying, holding a leaf in my hand as I gaze into a bowl of water or a mirror. The leaf's energy helps to focus my mind and open the channels of intuition, allowing me to receive clearer messages from the divine. I've also found that writing intentions or questions on a bay leaf and then burning it in a fire-safe dish can bring swift and insightful answers.

The medicinal uses of Bay Laurel are just as impressive. The leaves contain essential oils with anti-inflammatory and antimicrobial properties, making them a valuable addition to my herbal medicine cabinet. I often make a simple infusion by steeping the leaves in hot water, which I then use to soothe digestive issues or ease a stubborn cough. The scent alone is enough to clear my mind and relax my body, a gentle reminder of the plant's calming and protective nature.

However, as with all powerful herbs, Bay Laurel comes with its warnings. While it is generally safe for culinary and medicinal use, it's important to remember that the leaves should not be ingested whole, as they can be sharp and difficult to digest. I always remove the leaves from dishes before serving to avoid any potential issues. Additionally, some people may be sensitive to the essential oils in the leaves, so it's wise to test any topical applications on a small patch of skin first.

Bay Laurel's culinary uses are well known and celebrated. The leaves are a staple in my kitchen, where they infuse soups, stews, and sauces with their rich, earthy flavour. I love adding a couple of leaves to my slow-cooked dishes, knowing that they will impart a depth of flavour that is both comforting and complex. There's something deeply satisfying about using an herb I've grown and tended myself, knowing that it carries not just culinary benefits but also the energy of protection and wisdom.

One personal story that stands out in my mind is the time I used Bay Laurel in a protection spell for my home. It was during a period of upheaval and uncertainty, and I felt the need to create a strong protective barrier around my space. I gathered a handful of bay leaves, along with other protective herbs like rosemary and thyme, and created a wreath to hang on my front door. As I wove the leaves together, I infused them with my intentions for safety, peace, and stability. The wreath hung on my door for months, and every time I passed it, I felt a sense of calm and assurance, knowing that my home was guarded by the energy of these powerful plants.

In my small garden, container gardening has been a lifesaver, and Bay Laurel is particularly well-suited to this method. The plant can grow quite large, but by keeping it in a pot, I can manage its size and move it around as needed to catch the best sunlight. This also allows me to bring it indoors during the colder months, protecting it from frost and ensuring that it continues to thrive year-round. There's something incredibly satisfying about having such a versatile and ancient herb growing right on my windowsill, always within reach when I need it.

Beyond its magical, medicinal, and culinary uses, Bay Laurel has found its way into other areas of my life as well. The leaves make beautiful additions to homemade sachets and potpourri, filling my home with their warm, spicy scent. I've also used the branches in crafting, weaving them into wreaths or using them to decorate my altar during the darker months of the year. Their evergreen nature reminds me of the continuity of life, even in the midst of winter's chill.

There are several varieties of Bay Laurel, each with its own unique characteristics. The traditional Laurus nobilis is the one most commonly used in cooking and magic, but there are also variations like the 'Aurea,' which has golden-yellow leaves, or the 'Angustifolia,' with narrower leaves that are particularly fragrant. I've stuck with the classic variety, but I'm always intrigued by the different cultivars and their subtle differences.

My relationship with Bay Laurel has grown over the years, deepening as I learn more about this remarkable plant. It's become a symbol of protection and wisdom in my life, a green guardian that watches over my home and family. Whether I'm using it in a spell, a healing remedy, or a comforting meal, Bay Laurel never fails to bring a sense of peace and connection to the ancient world.

Looking back, I realize how much this plant has influenced my path as a green witch. It's taught me the importance of patience in cultivation, the power of intention in magic, and the deep satisfaction that comes from working with nature's gifts. Bay Laurel has become more than just a herb—it's a trusted ally, a source of strength, and a reminder of the enduring power of the natural world. As I continue to work with this plant, I'm constantly reminded of the ancient wisdom it holds and the many ways it can enrich my life, both in my practice and beyond.

The Witch's Botanical Apothecary

Bee Balm

From the moment I first encountered Bee Balm's vibrant blooms in a friend's garden, I was captivated. Its fiery red, pink, and purple flowers seemed to dance in the summer breeze, beckoning me closer. I felt an instant connection, as though the plant itself was calling to me, inviting me to explore its mysteries.

I admit I didn't know much about this herb so it required research. I learned that Bee Balm has a rich history, deeply rooted in the traditions of Native American medicine. The Native Americans revered this plant, using it to treat a wide array of ailments, from digestive issues to respiratory problems. The Oswego tribe, in particular, used the leaves to brew a tea, which the early European settlers later adopted, calling it "Oswego tea." This historical significance resonated with me, adding a layer of depth to my connection with the plant. It was as if, by cultivating Bee Balm, I was participating in an ancient tradition, tapping into the wisdom of the native Americans.

When I first decided to grow Bee Balm in my garden, I was both excited and a little apprehensive. I'd read about its tendency to spread rapidly if left unchecked, but I was determined to harness its energy. I started by selecting a sunny spot in my garden, knowing that Bee Balm thrives in full sunlight. The soil in that part of my garden was well-drained but rich, just the way Bee Balm likes it. I planted the seeds in early spring, gently tucking them into the earth with a silent prayer for a bountiful bloom. As the seedlings began to emerge, I felt a surge of excitement. Each tiny sprout was a promise of the vibrant, healing energy that would soon fill my garden.

Propagation of Bee Balm is relatively simple, which makes it a favourite among green witches like myself. I've propagated it both from seeds and by dividing established plants. Dividing Bee Balm is particularly rewarding because it allows me to share this beautiful plant with friends, fellow practitioners and it also sells well at the local farmers market in Guildford. There's something deeply satisfying about passing on a piece of a plant that has been nurtured in my own garden, knowing that it will continue to grow and spread its magic in someone else's sacred space.

One of the things I love most about Bee Balm is its versatility in both magical and medicinal uses. In my practice, I often use Bee Balm to enhance communication and understanding. The plant's vibrant energy is perfect for spells or rituals focused on strengthening relationships, whether they be with friends, family, or even within oneself. I often dry the leaves and flowers to create an incense blend that I burn during meditation or when I'm seeking clarity in my thoughts. The scent is uplifting and helps to open the mind, making it easier to connect with my inner voice and the energies around me.

Bee Balm is also a powerful ally in healing work. Its antiseptic properties make it an excellent addition to homemade salves and balms. I've used it to soothe minor cuts and scrapes, but above everything else it works wonders on insect bites. In the winter months, when colds and flu seem to be inevitable, I turn to Bee Balm for its antiviral and antimicrobial properties. A tea made from the leaves can help to ease congestion and sore throats, making it a staple in my herbal medicine cabinet.

One of the most meaningful uses of Bee Balm came when a dear friend of mine, decided to include it in her Christian wedding ceremony. She had always admired the way the Bee Balm flowers seemed to radiate energy and joy, and she felt that their presence would bring a special kind of magic to her wedding day.

When she approached me with the idea, I was thrilled and deeply touched. She asked if I could provide the flowers, knowing how much care and intention I put into growing them. We spent a sunny afternoon in my garden, surrounded by the vibrant blooms. Together, we chose the best flowers, ones that had opened fully and seemed to hum with life. As we harvested the Bee Balm, we shared stories and dreams for her future, laughing and crying as the flowers filled our baskets.

On the day of her wedding, the Bee Balm flowers took centre stage. We wove them into her hair, creating a crown that looked as though it had been plucked straight from a meadow. The bright, fiery reds and purples complemented her natural beauty, and as she walked down the aisle, I could see how much the flowers meant to her. They weren't just decorations; they were symbols of love, friendship, and the vibrant energy that she and her partner were bringing into their new life together.

During the ceremony, we placed the Bee Balm blooms on the altar, surrounding the couple with their protective and joyous energy. The scent of the flowers filled the air, mingling with the old smell of the church. It was a moment of pure magic, one that I will always cherish. Watching my friend exchange vows with the person she loved, surrounded by the flowers that we had picked together, somehow made me feel so much more a part of it.

In terms of maintenance, Bee Balm is relatively low-maintenance as long as its basic needs are met. Regular watering is important, especially during dry spells, but I'm careful not to overwater, as this can lead to root rot. I also make a point to deadhead the spent blooms throughout the growing season. Not only does this keep the plant looking tidy, but it also encourages more blooms, extending the flowering period well into late summer. Every few years, I dig up and divide the plants in early spring or fall to prevent them from becoming too crowded. This keeps the plants healthy and vigorous, and as I mentioned earlier, it gives me the opportunity to share the magic of Bee Balm with others.

While Bee Balm is a wonderful plant to have in the garden, it's important to be aware of a few warnings. The plant is a member of the mint family, which means it has a tendency to spread aggressively if not managed properly. This can be a blessing or a curse, depending on your perspective. For me, it's a reminder of the plant's vitality and resilience, but I also make sure to keep it in check by regularly dividing the plants and, when necessary, containing it within a specific area of the garden.

Another consideration is that while Bee Balm is generally safe, it's always wise to exercise caution when using any herb medicinally, especially if you're pregnant, nursing, or have any pre-existing health conditions. I always recommend consulting with a healthcare professional or a knowledgeable green witch before incorporating new herbs you haven't used before into your routine.

Bee Balm isn't just useful in the garden and in magic; it also has a place in the kitchen. The leaves and flowers are edible and can be used to add a unique flavour to a variety of dishes. I've used the fresh leaves to brew a refreshing tea, similar to the Oswego tea made by the Native Americans. The taste is somewhat reminiscent of Earl Grey, with a hint of citrus and spice. It's the perfect drink to enjoy on a warm summer afternoon, sitting in the garden surrounded by the very plants that made the tea possible. I've also added the petals to salads for a pop of colour and a subtle, slightly spicy flavour.

Bee Balm also lends itself beautifully to container gardening, which is a blessing for those with either limited space or if you like having pots around your outside table like I do. I've grown Bee Balm in large pots on my patio with great success. The key is to use a container that's large enough to accommodate the plant's root system and to ensure that the soil is well-draining. I like to mix a bit of compost into the potting soil to give the plants a nutrient boost. Container-grown Bee Balm requires a bit more attention to watering, as pots tend to dry out more quickly than garden beds, but it's well worth the effort. The sight of those bright blooms spilling over the edges of a pot brings me joy every time I step outside.

In addition to its magical and medicinal uses, Bee Balm has a variety of other applications. It's a fantastic plant for attracting pollinators, particularly bees and butterflies, which is how it earned its common name. I've often stood quietly in the garden, watching as bees buzz from flower to flower, collecting nectar.

In addition to its magical and medicinal uses, Bee Balm has a variety of other applications. One of its most delightful attributes is its ability to attract a wide range of pollinators, making it a vital player in the health of my garden ecosystem. It's no wonder Bee Balm earned its name—this plant is a magnet for bees, particularly honeybees and bumblebees, which are drawn to its vibrant, tubular flowers. The flowers are rich in nectar, providing a valuable food source that helps sustain bee populations, especially during the summer months when the blooms are at their peak.

But the appeal of Bee Balm doesn't stop with bees. Butterflies are also frequent visitors, especially species like the Monarch and Swallowtail. These elegant creatures are not only drawn to the bright, bold colours of the Bee Balm flowers but also to the nectar that lies deep within the blooms. Watching a butterfly delicately land on a flower, its wings slowly opening and closing as it feeds, is a sight that never fails to bring me joy and a deep sense of connection to nature.

Even creatures, like dragonflies and moths, are drawn to Bee Balm. They, too, visit Bee Balm for its nectar, playing a dual role in both pollination and pest management. Moths, especially those that are active during the twilight hours, find the scent of Bee Balm irresistible. As dusk falls, I sometimes catch a glimpse of these nocturnal visitors fluttering around the flowers, adding a touch of mystery to the evening garden.

"Saatat ajatella, että olemme vain tarinankertojia, mutta huomaa tämä, me olemme muinaisen voiman vartijoita."

"You may think we are just storytellers but mark you,
We are the keepers of ancient power."

Blackberries

Growing up in the countryside I was surrounded by fields and hedgerows, so was introduced to the wild beauty and untamed magic of blackberries at an early age. My mum, who had a profound connection to the land, was not just a gardener but a true steward of nature. Her love for hedgerows was a deep and abiding passion, rooted in her understanding of their importance to the ecosystem and the countless creatures that relied on them for survival. The hedgerows, with their intricate network of brambles, wildflowers, and sheltering branches, were a haven for birds, insects, and small mammals. Mum would often take me by the hand, leading me along the narrow, winding paths lined with these living walls, pointing out the nests of finches, the burrows of hedgehogs, and the delicate spider webs glistening with morning dew.

She was actually a bit annoyed as, over the years even in her lifetime, modern farming practices had led to the widespread disappearance of the hedgerows. The shift towards large, open fields devoid of these natural barriers had not only scarred the landscape but also resulted in the decline of the wildlife that had once thrived in these green corridors. The fields of her childhood, once teeming with life, had become barren expanses where few creatures could find refuge. This loss weighed heavily on her heart, and she felt sad at the disconnection from nature that she saw taking root in the world around us.

Determined to make a difference, like her mum, my grandmother, she wasn't the type just to complain (although equally like my grandmother - she was very good at it) - she always had to do something. She approached a local farmer (without talking to my dad) and suggested he might sell her a field, one that had been stripped of its hedgerow's generations earlier. It was a time when we as a family were not in the best financial position and can remember her and my dad arguing "robustly" about the possible purchase - as I sat at the top of the stairs. Of course, she got her way and we forfeited our holiday to Broadstairs that year. She, well I mean my dad actually, divided it into smaller fields, each one bordered by new hedgerows that she designed and he carefully planted and nurtured. It was a labour of love, requiring patience and dedication, but my mother was undeterred. She knew that these hedgerows would take years to mature, but she was willing to wait even knowing some would not be where she would like them to be until after her death, understanding that the restoration of the land was a gift she could give not just to her family, but to future generations.

Her inspiration, I found out later, came in part from a television or radio program, where Prince Charles as he was then, now King Charles, spoke rather eloquently about his own love for hedgerows and the traditional craft of creating them. He described how these ancient, living fences were more than just boundaries; they were vital ecosystems in their own right, supporting a rich diversity of life. Mum, who had always been a great admirer of the Royal Family, felt a deep resonance with his words, almost as if it had been a message especially to her. No she didn't have visions of grandeur, but when people spoke, even on the radio, she always listened as if they were talking directly to her. "I'm the only one in the room" she would say "who else is he talking to?" when telling us about something she had heard on the radio. She could see in his words a reflection of her own beliefs and values, and it galvanized her resolve to restore this lost part of the countryside.

The project became a personal mission, one that she pursued with the same care and reverence that she brought to all her work with the land. As the hedgerows began to grow, they transformed the field into a patchwork of life. Birds returned to nest in the dense thickets, bees buzzed among the wildflowers, and small mammals found shelter in the underbrush. My mother's field became a sanctuary, a testament to her belief in the power of nature to heal and renew itself when given the chance. These little fields also became a magnet for the local wild deer who seemed to think it was their own little gardens.

In the midst of these hedgerows, the blackberry bush took on a special significance. With its thorny canes and sweet fruit, it became more than just a plant; it was a symbol of resilience, protection, and abundance in our family's practice of witchcraft. The blackberries that grew in the new hedgerows were different from those in the wild, nurtured by my mother's careful hand. She would often say that the hedgerows were not just a gift to the land, but also a way to reconnect with the old ways, the traditions that had been passed down through our family for generations.

The blackberry bushes, thriving in these newly planted hedgerows, were a living reminder of the balance between giving and receiving. Although we had great crops we always left most for the birds and other creatures who relied on them. She showed me how to weave the thorny branches into protective charms, to brew the leaves into healing teas, and to use the berries in rituals that celebrated the cycles of the seasons and the abundance of the earth.

Through these practices, I learned that the blackberry bush, like the hedgerows themselves, was a powerful ally in the craft, embodying the principles of protection, healing, and connection to the natural world. But more than that, it represented my mother's enduring love for the land and her unwavering commitment to preserving its magic for those who would come after her.

In the years that followed, the field my mother had transformed became a place of gathering for our family, a living classroom where we learned not only about the practical aspects of gardening and land stewardship, but also about the deeper, spiritual connections that bind us to the earth. My mother's vision had created a sanctuary where the old ways could flourish, a place where the wisdom of the past could be passed down and the future could be nurtured.

Walking through those hedgerows today, you will see little shepherds huts on wheels that we let out through Air B&B and actually make a useful little bit of income from it. Each hut has its own little field.

The history of blackberries in folklore and witchcraft is as tangled and rich as the brambles themselves. Ancient cultures, from the Celts to the Romans, recognized the blackberry's power and incorporated it into their spiritual practices. In Celtic tradition, the blackberry was associated with the goddess Brigid, who presided over healing, poetry, and smithcraft. The Celts believed that the blackberry bush was sacred and that its thorns provided protection against evil spirits.

In Roman times, blackberries were seen as a symbol of prosperity and fertility. The Romans would often use blackberry branches in their rituals to honour the gods of agriculture, hoping to ensure a bountiful harvest. The blackberry's ability to thrive in the wild, growing in abundance even in the most challenging conditions, made it a powerful symbol of resilience and survival.

As Christianity spread across Europe, many of the old pagan beliefs were either absorbed or demonized. However, the blackberry bush retained its mystical associations. It was believed that blackberries offered protection against witches (pah!) and evil spirits, and people would often hang branches over their doors or windows to ward off negative influences. Ironically, this protective plant became a vital tool in the practice of witchcraft itself.

Blackberries are one of the most versatile plants in the witch's arsenal, used in various forms, berries, leaves, and even the thorns, each with its unique properties. My mum, who rarely spoke of her craft, more of nature, taught me to see the blackberry not just as a plant but as a living entity, brimming with energy and purpose.

The thorny canes of the blackberry bush are perfect for protection spells. Their sharpness symbolizes the ability to keep unwanted energies at bay. A simple protective charm involves weaving a small circle of blackberry thorn canes and placing it near the entrance of your home. This creates a barrier that negativity cannot cross. In binding spells, the thorn cane when still green can be used to wrap around objects, symbolizing the binding of harmful intentions or the sealing of a promise.

I remember once in the school holidays my dad handed me a bundle of dried blackberry canes and instructed me to place them under my bed, telling me that the thorns would protect my dreams and keep my spirit safe during sleep. I was a bit annoyed at first as there was nothing wrong me, but that night, I slept more peacefully than I had in months, and I began to understand the subtle power that the blackberry held. Whether I had been a moody teenager that week or there was something else my dad noticed, I'm not sure, but it seems those thorns managed to take the prickliness out of me. I later learnt this folklore from Wales where he grew up.

The blackberry's leaves and berries are potent in healing magic. The leaves can be brewed into a tea, which is not only medicinal, soothing sore throats and aiding digestion, but also magical, used in rituals to promote physical and spiritual healing. The berries, bursting with sweetness and vitality, are often used in spells to restore energy, bring prosperity, and even attract love.

My mother would make blackberry jam as summer turned to autumn, filling the kitchen with the warm, comforting scent of bubbling fruit and sugar. She always saved a small jar of the first batch, placing it on the altar as an offering to the spirits and as a symbol of gratitude for the abundance that the blackberries brought to our family. We would use this special jam throughout the winter months in our rituals, spreading it on bread during celebrations or adding a spoonful to a cup of tea to invoke the blackberry's healing properties.

The blackberry bush is also associated with the spirit world. Its tangled branches and dark berries make it a perfect conduit for communication with ancestors and spirits. The berries, when dried, can be used in divination, added to a scrying bowl, or burned as incense to enhance psychic abilities. The leaves, when scattered around a sacred space, help to create a bridge between the physical and spiritual realms.

One of the most profound experiences I had with blackberry divination occurred on a misty autumn evening, during Samhain, when the veil between the worlds is at its thinnest. I had gathered a handful of dried blackberry leaves and berries, preparing to cast them into the fire as an offering to the spirits. As I watched the flames dance around the offering, I felt my ancestors, standing beside me, whispering their wisdom and guidance. The blackberry, with its roots deep in the earth and its branches reaching towards the sky, seemed to be a perfect symbol of this connection between the living and the dead.

Growing and harvesting blackberries is both a practical and spiritual act. The plant requires little care, thriving in the wild with minimal intervention. However, a few simple practices can enhance its yield and potency.

One of the techniques my family has used for generations to increase blackberry yield is intimately tied to the plant's natural two-year growth cycle. Blackberry bushes produce fruit on two-year-old canes, known as floricanes, while the new growth each year, called primocanes, focuses on establishing strong, healthy branches. To encourage the development of more fruit-bearing floricanes, we gently pinch the tips of the primocanes during their first year of growth. This practice stimulates the plant to produce more lateral branches, which will bear more fruit in the following year.

This method not only enhances the abundance of berries but also embodies the concept of nurturing growth and abundance in all areas of life, teaching us to invest care and attention today to reap benefits in the future.

I have fond memories of walking through the bramble patches with my dad, who would show me exactly where to pinch the canes. He always emphasized the importance of doing it with respect and intention, speaking softly to the plant as if coaxing it to share its bounty. Through this process, I learned a valuable lesson in patience and care, qualities that are not only essential for tending blackberry bushes but also for the practice of witchcraft and life in general.

When it comes to harvesting blackberries, timing is crucial. The berries should be picked when they are fully ripe, plump, and almost falling off the cane. My mum always insisted that we leave the first few ripe berries on the bush as an offering to the earth and the spirits of the land. This small act of gratitude ensured that the plant would continue to thrive and produce fruit in the years to come.

We would often make a day of it, venturing out into the hedgerows with baskets in hand, carefully selecting the ripest berries. The act of harvesting was almost ritualistic, with each berry picked in silence, acknowledging the life force that it carried. Once home, we would wash the berries and set them aside for various uses, some to be eaten fresh, others to be made into jams, and the rest to be dried or frozen for later use in our magical practices.

I was quite surprised to find out that not all blackberries are the same. It should be obvious I know but at first I just thought a Blackberry was a Blackberry, if you see what I mean. Over the years, I have learned to recognize the different varieties, each with its unique flavour and magical properties.

The wild blackberries, which grow in abundance along the hedgerows, are perhaps the most potent in magic. Their ability to thrive in the wild, often in the harshest conditions, makes them powerful symbols of resilience and survival. These berries are small, but their flavour is intense and concentrated, making them perfect for use in protective and healing spells.

There are also cultivated varieties of blackberries, which have been bred for their size, sweetness, and ease of picking. While these berries are less wild, they are no less magical. In fact, their cultivated nature makes them ideal for spells and rituals that involve nurturing, growth, and abundance. The larger, sweeter berries are often used in love spells, symbolizing the sweetness of love and the joy of a fruitful relationship.

A more recent addition to the blackberry family is the thornless variety, which, as the name suggests, lacks the sharp thorns that characterize wild blackberries. While some might argue that the absence of thorns diminishes their protective power, I have found that these berries are excellent for spells that require a softer, more nurturing energy. They are also easier to harvest, making them ideal for those who wish to work with blackberries but are wary of the thorns.

My relationship with blackberries is deeply intertwined with my family and our traditions. For us, the blackberry bush has always been more than just a plant, it is a living connection to our past, a symbol of the resilience and strength that has carried us through difficult times.

One of my very earliest memories is of blackberry picking with my mother and grandmother, three generations. We would set out early in the morning, the dew still fresh on the grass, and spend hours combing the hedgerows for the best berries. It was hard work, and we often came back with scratched arms and stained fingers, but there was something deeply satisfying about it. I am sure I ate as many as I picked. The berries would be turned into jams, pies, and syrups, but a portion was always set aside for our rituals and spells.

As I grew older and began to explore my own path in witchcraft, I found myself returning to the blackberry bush time and time again. It became a source of comfort and strength, a reminder of the powerful women who came before me and the wisdom they passed down.

I found this poem that I wrote at school when I can't have been more than ten years old. I'm sure it didn't win me any prizes!

> I'm sitting in the brambles, with raindrops on my head,
> The blackberries are juicy, and the sky is turning red,
> The rain's a steady drizzle, but I don't mind a bit,
> It's peaceful here among the thorns, so here I'll sit.
>
> The bushes are a-tangling, they're wrapped around my knees,
> But there's magic in the raindrops, and a whisper in the breeze,
> The earth beneath is soggy, but it's warm and it's alive,
> And I feel a sense of calmness as I breathe and I thrive.
>
> Now, some folks see the rain as just a wet old bore,
> But sitting here among the brambles, I see something more,
> There's power in the pitter-pat, there's wonder in the damp,
> And I'm sitting in a hedgerow that's a witch's summer camp!
>
> The thorns are gently poking, but they're guarding me, you see,
> They're keeping all the worries out, just letting me be me,
> And though the rain is soaking through, it's really rather nice,
> It's like a sprinkle from the sky, a cool, refreshing spice.
>
> So, I'll sit here with the blackberries, the rain upon my face,
> And feel the magic swirling round, in this cozy little place,
> For in the brambles, wet and wild, there's comfort, there's a spell,
> And though it's only rain and thorns, I'm feeling rather well!

"Phuv on minun alttarini, tähdet minun oppaani, eikä taika minussa koskaan puchukavel."

"The earth is my altar, the stars my guide, and the magic within me never hides."

Blackthorn

Growing up in a family where craftsmanship and tradition were passed down like heirlooms, I have vivid memories of my dad working tirelessly on his passion, creating walking sticks, staffs, and wands out of blackthorn wood. Our home was always filled with the scent of freshly cut wood, and the rhythmic sound of his tools as he carved and shaped each piece into something beautiful and functional.

Blackthorn, or *Prunus spinosa,* has always held a special place in our family, not just for its practical uses but for the deep-rooted tradition and folklore surrounding it. My dad was a master of this tradition, using his skills and knowledge to create walking sticks and staffs that were not only strong and durable but also imbued with the history and magic of the blackthorn itself.

His workshop as I have mentioned before was a place of wonder for me, filled with an array of traditional tools that looked as though they belonged in a museum. He was a firm believer in doing things the old-fashioned way, and his tools reflected that. He used hand saws, spokeshaves, and drawknives, tools that required patience, skill, and a deep understanding of the material.

The process of creating a walking stick or staff from blackthorn began with selecting the right branch. Blackthorn is known for its dense, twisted branches, which are perfect for making strong, sturdy walking sticks. However, finding a branch that was both straight enough and thick enough was no easy task. My dad would spend hours combing the hedgerows, sometimes with me in tow, looking for just the right piece of wood.

Once he found the perfect branch, the real work began. The first step was to remove the bark, which was done with a spokeshave, a small, handheld tool that allowed for precise control. After the bark was stripped away, the branch was left to cure, a process that could take several months. This curing process was crucial, as it allowed the wood to dry out slowly, preventing it from cracking or warping.

After the wood had cured, my dad would begin shaping it into a walking stick or staff. This was where his artistry truly shone. Using a combination of drawknives, rasps, and files, he would carefully carve the wood, smoothing out the rough edges and bringing out the natural beauty of the grain. Each stick was unique, with its own personality and character, shaped by the natural twists and turns of the blackthorn branch.

The curing process was something of a family secret, and I can't give that away completely but this I can say. My dad had a special place in the garden where he would store the blackthorn branches, stacked carefully in a crisscross pattern to allow air to circulate around them. The branches were left to dry out naturally, exposed to the elements but protected from direct sunlight and rain.

This slow curing process could take anywhere from six months to a year, depending on the thickness of the branch and the weather conditions. He was a patient man, and he understood that rushing the process would only result in inferior products. He would often say, "slow and steady wins the race" and he was right. The finished sticks were as strong as iron and would last a lifetime. Many lifetimes.

Once the sticks were finished, my dad would take them to local markets to sell. He had a small stall that he set up every weekend in August, and over the years, he built up a loyal customer base for the intricate carved versions. His walking sticks were popular with older folks mostly of course who appreciated the strength and durability of blackthorn, as well as with younger people who were drawn to the unique, rustic appearance of the sticks, especially the ones with animals carved in the handles. I can remember him getting calls from time to time from June at Fox's, a famous umbrella shop who made the brolly for John Steed in the Avengers, and his sticks have been seen in more than one movie when they needed something "very special". I was treated to my first umbrella from Fox's in Moorgate, which alas I fear is now a wine bar.

In addition to the markets, my dad also sold his sticks through word of mouth. He was well-known in our community as the man who made the best walking sticks around, and people would often come to our house to buy one directly from him. He took great pride in his work, and it showed in the quality of the sticks he produced.

In the late 1990s and early 2000s, something unexpected happened that gave my dad's business a surprising boost, the Harry Potter craze. With the release of the books and later the films, suddenly everyone wanted a magic wand, and my dad's blackthorn wands became highly sought after.

Now, my dad was very clear about one thing: his wands were not toys. They were beautifully crafted, made from the same cured blackthorn as his walking sticks, and they were designed for adults, not children. He would always chuckle when someone asked why the wands were "over 18s only." "These aren't for casting spells in the playground," he'd say. "They're for serious practitioners, or at least for those who appreciate the craft."

Despite his intentions, the popularity of the wands among Harry Potter fans led to a few amusing encounters. People would ask him all sorts of questions, usually if they were affiliated with a particular house at Hogwarts. My dad, always with a twinkle in his eye, would reply, "The magic is in the belief, not the wood."

For a few years, the wands sold like hotcakes. My dad could hardly keep up with the demand, and then as my dad's hands began to shake a little he employed my future husband to be their gardener and a kind of apprentice. As the Harry Potter craze began to wane, so did the demand for the wands. Still, they remain a unique part of our craft, a testament to how a simple piece of wood can capture the imagination and power.

The Gardener has a knack for marketing and was able to expand the business's reach, bringing in customers from all over the country. He set up a small online shop, which has become a surprising success, especially among those looking for traditional, handmade items. We'll never be millionaires from it, but it all helps.

While my dad worked with the wood of the blackthorn, the women in our family took charge of the fruit. Every late summer or autumn, ideally if we had an early frost, we would head out to the hedgerows to gather sloes. There's a certain satisfaction in plucking those small, dark fruits, knowing that they'll soon be transformed into something delicious.

Making sloe gin has been a family tradition for as long as I can remember. It's a simple process, really, sloes, sugar, and gin, left to steep together for several months. But, as with the walking sticks, there's an art to it. The sloes must be pricked with a needle before they're added to the gin, a task that we take great care with, as it allows the juices to infuse the alcohol more thoroughly.

We've always been a bit liberal with our sloe gin consumption, especially during the long, dark winter months. There's nothing quite like a glass of homemade sloe gin to warm you up on a cold evening. Of course, we also give bottles away as gifts and they sell pretty well through some local hotels, though I must admit, not without a pang of reluctance. We're a little selfish when it comes to our sloe gin!

Over the years, we've experimented with different recipes, adding unusual herbs and spices to give the gin a unique flavour. One of our favourites is a recipe that includes a touch of star anise, which gives the gin a subtle liquorice note. We've also made Blackberry and Damiana which has its own story (see the section on Damiana), each batch bringing its own distinct character.

There was one memorable year when we added rosemary to the mint to a huge batch, but it just tasted like mouth wash so we won't do that again!

When I look back on all these years, I see a family deeply connected to the land and to the traditions that have been passed down through generations. My dad's walking sticks, staffs, and wands are more than just pieces of wood; they're a testament to his skill, patience, and respect for the craft. Each one carries a piece of him, and now, through The Gardener's work, that legacy continues. The wands may have been a funny chapter in our lives, with all the strange questions and curious customers, but they also represent a moment when the world took notice of something we've always known, that blackthorn, with its history and magic, is a special wood, capable of creating more than just walking sticks.

As for the sloe gin, well, that's our little indulgence. It's a tradition that brings us together, a way of celebrating the harvest and sharing a bit of our bounty with friends and family. And yes, perhaps we do drink a little too much of it, but life is short, and some traditions are worth savouring.

Borage

"You know, sometimes all you need is 20 seconds of insane courage, just literally 20 seconds of embarrassing bravery, and I promise you something great will come of it." That quote from Benjamin Mee's *I Bought a Zoo* always hits home for me. It's such a simple idea, but it feels so true, right? Those little moments of courage can completely change the direction of your life. In Benjamin Mee's case, that first burst of courage was when he worked up the nerve to ask his future wife out. That 20 seconds of bravery set everything in motion for him, leading to love, family, and eventually, to buying a zoo and navigating all the challenges that came with it.

I've always been a huge fan of *I Bought a Zoo*. The story itself is amazing, how Mee and his family took over the struggling Dartmoor Zoological Park in Devon, but it's the heart behind it that I really connect with. It's not just about the zoo; it's about how courage, even in the smallest moments, can ripple out and shape your whole life. And sure, the film adaptation is great, with Matt Damon and Scarlett Johansson bringing that story to life on the big screen, but it's the book that I truly love. Mee's writing has this raw honesty to it, and it makes the whole experience feel real. You feel the highs and lows of what it was like for him to take such a huge leap into the unknown, time and time again.

The zoo in the book is more than just a quirky setting. It becomes this symbol of how unpredictable and wildlife can be. When Mee bought the Zoo it was barely holding on. The animals were there, sure, but the place was falling apart. It needed a lot of love and a lot of work. And the truth is, Mee didn't know the first thing about running a zoo, but he took a deep breath and went for it anyway. It wasn't just one brave moment, like when he asked his wife out. That was just the start. After that, he had to keep finding the courage to deal with everything that came next, his wife's illness, the financial struggles, and learning how to care for all these animals.

I think about that a lot when I'm working with Borage in my garden. Borage, or *Borago officinalis*, has been known as the "Herb of Courage" for centuries. The ancient Romans believed it could give their soldiers bravery before they went into battle, and I love that. It's got these beautiful, bright blue flowers that just seem to radiate strength. For me, Borage is like a little reminder from nature that we all have that inner courage, even when it feels like we don't.

Whenever I feel like I need a bit of extra strength or confidence, I turn to Borage. Whether I'm making a tea with the leaves or just sitting with the plant in the garden, there's this calm, steady energy it gives off. It's like a nudge, saying, "You've got this." I think of Benjamin Mee in those moments, too. The courage he had to muster wasn't just for the big, dramatic decision to buy the zoo. It was for the day-to-day struggles that came after, the endless challenges, the setbacks, the grief. That's where real courage shows up, in those quieter moments when you have to keep going, even when it's tough.

In my garden, Borage is one of those plants that just seems to know what it's doing. It's low maintenance, which I appreciate. Once you've planted it, it'll reseed itself and pop up year after year. It doesn't need much fussing over, and in that way, it kind of embodies what courage is—steady, reliable, and always there when you need it. Borage is one of my go-to plants when I'm making remedies for people who are going through hard times, too. It's soothing but strengthening, like a quiet kind of bravery that helps you keep putting one foot in front of the other.

And it's not just useful as a herb—it's also lovely to look at. Its star-shaped flowers bring a splash of colour to the garden, and they attract bees, which is always a good thing. I like to think that the bees, drawn to the Borage, are also taking in some of that courage as they buzz around, doing their important work. And I guess in a way, that's what we do as well. We draw on that same courage to keep going, to face whatever comes our way.

Just like Benjamin Mee didn't know where that 20 seconds of insane bravery would lead him when he asked his wife out, we often don't know where our own moments of courage will take us. For him, it led to a whole new chapter of life, full of challenges but also full of meaning. And for me, working with Borage, I've found that courage doesn't have to be this big, dramatic thing. Sometimes it's about those little moments, like making the decision to keep going when things feel tough, or taking a chance on something new, even if you're scared.

Every time I sip a cup of Borage tea or see those vibrant flowers bloom in my garden, I'm reminded that courage is something that keeps us going. It's what helps us push through the tough stuff and, in the end, leads to something great, even if we don't always see it right away.

I often include Borage in talismans or sachets intended to bolster one's courage or to provide emotional support during difficult times. If I feel anxious or overwhelmed, I'll make a tea with Borage leaves and flowers, believing that the herb imparts some of its bravery to me. It's also a wonderful herb to work with during the waxing moon, a time for growth, action, and moving forward with intention.

In addition to its magical properties, Borage is a remarkable medicinal herb. The leaves and flowers are traditionally used as a remedy for stress and adrenal fatigue. It has a cooling, soothing effect, and I often use it as a tea or infusion when I need to calm my nerves or support my emotional well-being. The tea has a mild cucumber-like flavour and is particularly helpful for those suffering from exhaustion or burnout. Borage also has anti-inflammatory properties, making it useful for treating conditions such as arthritis and respiratory inflammation.

One of the more modern medicinal uses of Borage comes from its seeds, which are pressed to produce Borage oil, rich in gamma-linolenic acid (GLA). This essential fatty acid is known for its benefits in treating skin conditions such as eczema and for its role in maintaining hormonal balance, particularly in women. I've found Borage oil to be a gentle and effective remedy for skin irritations and dryness, and I often recommend it to those seeking a natural approach to skincare.

One of the many reasons I love growing Borage is its natural resistance to pests and diseases. It's a hardy plant that generally doesn't suffer from the usual garden nuisances. In fact, Borage is often grown as a companion plant for this very reason. Its presence in the garden deters pests such as cabbage moths. I've found that planting Borage near my tomatoes and brassicas helps keep these plants healthy and pest-free.

Occasionally, Borage might fall prey to powdery mildew, especially in humid conditions or if the plants are overcrowded. To prevent this, I make sure to space my plants adequately and ensure good air circulation. If powdery mildew does appear, I usually treat it with a homemade solution of water and baking soda, which helps to keep it in check.

Borage is a low-maintenance plant, which is one of the reasons I recommend it to novice gardeners. Once established, it requires very little attention. Regular watering during dry spells is usually sufficient, and I rarely need to fertilise the soil. If anything, Borage seems to improve the soil it's planted in, thanks to its deep roots, which help to aerate and enrich the earth.

Throughout the growing season, I deadhead the spent flowers to encourage continuous blooming. This is one of my favourite tasks in the garden, as it allows me to spend time with the plants, connecting with their energy while also ensuring they remain vibrant and healthy. If the plants begin to look a bit leggy, I'll trim them back to promote bushier growth. In the late summer, as the plants start to go to seed, I let some of the flower heads dry out and collect the seeds for next year's planting.

While Borage is generally safe for most people, it's important to exercise caution, particularly with the leaves and stems, which contain small amounts of pyrrolizidine alkaloids (PAs). These compounds can be harmful to the liver if consumed in large quantities over an extended period. However, occasional use in teas or culinary applications is generally considered safe for most people. If you're pregnant, nursing, or have liver issues, it's best to avoid Borage or consult with a healthcare professional before using it.

Borage isn't just a medicinal and magical herb; it also has a place in the kitchen. The fresh leaves have a crisp, cucumber-like flavour, making them a wonderful addition to salads, sandwiches, and cold drinks. In the summer, I often add Borage leaves and flowers to a jug of water with lemon slices for a refreshing and slightly herbaceous infusion. The flowers are edible as well and make a stunning garnish for desserts and cocktails. I love to sprinkle the vibrant blue blossoms over salads or freeze them in ice cubes for a visually striking addition to summer drinks.

One of my favourite traditional uses for Borage is in Pimms, a classic British summer drink. The flowers, with their delicate flavour and bright colour, add a touch of elegance to the glass. In addition, I've experimented with using Borage in soups and stews, where its cucumber-like taste adds a fresh note. However, it's important to note that the leaves become quite bristly when mature, so they're best used when young or finely chopped.

"Voro alhaalla taivaaseen ylhäällä, minä loitsun voimalla, viisaudella ja camelos."

"From the roots below to the skies above, I cast with strength, wisdom, and love."

The Witch's Botanical Apothecary

Candy Leaf

Candy Leaf

You know how some plants just feel like little miracles? Well, that's how I feel about candy leaf, or stevia. It's one of those wonder plants that seems almost too good to be true. I mean, the leaves are 200 times sweeter than sugar, seriously, 200 times! And the best part? It has zero calories. Yep, none, nada. It's like nature decided to give us the perfect sweetener without any of the guilt.

Whenever I tell people about it, they're always sceptical at first. Like, "How can something that sweet be good for you?" But that's the magic of stevia, it's this unassuming little plant that packs a punch. And, honestly, it's become one of my favourite herbs to work with in my garden, my kitchen, and even my magic.

The real kicker is the science behind how we get that insane sweetness from the plant. You see, it's all about these compounds in the leaves called steviol glycosides. Those are what make the leaves taste so sweet. When you use the raw leaves, you'll definitely notice the sweetness, but to get that intense sugar-like flavour, you have to extract it. The process is actually pretty simple, they just steep the leaves in water, then filter and purify the glycosides. It's like making a tea, only the end result is this pure, concentrated sweetness that's ready to use.

So, stevia is pretty much a wonder plant in my book. Whether I'm tossing a few leaves into my tea or using it in a spell to sweeten life's tough moments, it's always surprising me with how much it has to offer. And the best part? It doesn't mess with your body the way sugar does. It's all the sweetness with none of the downside. How could you not love that?

Growing candy leaf (stevia) is like welcoming a sweet little friend into your garden, one that doesn't demand too much but gives back so much in return. It's super easy to cultivate if you've got the right conditions. Stevia loves full sun and well-drained soil, and it thrives in warmth, think summer sunshine. But don't worry, even if you're in a cooler climate, you can still grow it. Just treat it as an annual or bring it inside when the weather cools down. Stevia is super sensitive to frost, so that's something to keep in mind.

When I first started growing it, I was amazed at how quickly it took off with just a little love. I like to propagate my plants, and stevia is no exception. It's ridiculously easy to propagate from cuttings. You just snip a healthy stem below a leaf node, remove the lower leaves, and stick it in water or directly into some moist soil. In no time, you'll see roots forming, and you'll have a brand new stevia plant ready to add to your collection. Propagating plants always feels like a small, personal victory, like you're growing your garden family and abundance at the same time.

To me, propagation has this lovely symbolic energy. It's all about taking something small, nurturing it, and watching it flourish into something new and whole. I like to think of it as a form of manifestation in action. Plus, who doesn't want more of a good thing, especially when that thing is sweet candy leaf?

Magically speaking, candy leaf is a dream to work with! Its sweetness makes it perfect for any type of spell where you want to sweeten a situation, whether that's relationships, self-love, or even just bringing more positivity into your life. In love spells, I like to add dried stevia leaves to a sachet or charm bag alongside roses and lavender. It helps bring a kind, nurturing energy that softens even the toughest of hearts (including your own).

And here's where it gets interesting. You know those purified steviol glycosides I mentioned earlier, the ones that are 200 times sweeter than sugar? Well, you can use those in magic too! When you need to really amplify the sweetness in a spell, a few drops of liquid stevia extract can work wonders. It's like turbo-charging the energy of the spell. I've used it in jar spells for love and abundance where I needed a big, bold, sweet energy boost, and it's never let me down.

On the medicinal side, stevia has some amazing properties. It's great for people with blood sugar issues, like diabetes, because it provides sweetness without spiking insulin levels. I make teas with the fresh leaves for digestive support, or sometimes I'll add it to a bitter herbal blend to balance out the flavours. It's nice to have something so versatile, it's sweet and healing at the same time. Like a magical little helper!

I absolutely love using candy leaf in the kitchen. You can use the fresh leaves, dried leaves, or even the purified stevia extract, and each one has its own charm. The fresh leaves are great for sweetening teas. I'll throw a couple of leaves into a cup of hot water with some mint or lemon balm, and it adds the perfect natural sweetness without any sugar crash later.

When it comes to baking or more involved recipes, I lean towards using the purified stevia extract. It's a bit trickier to cook with since it doesn't act like sugar (no caramelization, for example), but once you get the hang of it, it's awesome. You only need a teeny, tiny bit, like a few drops or a small pinch, and it gives you all the sweetness you need. I've made cookies, cakes, and even jams with stevia, and they turn out delicious every time. One thing to remember is that it pairs really well with strong flavours, like cinnamon, chocolate, or citrus, because it complements rather than competes with them.

One of my favourite recipes is a stevia-sweetened lemonade. I just make a simple syrup using dried stevia leaves, mix it with fresh lemon juice and water, and voila! It's the perfect refreshing summer drink, and I don't miss the sugar at all.

If you don't have a garden or live in a place with unpredictable weather, don't worry, candy leaf is perfect for container gardening. I've got a couple of stevia plants growing in pots right on my sunny kitchen windowsill, and they're thriving. The key to growing stevia in containers is to give it plenty of light and make sure the soil drains well. Stevia doesn't like soggy roots, so use a pot with good drainage holes, and water it just enough to keep the soil moist but not soaked.

One trick I've learned is to use a slightly bigger pot than you think you need. Stevia can develop a decent root system, and it'll appreciate the extra room to grow. And the great thing about growing it in a pot is that you can bring it indoors when the weather gets colder, extending its growing season.

Container gardening also makes it super convenient to snip a few fresh leaves whenever you want. I can't tell you how many times I've wandered into my kitchen to make tea and thought, "Oh, I'll just grab a couple of fresh stevia leaves," because they're right there. It makes incorporating this magical plant into your daily life so easy.

Aside from its magical and medicinal uses, Candy Leaf has found its way into some surprising areas of my life. One thing I love to do is use it in homemade beauty products. Stevia has a soothing quality, so I'll mix some dried stevia leaves into a homemade sugar scrub or add a bit of stevia extract to a face mask for a little extra skin-softening magic. It's a fun and easy way to add a touch of sweetness to my self-care routine.

Another thing I've experimented with is using Candy Leaf in DIY dental care products. Because it's naturally sweet without feeding bacteria like sugar does, it's perfect for homemade mouthwash or even toothpaste. It gives you that clean, sweet taste without the risk of cavities. Plus, it just feels good to know that something so natural and wholesome is doing good things for my body.

It's a plant that reminds me of the power of sweetness, both in magic and in everyday life. And whether I'm working with the raw leaves or the super-sweet stevia extract, it never fails to surprise me with just how much it has to offer.

If you haven't yet invited stevia into your practice or your kitchen, I highly recommend it. It's one of those herbs that's both simple and powerful, and once you start working with it, you'll wonder how you ever did without it. After all, who couldn't use a little extra sweetness in their life?

The Witch's Botanical Apothecary

Chamomile

Chamomile

Does this make sense to you? Whenever I work with Chamomile I get this eerie essence of calmness, healing, and that nurturing, grandmotherly kind of energy that we all need from time to time, or at least I do. It feels like a hug.

Chamomile has been revered for thousands of years. Its name is derived from the Greek word "chamaimelon," meaning "ground apple," which is fitting because its small white flowers have a scent that's faintly apple-like. The Egyptians valued it so much that they dedicated it to the sun god, Ra, and used it for treating fevers. In medieval Europe, chamomile was a key ingredient in many remedies, and it became known as the "plant physician" because people believed it could heal other plants that were ailing when grown nearby, which from my experience I believe is true. Even today, chamomile is known for its strong healing properties, both physically and energetically.

Growing chamomile is fairly straightforward, making it an excellent herb for beginners. I mostly grow two types: German chamomile (Matricaria chamomilla) and Roman chamomile (Chamaemelum nobile). Both are wonderfully easy to cultivate, but they each have their quirks.

German chamomile is an annual, which means it lives for one season, but it self-seeds like crazy. I usually don't have to worry about replanting it each year because it takes care of that for me. It grows taller and more freely than Roman chamomile, and I tend to use it more often in teas and remedies because its flowers are a bit more prolific.

Roman chamomile, on the other hand, is a perennial, and it grows lower to the ground like a creeping mat. It has these cute, daisy-like flowers that just feel so whimsical. This type is what you'll want to grow if you're looking for a ground cover or something that's a bit more permanent. I use Roman chamomile in more magical work and for my garden spaces since its soothing presence keeps the energy calm and serene.

Chamomile likes well-drained soil and plenty of sunlight, though it will tolerate partial shade. I've found it to be fairly low-maintenance as long as it gets a good amount of light and isn't waterlogged. Over the years, I've grown it from seed, which can be a bit tricky because the seeds are so small, but with patience and a gentle hand, you'll have seedlings sprouting up in no time. Just make sure not to cover them with too much soil—they like light to germinate.

In witchcraft it's known for its ability to dispel negative energy and create a peaceful environment. I'll often burn dried chamomile flowers in my rituals when I feel I need to clear out stagnant energy or when I'm preparing a space for meditation or healing work.

One of my favourite ways to use chamomile in magic is through teas or bath infusions. When you sip chamomile tea with intention, you're not just drinking a cup of warmth, you're also drinking in peace and protection. I think this last bit is what people miss all the time, drinking chamomile is pleasant but will do nothing without intention! I've used chamomile tea in rituals to soothe emotional pain or grief, as its energy is so nurturing. There's something about sipping chamomile tea during a quiet evening that feels like an act of deep self-care and reflection. It's also said to attract money and good luck, so I've included it in charm bags or used it to wash my hands before a big decision or a new venture.

Medicinally, chamomile has been a life-saver for me. It's incredibly gentle, which makes it perfect for soothing digestive issues like bloating, indigestion, or cramps. If you've had too much coffee or your stomach is in knots from stress, a simple cup of chamomile tea works wonders. I've also used chamomile tea or oil infusions as a topical remedy for skin irritations, like eczema or minor burns, as it's anti-inflammatory and soothing.

And let's not forget its role as a sleep aid. I don't know how many sleepless nights chamomile has saved me from! A cup of chamomile tea before bed is a ritual that I swear by. Its mild sedative effect is perfect for winding down without feeling groggy the next day.

Chamomile is pretty low-maintenance once it's established. For the German variety, I allow it to self-seed and just thin the seedlings if they start to overcrowd the garden. Roman chamomile does best with regular trimming to keep it neat and bushy, especially if you're using it as ground cover. I usually deadhead the flowers to encourage more blooming throughout the season.

Watering is important, but like I mentioned earlier, it doesn't like to have soggy roots. I let the soil dry out a bit between waterings, and this routine seems to keep my chamomile happy.

Although chamomile is generally safe, it's always a good idea to exercise some caution. It's part of the daisy family, so anyone with ragweed allergies might have a reaction to it. I've heard of people having skin irritations from handling fresh chamomile, so I always recommend doing a patch test if you're using it topically for the first time.

Chamomile can also have a mild blood-thinning effect, so it's not recommended for people on blood thinners or anyone about to undergo surgery. And as always, if you're pregnant or nursing, it's best to check with a healthcare professional before using chamomile medicinally.

Chamomile has a gentle, floral flavour that's lovely in more than just tea. I've infused honey with dried chamomile flowers, and let me tell you, it's divine drizzled over toast or stirred into oatmeal. You can also use chamomile to infuse syrups or make calming, aromatic desserts. I've added it to shortbread cookies and even made a chamomile ice cream that was just the right blend of sweet and soothing.

It's also wonderful when paired with citrus, so I'll sometimes add a bit of dried chamomile to lemonades or cocktails for a calming twist.

If you don't have a lot of space or you're growing chamomile on a balcony or patio, it does wonderfully in containers. Both German and Roman chamomile can be grown in pots, but I recommend choosing a slightly larger container if you're growing German chamomile, as it can get a bit taller and bushier.

Make sure the pot has good drainage and use a well-draining potting mix. I've found that chamomile doesn't like its roots to sit in water, so keeping the soil lightly moist but not soggy is key. You can even create a little chamomile container garden mixed with other calming herbs like lavender, lemon balm, and mint for a small but powerful calming corner.

Chanterelles

Chanterelles

As a child, I was utterly enchanted by the idea of a world filled with fairies, mischievous pixies, and all sorts of magical creatures hiding just beyond the veil of what we could see. I can vividly remember the stories my grandmother would tell me about how the fairies lived in the garden and the woods, watching over everything, making flowers bloom and guiding the seasons. I would run outside after the rain, convinced I could catch a glimpse of them darting between the petals, especially when the air was still misty and the light shimmered through the leaves. The world felt so alive with possibilities, and I was certain the fairies were part of that magic.

The pixies, on the other hand, were a bit of a different story. In my young mind, they were the ones who caused all sorts of mischief. If something went missing around the house, a hairbrush, a favourite toy, or, most frustratingly, a shoe, it was always the pixies to blame. We'd laugh and say the pixies must've taken it, hiding it away in some secret spot just to watch us scramble around looking for it. Sometimes, in the spirit of fun, I'd leave little offerings of buttons or pebbles for them, hoping they'd return what they'd taken in exchange. Sure enough, after a while, the missing object would always turn up in the most unexpected place, and I'd smile, convinced that the pixies had finally tired of their game.

But the fairies were different. They didn't take things away; instead, they were the ones who seemed to make the world a little more magical, a little kinder. If something unexpectedly went right, a surprise gift from a relative, a particularly lovely day where everything felt perfect, or even something small like finding a shiny coin on the ground, we'd whisper that it must've been the fairies. They were the benevolent spirits who watched over us, leaving little gifts or blessings when we least expected it. I remember one time when, after days of relentless rain, the sun finally broke through, and a perfect rainbow stretched across the sky. My friends and I were convinced that it was the fairies' doing, and we spent the rest of the afternoon searching for where they might be hiding, hopeful for just a glimpse of their magic.

When I first learned about chanterelle mushrooms, the idea that fairies might use them as tiny cups to drink dew from felt so perfectly in line with that childhood sense of wonder. I mean, can't you just imagine it? These little golden mushrooms, sprouting up like tiny goblets in the forest, catching the morning dew, if anything could be a fairy's cup, surely it would be a chanterelle. Their bright, golden colour, the way they seem to glow even in the shaded forest, all of it feels like something from a fairy tale. And of course, the idea that forest spirits might leave them as gifts for those attuned to nature feels just right, too. After all, when you stumble upon a patch of chanterelles in the wild, especially when you weren't expecting it, it does feel like a little gift from the earth, a small blessing for those of us who pay attention.

Even now, as an adult, there's a part of me that can't help but smile when I find chanterelles shimmering in the forest light. Whether the folklore is true or not, there's a magic to the moment. It transports me back to that time when I believed wholeheartedly in fairies and pixies, when the world was alive with unseen wonders. And maybe, just maybe, the fairies and pixies are still there, watching, playing their tricks, and leaving their gifts for those of us who still believe in a little bit of magic. There is a strength we lose when we grow up, of that assurance of the unexplained. The belief in magic for some changes to religion, and for some of us, we never grow up! There is a advertising board outside a coffee shop down The Strand near Charring Cross station in London that says "Don't grow up – It's a trap". I have a photo of it on our cork board in the kitchen.

The chanterelle mushroom, *Cantharellus cibarius*, is a beloved species that we have known about for centuries but may have been with us since the dawn of time. It's celebrated not just in the culinary world but also by herbalists and witches like myself for its magical properties. There's something almost otherworldly about them, and I can't help but believe that ancient peoples felt this too.

Traditionally, chanterelles have been prized across Europe and North America, especially in places like Scandinavia and France. Historically, foragers in these regions would gather them to sell in bustling market squares or dry them to preserve for the colder months. They've always been considered a bit of a delicacy, and their buttery, slightly peppery flavour has earned them a spot in gourmet kitchens. But beyond their culinary value, chanterelles have medicinal and magical properties that often get overlooked.

The hunt for chanterelles is, for me, part of the magic. They're not the easiest mushrooms to find, but that's part of the allure. I like to think of chanterelles as the forest's way of rewarding those who respect and appreciate the land. You can't just go marching into the woods expecting to find them right away. You have to slow down, observe, listen, and let the forest guide you. A friend sent me this on a postcard long long ago.

Hwilc hīe behydath for gamene,   Are they hiding just for fun,
Oþ þæt dæg swīge hæfþ ende?   Until the quiet day is done?
Oþþe is hit þæt se wudu cann,   Or is it that the forest knows,
Þam þe hīe gehyrað, hēo forgiefþ?   To those who listen, she bestows?

Chanterellan, dīgle gemet,   Chanterelles, a secret found,
Þonne nænig word sōna cweþ.   When not a single word is sound.

Chanterelles tend to grow in specific habitats. You'll often find them near hardwood trees, especially oaks and birches, in areas with plenty of shade and a rich, moist ground. They prefer the undisturbed parts of the forest, so if you're in a heavily trafficked area, you might be out of luck. I've also found that they tend to pop up after a good rain, especially in late summer and early fall. It's like the moisture activates something in the earth, coaxing them to the surface.

One of the first things you'll notice about chanterelles is their vibrant, golden-yellow colour. It's this almost glowing hue that makes them relatively easy to spot once you're in the right environment. However, as with any wild foraging, it's essential to be certain of what you're picking. There are a few look-alikes, like the false chanterelle (*Hygrophoropsis aurantiaca*), but thankfully, there are some key differences.

The true chanterelle has a distinctive wavy cap with a trumpet-like shape. The underside of the cap isn't gilled like many mushrooms; instead, it has ridges that are forked and run down the stem. These ridges are soft to the touch, not sharp or blade-like. The stem itself is solid and firm, not hollow. When you cut into a chanterelle, the flesh should be white, and there's a subtle but distinct fruity smell. If you can't smell a note of apricot or peach then throw them away. That scent is one of my favourite things about chanterelles, it feels like the earth's way of adding a little extra magic to the experience.

If you're ever in doubt about whether you've found a real chanterelle or not, a simple spore print test can help. To do a spore print test on a chanterelle mushroom, all you really need is a fresh mushroom and a bit of patience. It's a simple process that can confirm whether what you've found is a true chanterelle or possibly one of its look-alikes. First, pick a mature mushroom with a fully opened cap, this is important because younger mushrooms might not drop enough spores for you to get a clear print.

Once you've got your mushroom, carefully cut off the stem, leaving just the cap to work with. Then, place the cap face down on a piece of paper. Since chanterelle spores are pale, using both a white and a black piece of paper can be really helpful, as the contrast will make it easier to see the spores. Now, to prevent any breeze from disturbing the spores, you can cover the mushroom cap with a bowl or a glass. This also keeps the moisture in, which helps the spores drop more easily.

Now comes the waiting game. Leave the mushroom undisturbed for at least 6 to 12 hours—overnight is even better. When you lift the cap in the morning, you should see a spore print on the paper. If it's a true chanterelle, the spores will usually be white or a very pale yellow. This is your confirmation. However, if the spore print comes out orange or darker, you might be dealing with a false chanterelle, which isn't poisonous but can cause digestive upset if eaten.

It's an easy, effective way to double-check your find, especially if you're feeling uncertain about its identification. And there's something quite magical about lifting the cap and seeing those delicate spores left behind like a signature from the forest itself. Just another little mystery of nature unravelled.

In my practice I see chanterelles as a symbol of abundance, connection to nature, and quiet resilience. These mushrooms don't grow quickly or in easily accessible places. They take their time, flourishing in symbiosis with the trees around them, and they remind me that sometimes, the best things in life take patience and a little effort to find.

Magically, I use chanterelles in rituals related to grounding and strengthening my connection to the earth. Their vibrant colour makes them ideal for working with solar energy or invoking warmth and positivity. I've dried them and used the powder as an offering during rituals to honour forest spirits, and I've also placed fresh chanterelles on my altar during the autumn equinox to celebrate the abundance of the season. The chanterelle's fruit-like scent carries with it a sense of lightness and joy, so I often include it in charm bags or potions aimed at boosting creativity, joy, and personal growth.

One thing that fascinates me is how chanterelles grow in a mycorrhizal relationship with trees. I know that's a big word but what it means is they don't just survive on their own—they thrive by working in harmony with the roots of trees, exchanging nutrients in a mutualistic relationship. This quality makes them a potent symbol in spellwork involving relationships, cooperation, and mutual growth. If I'm working on strengthening a friendship or fostering collaboration, I might incorporate chanterelles into my ritual as a reminder of the power of interdependence.

From a medicinal perspective, chanterelles have more to offer than just their beauty. While they're not the most potent medicinal mushroom out there, they do have some health benefits. They're rich in vitamins, particularly D and B, and contain compounds that are believed to support immune function. I've also read that chanterelles have mild anti-inflammatory properties, making them a useful ally in soothing minor aches and pains. However, I must say that I primarily use them for their magical and culinary qualities more than anything medicinal.

As with any mushroom foraging, it's essential to approach chanterelles with respect and caution. While chanterelles themselves are edible and delicious, there are a few look-alikes that can cause trouble. As I mentioned earlier, the false chanterelle is one such imposter. It looks quite similar but can cause stomach upset if consumed, so it's essential to make sure you're confident in your identification before eating anything you forage.

Another word of caution: even true chanterelles can cause issues for some people, particularly if they're eaten raw. I always recommend cooking chanterelles thoroughly, as this helps to break down any compounds that might cause digestive discomfort. If you're new to chanterelles, it's wise to try just a small amount at first to ensure that your body agrees with them.

Finally, I like to remind fellow foragers to take only what you need. Chanterelles, like many wild foods, are part of a delicate ecosystem. Over-harvesting can harm both the local mushroom population and the health of the trees they support. When I forage, I follow the "rule of thirds": I take one-third of what I find, leaving the rest to continue growing and reproducing. This ensures that future generations of both mushrooms and foragers will be able to enjoy the bounty of the forest.

Now, I know I've been going on about the magical side of chanterelles, but let's not forget how incredible they are in the kitchen. Chanterelles have this buttery, slightly peppery flavour that pairs well with a wide range of dishes. They're one of the first wild foods I ever cooked with, and to this day, they remain one of my favourites.

One of the simplest ways to prepare chanterelles is to sauté them in butter with a bit of garlic and fresh herbs. The mushrooms absorb the butter, lots of butter, becoming even more rich and flavourful, while the garlic adds a lovely, savoury note. I'll often toss this mixture with fresh pasta, a sprinkle of parmesan, and maybe a few toasted pine nuts if I'm feeling fancy. It's simple, but it highlights the natural flavour of the mushrooms in the best way.

I've also used chanterelles in soups, where their delicate texture adds depth without overpowering the broth. They're particularly lovely in a creamy mushroom soup with a splash of sherry or white wine. If you're lucky enough to find a big haul, they dry well, and dried chanterelles can be rehydrated and used in all kinds of dishes throughout the year.

Chanterelles also have a special place in my seasonal celebrations. During the autumn equinox, I'll often bake a savoury chanterelle tart or prepare a chanterelle risotto to share with friends and family. There's something about incorporating wild, foraged food into these celebrations that makes the meal feel even more meaningful. It's a way of honouring the gifts of the earth and giving thanks for the abundance of the harvest season.

Cherry

There are some trees that seem to whisper secrets, hidden just beneath their leaves or roots, waiting for those who are willing to listen. One of my absolute favourites is the English Cherry. It's such a beautiful, versatile tree, and if you take the time to understand it, it can become a true ally in both magical and medicinal practices

Before I dive into the specifics of how I use cherry trees in my practice, I want to share a little history, both about the cherry itself and how it's rooted in my own family's story.

The English Cherry tree has been an important part of our landscape for centuries. Though cherries were first cultivated in the Mediterranean and later spread across Europe by the Romans, their presence in England has become deeply embedded in the natural environment. While I can't claim that the cherry trees in my garden were planted by Roman hands, it's entirely possible that the cherries on our land are descendants of those ancient trees, either self-seeded over the generations or purposefully planted by people who lived here long before my family did or evolved into our family.

One of the trees in our garden is incredibly old, possibly over a hundred years, which is old for a Cherry Tree but is still covered in fruit in the summer. It stands as a sentinel, watching over our home as it has done all my life. This particular tree is very special to me. I've written about it elsewhere in this book, but it's worth mentioning again. My dad, with his deft hands and love of tradition, once made a pipe from its wood. He understood the magic and history in that tree. The pipe became a cherished family item, something that carried not just his craftsmanship but the energy of that ancient cherry tree and the love through his hands and craftsmanship.

Every time I look at that old cherry, I feel a sense of connection, not just to my dad and the generations before me, but also to the earth beneath my feet. This tree and it's forebears has seen so much, weathered countless seasons, and continues to thrive. There's something incredibly grounding about that, something that reminds me of the cyclical nature of life and the deep roots we share with the land.

The cherry tree is a true representation of the changing seasons, and each phase of the year brings new gifts from it. In the spring, when the tree is covered in delicate blossoms, I can't help but feel the stirrings of new energy in the air. There's something almost ethereal about cherry blossoms, the way they catch the light and float softly to the ground. In the past, I've collected these petals to dry and use in love spells or rituals of renewal. The blossoms are symbols of new beginnings, so I'll often place them on my altar when setting intentions for the coming months.

By summer, the blossoms give way to fruit and come early June (it used to be late June), they're weighed down with clusters of dark red cherries, their branches bending slightly under the weight. This is the time of year when I harvest the fruit, some for drying, others for culinary purposes. There's an abundance of cherries, and I like to think the trees offer more than enough to sustain both the people and the birds that flock to them.

We often end up with a wasps' nest or two in our cherry trees here in Surrey, usually common wasps (Vespula vulgaris) or sometimes the German wasp (Vespula germanica). Now, I know wasps don't have the best reputation compared to bees, but they actually do their part. While they might not be as efficient at pollination as bees, they still help out. What's really great, though, is how they help keep pests in check. Wasps feed on insects like aphids and caterpillars that could reduce the crop. So, even though they can be a bit annoying, they're actually a valuable part of the garden's balance, helping us get a better cherry harvest in the end.

As autumn arrives, the leaves turn a vibrant gold and crimson, reminding me of the tree's connection to the cycle of life and death. I gather the fallen leaves, drying them for teas and rituals that honour change and transformation. Finally, when winter comes, the cherry tree seems to stand quietly, almost waiting for the return of warmth and light. During this time, I collect fallen branches to use in crafting magical tools, wands, and talismans.

One of the simplest tests to ensure you're working with an English Cherry tree is to crush a leaf or a small twig and take a sniff. You'll notice a faint almond-like scent, which comes from cyanogenic compounds naturally present in the tree. It's a subtle reminder of the balance of life and death, as these compounds are toxic in large amounts. This is also why I always wash my hands after handling the fresh leaves or twigs.

The cherry tree is an absolute treasure trove for magical uses. In my green witch practice, I often associate the tree with love, transformation, and protection. There's something undeniably powerful about the energy of the cherry tree—it carries both lightness and depth, much like life itself. I frequently use dried cherry blossoms in love spells. If I'm working with a client to attract love or rekindle passion in a relationship, I'll combine the blossoms with other love-associated herbs, like rose petals and lavender, along with a little bit of honey or Candy Leaf to sweeten the outcome.

But it's not all about love spells. The cherry tree also lends itself well to protection magic. I sometimes craft protective amulets or charms using cherry wood. When carved with symbols of strength and intention, cherry wood can serve as a powerful talisman. I may not be as good turning wood as my dad or The Gardener but I'm quietly proud of what I can make.

Medicinally, the cherry tree has much to offer as well. Cherry bark has long been used in folk medicine to treat respiratory issues, especially coughs. I often make a cherry bark syrup, mixing it with honey and a bit of ginger for a warming, soothing remedy. It's my go-to during the colder months when colds and coughs seem to linger. Cherry leaves can also be used for digestion, and I'll sometimes blend them into a tea when I need to calm my stomach. As you can tell we buy very little from Boots the Chemist!

It's also important not to strip too much bark from a living tree, as it can cause lasting damage. I prefer to gather fallen branches or pruned sections of the tree to use in my magical and medicinal work, always with the understanding that the tree's well-being must come first.

I'd be remiss if I didn't mention the culinary side of cherries. Beyond their magical and medicinal uses, cherries are simply delicious! In the summer, my garden is overflowing with cherries, and I make use of them in every way I can. One of my favourite recipes is cherry jam, which I make with fresh cherries, sugar, and a touch of lemon juice. It's a family favourite and always reminds me of the sweetness that nature has to offer. And… before you ask if you have just read the section on Candy Leaf - Yes, you can definitely use candy leaf extract instead of sugar in jam, but there are a few things to think about. Candy Leaf is way sweeter than sugar, so you'll only need a small amount, which is great if you're cutting back on sugar. But sugar does more than just sweeten, it also helps with the texture and thickness of the jam, and it acts as a natural preservative.

If you switch to Candy Leaf extract, you'll probably need to make some tweaks. For example, you'd want to use a low-sugar or no-sugar pectin because regular pectin needs sugar to set the jam. Without sugar, the texture might be a little runnier, so you might have to add extra pectin or I would suggest something like chia seeds to thicken it up.

Also, Candy Leaf can sometimes leave a hint of a bitterness which I really like, but you might want to balance it out by mixing it with fruit juice concentrate. And since sugar helps preserve the jam, you'll need to either keep it in the fridge or freeze it, unless you're going through the proper canning process.

It's totally doable with a few adjustments, and the end result can still be a delicious, lower-sugar jam!

Another personal favourite is cherry cordial. I make it by pitting fresh cherries and placing them in a jar with sugar and brandy. After a few weeks of steeping, the result is a rich, sweet liqueur that I sip during the colder months. It's a way of preserving the warmth and energy of summer, something to carry me through the darker days.

Dried cherries are also a staple in my kitchen. They're perfect for adding to bread or cakes, or simply snacking on when I need a quick pick-me-up. Packed with antioxidants and vitamins, they're a healthy treat that never fails to brighten my day.

The English Cherry is more than just a tree in my garden, it's a connection to my past, my family, and the land itself. From the ancient tree that has watched over our home for over a century to the delicate blossoms that herald the arrival of spring, the cherry tree is a constant source of magic, medicine, and beauty in my life. Whether I'm using it in spellwork, crafting remedies, or simply enjoying the fruit, the cherry tree reminds me of the cyclical nature of life, love.

"Kuun tšingarimos, taika liikkuu ja noita pachavel."

"In the silence of the moon, the magic stirs and the witch awakens."

Cowslip

I absolutely love telling my son and daughters about the magic of plants in our garden, and cowslip is one of our favourites. There's something so enchanting about passing down this knowledge, especially when you can see the same wonder in their eyes that I used to have (and, let's be honest, still do) when hearing stories about fairies.

When we're out in the garden, they always want to know the stories behind the flowers, and we tell them that absolutely every living thing has its own story. Cowslip, with its ties to the fairy world, is a perfect one to share. I kneel down next to my daughters (my son is more into trucks at the moment!), and we pick a few of the yellow flowers together, making sure to leave enough for the bees. I tell them about how, in the old days, people believed cowslips were the keys to fairyland. Their eyes get wide and look around as if expecting a little fairy to flutter by at any moment. It takes me right back to my own childhood, where I used to do the same, looking for just the right patch of flowers that might open a door to a magical world.

I tell them how, if you find the right cluster of cowslips, fairies might reveal a hidden treasure or lead you into their secret world. I explain that some old stories say fairies use the cowslip flowers as tiny golden goblets, drinking dew from them in the early morning. It's like I can see their imagination whirring as they picture it all, the delicate yellow petals as fairy cups, the dew sparkling like magic. They're mesmerized, just like I was when my grandmother used to tell me these same stories. The fairies felt so real to me back then, and I can see my daughters believe in them too, at least for now.

We often sit together, all the kids, The Gardener and me in the grass, talking about how if we're really quiet, maybe, just maybe, we might catch a glimpse of a fairy. They are completely captivated by the idea, we all get caught up in it. There's something so special about seeing the world through children's eyes, where every flower has a story and every patch of garden could hide a secret. I explain that, according to some legends, cowslips were hung in front of windows or doors to keep out mischievous spirits and invite fairies to bless the home. I can tell my youngest loves this idea, she's always asking if we can make little cowslip wreaths for the doors.

I also teach them the old rhyme about cowslips and fairies, the one I love so much:

> *"The Cowslip tall, her pensioners be,*
> *In their gold coats spots you see;*
> *Those be rubies, fairy Favours,*
> *In those freckles live their savours."*

They repeat it back to me, voices full of excitement. The way their young voices say it, like it's a spell or a secret code, just makes the moment feel even more magical. They ask about the "fairy favours" in the rhyme, and I tell them how the little red spots on some of the cowslip petals are said to be fairy gifts, tiny rubies given to the flowers by the fairies as thanks for letting them use the blooms as their cups.

Sometimes, when we're in the garden at dusk, I tell them stories about how, if we're lucky, the fairies might come out for a dance among the cowslips when the sun sets. We sit together, watching the flowers sway gently in the breeze, and even though we never actually see any fairies, it feels like they're there, just out of sight. I tell them how I used to do this as a child, sitting by the flowers, hoping for a glimpse of magic, and I can see that same quiet anticipation. I have been asked of course if I have ever seen one, but always say that fairies cast magic so even if you did see one, their spell would make you forget, but I "feel" that I might have, when I was their age.

One of my favourite things to do with them is to make cowslip wine, which adds yet another layer of wonder. They help me pick the flowers, and I tell them how, just like people used to make fairy drinks from these flowers long ago, we're continuing a tradition that's been passed down for generations. Even though they are too young to drink the wine, they love helping with the process, especially since I keep the fairy theme going, telling them that we're making something special that the fairies would enjoy, too.

We gather the cowslips together, and I tell them to pick only the best flowers, because the fairies appreciate care and thoughtfulness. We wash the flowers gently, making sure to remove any bugs or dirt, and as we do, I tell them more stories about how these flowers are believed to hold magical properties, especially when picked with love. As the water boils, I tell them that this is where the magic happens and to "shoosh quiet" and see if they can hear the magic happening when we pour the hot water over the flowers, it's like we're releasing all the energy and goodness stored in the petals.

We add the lemon and orange zest, and I explain how the citrus helps to balance the sweetness, just like how the fairies bring balance to nature. Then comes the sugar, which they take turns helping to stir in, and I tell them that the sweetness is what gives the wine it's power, it's what transforms the flowers into something delicious and unique. They are always so proud to help, knowing that what we're making isn't just wine, but something with a story behind it, something connected to the fairies.

When we add the yeast, I say this is where the fairies start to help us, the fermentation, the fairies visit at night to stir the mixture. Over the next few days, we check on the mixture together, watching it bubble and change. To them it's like a spell in motion, and honestly, it feels that way to me too.

Once the wine is bottled, I set it aside to mature, and even though it'll be months before it's ready, they're always asking me if the "fairy wine" is ready yet. I love that this simple process, something that's been done for centuries, has become a little piece of magic in their world as well as mine.

Sharing cowslip with my kids, from its folklore to its real-world uses, brings us closer. It's not just about the flowers; it's about passing down that sense of wonder, of magic, and of believing in something beyond what we can see. Every time I watch them gaze at the cowslips, eyes full of awe, it feels like I'm giving them the same gift I was given as a child, the belief in fairies, in magic, the hidden beauty of nature and the gift of childhood. This bond is beautiful and whether you believe in magic or not, there is a little piece of beauty being created right here with my children. What more proof of magic do you need?

Damiana

Damiana is quickly becoming one of the most lucrative herbs in any commercial witch's practice, and for good reason. As the sensual knowledge of this herb spreads, more and more people are discovering its incredible potential. Damiana's reputation as a powerful aphrodisiac has taken off, making it a popular choice for anyone looking to enhance passion, intimacy, and self-love rituals. Its ability to tap into our deeper, more sensual energy has caught the attention of modern witchcraft communities, wellness enthusiasts, and even those simply curious about natural ways to boost their love lives. Whether in teas, spell bags, or even oils, Damiana's allure is undeniable, and it's no wonder it's become such a high-demand herb in witchy circles.

So, let's get right into the juicy part: its aphrodisiac properties. This little herb has been used for centuries to spark passion and sensuality. Whether you're in a relationship, or just want to connect with your own inner sensual energy, Damiana is the perfect herb to help you tap into that. I've found that it works in this wonderfully subtle way, it's not like an instant switch, but more of a gentle awakening of your senses, a slow burn that brings you back into your body and your desires.

I love to use Damiana in tea blends when I'm getting ready for a special evening or just want to feel more connected to my own sensuality. If I'm preparing for a date night, or a full moon ritual, forget breaking out the bubbly, I'll brew up some iced Damiana tea served in a wine or champagne glass with a bit of cinnamon or rose petals instead. It creates this sharp, loving energy that just sets the perfect mood. There's something about the way Damiana works—it's not just physical, it's emotional and even spiritual. It helps you drop the barriers, relax into your body, and feel more open to intimacy.

And if you're feeling a little playful (or adventurous), Damiana can also be used in smoking blends. Now, I don't do this often, I do have work to do! - but when I want to really deepen the mood or meditate on sensuality, I'll mix it with other herbs like mugwort or lavender. The effect is so dreamy, it helps you feel more relaxed and in tune with your desires, without overwhelming you.

In my green witch practice, I turn to Damiana not just for its aphrodisiac properties, but for the way it helps me connect with myself on a deeper level. I'll often make a little spell bag with Damiana, rose quartz, and other herbs like jasmine or vanilla, and keep it under my pillow or on my altar. It's perfect for setting intentions around love, whether that's love for another person or just deepening your own relationship with yourself.

For me, Damiana is all about embracing the sensual side of life. It reminds me that feeling good in your own skin is something to celebrate. Whenever I feel like I'm stuck in that Groundhog Day of routine same ole same ole, a little Damiana goes a long way. Sometimes I'll make a massage oil with Damiana-infused olive oil, adding a few drops of essential oils like ylang-ylang or sandalwood for an extra boost of sensuality.

Damiana's reputation as an aphrodisiac goes way back. The Mayans and Aztecs were known to use it to increase libido and boost overall vitality. There are even stories about women using Damiana tea to seduce their lovers or to strengthen the bond between them. There's something so intoxicating about the energy of this herb. It's like it helps you let go of all the mental clutter and just be present in the moment, which is exactly what you need to feel connected to yourself and others.

It's not just about the physical though, Damiana has this beautiful way of helping you open up emotionally too. It's said to deepen emotional intimacy, which is just as important as the physical side of things, right? I've read that in some cultures, Damiana was sprinkled around the bed or used in love spells to attract passion and love. Whether you believe in love spells or not, as I assume not everyone reading this book is a believer, I think there's something really powerful about using herbs like Damiana with intention. It's all about creating the energy you want to invite into your life.

Now, while Damiana is famous for its aphrodisiac properties, it's also been used medicinally for a ton of other things. It's a great mood lifter, and I personally love using it when I'm feeling a bit low or stressed. It has this calming yet energizing effect, so it's perfect for those days when you need a little emotional boost but don't want to feel drowsy. It helps with anxiety, depression, and even nervous tension, which can sometimes be the very things that get in the way of feeling sensual or connected.

On top of that, Damiana has been used for digestive issues, particularly after a heavy meal. It's mildly diuretic, which means it can help if you're feeling bloated or sluggish. And while I mostly use it for its magical properties, it's nice to know that it has all these other practical benefits too.

You can also use Damiana in culinary ways, though it's not as common as some other herbs. In Mexico, they make a Damiana liqueur, which is sweet, herbal, and perfect for cocktails. I've even tried making my own Damiana-infused honey, which is incredible drizzled over warm bread or stirred into tea. There's something so indulgent about it, it's like adding a little extra magic, a little razzle-dazzle into whatever you're making.

If you're into mixing your own herbal cocktails, Damiana is a fun ingredient to play with. I once made a cocktail with Damiana syrup, a splash of tequila, and a bit of lime juice, and it was an absolute hit! It's got this slightly bitter, sweet taste that's really unique, and it works so well with other bold flavours.

If you haven't worked with Damiana yet, I can't recommend it enough. For me, Damiana is a reminder to embrace my sensual side, to connect with my body, and to celebrate the pleasure and joy that life has to offer. Whether you're drinking it in iced tea, using it in a ritual, or simply enjoying its energy, it has this way of helping you feel more in tune with yourself and your desires. And honestly, who doesn't want a little more of that in their life?

"Voimaa ei anneta; se otetaan, viljellään kuin juuret maan alla. Kuuntelen henkiä, kuljen näkymättömien kanssa, ja heidän kuiskauksillaan muovaan maailmaa ympärilläni."

"Power is not given; it is claimed, cultivated like the roots beneath the soil. I listen to the spirits, walk with the unseen, and with their whispers, I shape the world around me."

The Witch's Botanical Apothecary

Dandelion

Dandelion

Poor Bridget. I've spent a lot of time writing about the lovely fairies, the ones that flit about in our gardens, bringing magic and mischief into our lives. But, as with most things in folklore, there's a darker side too. Not all fairies are friendly, and some tales are more terrifying than charming. One such story is that of Bridget Cleary, a young woman in Ireland who was tragically caught up in the beliefs of her time. Her story isn't just about fairies; it's about fear, superstition, and the dark consequences of those beliefs. Poor Bridget, indeed.

Bridget Cleary was a seamstress living in rural Ireland in the late 19th century. By all accounts, she was a strong, independent woman, known for her skill with a needle and her fashionable, somewhat modern lifestyle. Perhaps it was this independence that made people uneasy or even envious of her. Life in rural Ireland was tough, and those who stood out were often looked at with suspicion. When Bridget fell ill in March 1895, what followed was a tragic mix of folklore, fear, and fatal misunderstanding. Don't forget 1895 wasn't the dark ages, by this time we had discovered X Rays, Radioactivity, Motion Pictures, Radios, Vaccination.

You see, Bridget wasn't just suffering from any ordinary sickness. Her symptoms: fever, delirium, and general weakness, led some in her community to believe that she wasn't herself. Have you ever heard that expression "not feeling yourself"? And this is where the belief in changelings comes into play. In Irish folklore, changelings are fairies that have swapped places with a human, leaving behind a fairy in disguise while the real person is spirited away to the fairy world. The belief in changelings was particularly strong when someone exhibited behaviour that was unexplainable or frightening, like sudden illness or madness or epilepsy. To those who believed, it was as though an otherworldly being had taken the place of their loved one, and they were not themselves.

Bridget's husband, Michael Cleary, was among those who became convinced that the woman in his home was not his wife but a changeling. The desperation to rid his home of this perceived fairy intruder led to a series of increasingly violent "cures." One of the methods used was a mixture of dandelion root, nettle, and wormwood. These herbs were commonly associated with purification and protection in folklore. Dandelion root can be used to drive out malevolent spirits; nettle was known for its ability to repel evil; and wormwood was often used in rituals to ward off witches and dark magic. (We are so often typecast!). In this context, forcing Bridget to eat this mixture was thought to be a way to banish the changeling and bring the real Bridget back. It's heartbreaking to think they didn't give the treatment enough time, as the logic of the combinations I can relate to.

The idea was that if the changeling could be made uncomfortable enough, through a variety of harsh treatments, including these herbal remedies, it would reveal itself and flee, allowing the true person to return. She didn't! This belief was deeply ingrained in the community, where fear of the supernatural was intertwined with daily life. But poor Bridget was not a changeling; she was simply a sick woman. The situation escalated, fuelled by fear and ignorance, leading to an outcome that was nothing short of tragic.

The culmination of this tragic tale came when Michael Cleary, in a fit of desperation and belief in the fairy myth, went to extreme lengths. After forcing Bridget to eat the herbal concoction, he and others subjected her to a ritual that involved burning. They believed that the flames would drive out the fairy spirit, but instead, it resulted unsurprisingly, in Bridget's death. When her body was found, the community was shocked, and the authorities stepped in.

Michael Cleary was put on trial, but here's the part that might make you shake your head in disbelief: he was found guilty of manslaughter, not murder. The court recognized that he had genuinely believed he was dealing with a changeling and not his real wife. In their eyes, this belief somewhat excused the severity of his actions, at least to the point of not convicting him of murder. Manslaughter, by definition, is the unlawful killing of a person without the intent to kill. The verdict implies that Michael did not set out to kill his wife but rather to "save" her from what he believed was a supernatural threat. It's a chilling reminder of how powerful beliefs can be, especially when they lead to tragic outcomes.

During the trial, it came to light that Michael Cleary had sought help not just from the local priest but also from a "wise woman," a figure who was likely considered a witch in those days. In 1800s rural Ireland, such "wise women" were often seen as protectors against supernatural forces like fairies, drawing on ancient knowledge of herbs and charms. This particular wise woman, known locally as Máiréad Ní Chathasaigh, suggested hanging aromatic herbs, such as dandelion, rosemary, thyme, and elderflower, around Bridget's bedroom to ward off the malevolent fairy presence. Aromatic herbs were believed to create a protective barrier against dark forces. However, the local priest, reflecting the deep-rooted belief in fairies that even the Church shared, advised a far more drastic measure. He suggested that fire was the only way to rid the fairy for good, reinforcing the idea that supernatural problems required extreme solutions. In the end, it was this mingling of folklore, religion, and fear that tragically sealed Bridget's fate.

Bridget Cleary's story is a stark contrast to the whimsical tales of benevolent fairies we've grown up with. It shows the other side of folklore, the side that's rooted in fear, superstition, and sometimes, the darker parts of human nature. Poor Bridget wasn't the victim of fairy magic, but of the human capacity for misunderstanding and cruelty cloaked in the guise of superstition. It's a haunting tale, one that lingers in the shadows of history as a reminder of the dangers that can arise when belief turns into fanaticism.

So, while we often like to think of fairies as whimsical beings who dance under the moonlight and grant wishes to the pure of heart, stories like Bridget Cleary's remind us that the folklore surrounding these beings is complex. It's filled not just with light and laughter, but also with darkness and fear. And sometimes, it's the stories of the "not-so-nice" fairies that tell us more about ourselves and the world we live in than the charming ones do.

Dandelions are some of the most underrated plants, don't you think? In my little wildlife garden, I have a dedicated area where wildflowers and plants like dandelions thrive. I know some people see them as pesky weeds that need to be pulled up, but I've always seen them as little spots of sunshine that bring life to the garden. Over time, I've discovered not only their beauty but also their versatility. Dandelions aren't just for bees to enjoy; they can be used in a variety of ways, from creating a delicious sparkling drink to using the roots in herbal remedies.

Every spring, my garden becomes a haven for dandelions. They pop up with their bright yellow heads, attracting bees and other pollinators. I let them grow freely, especially in my designated wildlife area. I love watching the bees buzzing around, doing their essential work, and I always make sure to leave plenty of dandelions for them. But I also like to harvest some for my own use. It's a delicate balance between keeping the wildlife happy and making the most of what nature offers.

One of my favourite things to do with dandelions is to make a sparkling drink. It's a simple, refreshing beverage that captures the essence of spring. Here's how I usually go about it: I start by picking the flower heads, making sure they're from an area of the garden that's free from any pesticides or chemicals. You only need the yellow petals, so I spend a bit of time carefully removing them. It can be a bit tedious, but there's something quite therapeutic about it. Once I have a bowl full of petals, I add them to a pot of boiling water, along with some sugar and a squeeze of lemon juice. The mixture simmers gently for a while, releasing the dandelions' subtle flavour. After it cools, I strain the liquid and pour it into bottles, adding a bit of yeast to get the fermentation going. Then, I let it sit for a few days. The result is a lightly sparkling drink with a delicate, slightly sweet flavour that reminds me of the garden itself.

The first time I made this sparkling dandelion drink, I wasn't sure what to expect. I'd read about it in an old herbal book and thought, "Why not give it a try?" To my surprise, it turned out to be a delightful treat. Now, it's become a bit of a springtime tradition for me. I love pouring a glass of it on a warm afternoon and sipping it in the garden, surrounded by the very plants that made it possible. It's like bottling up a little bit of the season to enjoy.

But dandelions aren't just about the flowers. The roots, in particular, are known for their medicinal properties. I've dabbled a bit in herbal remedies, and dandelion root is one of those go-to ingredients I always like to have on hand. Digging up the roots can be quite the task—they're long and stubborn, just like the plant itself! Once I have a decent batch, I wash them thoroughly and then dry them out. You can use the fresh roots but drying them helps to preserve their potency. After they're dried, I chop them up and store them in a jar.

One of the most common uses for dandelion root is as a herbal tea. I often make a cup when I'm in need of a gentle detox or just something soothing to sip on. The root is known for its diuretic properties, helping the body flush out toxins. It's also thought to support liver health, which is why it's often included in detox blends. To make the tea, I simply steep a teaspoon of dried root in hot water for about 10 minutes. The taste is earthy and slightly bitter, so sometimes I add a bit of honey to soften the flavour. It's a bit of an acquired taste, but I've come to enjoy it. There's something grounding about drinking a tea made from a plant that grows so abundantly in my own garden.

I've also experimented with roasting the roots to make a coffee substitute. It's a bit of a process, involving chopping the roots into small pieces, roasting them in the oven until they're dark and fragrant, and then grinding them up. The result is a drink that's somewhat reminiscent of coffee, with a deep, roasted flavour, but without the caffeine kick. It's not quite the same as a morning cup of coffee in my view, but it has its own unique charm.

What I love most about using dandelions is the sense of connection it gives me to my garden. It's incredibly satisfying to be able to use something that grows so freely and abundantly around me. Dandelions are often overlooked, dismissed as weeds, but they're actually little powerhouses of nutrition and health benefits. Their leaves are packed with vitamins A, C, and K, and their roots have been used for centuries in traditional medicine.

In my garden, dandelions have become more than just wildflowers. They're a reminder of nature's generosity, offering so much if we just take the time to look. Every spring, as they begin to bloom, I know it's time to start gathering and creating. Whether it's a sparkling drink to enjoy on a sunny day or a cup of tea to warm up on a cool evening, dandelions have a way of bringing a bit of wildness into my everyday life. So, the next time you see a dandelion, perhaps you'll think twice before pulling it out. You never know what kind of magic it might hold.

A fact for down the pub: Continental, a German tire manufacturer, has been developing tires made from dandelion rubber as part of their "Taraxagum" project. They aim to produce sustainable and eco-friendly tires by using dandelion-derived latex. The Fraunhofer Institute for Molecular Biology and Applied Ecology in Germany is also involved in research to optimize the cultivation of Russian dandelions for rubber production.

"Varo voimaa jumalallisessa feminiinissä, sillä siinä on sekä luominen että tuho. Kulkea noidan polkua on kunnioittaa jumalatarta, joka asuu sisällä ja ympäröi meitä, voima joka on yhtä hoivaava kuin se on raivokas."

"Beware the power within the divine feminine, for it holds both creation and destruction. To walk the path of the witch is to honour the goddess that resides within and surrounds us, a force as nurturing as it is fierce."

The Witch's Botanical Apothecary

Dittany of Crete

Dittany of Crete

Right, it's time. Let me tell you about Dittany of Crete, one of the most magical herbs I've ever worked with. I've been excited waiting to get to this herb. Honestly, if I had to pick a favourite plant, this would be somewhere right at the top. Dittany is pure magic! People have been using it for centuries, and in the days before emails, WhatsApp and instant messages, when people actually took the time to write proper letters, Dittany was often used to influence whoever was reading those letters. Witches didn't just send their words; you sent a bit of magic too.

Dittany has this amazing quality where, when you heat it up, it releases a vapour filled with volatile organic compounds (or VOCs, if you're feeling fancy). These VOCs carry the plant's essence into the air, and here's the kicker: it acts like a carrier gas. That means when you combine it with other herbs, it helps their magic and properties spread too, making the whole thing way, way more powerful. You're basically creating a magical potion in the form of vapour, which can then be infused into things like letters or ritual objects. It's like turning your words into a spell that clings to the paper. How exciting is that?

Now, the magic of Dittany really comes alive when you start mixing it with other herbs. I've found that the sweet spot is about two-thirds Dittany and one-third of whatever else you're using. The Dittany takes the lead, while the other herbs add their own unique flavour to the mix.

If you're going for love or something a bit softer, lavender and rose petals are perfect. The Dittany carries the romantic, calming vibes of the lavender and the heart-opening energy of the rose, making the whole thing much more intense. It's like sending a love spell through the post. Proper magical! The person on the other end will feel more than just the words, they'll feel the love and "your intention" radiating from the paper itself.

On the other hand, if you want to dabble in something a little stronger and darker, you can mix in Broomrape. Now, Broomrape's power isn't about luck or wealth coming your way out of nowhere, it's about stealing what someone else has. Whether it's their money, their business, or even their lover. Broomrape has a history of stealing someone else's good fortune. Add that to the Dittany, and you've got a spell that's not messing around.

Then there's Bee Orchid, which is all about deception. This plant's a bit of a trickster, it mimics a bee to fool other insects, and in magic, it's used to cast illusions or trick someone into believing something that's not true. When you blend it with Dittany, you're creating a spell for pulling the wool over someone's eyes, making them see what you want them to see. It's the kind of herb you'd use if you were trying to send a message that's not quite what it seems, cheeky perhaps, dark definitely, but powerful.

Is that immoral? I expect some will judge that it is. I don't practice dark magic, meaning the use of magic for malevolent purposes, and I have no desire to use my knowledge to control, dominate, or harm others. But here's the thing, there is a line, even I will cross when I believe a wrong has been committed that needs to be righted. Life isn't always so black and white, is it? There are times I've encountered a soul burdened by something so deeply wrong that I feel, to truly help them, it's right to do wrong. If that makes any sense at all. I know two wrongs don't make a right, except for me, if the wrong is big enough then fill your boots!

Now, does that make me immoral? I'm not trying to dance with the devil or anything. It's more about striking a balance, sometimes, bending those so-called rules feels like the only way to tip the scales back to justice. Perhaps that's a topic better suited for a long, winding conversation with some friends down at the pub. Because, let's be honest, morality has a funny way of shifting depending on who you're talking to.

Alright, time for a little bit of science (don't worry, I'll keep it simple). VOCs, or volatile organic compounds, are the chemicals that plants release into the air when they're heated up. These are what give plants their smells, and in the case of herbs like Dittany, their magical properties. When you heat Dittany, its VOCs mix with the VOCs of any other herbs you add to the mix, and here's where the real magic happens …they react.

Under the right conditions, like a bit of heat or light, these VOCs can actually form brand new compounds. You're not just mixing scents or properties; you're creating something entirely new. That's why Dittany is so special as a carrier gas, it helps those other herbs' properties evolve and become something more than they would be on their own. The vapour becomes this living, breathing thing, carrying the magic through the air and into whatever you're working on.

For example, when you blend Dittany with rosemary or lavender, the VOCs from both plants can react to boost their antimicrobial and antioxidant effects. That's why certain herb combinations have been used for healing for centuries, it's not just about the individual plants, it's about the magic they create together.

So, how do you use this magic? One of my favourite ways is to infuse letters with Dittany's vapour. I've got a little ritual that I follow, heat up some Dittany on a hot plate above a candle or alcohol burner, maybe add a few other herbs depending on what I'm aiming for, and let the vapour rise and collect in a bell jar which contains my letters. I'll leave the letters in there for a few minutes, just long enough for it to absorb the vapour but not too long that it gets soggy or overwhelmed.

When I take it out, the paper smells faintly of the herbs, I read the letter out loud and emphasise its intent, as I have said many times in this book, without "intent" you will not achieve anything. I know that whoever opens the letter will feel the magic even if they do not recognise it as that.

Whether it's a letter to a friend, a love note, or even a spell of protection, the Dittany carries the energy and intention I've poured into the letter. It's like sending a bit of myself with every word.

Wren is the name of our family grimoire which I write about in much more detail in Chapter 9. I should more accurately say that the grimoire (spell book) known as Wren, (no I don't know why it's called Wren) belongs to our "house" and does not belong to our family. It has a presence that commands reverence, but more of that later. It's not just a collection of spells; it holds the essence of the lineage of those who lived in that house, and with it, a peculiar enchantment inscribed on the very first page. The spell is clear: Wren must never be removed from this house. Destruction is allowed, but only within the grounds. The idea of taking it beyond the walls of the house is strictly forbidden, as if the book itself is bound to the home or possibly the other way around. I often wonder if the pages were prepared with vapours and intent, infused with purpose in the same way I use herbs like Dittany in my rituals. It's likely that every sheet carries the energy and intent of our ancestors, or the owners of this house, sealed in with their breath and woven into the very fibres of the book, making Wren as much a part of this place as the foundation stones themselves. Anyway, look at Chapter 9 if you want more on Wren!

Now, here's something that might just intrigue you, if you're into that sort of thing of course. Honestly, I'm not sure how I feel about it myself. You've probably seen those old-school crystal balls used for scrying in films, looking into the future or past, or maybe Harry Potter, right? Well, here's where it gets interesting. Instead of a solid crystal ball, my family, my mother, her mother before her, and so on, have always used something a bit more... unique. A simple glass jar, domed and unassuming, but when filled with the smoke of Dittany, it becomes something entirely different.

Picture this: you heat the herb beneath the jar, and as the smoke rises, it swirls inside, creating these hypnotic, ever-changing patterns. It's like the very air inside is alive, whispering secrets, revealing glimpses of something beyond. You can't help but feel that, for just a moment, you're peering into another world, a place where magic is not only possible but palpable.

But here's the kicker: when you mix Dittany with herbs like sage or mugwort, something stirs. The air thickens. Sage purifies, clears away the dark energy like it's sweeping a room. Mugwort? That sharpens the senses, opening doors to dreams and visions. But when you combine them with Dittany, something else entirely happens. The smoke curls and twists, hanging in the air like a veil between worlds, and if you stare long enough, you start to feel... something. The longer you watch, the more it feels like the future is whispering, just out of reach, unfolding before you.

I've seen it done. My mother was a master at it, in the way I check the weather app on my phone, she would gaze into the mist, reading the patterns for signs, answers. But I've always kept my distance. Something about it makes me uncomfortable, same with Ouija boards. Maybe it's the power in that smoke, the way it feels like it can pull you in, show you things you can't unsee. Or maybe it's the fear of knowing what comes next… especially if it's bad news. I can't quite tell you which.

I remember, as a young girl, watching Mum sit there for hours, eyes lost in the mist. It made me restless, agitated even, as if the room was filled with something I couldn't touch, a place she had gone to that I wasn't allowed to follow. Wherever she went, it was private, she became closed, distant, like she had slipped somewhere between here and there. She never talked about it, never shared what she saw. Except once. I asked her, half-joking, where she went when she gazed like that. She just looked at me as if I had intruded, and said, "Where I always go." That was it. She wouldn't share more.

It stopped when I was 15. I heard my mum and dad arguing and the next day she stopped.

But here's the thing, I always had this feeling, like she was meeting someone, in the smoke, does that sound insane? I don't know why I say that, it was just a sense I couldn't shake. You know like that feeling that someone else was in the room. Maybe it was nothing, or maybe it was everything. I'll never know for sure.

At the end of the day, Dittany of Crete is one of those herbs that truly transforms any magic you're working with. Whether you're writing letters, creating spells, or divining the future, Dittany elevates everything it touches. It's more than just a herb, it's a bridge between the physical and magical realms, allowing you to create something truly unique and powerful every time you use it.

If you've never worked with Dittany before, now's the time. Trust me, tell me, once you start using it, you'll wonder how you ever did magic without it. Whether you're sending a letter infused with love or creating swirling clouds of magical smoke in a bell jar, Dittany of Crete will take your practice to a whole new level. My only advice is treat it with much, much more respect than you think it deserves.

"Katso tarkasti varjojen puita. Ne katsovat sinua ja odottavat, että paljastat kuka olet."

"Watch closely the trees in the shadows. They are watching you and waiting for you to show who you are."

The Witch's Botanical Apothecary

Elderberry

Known as the "Witch's Tree" or "Tree of Witches," the elder tree has a long history steeped in folklore and magic. Every year, I have my own little ritual involving elderberry, something that's become as traditional and significant as putting up a Christmas tree.

The elder tree has been called the "Witch's Tree" for centuries, and it's not hard to see why. It has an aura of mystery about it, with its twisting branches, clusters of creamy white flowers, and dark, almost ominous berries. According to folklore, the elder tree is inhabited by a powerful spirit known as the "Elder Mother" or "Hylde-Moer." In many European traditions, this spirit is considered a guardian of the tree and a protector of those who respect it. The Elder Mother is both a wise and sometimes vengeful figure, embodying the duality of nature, nurturing and fierce, generous yet demanding respect.

The belief in the Elder Mother means that elder trees are not to be tampered with lightly. Cutting down an elder tree, or even pruning it, without asking for the spirit's permission is said to bring bad luck or the wrath of the tree's spirit. This belief has been so strong that people would perform a small ritual or utter a prayer before taking anything from the tree. A common phrase whispered in the old days was, "Elder Mother, please give me thy wood, and I will give thee mine when I grow into a tree." It's a small offering of respect, a way to acknowledge the spirit within the tree and seek her blessing.

Hans Christian Andersen's fairy tale, "The Elder Tree Mother," centres on the magical and protective qualities of the elder tree. In the story, an old man shares a tale about the Elder Tree Mother, a spirit who lives in the elder tree and comes to life when the tree is respected and cared for. The story reflects the traditional European folklore that views the elder tree as a sacred and protective presence, often believed to house a spirit that could offer protection or wisdom.

Every year, as reliably as hanging baubles on a Christmas tree, I have a ritual of hanging elder branches over my doorways. This practice is rooted in ancient customs where elder branches were used as a protective charm. The belief is that the elder's powerful spirit wards off evil and malevolent forces. By hanging the branches over doors and windows, you create a boundary that negative energy cannot cross.

For me, this ritual usually happens in late spring or early summer when the elder tree in my garden is in full bloom. I carefully choose a few branches, always asking permission from the tree as I was taught. I whisper a small prayer to the Elder Mother, thanking her for her protection and explaining why I need to take these branches. It's a moment of mindfulness, a way to connect with the natural world and acknowledge the sacredness of the act. Once I have the branches, I bring them inside and hang them over the main entrance and a few windows. The fragrance of the elderflowers fills the house, and it feels like a shield of nature's magic is wrapping around my home. Of course there is science around this too, filling your house with the anti-inflammatory and antioxidant properties has a lift to the whole house.

During the Black Death, which claimed millions of lives, people sought protection from the disease in any way they could, often turning to plants and herbs with traditional protective associations. The elder tree was thought to have the ability to ward off evil spirits and malevolent forces, which included illnesses like the plague. It was common practice to hang branches of elder over doorways and windows to keep the disease at bay. This ritual was based on the belief that the elder tree's spirit, the Elder Mother, would provide a protective barrier. People believed that this would prevent the plague, seen as an evil entity, from entering the home.

This act has become a cherished ritual for me. It feels like I'm participating in an ancient tradition, a link to those who came before me and believed in the elder tree's power. It's not just about protection; it's also about inviting a sense of magic and wonder into my life. The branches stay up until Christmas, reminding me of the cycle of nature and the unseen forces that surround us.

Elder trees are often thought to be gateways or bridgeways to the fairy realm. In many folktales, elder trees are said to be sacred to the fae, acting as portals between our world and theirs. It's believed that if you sit quietly under an elder tree at twilight or during a full moon, you might catch a glimpse of the fairies or hear their whispers. This idea of the elder tree as a doorway to another world has always fascinated me and my daughters as you would have read in earlier chapters.

I sometimes like to sit beneath my elder tree in the quiet of the evening, letting the day fade away and the sounds of the garden come alive. There's a certain magic in the air, a feeling that you're not quite alone, that if you sit still enough, you might see something extraordinary. While I've never personally seen fairies flitting about, I have felt an undeniable sense of peace and connection to something greater. It's as if the tree itself hums with an ancient energy, a reminder of the mysteries that lie just beyond our ordinary perception.

Every living organism, including trees, emits a natural vibrational frequency. In the realm of scientific study, this can be related to the concept of bioelectricity. Trees have a measurable bioelectric field that results from the various physiological processes happening within them, like the flow of water, nutrient transport, and cellular activity. Research has shown that trees can generate specific bioelectrical signals in response to environmental stimuli like light, temperature changes, and mechanical damage. Some studies have shown that plants can react to touch, including gentle stimuli like a breeze or the touch of a hand. While these reactions are more observable in certain plants (like the Venus flytrap or Mimosa pudica), the underlying electrical signalling pathways are present in most plants, including trees. There is also the concept of "grounding" or "earthing," which suggests that physical contact with the earth or living plants can have health benefits by transferring electrons from the ground to the body. While this concept is somewhat controversial and not fully understood, some studies suggest that direct contact with the earth can help neutralize free radicals in the body, potentially reducing inflammation and stress.

When you sit close to a tree, especially with your feet or hands in contact with the ground, you might be engaging in a form of grounding, which can promote a sense of balance and well-being. This is where centuries of observational science can create knowledge, because we have seen the effects, now tie in with modern science and scientists who are just starting to be able to explain the things we already know.

Elder wood has long been used in the crafting of wands, amulets, and other magical tools. In many witchcraft traditions, elder wands are considered particularly powerful and are often associated with protection, healing, and transformation. The wood's connection to the spirit world and its reputation for warding off evil make it a favourite among those who practice magic.

However, working with elder wood is not taken lightly. Because of its sacred status, crafting a wand from elder requires careful preparation and respect for the tree.
If I ever find a naturally fallen branch in my garden, I take it as a gift from the Elder Mother. The Gardener will clean and sand it, shaping it into a wand, all the while keeping the intention of protection and respect in mind. Elder wands are known to be temperamental, much like the spirit of the tree itself. They're not tools to be wielded carelessly, and it's said that the elder wand chooses the witch, not the other way around. (I think this concept is well known to those of you who read harry Potter, but the practice of the wand choosing its master has been there for centuries. When treated with respect, an elder wand can be a powerful ally in both protective and transformative spells.

One of the most important taboos surrounding the elder tree is that you must never burn its wood. Burning elder is said to release the spirit within, which can result in misfortune or attract unwanted supernatural attention. In some traditions, it's believed that burning elder can summon the Elder Mother in her more vengeful form, as the smoke releases her protective energy in a way that's not intended. This could lead to bad luck or even a curse upon the person who burned it.

In my own practice, I make sure to honour this belief. If I need to dispose of elder branches, I do so by burying them back into the earth rather than burning them. This is another small ritual of respect, a way of returning the elder to the ground from which it grew. It's a practice that reinforces the idea that we are stewards of the natural world, and our interactions with it should be guided by care and reverence.

Making elderberry wine is one of my favourite yearly traditions. It's a way to connect with the natural rhythms of my garden and transform the elderberries that grow in abundance into something special to enjoy through the colder months. Elderberries have a deep, rich flavour that makes for a surprisingly robust and flavourful wine. Here's how I go about making it:

The first step, of course, is harvesting the elderberries. I usually do this in late summer or early autumn/fall when the berries have turned a deep, dark purple and are hanging in heavy clusters. I always make sure to leave some for the birds and other wildlife, as well as a few clusters to reseed for next year. When harvesting, I cut the whole cluster of berries using garden shears and place them gently into a basket.

Once I've gathered enough elderberries, it's time to prepare them for the wine. Elderberries need to be destemmed, which can be a bit of a tedious task, but I find it quite meditative. I use a fork to gently pull the berries off the stems. It's important to remove all the stems because they contain compounds that can be toxic if ingested.
After destemming, I rinse the berries thoroughly to remove any dirt or insects. Then, I place them in a large pot and crush them lightly with a potato masher to release their juices. At this point, the kitchen starts to fill with a lovely, earthy aroma that hints at the rich wine to come.

Here's the step-by-step process I use to make elderberry wine:
1. Ingredients and Equipment: For this recipe, I usually use about 3-4 pounds of elderberries, 3 pounds of sugar, a gallon of water, the juice of one lemon, and wine yeast. You'll also need a fermenting bucket, a demijohn (glass fermenter), an airlock, and sterilized bottles for the finished wine.
2. Boiling the Berries: I transfer the crushed berries to a large pot and add about half the water (around half a gallon). I bring this mixture to a boil and let it simmer for about 20 minutes. This helps to extract the juice and sterilize the berries.
3. Adding Sugar and Lemon Juice: After simmering, I turn off the heat and add the sugar to the hot berry mixture, stirring until it's completely dissolved. Then, I add the lemon juice, which helps to balance the flavours and acidity of the wine.
4. Fermenting: I let the mixture cool down to room temperature before transferring it to a sterilized fermenting bucket. Once it's cooled, I add the wine yeast and the rest of the water to make up to a gallon. I cover the bucket with a clean cloth and let it sit in a warm place for about a week, stirring it daily. During this time, the yeast will start fermenting the sugars into alcohol, and the mixture will bubble and fizz as it ferments.
5. Straining and Secondary Fermentation: After the initial fermentation period, I strain the mixture through a fine mesh strainer or cheesecloth into a demijohn, discarding the solids. I fit the demijohn with an airlock to allow gases to escape without letting any contaminants in. The wine continues to ferment for about 4-6 weeks or until the bubbling in the airlock slows down significantly.
6. Racking and Aging: Once the fermentation has mostly stopped, I siphon (or "rack") the wine into a clean demijohn to leave any sediment behind. I may repeat this process a couple of times over the next few months to further clarify the wine. Elderberry wine benefits from aging, so after the final racking, I usually let it mature for at least 6 months to a year in a cool, dark place. The longer it ages, the more the flavours develop.
7. Bottling: When I'm satisfied with the taste, I siphon the wine into sterilized bottles and cork them. Then, it's just a matter of labelling the bottles and storing them in a cool place. If I can wait, I try to let the wine age in the bottle for a few more months before enjoying it.

There's something incredibly satisfying about uncorking a bottle of elderberry wine that I've made myself. The wine has a deep, rich colour and a complex flavour—sweet, earthy, and slightly tannic, almost like a young red wine. It's the perfect drink to enjoy on a cold evening, a little taste of summer preserved in a bottle. I often pour a glass and sit in the garden, surrounded by the plants and trees that make such creations possible. It's not just about the wine itself, but the entire process that brings me closer to nature and the cycles of the seasons.

Tip: Poached Pears in Elderberry wine is the absolute best …I simmer the wine with a bit of sugar, a cinnamon stick, a few cloves, and a strip of orange zest until the mixture is fragrant. Then, I add the peeled pears and let them gently cook until they're tender and have absorbed the deep, rich hue of the wine. Once the pears are done, I remove them and reduce the poaching liquid to concentrate its flavours. I love repurposing this luscious, spiced syrup as a cocktail mixer. For an elderberry wine spritzer, I mix a few spoonfuls of the syrup with sparkling water and a splash of lemon juice, adding a splash of gin or vodka for an extra kick. It's a beautiful way to enjoy the essence of the poached pears long after the dessert is gone. Another tip is using in the sauce for spaghetti bolognaise.

I also love using elderberry juice as a natural dye. It's incredibly simple to make and offers a beautiful, rich purple hue that can be used for a variety of purposes. To create the dye, I start by simmering fresh elderberries in a pot with a small amount of water. As the berries heat up, they release their deep, purple juice. After about 20 minutes, I strain the mixture to remove the pulp, leaving behind a concentrated, vibrant dye. We use this to paint each other's bodies for Mabon, our celebration of the autumn equinox and dance the night away.

The use of elderberry juice as face paint has roots in history, particularly among the Germanic tribes who fought against the Romans. These tribes were known to paint their faces and bodies with natural dyes, including those from elderberries, to appear more intimidating in battle and to invoke the spirit of the wild. The dark, fierce appearance created by the elderberry dye served both as psychological warfare and as a symbol of their connection to the natural world.

The Witch's Botanical Apothecary

Hop Vines

Hops

Hops may be best known for their role in brewing beer, but for those of us involved in the world of magic and healing, they hold a much deeper significance. When everything else seems to fail, when someone is deeply troubled emotionally, and no other remedy has brought them peace, I often turn to hops to help them heal. There's something about their calming, nurturing energy that can reach even the most restless of minds. I use hops not just for physical relaxation but also for entering the dream space, where true, deep healing can begin.

This practice reminds me of the Māori concept of dreams, where dreams are seen as a direct connection to the spiritual realm. For the Māori, dreams provide a way to communicate with ancestors, seek guidance, and resolve emotional conflicts. Similarly, when I use hops to delve into dreamtime, I'm tapping into that subconscious space where we are most vulnerable and where profound change can occur. Hops, with their dream-inducing magic, act as a bridge between our waking struggles and the subconscious truths we often bury.

Hops possess incredible elemental energies, aligned with Water and Earth. Water imparts its soothing, calming influence, making hops perfect for spells and rituals involving relaxation and dream work. They are also deeply rooted, thanks to their Earth element, providing balance for those who feel emotionally scattered or ungrounded.

Hops are governed by Venus, the planet of love, harmony, and peace. They are naturally suited for spells or rituals that focus on emotional healing, self-love, and inner balance. While we might not initially associate hops with beauty or romance, they carry a Venusian energy, particularly when it comes to bringing peace to a troubled heart. Their feminine energy makes them nurturing and protective, traits I rely on when helping those who are emotionally raw. Hops can soothe and restore balance, both physically and spiritually, much like a loving, protective embrace. I often link them with Cancer, the zodiac sign connected with home, emotions, and intuition, ruled by the Moon. Hops are perfect for those in need of emotional security or who seek to connect more deeply with their inner selves.

In mythology, hops are associated with goddesses like Aphrodite, Venus, and Hathor, who embody love and fertility, as well as lunar deities like Selene and Hecate, thanks to their dream-inducing magic. This makes hops powerful allies when working on emotional healing or spiritual protection spells.

For me, hops truly shine in sleep and dream magic. Their natural sedative properties are well-known in herbal medicine, but their use in magical practices goes further. Hops help create a peaceful space for exploring the dream world, enhancing psychic visions, and even processing emotional traumas. When working with someone who is emotionally troubled and struggling to find clarity, I often turn to hops to help uncover what's truly happening beneath the surface.

If someone is struggling with nightmares or restless sleep, I'll create a sleep pillow filled with dried hops, often combined with lavender, blackberry leaves or chamomile. The calming scent acts like a gentle nudge into dreamland. Many people have told me that their sleep becomes peaceful after keeping one of these pillows near their bed. The pillow serves as a physical manifestation of comfort, protection, and peace, guiding the mind into a restful state where healing can occur.

Sometimes, I'll burn hops as part of a sleep spell. Smudging a room with hop smoke not only clears negative energy but also creates an inviting space for peaceful, restorative sleep. This sets the stage for deep dream work, especially when paired with moon rituals. Hops help open the door to those subconscious realms where profound healing takes place.

I also use hops to enhance psychic visions and lucid dreaming. If I'm working with someone who needs to tap into their subconscious, I often have them drink a tea made from hops, mugwort, and chamomile before bed. This blend acts as a key that unlocks the door to the dream world. Once there, we can explore their emotions, receive guidance from spirit guides, or work through issues that are too painful for the conscious mind to process.

I've also found that carrying a small charm bag of dried hops can be incredibly powerful for those dealing with anxiety or emotional turmoil. Keeping hops close to the body harnesses their calming energy throughout the day, creating a personal bubble of peace and protection.

Hops aren't solely for healing; they are also excellent for protection. In folklore, hops were believed to ward off evil spirits and keep negative energies at bay. I sometimes use dried hops in protection spells, scattering them around the perimeter of a house to create a barrier against unwanted energies. Hanging hop garlands over doorways is another simple yet effective form of protection, plus they are very pretty.

Due to their connection with Venus, hops are fantastic for love magic. Whether someone is looking to attract new love or restore harmony in a troubled relationship, hops are the herb to turn to. I've created love charms with dried hops, rose petals, and cinnamon, placing them under pillows or carrying them in a pink sachet to promote emotional healing and connection. It's about bringing that calm, loving energy back into relationships.

Hops are also used in spells for luck and fertility. In some traditions, hops were thought to bring good fortune, especially in competitive situations. Carrying a hop sachet for protection during stressful events can help ensure a smooth and successful outcome.

In weddings, both Christian and pagan, hops have symbolised fertility and abundance. I've used hop garlands in handfasting ceremonies to bless a couple's union, wishing them prosperity and balance. The idea is that the grounded energy of hops will help their relationship flourish, much like the plant itself.

For me, hops are more than just a plant, they're a guide, a protector, and a healer. When someone is emotionally troubled and nothing else seems to work, I turn to hops to help enter their dream space and begin the healing process. From enhancing dreams to protecting homes, hops are a versatile and powerful ally in witchcraft. They've been my go-to for helping people find peace when they need it most.

Horseradish

Horseradish has always had a special place in both my kitchen and my magical practices. There's something about its sharp, spicy kick that I love, not just for adding flavour to dishes, but for its potent energy in spells and rituals. It's a plant with a rich history that goes back thousands of years, celebrated not just for its culinary uses but also for its healing properties. I often find myself grating up a fresh root in the autumn to make a homemade horseradish sauce, which I use for everything from spicing up meals to warding off negative energy.

The history of horseradish is quite fascinating. First tales appear over 3,000 years ago in Eastern Europe and it made its way to ancient Egypt and Greece. The Greeks were some of the first to recognise its medicinal value, using it to treat back pain and even considering it an aphrodisiac. There's a bit of Greek mythology that says the Delphic Oracle claimed horseradish was worth its weight in gold. That might sound like an exaggeration, but if you've ever grated fresh horseradish and felt its fiery heat hit your senses, you might agree there's something almost magical about it. By the Middle Ages, horseradish had spread across Europe, becoming a staple for both seasoning food and treating ailments like respiratory issues and digestive problems. In Germany, it was called "meerrettich," meaning "sea radish," because it often grew near coastal areas. When it crossed over to England, it became "horseradish," with "horse" indicating its strong, robust nature.

In my own kitchen, making homemade horseradish sauce is a yearly occurrence, especially in the cooler months. The process is simple but powerful. I start by digging up the roots, giving them a good wash, and peeling them. Then comes the grating, this is where you need to brace yourself because the heat and pungency that rises from freshly grated horseradish can be quite intense. I mix the grated root with vinegar, salt, and a touch of sugar. Sometimes I add a bit of mustard or cream to smooth it out. The result is a fiery, tangy sauce that I use to add a punch to meats, sandwiches, or even soups.

But horseradish sauce isn't just for eating. In witchcraft, horseradish has long been used for its protective and purifying properties. Its sharpness and heat are believed to create a barrier against negative energies and harmful influences. When I make a batch of horseradish sauce, I often set some aside for magical use. For instance, I'll take a small dab and place it on the perimeter gates of my home. This is my way of asking the fiery spirit of horseradish to guard the space, almost like saying, "Only good vibes are welcome here." It's like setting up a spicy boundary around the home.

Horseradish also comes in handy when I need to banish negativity or clear out stagnant energy. Its intense nature can help "burn away" anything that's holding you back. Sometimes, I'll write down what I want to release, whether it's a bad habit, a negative thought pattern, or a toxic influence, and I'll use a small dab of horseradish sauce on the paper.

Then, I'll bury the paper outside, visualizing the horseradish's fiery energy consuming and transforming the negativity into something that can nourish new growth. It's a simple but powerful ritual that makes me feel like I'm actively clearing the way for positive change.

When it comes to healing, horseradish has a lot to offer. Historically, it was used to clear congestion and stimulate circulation, and I use it with the same intention in my magical practice. If I'm feeling a bit under the weather or want to boost my immunity, especially during cold season, I'll make a batch of horseradish sauce infused with garlic and honey. I take a spoonful daily, imagining it burning away any illness or sluggishness in my body. It's like taking a fiery tonic that warms you from the inside out.
Horseradish is also great for spells related to personal empowerment and inner strength. Its bold, fiery energy can be harnessed to boost confidence and courage. Before a big event where I need an extra push, I'll take a tiny bit of horseradish sauce and place it on my tongue. As the heat spreads through my senses, I visualize it igniting a fire within me, burning away any self-doubt and filling me with determination. It's a simple act, but it has a way of making me feel ready to take on anything.

There's a lot of folklore around horseradish too. In European traditions, it was often used to ward off evil spirits and protect homes. People would plant it around their gardens or hang it in their kitchens, believing its pungent scent would keep malevolent forces at bay. Its association with Mars, the planet of war and protection, ties it to themes of strength and defence. I like to think of horseradish as a fiery guardian that doesn't shy away from taking on negative energy head-on.

For me, horseradish is one of those plants that carries a fiery spirit within it, ready to cut through negativity and bring a sense of boldness to any situation. Whether I'm grating it into a sauce to spice up a meal or using it in a protective spell around my home, horseradish always makes its presence felt. Its history as a medicinal and magical herb makes it a valuable ally, reminding me that sometimes a little spice is exactly what we need to clear the air, protect our space, and ignite our inner fire!

"Mistä tiedät, että se mitä näet on totta, katso kahdesti! Varotin sinua."

"How do you know what you see is to be believed, look twice! I warned you."

The Witch's Botanical Apothecary

Lavender

Lavender

Lavender, or Lavandula angustifolia, has always fascinated me with its striking purple flowers and soothing fragrance. Its rich history, spanning several millennia, only adds to its allure. Lavender's versatility, encompassing beauty, medicinal, magical and aromatic properties, has cemented its place in cultures throughout history.

The name "lavender" derives from the Latin word "lavare," meaning "to wash," highlighting its ancient use in Roman baths. The Romans infused their bathwater with lavender for its relaxing and antiseptic properties. It was also used in perfumes, cosmetics, and as an insect repellent. Its popularity surged across the Roman Empire, becoming a staple in personal care and household use.

Roman soldiers carried lavender with them, using it to clean wounds and prevent infection due to its antiseptic properties. This practical application made lavender an essential part of Roman military gear, beyond its pleasant scent. If the lavender in my garden has worked its way down the centuries from the Romans who had lived on this land I really don't know, I do like to think so.

Lavender thrived in England after being introduced by the Romans. By the medieval period, it was widely cultivated in monastery gardens, used by monks and nuns for medicinal purposes, culinary dishes, and as a natural air freshener. Historical records from the 13th century document its use in apothecaries and herbal remedies.

The lavender fields of England, particularly in Kent, Surrey, and Norfolk, became renowned for their well-drained soil and ample sunlight, ideal for lavender cultivation. Before reaching London, lavender was primarily grown in these rural areas, harvested, and processed into oils, sachets, and other products.

In the 16th century, lavender's popularity in London soared. The city's growing population and increased interest in personal hygiene made lavender highly sought-after. Lavender street sellers became common, and Elizabeth I always asked for daily fresh lavender flowers.

During the Victorian era, lavender saw another surge in popularity, used in soaps, perfumes, and cleaning agents. Lavender farms near London expanded to meet the demand, and the herb became a British household staple. Its soothing properties were utilized in hospitals and homes to promote relaxation and sleep.

Today, lavender continues to be celebrated for its diverse uses. It's a favourite in gardens for its beauty and drought resistance, and its essential oil remains key in aromatherapy, cosmetics, and natural remedies. Lavender festivals and farms, especially in regions like the Cotswolds and Norfolk, attract tourists seeking the sight and scent of blooming lavender fields. If you do find yourself travelling around Surrey do look up Mayfield Lavender in Banstead and book yourself a bee safari! Also, Castle Farm in

Shoreham in Kent, is very pretty. I used to work as a fruit picker in my school summer holidays around Shoreham and it's a very special place to me.

In my own garden, lavender holds a special place. I've always been drawn to its calming scent and beautiful blooms and plant along pathways and near windows, its fragrance filling the air creating a peaceful and inviting atmosphere. There's something incredibly soothing about stepping outside and being greeted by the gentle aroma of lavender and the gentle hum of the bees, especially in the early morning when dew clings to the petals.

One of my favourite activities is making my own lavender pouches. The process itself is therapeutic: gathering the flowers, drying them, and sewing little fabric bags to fill with the dried blooms. I place these sachets in closets, drawers, and even under my pillow to help me sleep. The subtle, continuous release of lavender's scent keeps my home feeling fresh and serene. Also see the Commercial Witch section later in the book.

I also enjoy making my own essential oils. It's a tad time consuming but the end result is worth it. I use the oil in various ways around the house. A few drops in my diffuser create a calming environment, perfect for unwinding after a long day. Diffusing lavender oil not only helps me relax but also keeps annoying midges and Horse Flies at bay, making summer evenings on the porch much more enjoyable.

Lavender tea has become a personal favourite, providing a soothing end to a busy day. Brewing a cup of tea from lavender I've grown and dried myself brings simple pleasure. The tea's gentle, floral flavour is calming and refreshing, my go-to beverage when I need to de-stress or prepare for a good night's sleep.

During stressful times, a lavender-infused bath is my sanctuary. I add a few drops of lavender oil to the bathwater with some Epsom salts. The warm, fragrant water helps me relax and unwind, melting away the day's tension, and I can start to forget the kids arguments, of who said what to who or who's turn it should have been for this of that. When I watch the world news I know the problems I have are nothing compared to the poor families elsewhere but even so it's a cherished ritual, providing respite from daily life.

Incorporating lavender into my skincare routine has been great for me. Lavender oil's antiseptic and anti-inflammatory properties keep my skin healthy. When I was little I had a little Rosacea and my mum would rub in some Aloe Vera and lavender Oil which seemed to help. Now I mix a few drops with a carrier oil like jojoba or almond oil and apply it to my skin before bed. It soothes irritation, leaving my skin soft and rejuvenated by morning.

Growing lavender is straightforward: it thrives in well-drained soil and full sun, preferring slightly alkaline soil. Minimal watering is needed once established. Pruning after flowering maintains its shape and encourages new growth.

Harvesting is deeply satisfying, preserving its scent and beauty for months. I harvest early in the morning after the dew has dried but before the heat sets in, when essential oils are most concentrated. Using sharp pruning shears or scissors (which are easier to keep sharp), I cut the stems when about one-third of the flowers on the spike have opened, ensuring the lavender is in full bloom for the best colour and scent during drying.

I gather the stems into small bundles, securing them with rubber bands for good air circulation, preventing mould and ensuring even drying. I hang the bundles upside down in a cupboard next to the garage, its dark, dry, well-ventilated space preserves the lavender's vibrant colour and prevents moisture buildup. After two to four weeks, the flowers and stems are dry and brittle, and the scent is intense. I gently strip the flowers from the stems and store them in airtight containers away from direct sunlight, keeping the lavender fragrant for long use in sachets, potpourri, and homemade beauty products.

Propagating lavender from seeds I'm afraid is not for me, I try and try but always fail. If you can grow from seed then tell me how, I've read every book, seen every YouTube video and it should be easy right? I sow seeds in well-draining seed mix, keep the soil moist but not waterlogged, and provide ample light. Germination should take two weeks to a month but whatever I do I have just an empty patch.

Taking cuttings however does work! Cut from healthy, non-flowering stems below a node, remove lower leaves, dip the cut end in home-made rooting hormone, and place in a pot with fine gravel and potting soil. Keep moist and in indirect light until roots develop, then transplant. The fine gravel I steal! I know I shouldn't but there it is, I admit it! On my morning walk with Bunny, our Golden Retriever, we often stop for her to paddle in a ford of a small river that when the water level is low enough cars can drive through. At the edges of the river there is a lovely fine gravel, river gravel, more rough then sand. I always have dog poo bags with me and I reach down and grab a handful. It's the same gravel I use for potting Fennel or my herb that resembles Silphium. So, if anyone spots me on the way home they think I'm a good citizen clearing up after my dog, rather than the gravel thief I'm afraid I really am.

I don't seem to get many bugs in my garden that feast on Lavender (They can have a banquet elsewhere mind!). If you get aphids. treat with soapy water of give a bit of blast with your hose spray.

Burning lavender incense during meditation, as part of incantations, or before bed creates, for me at least, a clarity of thought, a cleansing of those thoughts that seem to clog up the brain, leaving it free to fill up with new or refreshed thinking. Its purifying properties cleanse spaces of negative energy and its protective qualities are used in charms or sachets to ward off negative influences. I do recommend placing lavender under pillows if you're having nightmares or you have other grief in your life that is stopping you sleeping properly.

Historically, lavender treats anxiety, depression, and insomnia, with its calming properties relaxing the nervous system. Used in baths, teas, and inhalations, it alleviates symptoms. In love spells and sachets, lavender's aroma attracts love and enhances romance. Brides often carry lavender in wedding bouquets for love and devotion.

Modern applications include aromatherapy to reduce stress and promote relaxation. Lavender oil in diffusers, baths, or massage oils lowers blood pressure and heart rate, providing calm. Its soothing properties treat skin conditions, with lavender oil added to lotions, creams, and balms. Lavender enhances sweet and savoury dishes in culinary applications.

Lavender's mosquito-repellent properties come from compounds like linalool, linalyl acetate, and camphor, disrupting mosquitoes' sensory reception. That sounds very clinical doesn't it, but don't forget plants are the basis for most medicines. Mosquitoes and midges are attracted to lots of things but did you know the thing they like most is carbon monoxide, or the stuff we breathe out. So, unless you want to turn into a balloon, we can't stop breathing out, but we can mask the carbon monoxide. Apparently, they can detect us breathing from 150 feet away, so planting lavender around our outside table does seem to create that bubble to keep those annoying midges away. We plant around pathways, but also have in pots on the patio to create natural barriers.

Lavender attracts beneficial insects like bees and butterflies, supporting the local ecosystem. Its versatility and beauty make it indispensable in my life, both in magical practices and everyday use. Lavender's presence in my home and garden creates tranquillity and peace. It reminds me to appreciate small moments, bringing calm and self-care.

A favourite lavender recipe is Lavender Shortbread Cookies. The ingredients include 225g unsalted butter, 100g sugar, 250g all-purpose flour, 2 tablespoons dried lavender flowers, and 1 teaspoon vanilla extract. Cream the butter and sugar, add vanilla, mix in flour and lavender, roll out dough, cut into shapes, bake at 165°C for 20-25 minutes until lightly golden. These cookies are yummy! Crumbly and melt in the mouth.

There was a poignant time in my life when school was ending, and my friends and I were all preparing to go our separate ways, starting new phases of our lives, including my best friend, Sophie. The thought of us scattering in different directions filled me with a deep sense of loss and uncertainty. Simply I guess I was sad. I should have been excited about what lay ahead but I wasn't feeling that. My friends knew my "witchy" inclinations and "weird family!" but they all came around never-the-less to join me in performing a spell as a way of bonding before our big farewell. Our school only went up to the age of 16 so we were too young to go to the pub or celebrate in that way and this felt personal.

On the evening before our last school day, we gathered at my house. The atmosphere was a mix of sadness and excitement for the unknown future. My mum had suggested; actually that's not true. My mum and grandma had been arguing all afternoon which was the right "binding" spell, but they ended up, eventually, agreeing on one that would bring us peace and help us stay connected despite the miles that would soon separate us.

We began by selecting our ingredients. Lavender, my mother explained, was essential for its calming and protective properties. We also chose Mugwort to enhance our intuition and clarity, Rue for its protective qualities to guard our friendship, and Lemon Balm to uplift our spirits and promote emotional healing. The combination of these herbs would mean that our bond would remain strong and harmonious.

As the sun started to go down, we prepared a sacred space. My mother lit a white candle and placed it at the centre of our circle, its gentle light casting a warm, comforting glow. Then me and my friends arranged fresh purple sprigs of lavender around the candle.

In a small saucepan, we mixed the dried herbs: lavender, mugwort, rue, and lemon balm. My mother guided us as we combined them, her hands steadying ours, helping us to feel the energy emerging from each herb. We held the saucepan handle together, closed our eyes, and took deep breaths, letting the calming scents fill our noses and senses.

Mum gave me a piece of paper which she had written the incantation upon and we all had to pass it around and read it aloud one by one.

> *Bound by friendship, strong and true, We carry this love in all we do.*
>
> *Though we journey far and wide, Our spirits stay connected, side by side.*
>
> *Just look for the North Star's guiding light, It keeps watch over us all, in it's sight.*
>
> *Protected always, near and far, Bound by love, we know who we are.*

After the incantation, we placed the saucepan at the centre of our circle, letting the herbs steep in some walnut oil above the candle. Whether any of my friends believed or didn't in any form of witchcraft of spirituality you could feel the emotion tingling as we all read, some chirpy, some quite emotional. I thought I would be the emotional one, but the ones who I thought would be the most confident in their future were the ones whose voices seem to crack or stumble the most.

When that was over it was like a huge relief and we giggled so much that if our school teacher had seen us he would have thought we were drunk. We all took small handfuls of the mix of herbs in oil and squished it into a small lump of cake and stuffed it in little cloth pouches. I thought the oil would stain or mark the pouches but it never did.

In the days that followed, we each carried our small pouch of our herb cake, a personal reminder of the spell and our friendship. Whenever I felt the sting of loneliness or doubt, I would hold the pouch, take a deep breath, look for the North Star in the night sky, and each time, the soothing scent of lavender and the combined energies of the herbs grounded me, bringing peace and clarity. It was probably one of the first times I realised that having people around me who all had wanted the same thing, all who had the same emotion welling up inside that they wanted to share, was incredibly powerful. I now know how the emotion of others in a circle with you can amplify your own emotions and bond to them. It's not just about herbs, potions, words or incantation, it's about people, the energy, feelings, desires and kindness of other people. In a small way, and perhaps even though I was the only witch, it had been my first coven.

It feels like a long time ago and at the same time no time at all. Not all my friends are still here, we lost one tragically, maybe, perhaps I'll write about that somewhere later in the book or perhaps not at all, I'll see how I feel. What I do know is that at her funeral each of us had our binding herb pouches with us, and Sophie's will now lay with her by her side for all time.

"Jokainen tuulenhenkäys kantaa viisautta, ja maa itse on loputon taikuuden lähde."

"Every breeze carries wisdom, and the earth herself is a boundless source of magic."

Lions Mane

Throughout time, people have relied on observational science to understand the world around them. Before modern scientific methods and advanced technology, our ancestors used keen observation and practical experience to learn about plants and fungi. Lion's Mane mushrooms are a prime example of this. Observers noticed that this peculiar mushroom, with its cascading, shaggy white spines, seemed to benefit those suffering from what we now call memory loss, cognitive decline, and neurodegenerative diseases like Alzheimer's and Parkinson's. This wasn't based on laboratory tests or clinical trials but rather on years of observing how those who consumed Lion's Mane seemed to maintain sharper minds and better memories as they aged.

In my family, we've been fortunate never to have experienced Alzheimer's, Parkinson's, or other severe memory-related diseases. We've always chalked this up to our DNA or regular use of Lion's Mane mushrooms in our cooking and sometimes in teas. It has been a long-standing tradition passed down through generations. We didn't think of it as a "preventative" per se, it's just something we did because it tasted good and made us feel good. But now, as modern science starts to back up those old observations, it feels like there's more to our family habit than just a coincidence.

Traditional Chinese and Japanese medicine included Lion's Mane as a natural remedy for a variety of ailments, particularly those related to the mind and nerves. Monks would brew it into teas to help with concentration during long meditation sessions. Healers recommended it to the elderly to help ward off the "fog of old age." There was a growing understanding, simply through generations of watching and noting, that people who consumed Lion's Mane regularly seemed to retain their cognitive abilities longer. It was noticed by different cultures all around the world.

In today's terms, they might have been looking at early symptoms of what we now know as Alzheimer's and Parkinson's, confusion, forgetfulness, difficulty with basic tasks. These ancient healers didn't know about neurodegenerative diseases in the way we do now, but they could see that the mind and body were interconnected. They recognized that certain foods, herbs, and fungi had effects on the mind, and they leaned heavily into using these natural remedies to maintain mental acuity.

Fast forward to today, and science is beginning to catch up with what these ancient traditions have known all along. Modern research has shown that Lion's Mane contains bioactive compounds, notably hericenones and erinacines, which have a unique ability to cross the blood-brain barrier and promote the production of Nerve Growth Factor (NGF). NGF is crucial for the growth, maintenance, and survival of neurons, the cells that make up our brain and nervous system.

Neurons are like the wiring in our brains, and as we age, some of this wiring can get damaged or start to break down. This is where diseases like Alzheimer's and Parkinson's come into play; they're essentially conditions where the neurons degenerate, leading to memory loss, cognitive decline, and a host of other symptoms. Lion's Mane, by promoting the production of NGF, supports the maintenance and repair of these neurons. It's like giving your brain a little bit of a tune-up, encouraging it to produce more of the chemicals that keep it healthy and functioning. When I explained this to my son he simply called it "brain fertilizer", which is probably a better description then any of the text books can claim.

In our family, we've always included Lion's Mane in our diet. My grandparents used to actively grow it , and it was as common as any other vegetable in the kitchen. I remember my grandmother adding it to soups and stews, sautéing it with garlic and herbs, and sometimes drying it to make tea. As kids, we were just told it was good for us, and we never questioned it. We never thought about cognitive decline or memory loss; we just knew that it was a delicious part of our meals.

To grow Lion's Main, you can either grow them indoors using sawdust or head outdoors and grow them on logs. We have done both over the years, and everyone has different luck depending on the conditions, so there is no wrong or right answer but we seem to have been more successful growing them directly on logs. We have a quiet, shaded corner with just the right amount of dampness, a haven for mushrooms. It seems ideal for stacking old hardwood logs and just letting nature take over.

If you're going the sawdust route, it's pretty straightforward. You start with some hardwood sawdust or pellets, soak them until they're damp but not sopping wet, and then mix in the Lion's Mane spawn. The whole mixture goes into a bag with some small holes cut in it, and then you place it in a warm, dark place to incubate. The mycelium, the "roots" of the mushroom, spreads through the sawdust over the course of a few weeks. Once the bag is fully colonized with white, fluffy mycelium, you move it to a place with indirect light and high humidity. Before you know it, those shaggy little mushrooms start poking out through the holes.

But our favourite method has been growing them on logs. There's something really satisfying about seeing these mushrooms pop up in a more natural setting. My Great Grandparents found the perfect spot in the garden and we have been using it ever since. We gather old hardwood logs around January/February whilst the trees are still dormant, oak and beech work best, ideally fresh cut logs 6 weeks previous, as logs that are too old or dry will not promote growth of the mycelium effectively. Aim for logs approx. 6 inches in diameter, and drill holes in them 1 inch deep and 6 inches apart to insert the spawn. We then sealed the holes with wax to keep the spawn moist and protected. We throw the logs on top of the others in the shady rotten wood pile, stacking them in a way that allowed air circulation but still kept them off the ground. And then, we just let nature take its course.

The logs take a bit longer than sawdust to produce mushrooms—it can be several months before you see any signs of growth, but it's worth the wait. When the conditions are just right, you'll start to see the white, cascading spines of Lion's Mane emerging from the logs. It's like a little bit of magic happening in the corner of the garden. Not only does it feel more natural, but it also creates this sense of discovery every time you check on the logs.

Both methods have their charm. Growing on sawdust is quicker and more controlled, while logs take more patience but feel wonderfully organic. Finding that perfect spot for the logs is key but it can use the most under used part of your garden and turn it into a little mushroom sanctuary.

Over the years, we've watched as friends and acquaintances have struggled with the mental decline that comes with age. In our family, we've stayed remarkably sharp, even into old age. Now, I'm not saying Lion's Mane is a miracle cure or that it's solely responsible for our cognitive health, but I can't help but wonder if our family's regular consumption of this mushroom has played a role. After all, it aligns with what ancient wisdom and modern science are telling us: Lion's Mane has properties that support brain health.

We still use Lion's Mane regularly. When it's in season, we sauté it with a bit of olive oil, garlic, and thyme. It has a wonderful, almost seafood-like flavour and a texture that's both hearty and satisfying. We add it to stir-fries, soups, and stews, blending it seamlessly into our meals. On colder days, we sometimes brew a pot of Lion's Mane tea. It's a bit earthy, but adding a slice of fresh ginger or a bit of honey makes it a comforting and warming drink.

The modern studies around Lion's Mane are promising. While more extensive research is needed, particularly in human clinical trials, what we've seen so far suggests that this mushroom could be a powerful ally in maintaining cognitive health. It's exciting to think that something as simple as a mushroom could have such profound effects on the brain. It's a testament to the wisdom of those who came before us, who observed the natural world with such clarity and passed down their knowledge through the generations.

So, whether it's a coincidence or a testament to the power of Lion's Mane, my family continues to enjoy this mushroom in our meals. We don't treat it as a medicine, but rather as a delicious and healthy part of our diet. And if it happens to be contributing to our mental sharpness as we age, well, that's just another reason to keep cooking with it.

The Witch's Botanical Apothecary

Mullein and Coltsfoot

Growing up, my father was a man of many hobbies, but one of the most fascinating to me was his ritual of making his own pipe tobacco. He had a unique blend that included Mullein, Coltsfoot, and traditional tobacco plant leaves. The process he followed was a mix of science, patience, and a touch of magic, creating memories that have stuck with me as I grew up.

Our garden was always teeming with life and purpose. Dad had a special section dedicated to his tobacco-making herbs. The Mullein grew tall and stately, with its large, soft leaves that felt like velvet. Coltsfoot, with its broad, heart-shaped leaves, provided a nice contrast and was often mistaken for weeds by unknowing visitors. And then there were the tobacco plants, which, though not as tall as the Mullein, had a robust presence with their large, sticky leaves and tall, flowering stems.

Every spring, my father would prepare the soil meticulously. He believed in the old ways, turning the soil by hand, adding compost he had nurtured all year, and talking to the plants as he set them into the ground. He'd plant the Mullein and Coltsfoot first, as they were more resilient to the early spring chills. The tobacco plants would start indoors and then go a bit later when he was sure the last frost had passed. Watching him in the garden was like watching an artist at work, each movement deliberate and filled with care.

Throughout the summer, the garden would flourish under his watchful eye. Mullein's tall stalks would shoot up, and Coltsfoot would spread its leaves wide. The tobacco plants, with their large leaves, needed more attention. Dad would often be out there, inspecting them for pests, removing the occasional caterpillar and throwing them into the meadow, and ensuring they got just the right amount of water. He'd tell me stories as he worked, of his own father and grandfather, who had passed down the knowledge of tobacco growing and preparation. I liked the thought of my grandad wandering around the same paths with a pipe.

Come late summer, it was harvest time. This was always an exciting period. Preparations would start in Lammas, also known as Lughnasadh on the 1st of August when my mum would hang the corn dollies all around the garden. Dad would carefully inspect to see if the Mullein leaves were mature but still vibrant green. They should be large and soft, with a slight fuzziness on the surface. He cut the Mullein leaves first then a week later the Coltsfoot, laying them out on racks to dry in our old shed. The tobacco leaves required a bit more finesse. They had to be picked at just the right time, when they were mature but before they started to yellow too much. These too were hung in the shed, but unlike the other herbs, the tobacco leaves had to be cured.

Curing tobacco was a slow process that required patience. The shed would be filled with the sweet, earthy smell of drying leaves. Dad had rigged a simple but effective curing system with a small heater and a fan to keep the air circulating. For all three types of leaves, he let them wilt slightly for a day or two in a shaded area before moving them to the drying shed and then checked the leaves daily, ensuring they were drying evenly. The scent that filled the shed was intoxicating, a mix of the grassy freshness of the Mullein, the slightly medicinal aroma of Coltsfoot, and the rich, complex fragrance of the curing tobacco.

Once the leaves were fully dried, around 2 weeks for the Mullein and Coltsfoot and around 6 weeks for the tobacco, Dad would move on to the blending stage. He had a special table in the shed for this purpose, covered with old newspapers (usually The Sun). The dried leaves would be carefully crumbled by hand. He had a specific ratio he followed: two parts Mullein to one part Coltsfoot and one part tobacco. This blend, he said, had been perfected over years of trial and error. The Mullein provided a smooth, mild smoke, the Coltsfoot added a bit of "bite" or flavour and acted as a natural expectorant, and the tobacco gave the mix its traditional richness.

Watching him blend the leaves was mesmerizing. He'd crumble them gently, almost reverently, mixing them thoroughly. The final blend was stored in glass jars with tight-sealing lids to keep the moisture out. These jars were then placed on a high shelf in the shed, away from direct sunlight. Each jar was labelled with the date and blend ratio, though he hardly needed the labels, as he could tell just by the smell and texture.

The shed was a sanctuary of sorts. On quiet afternoons, I'd join him there, sitting on an old wooden stool while he filled his pipe with the freshly blended tobacco. The ritual of packing the pipe was precise. He'd tap the pipe lightly to settle the tobacco, strike a match, and take a few gentle puffs to get it going. The smoke that wafted through the air was aromatic and comforting, a blend of the earthy, herbal notes of Mullein and Coltsfoot with the rich, smoky undertone of tobacco.

Some of my fondest memories is sitting in that shed with him, the two of us surrounded by the scents of drying herbs and curing tobacco. He'd tell me stories about his childhood, about the traditions of tobacco growing in our family, and about the significance of each herb in the blend. Those moments felt timeless, bridging the gap between generations.

The pipe tobacco he made wasn't just for his own use. He'd often share it with friends and family. I remember our home being a gathering place, especially during the Christmas holidays. There was something special about those gatherings, the smell of his tobacco blending with the scent of mulled wine and roasting chestnuts. It created an atmosphere of warmth and family. Memories can be sparked by so many things; it seems smell is the strongest for me. Our family has a unique smell, now that can be taken both ways I guess, but I mean in the most loving way.

As I grew older, I came to appreciate not just the end product, but the entire process. It taught me the value of patience, the importance of tradition, and the joy of creating something with your own hands. Dad's pipe tobacco was more than just a hobby for him; it was a connection to his past, a way to remember his dad, and a method to create something unique and very personal.

Even now, whenever I catch a whiff of Mullein or Coltsfoot smoke, I'm transported back to those days in the garden and the shed. It's a scent that carries memories of my father's voice, the stories he told, and the lessons he imparted. Clearly his passion for growing and blending his own tobacco left an indelible mark on me, one that I carry with me and hope to pass down to my own children someday (as long as the Health and Safety police don't get me first!)

It was a labour of love, a pure example of a green craft honed over years, and a testament to the simple joys of working with nature to create something truly special. We witches often talk about "smudging" and I'll cover more of that later, but this was a recipe for love and happiness and remembering the people who loved us first.

I vividly remember a time, I can't have been more than 10 years old, when sitting with my dad sunder the old Cherry tree in the centre of the garden, he shared with me the story of his two favourite pipes, explaining how the shape of each pipe impacted the flavour, the way the tobacco burned, and even the smell of the smoke. It must have been early July as I remember the Cherries were red on the tree but not quite ripe, and the familiar scent of his pipe tobacco mingling with the fresh air, as he carefully packed his old Churchwarden pipe from the little dented tin with an edelweiss scored into its lid that he always carried in his pocket.

He held the churchwarden up, its long stem and elegant curve catching the light. "This pipe," he said with a twinkle in his eye, "is something special. The long stem cools the smoke before it reaches your mouth. It brings out the subtle nuances in the tobacco blend, making each puff smoother and more flavourful. Plus, keeping the smoke away from your face makes the whole experience more pleasant." Or words to that affect.

"You sound like a hobbit," I teased, having been immersed in "The Lord of the Rings" at his recommendation.

He laughed heartily. "Is it like Old Toby?" I asked, my curiosity piqued.

"I wish I knew," he replied with a wink, "but I think mine would be better."

Then he took out his Rhodesian pipe, the one with a rounded bowl and short, thick stem. He knocked the base against his shoe to clean it out. "Your granddad made this," he said, his voice softening. "He carved it from this tree," he added, pointing up at the cherry tree above our heads that stood proudly in the centre of our garden.

He explained that the shape of the Rhodesian pipe allowed for a more even burn, enhancing the depth and richness of the tobacco's flavour. "And the cherry wood," he added, "gives the smoke a slight sweetness. It has a unique aroma that you can't find in any other pipe."

Listening to him, I could sense the deep connection he felt with these pipes, each one not just a tool for smoking but a piece of our family's history. Sitting there, I realized that these moments, filled with stories and laughter, were just as special as the pipes themselves.

I know it's probably not lady like and possibly not exactly healthy, but I do smoke a pipe in the garden too, usually when my kids aren't looking. I do end up arguing the healthiness of it with my children, usually losing, that the Coltsfoot helps soothe the respiratory system and acts as a natural expectorant. I think more so they know it reminds me of my dad, and that makes me both happy and sad, but in a good way, if you know what I mean. When I came home from Portland when my parents died, it was one of the mysteries where dad had put his pipes. He had two because he was always putting one down and forgetting where he put it. One day they'll turn up, probably a time when I need him the most. Don't tell me magic doesn't exist, I know better!

"Kuuntele varjoja, haista ilma, ja tanssi tanssisi maailmojen välillä."

"Listen to the shadows, smell the air, then dance your dance between the realms."

The Witch's Botanical Apothecary

Pumpkin

As you would expect Halloween is, without a doubt, the most exciting time of year for our family, probably matched only with Christmas. The energy in the house shifts as October rolls around; you can feel it in the air, this blend of anticipation, mystery, and joy. The kids start planning their costumes weeks in advance, and I find myself caught up in it all, from decorating the house to baking treats. But for us, Halloween is more than just a night of dressing up and collecting sweets. It's a time steeped in tradition, magic, and a connection to the unseen world. As a witch family, Halloween, or Samhain as we also call it, holds a very special place in our hearts and sits at a significant point in the witch's calendar.

The build-up to Halloween in our home is a mixture of excitement and reverence. We begin preparing early in October, decorating the house with pumpkins, corn stalks, and candles. The house takes on a warm, cozy glow as we light candles in every room, their flickering flames a reminder of the thinning veil between our world and the spirit realm., a time to honour those who have passed and to celebrate the magic that surrounds us every day but is especially potent on this night.

Halloween has long been associated with witches, and for good reason. The origins of Halloween trace back to the ancient Celtic festival of Samhain, which marked the end of the harvest season and the beginning of winter, a time when the world was believed to be more vulnerable to the supernatural. Witches were considered wise keepers of ancient knowledge and were often the ones who led the rituals and celebrations during this time. Samhain was seen as a night when the veil between the worlds was paper thin, and witches, with their understanding of the natural and spiritual worlds, were believed to have the power to communicate with spirits and perform magic more effectively.

For our family, it's a time of reflection, of looking back at the year that has passed, honouring our ancestors, and setting intentions for the year ahead. We embrace the witchy aspects of Halloween wholeheartedly, not just as a fun costume idea, but as a way to connect with the traditions and magic that have been passed down through generations.

Our Halloween celebrations are filled with both the playful and the mystical, blending childhood games with ancient customs. One of the first things we do is carve pumpkins. Every year, we gather around the kitchen table, each of us armed with a pumpkin and a carving knife. We carefully scoop out the seeds, saving them to roast later, and then set to work carving faces into the pumpkins. The children's designs range from the traditional jack-o'-lantern faces to more intricate designs, last year featuring Scooby Doo, while I usually carve symbols that have personal meaning. The flickering candle inside each pumpkin is more than just a light; it's a beacon to welcome the spirits and protect our home from any malevolent forces.

Once the pumpkins are lit and placed outside, we move on to one of our favourite games: apple bobbing. There's something delightfully simple and timeless about dunking your head into a bowl of water to catch an apple with your teeth. It's a tradition that dates back to ancient Roman times, symbolizing the abundance of the harvest and the cycles of life and death. We also play another game with apples: peeling them in one long strip. Whoever manages to peel the longest strip gets to toss it over their shoulder, and the shape it lands in is said to reveal the first initial of their future love's name. It's all in good fun, and even though we laugh at the results, there's always a sense of magic in the air.

One of the spookier traditions we engage in is mirror gazing. Once the children are settled with their treats, those of us who are feeling brave will sit in front of a mirror in a dimly lit room, usually with a single candle burning. The idea is to gaze into the mirror and see if a vision appears. It's said that on Halloween night, you might catch a glimpse of your future or see the faces of spirits. Even for me, who should have no qualms, I still think it's an eerie practice, and I'll admit that it sends shivers down my spine every time. I'm such a wimp as a witch! It's not something we take lightly, as we respect the power of the night and the spirits who might be passing through.

We also leave a space at the dining table for the spirits of our home and our ancestors. On Halloween night, we set an extra place at the table with a plate of food and a drink. This gesture is our way of honouring the spirits who dwell with us and those who have passed on. It's a quiet moment amidst the evening's festivities, a chance to connect with the unseen and acknowledge their presence in our lives. We always toast to "Betty or Berty" the missing guest. No, I have no idea why either.

One of the more old-fashioned traditions that I can remember we used to do as children, but not sure if this was only our family, or if many do, is nut-cracking. Nut cracking is a bit of divination fun. We take two hazelnuts and name them for a couple, placing them near the fire. If the nuts stay close together as they roast, it's said that the couple will have a strong relationship. If they crack apart, well, it might mean trouble. It's a simple yet intriguing way to engage with the magic of the evening.

Cabbage stalk pulling is another quirky tradition. We go out into the garden, and each person pulls up a cabbage stalk in the dark. The shape and condition of the stalk are said to predict the future, particularly in matters of love and marriage. If it's straight and sturdy, it's a good omen; if it's twisted or broken, it might mean a more challenging year ahead. It's all in the spirit of fun and a reminder of the old ways when people turned to nature for signs and omens.

As a witch family, Halloween is the pinnacle of our year. Beyond the games and laughter, there's a deeper sense of ritual and magic. We take this time to perform our own Samhain rites, which are both personal and sacred. We light candles and incense, casting a circle to protect and honour the space.

We perform rituals to honour our ancestors, sometimes using photographs, keepsakes, and mementos of those who have passed. We speak their names aloud, inviting their spirits to join us if they wish, and leave offerings of food and drink as a token of our love and remembrance.

We also take this time to perform divination for the year ahead. Tarot cards, runes, or scrying are all part of our Halloween night. This is the time when we feel closest to the spirit world, so it's the perfect opportunity to seek guidance and wisdom for what lies ahead. As the evening draws on and the night grows darker, when the kids are sleeping off their sugar infused highs, there's a quiet, almost sacred stillness that settles in the house. We sit together, talking about the past year, our hopes, and our fears, finding comfort in the knowledge that we are surrounded by love, both from those here with us and those who have passed on.

In the witch's calendar, Halloween, Samhain, is one of the most significant Sabbats. The wheel of the year turns, marking the end of the harvest and the start of winter. It's a time to honour death as a natural part of the cycle of life and to reflect on the past year. For us, it's not just about the ghosts and the spooky tales; it's about recognizing the ever-present connection between the living and the dead, the seen and the unseen.

Whenever autumn rolls around, and I've got a pile of pumpkin seeds left over from carving pumpkins, I love making something a bit different with them, Spicy Pumpkin Seed Brittle. It's become a bit of a seasonal tradition for us. It's not your usual roasted pumpkin seeds; this is sweet, spicy, crunchy, and completely addictive.

First things first, I start by toasting the pumpkin seeds. I throw about a cup of raw seeds into a dry pan over medium heat and let them toast for a few minutes. You have to keep an eye on them because they can go from perfectly golden to burnt pretty quickly. As soon as they start to smell nutty and get a nice golden colour, I take them off the heat and set them aside.

Now comes the fun (and slightly nerve-wracking) part: making the caramel. In a medium saucepan, I combine a cup of sugar, a quarter cup of water, and a quarter cup of light corn syrup. If you don't have corn syrup, honey works just as well. I stir this over medium heat until the sugar dissolves. Then, I crank up the heat to medium-high and let it boil away without stirring it. This is the part where you need to be patient and hold your nerve. The sugar mixture will start to bubble and change colour. I keep a close eye on it until it turns a deep golden amber colour, this usually takes about 8 to 10 minutes.

Once the caramel hits that beautiful golden stage, I quickly remove the saucepan from the heat and toss in 2 tablespoons of butter, the toasted pumpkin seeds, half a teaspoon of sea salt, half a teaspoon each of ground cayenne pepper, smoked paprika, and cinnamon. The spice combo is what makes this brittle special. The cayenne gives it a bit of a kick, while the smoked paprika adds a subtle depth. I mix everything together really well to coat the seeds in that spicy, sugary goodness.

Almost forgot. After I've got my pumpkin seeds toasted and the caramel bubbling away, I get the dried cherries ready. I usually use about a half cup of dried cherries. You can chop them up into smaller pieces if you want them to spread more evenly throughout the brittle, but I often just leave them whole because I like those occasional bursts of tartness.

Once I've mixed the toasted pumpkin seeds with the butter and spices into the caramel, I toss in the dried cherries right before adding the baking soda. This way, the cherries get coated in that hot, spicy caramel along with the seeds, and everything mixes together nicely. The key here is to stir quickly, making sure the cherries are evenly distributed.

Then, I quickly pour the mixture onto a baking sheet lined with parchment paper. You have to move fast here because the brittle will start to set almost immediately. I use a spatula to spread it out into a thinnish, even layer. If I'm feeling fancy, I'll sprinkle a bit of flaky sea salt over the top for that perfect sweet and salty contrast.

After that, it's just a matter of waiting for it to cool and harden, which usually takes about 20-30 minutes. Once it's completely set, I break it into pieces. There's something so satisfying about cracking it into shards and sneaking a piece while it's still fresh. It's sweet and spicy with this great crunch, and it's so much better than the store-bought stuff. I have a stone floor in the hall and I must admit (close your ears hygiene police) I lift the brittle up high and let in fall to the ground where it cracks. It's a nice sound, I suppose with the same satisfaction as the Greeks have smashing plates. It does also remind me of the day I dropped my iPad on the stone floor but best skip over that.

We usually end up snacking on it throughout the day, but it's also great crumbled over ice cream or served on a cheese board if you want to get a little fancy. I store the leftovers (if there are any) in an airtight container, and it stays fresh and crunchy for up to two weeks, though it rarely lasts that long around here.

Ooooh - I forgot to mention Doughnut bobbing – I can't claim it's anything magical but we have a pile of round doughnuts, the ones with a hole in the middle, through which we tie a string between two trees. We have to eat our own individual doughnut, hands behind our back without it falling off onto the floor, in which case we have a rather happy tubby Golden Retriever prowling the line getting in everyone's way. I am sure he does it on purpose and every year perfects the "accidently "stumbling into our knees technique.

"Elä harmoniassa luonnon rytmin kanssa, hoivaten sekä ympäröivää maailmaa että sisäistä henkeä."

"Live in harmony with the rhythm of nature, nurturing both the world around us and the spirit within."

The Witch's Botanical Apothecary

Romanesco

Romanesco

There's something magical about the way numbers and nature intersect, and nowhere is this more evident than in the Fibonacci sequence. This sequence of numbers: 1, 1, 2, 3, 5, 8, 13, 21, and so on, where each number is the sum of the two preceding ones, has captivated mathematicians, scientists, and yes, even witches for centuries. The Fibonacci sequence appears in the natural world in such a mysterious and wondrous way that it's hard not to see it as part of the magical fabric that underlies our universe. One of the most stunning examples of this is the plant Romanesco, a vegetable that almost seems to defy the natural order with its perfect spirals and fractal patterns, all of which are intricately linked to the Fibonacci sequence.

For those of us who practice witchcraft, the Fibonacci sequence isn't just a mathematical concept; it's a symbol of the deep, underlying order in the universe. It's the way nature seems to whisper to us about the patterns that connect all things. In witchcraft, we often seek to align ourselves with natural energies, understanding that the universe is full of rhythms and cycles. The Fibonacci sequence, appearing in the spirals of shells, the arrangement of leaves, the flowering of plants, and even in the stars, serves as a reminder that there is a hidden structure to everything.

In my practice, I often use the Fibonacci sequence as a tool for meditation and spellwork. It's a way to connect to the idea of balance and harmony. When I set up my altar or perform rituals, I sometimes use the sequence as a guide. For example, I might arrange objects, candles, crystals, or herbs, in a spiral pattern that follows the Fibonacci sequence. There's something deeply calming about working with this natural pattern; it's as if by aligning with it, I'm tapping into a universal rhythm that extends far beyond myself.

The spiral, a shape frequently associated with the Fibonacci sequence, is also a powerful symbol in witchcraft. Spirals represent growth, cycles, and the journey inward and outward. When I incorporate spirals into my rituals, I feel like I'm honouring the endless cycles of nature, birth, death, and rebirth, the waxing and waning of the moon, the turning of the seasons. It's a visual and energetic representation of the interconnectedness of all things.

One of the most incredible manifestations of the Fibonacci sequence in nature is the Romanesco vegetable. It's almost as if this plant was created to showcase the magic of mathematics. Romanesco's vibrant green head is composed of a series of spiralling florets, each smaller version a perfect miniature of the whole. When you look closely, you can see that these spirals follow the Fibonacci sequence exactly. The number of spirals on a Romanesco head is always a Fibonacci number 5, 8, 13, 21 each arranged in a precise logarithmic spiral. It's like holding a piece of nature's blueprint or DNA in your hands.

When I first encountered Romanesco, I was struck not just by its beauty, but by the sense of wonder it evoked. Here was a plant that looked like it belonged in a fantasy world, its intricate fractal design defying simple explanation. Yet, it was a natural creation, formed by the same rules that govern the rest of the universe. For me, Romanesco became a symbol of the harmony between the mundane and the mystical, a reminder that the natural world is full of hidden mysteries that straddle the line between science and magic.

The Fibonacci sequence is often linked with growth patterns in nature, from the branching of trees and the arrangement of leaves on a stem, to the flowering of an artichoke or the way Romanesco grows. It's as if nature uses this sequence as a template for growth, achieving a balance that is both efficient and beautiful. In witchcraft, we can harness this energy by working with plants like Romanesco, recognizing them as physical manifestations of universal principles.

When I grow Romanesco in my garden, it feels like cultivating a little piece of cosmic magic. Watching the plant develop from seed to this incredible fractal form is a process that never ceases to amaze me. I use the Romanesco in my spellwork, especially in rituals focused on growth, expansion, and transformation. Because it embodies the principles of the Fibonacci sequence so perfectly, it carries the energy of balanced growth. Whether I'm using it as an offering on my altar or incorporating it into a ritual meal, Romanesco becomes more than just a vegetable, it becomes a conduit for the magical patterns of the universe.

The Fibonacci sequence can be a guide for spellwork as well. In crafting spells, particularly those related to growth, prosperity, or change, I sometimes use the sequence as a framework. For instance, in a spell for abundance, I might light candles or place stones in a spiral pattern, each one representing a number in the sequence. This pattern not only aligns with the natural flow of energy but also creates a visual and energetic representation of continuous growth and expansion.

I also find that meditating on the Fibonacci sequence, or simply tracing its spiral pattern with my finger, helps me to centre and ground my energy. It reminds me that the world operates on patterns and cycles that are both infinite and interconnected. In times of chaos or uncertainty, the Fibonacci sequence offers a glimpse of the order that exists within the universe, a reassuring whisper that everything is unfolding as it should.

What fascinates me most about the Fibonacci sequence and its connection to plants like Romanesco is how it bridges the gap between the logical and the mystical. Mathematics is often seen as the domain of cold, hard logic, while magic is considered the realm of intuition and the unseen. Yet, the Fibonacci sequence shows us that these two worlds are not separate. The same mathematical principles that govern the growth of a Romanesco floret also guide the flow of energy in the universe. In this way, the Fibonacci sequence serves as a beautiful reminder that magic and mathematics are simply two languages describing the same underlying reality.

Romanesco, with its mesmerizing spirals, is a living example of this union. It's a plant that, in its very structure, reveals the harmony and balance that exist in nature. When we look at it through the eyes of a witch, we see not just a vegetable, but a manifestation of the sacred geometry that weaves through all of existence. It's a reminder that magic isn't just something that happens in rituals or spells, it's all around us, hidden in the patterns of the natural world, waiting to be noticed and appreciated.

The Witch's Botanical Apothecary

Rowan Berry

Rowan Berry

The first Rowan that really caught my attention stood just off a trail I often walked on the South Downs. It was relatively small, almost unassuming among the towering trees surrounding it. Yet there was something about it that drew me in. Its bright red berries were hanging in clusters, glowing like rubies in the late afternoon sun. The leaves, so fine and delicate, shimmered in the breeze. There was an otherworldly air about it, as if the tree had chosen this spot to make itself known to those who might appreciate its secrets.

At that moment, I felt as if the Rowan was offering me a silent invitation, pulling me into a deeper connection with nature. There was something alive and ancient in the way its branches danced in the wind, something that called to me beyond just its beauty. It felt as though the tree was waiting for me to notice, to understand the significance it held. It wanted me to notice it. It had in its own way, ensnared me. And so began my fascination with the Rowan tree and its history, a journey that led me to uncover the tree's storied past, its associations with magic, protection, and even ensnarement.

In ancient Celtic tradition, the Rowan was considered a sacred tree, often planted near homes and at the edges of property to ward off evil spirits. Its red berries, considered a symbol of protection, were thought to have the power to repel malevolent forces. The Celts believed that just having a Rowan nearby could shield a household from dark energies.

I found this notion fascinating. It struck me that perhaps, on some level, I had been instinctively drawn to the tree for its protective energy. After all, the Rowan's reputation as a guardian was not confined to the Celts alone. In British and Scandinavian folklore, it was thought to ward off witches and other supernatural threats. (hmmm here we go again!) People would make crosses from Rowan twigs and hang them above doorways or wear them as talismans, confident that the tree's power would keep them safe from harm.

Yet, as I dug deeper into the folklore surrounding the Rowan, I discovered that its associations went beyond protection. The very name *Sorbus aucuparia*, which the tree bears in Latin, gives a clue to its more cunning side. *Aucuparia* comes from the Latin words for "bird-catching," as the Rowan berries were often used to ensnare birds. While it's true that birds, especially thrushes, are drawn to the berries, the berries were historically used as bait in traps. But what struck me as even more intriguing was how this ensnaring quality extended beyond the animal world, and to that I'll explain more later.

As much as the Rowan protected against dark forces, it also had the power to ensnare and bind. In witchcraft, the Rowan berry was sometimes used not to capture birds or animals, but to ensnare humans. These magical practices were meant to bind the will of another, to subtly trap them in emotional or psychological ways. I remember feeling a chill when I read about these practices. How could something so vibrant and beautiful as the Rowan berry, something that glows like a jewel, be used for such a dark purpose?

Yet, this darker aspect of the Rowan only added to its complexity in my mind. Like many things in the natural world, the tree had a dual nature. It could protect and heal, or it could bind and control, depending on the intentions of the one who wielded its power. The Rowan was not just a passive guardian, it was a powerful force that, when used with ill intent, could ensnare the unwary.

I began to think about how the Rowan tree might have been viewed by those who practiced the old ways of magic. The berries, with their bright colour and hidden pentagram shape, would have been irresistible to those who sought to harness the Rowan's energy. Perhaps they saw in the berries a way to trap others in a web of their own making, just as the tree itself had been used to lure and capture birds. It was a sobering thought, yet it made me appreciate the Rowan even more. This was not a simple tree; it was layered with power and meaning, a living symbol of both protection and peril.

One of the most captivating details about the Rowan berries is the tiny five-pointed star, or pentagram, that you can see when you cut the berry in half. The pentagram is an ancient symbol of protection, and its presence within the berry only deepened the tree's reputation as a guardian against evil. But this symbol also seemed to hint at something more, a hidden secret, a connection to the mystical and magical realms.

It was easy to see why this tree had been revered in magical traditions for centuries. The pentagram, hidden within the bright red fruit, was a clear sign that the Rowan had a connection to the spiritual and the magical. In some traditions, the Rowan was even believed to be a portal to higher consciousness, a bridge between the world of the living and the world of spirits. Druids often planted it near places of learning, believing that the tree's presence would help guide them toward wisdom.

Even in ancient Rome and Greece, the Rowan was believed to be a tree of divination, a tool for revealing truths hidden from ordinary sight. It was said that oracles would use the Rowan to help them see the future, and in some traditions, the tree was thought to have the power to reveal deep truths to those who knew how to look. This only deepened my fascination with the tree. The Rowan wasn't just a protector, it was a guide, a teacher of hidden knowledge.

One of the most intriguing stories I can tell you of the Rowan tree, and perhaps the moment I began to feel truly connected to its mysterious nature, comes from a day spent with my grandmother when I was in my teens. She was French, with a love for history and magic that matched my own. What am I saying of course she was, she was a witch! Every now and again she would take me on train up to London to visit Hamleys or Harrods or some of the markets, usually including exploring some of the amazing places hidden there, more of which I'll write later. On this day we had taken the tube from Waterloo Station into central London, and when we emerged into the cool autumn air near Leicester Square, I remember the excitement bubbling up in me. She had promised to take me to a street full of old bookshops, and I had no idea what to expect. When we turned into Cecil Court, it was like walking into another time. The street was narrow, the bookshop windows filled with treasures, ancient, leather-bound volumes, faded maps, and delicate trinkets. The air smelled of musty paper, dust, and something earthy, like history itself. There was nothing that was new to be found anywhere.

We spent hours wandering from shop to shop. My grandmother would pause, fingers brushing over the spines, murmuring quietly in French about the wonders contained within those pages. There was something magical about it, about her knowledge and the way she moved through those small, cozy shops as if she belonged to them. I remember the creaking floors and the quiet murmur of conversation between book collectors, each of them reverent, as if they were in a church or plotting some devious plan.

We came across a really old leather book, written in French that seemed to suddenly really excite her. It was a hundred pounds, which was incredibly expensive in those days, and grandma usually didn't like spending much at all. Her favourite phrase was "I'm just looking" rather than buying, so this was a big thing. The book was well-worn, its pages yellowed and fragile, the kind of tome that looked as if it had passed through many hands over the centuries. I remember the way the scent of old parchment mixed with the perfume of the wildflowers she kept in her window.

What made this book special wasn't just its age or the mystery it held within its pages. It was written in a style of French that even my grandmother, with all her fluency and grace in the language, found difficult to decipher. It was old French, archaic and dense, and together we struggled to make sense of the strange, curling letters and the archaic phrasing. But that challenge only made the experience more thrilling, as though we were uncovering long-lost secrets buried in time.

It was a grimoire, I don't know if it was an original or if it had been copied, but if copied it must have been done hundreds of years ago. On the journey home on the train I could tell she was excited, twitching to get it open and look through, but she was going to savour it in her own way when she had a large Gin in her hand. Laid out on the kitchen table with my grandma and my mum and me all pouring over it, one spell in particular caught our attention that day, and it has stayed with me ever since. It was a curious spell involving Rowan berries, but this was no simple charm for protection or healing. The spell seemed to hint at something darker, something tempting and dangerous. It spoke of using the berries to attract the greedy, particularly women who lusted after princely jewels. We sat huddled over the page, tracing the faded ink with our fingers, trying to understand the old French that described how the berries could be transformed, or perhaps how they could transform something else.

The grimoire hinted at turning the berries into a necklace of rubies, dazzling enough to catch the eye of anyone with a greedy heart. Or, it might have been a spell to cast upon an already existing necklace, enchanting the jewels to tempt and ensnare those who were drawn to wealth and luxury. We weren't sure. The language was vague, almost purposefully so, as if the author had intended the spell to be cloaked in ambiguity, leaving the caster to determine its true meaning.

I remember my grandmother frowning slightly as we worked through the words, her brow furrowed in concentration. She was a woman who believed in the power of intent, and the idea that these seemingly innocent berries could be used to entice and bind others, especially through their desires, gave her pause. She explained to me that magic often worked in subtle, unseen ways, and that such a spell might not only trap the greedy but might also backfire, entangling the one who cast it in their own web of desires.

Still, the image the grimoire painted was a vivid one. I could almost see the row of bright red berries, glistening like rubies on a chain, their alluring glow irresistible to anyone with a taste for opulence. The fact that I caught myself imagining the necklace of rubies around my own neck suddenly gave me a start. The way the spell described the berries, it was as if they could shimmer with an otherworldly light, drawing in those who couldn't resist the temptation of jewels fit for royalty. But with that temptation came danger. The more we read, the more it seemed that the berries, once enchanted, wouldn't just be a beautiful adornment, they would become a trap, a snare for the soul of whoever wore them.

I found the notion both fascinating and unsettling. Rowan berries, which I had always seen as protective symbols, could also be used to lure and entrap. It added another layer of mystery to the tree, deepening my understanding of its dual nature. While the Rowan protected against evil, it also held the power to ensnare, to bind others through their weaknesses. That ancient grimoire had revealed a side of the Rowan that I hadn't considered before, a side that made me see its bright berries in a new, more complex light. But what we did understand was the spell's intent: to attract those who were driven by greed and vanity, to weave a web of allure that could trap even the most cautious of hearts.

That day with my mum, grandmother and me, leaning over the kitchen table, the old French grimoire spread open between us, remains one of my fondest memories. It was as if the Rowan tree itself had guided us to that spell, revealing to us another piece of its enigmatic puzzle. Even now, when I see Rowan berries glinting in the sunlight, I can't help but think of that spell and the hidden power that the tree holds. There is something both beautiful and dangerous about the Rowan, and I love it all the more for that very reason.

Sea Buckthorn

I'm sitting in my kitchen today with my laptop on the table and watching the wind and rain smatter across the window above the sink. It's taken me so long to write this book I must have passed through all the seasons. I suspect the weather outside influences how I write inside, and gives its own flavour to my writing, jolly or dramatic, whimsical or factual. When I've been writing about some of the herbs in this book, I've had to go and stand by them for a while, or pick a stem, or steal a fruit. It helps me to remember what little I know about them. As you can tell this isn't a scientific journal but mostly stories and memories.

Today I have a little pile of orange berries on the table in front of me, still wet from the rain.

Sea Buckthorn has always fascinated me—its vibrant orange berries glowing like tiny orbs of sunlight on silvery branches. But beyond their beauty, these berries are powerhouses of nutrition, especially when it comes to Vitamin C and antioxidants. It's no wonder that in the past, wise women, those who were often dismissed as witches, treasured Sea Buckthorn for their potions and remedies. They may not have known the science behind it, but they certainly understood the profound impact these berries could have on health and healing.

Today, we know that Sea Buckthorn is rightly called a superfood. When I hear the term "superfood," it conjures images of exotic ingredients packed with nutrients that promise to transform health, and Sea Buckthorn certainly fits the bill. It's bursting with Vitamin C in astonishing quantities. To give you an idea, Sea Buckthorn berries can have up to 15 times more Vitamin C than oranges. That's an enormous amount, considering we've long been told that oranges are the gold standard for this essential vitamin. Just a small handful of these berries can provide more Vitamin C than you'd get from an entire basket of citrus.

But the story doesn't end with Vitamin C. These berries are also rich in a variety of antioxidants, particularly flavonoids and carotenoids, which play a vital role in protecting our cells from damage caused by free radicals. Flavonoids are a group of compounds responsible for giving plants their vibrant colour like red, purple, yellow, and blue. They're found in foods like berries, citrus fruits, tea, and dark chocolate. In our bodies, flavonoids act as antioxidants, which means they help neutralize harmful molecules called free radicals that can damage our cells. This helps reduce inflammation, improve heart health, and even support brain function. Carotenoids on the other hand are pigments that can be converted into Vitamin A in the body, which is crucial for vision and skin health. Free radicals are the unstable molecules that can lead to everything from aging to diseases like cancer. Antioxidants act like a shield, neutralizing these harmful agents and promoting overall health and vitality. Ok I had to look that up too!

So, while today we understand the biochemistry of how these antioxidants work, our ancestors, the wise women of old, already grasped the power of Sea Buckthorn in a very different way. They might not have known about free radicals or flavonoids, but they certainly knew that these berries had potent healing properties. They saw the results in the people they treated, and those who consumed the berries or the potions made from them seemed to recover faster, their vitality returning in a way that seemed almost magical.

I often think about those wise women, those who understood nature in a way we've largely forgotten. They were the healers, the ones who knew which plants to gather and how to prepare them. They may not have had microscopes or scientific studies to back up their practices, but they had centuries of knowledge passed down through generations. They knew that Sea Buckthorn berries could be made into potions that promoted healing, strength, and resilience.

Imagine one of these gnarly, weatherbeaten women gathering Sea Buckthorn berries on a cold autumn day like I was doing this morning, (yup that's how I feel today a bit gnarly!) her basket filled with the glowing orange fruits. She would have known by instinct, and by experience, that these berries were more than just food. They were medicine, potent and powerful. She might not have known it was the Vitamin C that gave them their healing properties, but she could see the results in the people she treated. Those who were weak, run-down, or recovering from illness would perk up after consuming her potions. Their skin would brighten, their energy would return, and their bodies would begin to heal. In their world, it seemed like magic, and in a way it is, magic of nature, magic of knowledge!

Vitamin C is crucial for so many bodily functions, from boosting the immune system to promoting skin health by stimulating collagen production. Conditions like scurvy, a disease caused by Vitamin C deficiency, were well known throughout history, especially among sailors and others with limited access to fresh fruits and vegetables. The wise women may not have known about scurvy in clinical terms, but they would have recognized the symptoms: bleeding gums, weakness, fatigue, and slow healing wounds. They would have seen the remarkable turnaround after treating their patients with a potion rich in Sea Buckthorn berries.

Today, we understand the science behind why Vitamin C is so crucial, and it's fascinating to think about how our ancestors knew, even without that science, which plants held the key to healing. Vitamin C plays an essential role in maintaining the immune system. It helps the body produce white blood cells, which are responsible for fighting infections. During times of illness, our bodies need even more Vitamin C, as it gets used up quickly in the battle against invading pathogens.

But it's not just about warding off colds and flu. Vitamin C has been shown to help in wound healing, which ties in perfectly with the way the wise women used Sea Buckthorn. It promotes the production of collagen, a protein that's vital for the repair of skin, tissues, and bones. Anyone suffering from cuts, bruises, or burns would benefit from the healing properties of Sea Buckthorn, as the berries would speed up the repair process, knitting wounds together faster than they would on their own.

Interestingly, Sea Buckthorn isn't just rich in Vitamin C, they also contain Omega-7, a rare fatty acid that further supports skin health. When you combine the Vitamin C with these fatty acids, it's no wonder Sea Buckthorn was often used to treat burns, rashes, and other skin conditions. After the terrible incident at Chernobyl the Russians were bringing down lorry loads of Sea Buckthorn from Siberia where it grows really well, and it was also taken into space by the Russian cosmonauts, why? Because in both cases the berries were used to create a salve to tend radiation burns and protect from radiation sickness. The wise women might not have thought of sending the berries up into space but they would have seen firsthand how applying Sea Buckthorn oil or a berry paste could soothe inflamed skin and promote rapid healing.

Beyond its healing properties, Sea Buckthorn has long been associated with longevity and vitality. The antioxidants in the berries, especially these flavonoids and carotenoids, (see the science just rolls off the tongue now), play a major role in combating the effects of aging.

Sea Buckthorn berries would have been especially valuable in times of hardship, during the long winter months when fresh food was scarce, or when people were recovering from illness or injury. The berries are not just full of Vitamin C; they are also packed with Vitamin E, Vitamin A, and B vitamins. Together, these nutrients support everything from eye health to skin regeneration to overall energy levels.

Don't forget Oranges didn't appear in England until the 1400's or 1500's and even then they were only for the very rich. You had to wait until the 18th century before oranges were available to the common people. Sea Buckthorn, is as native as it comes.

Hair Growth Salve with Sea Buckthorn

Sea Buckthorn berries are packed with Omega-3, Omega-6, and especially Omega-7 fatty acids, which are known for promoting hair health, strengthening hair follicles, and nourishing the scalp. The oil extracted from these berries can be used to create a potent hair growth salve, providing essential nutrients to encourage thicker, healthier hair.

Here's how I make a simple but effective Sea Buckthorn hair growth salve:

Ingredients:

- **Sea Buckthorn oil** (2 tablespoons) – You can extract the oil from the berries by cold-pressing them or buy it from a natural food store if you prefer.
- **Coconut oil** (2 tablespoons) – Provides hydration and serves as the base of the salve.

- **Castor oil** (1 tablespoon) – Known for promoting hair growth and increasing hair thickness.

- **Rosemary essential oil** (5 drops) – An essential oil renowned for stimulating blood circulation in the scalp.

- **Beeswax** (1 tablespoon) – To give the salve a solid consistency.

Instructions:

1. **Melt the beeswax and coconut oil** together using a double boiler until fully liquefied.

2. **Remove from heat** and let it cool for a minute before stirring in the Sea Buckthorn oil and castor oil.

3. Add **5 drops of rosemary essential oil**, which is a known stimulant for hair follicles.

4. Stir everything together until it is well combined and then **pour into a small jar**. Let the mixture cool and solidify.

5. **To use**: Apply the salve directly to your scalp before bed, massaging it into your roots to stimulate circulation and absorption. Leave it on overnight and wash it out in the morning.

The blend of oils, especially the Omega-7-rich Sea Buckthorn, will help rejuvenate the hair follicles, strengthen roots, and improve scalp health over time.

I also use to make anti-ageing eye treatments, applying a tiny amount around the eyes at night can help reduce the appearance of fine lines, crow's feet, and dark circles, while also nourishing the delicate skin in that area. And wait for it…… one of my most profitable lines as a commercial witch is selling small bottles to tattoo shops, yes really! Sea Buckthorn oil can be a great aftercare treatment. Its natural ability to promote skin healing, reduce inflammation, and prevent infections makes it an ideal oil to apply to healing tattoos. It can help soothe irritation, speed up the healing process, and even enhance the colour retention in tattoos, thanks to its regenerative properties.

"Kuulitko hiljaisuuden, älä anna sen hämätä, kun kaikki on hiljaa, olemme vahvimmillamme."

"Can you hear the silence, be not fooled, when all is still we are at our most fierce."

The Witch's Botanical Apothecary

Silver Birch

Silver Birch

Spring has arrived! Every spring, there's a certain day that all my friends and I look forward to with a kind of quiet anticipation, a day that's marked on our calendars well in advance. Birch-Day! It's a ritual of sorts, one that draws us into nature just as winter begins to loosen its grip. That day is when we head out into the woods to tap the silver birch trees, harvesting the precious sap that's been quietly gathering strength beneath the bark. For us, it's more than just a task, it's a celebration of the changing seasons, a reconnection with the earth, and a tradition that brings us together every year.

The first time we tapped a silver birch, it felt like we were participating in an ancient rite, one that had been passed down through generations. It's said that people have been collecting birch sap for centuries, particularly in northern Europe, Russia, and parts of Scandinavia. Even then, there was an understanding of how special this sap was, both for its healing properties and its magical qualities. But for us, it began as a curiosity, a desire to step away from the modern world and engage in something elemental, something timeless.

As with many things in nature, timing is crucial when it comes to tapping a birch tree. The sap begins to rise in early spring, usually between late February and April, depending on the climate. The best time to tap is when the days start warming up, but the nights are still cold, typically when temperatures hover close to freezing at night but rise to a comfortable 5-10°C (41-50°F) during the day. This fluctuation creates pressure in the tree, causing the sap to flow upward from the roots, where it has been stored throughout the winter.

We've learned to watch for the signs: the subtle greening of the landscape, the first tentative buds on the trees, and that unmistakable freshness in the air that signals spring is on its way. It's a brief window, usually just two or three weeks, when the sap is at its peak, and missing it means waiting an entire year for another chance. That's why we plan carefully, checking the weather forecasts and making sure everyone's schedules align. There's a certain thrill in knowing that this event is dictated by nature, not by us.

When the time is right, we head out to the woods with our gear, a collection of taps, buckets, and drills, all simple tools that get the job done without harming the trees. The first step is choosing the right tree. A silver birch should be mature, with a trunk at least 8 inches in diameter. Younger trees need time to grow, so we always choose ones that can handle being tapped without stress.

Standing beneath a towering silver birch, you can feel its energy, the sap rising just beneath the surface of the bark. Put your hand on the trunk can you feel it? We debate this often. There's a reverence in the moment before drilling into the tree, a quiet understanding that we are taking something, and we must do it with respect and wary not to hurt. We carefully drill a small hole, about 2-3 inches deep, at a slight upward angle. The hole is usually positioned about 2-3 feet from the ground, on the south-facing side of the tree where the sun can warm it.

As soon as the drill bites into the wood, there's a pause, a second of stillness, and then the sap begins to flow. It's clear, like water, but there's something almost magical about the way it drips steadily from the tree, a reminder that this is nature's life force. We insert a metal or wooden tap into the hole, gently tapping it into place, and hang a bucket below to catch the sap as it flows.

The first few drops are always exciting, like witnessing the opening notes of a song we've been waiting to hear all winter. The sap flows slowly, a steady drip that will continue for hours, sometimes days. Each tree can produce up to 10 litres of sap over the course of a few days, and we're careful not to take too much, ensuring the tree isn't harmed by the process. Once the sap has been collected, we plug the hole with a small wooden dowel to allow the tree to heal naturally. The trees we tap every year look the strongest in the forest.

Birch sap is delicate, refreshing, and slightly sweet, like the essence of spring captured in liquid form. When you drink it fresh from the tree, there's a crispness to it that's hard to describe, something pure and invigorating. Over the years, we've discovered countless ways to use the sap in our kitchens, and it's become a staple in our springtime diets.

One of the simplest ways to enjoy birch sap is to drink it straight, chilled and pure. It's a wonderful tonic, full of vitamins, minerals, and antioxidants. Some say it's good for detoxing the body after the long winter months, cleansing the system and boosting energy levels. We've come to think of it as a kind of spring elixir, one that helps us shake off the sluggishness of winter and step into the new season with vitality.

But the culinary uses of birch sap go far beyond just drinking it. Over the years, we've experimented with using it in a variety of recipes. It can be used as a base for soups, lending a subtle sweetness to dishes like leek and potato or spring vegetable broth. We've also tried using it in smoothies, mixing it with fruits and leafy greens for a fresh, nutrient-packed drink.

One of my favourite ways to use birch sap is to reduce it into a syrup. By gently simmering the sap, you can concentrate its sweetness into a golden, slightly caramel-flavoured syrup that's perfect for drizzling over pancakes or adding to desserts. It's a bit like maple syrup, but lighter, with a more delicate flavour. We also use the syrup as a glaze for roasts, brushing it over meat or vegetables for a subtle, earthy sweetness.

Birch sap can even be fermented to make birch wine or birch beer, both of which have a long history in parts of northern Europe. The fermentation process gives the sap a slightly fizzy, tangy flavour, and it's a wonderful way to preserve the sap for later use. We've tried making small batches of birch wine, and it's become a yearly tradition to open a bottle during midsummer celebrations, a reminder of the early spring days when we gathered the sap. You lot reading this will by now probably assume we make wine, gin or beer out of everything! True!

Beyond its culinary uses, birch sap holds a special place in the world of magic and healing. The birch tree itself is considered sacred in many cultures, often associated with new beginnings, protection, and purification. In ancient times, wise women and healers would use birch sap in their potions and rituals, recognizing its ability to cleanse and renew both the body and spirit.

For me and my friends, tapping the birch trees has become more than just a way to gather sap, it's a way of connecting with the earth's cycles, of participating in the ancient rhythms of nature. The fact we do it together feels important too. We've come to see the sap as a symbol of rebirth and renewal, flowing from the tree just as the earth wakes up from its winter slumber. It's no surprise that birch sap has been used in witchcraft for centuries, often in spells for cleansing and purification.

One of the ways we use birch sap in our own rituals is to incorporate it into cleansing baths. A few drops of the sap added to bathwater can help wash away negativity, leaving you feeling refreshed and revitalized. The sap is also said to enhance psychic abilities and can be used in rituals for opening the third eye or deepening one's connection to the spiritual world.

In healing, birch sap has long been considered a powerful remedy. Its natural diuretic properties make it useful for treating kidney and bladder issues, while its high levels of minerals like potassium and magnesium support overall health. We've also used birch sap in skin care, applying it to soothe irritated or inflamed skin. It's a natural moisturizer and can help promote the healing of wounds and scars.

For protection, birch sap can be used in protective charms or sprinkled around the home to ward off negative energies. Some traditions even suggest writing a wish or intention on a piece of birch bark and anointing it with the sap before burying it in the earth, allowing the tree's energy to help manifest your desires.

Tapping birch trees has become an annual ritual for us, something that marks the transition from winter to spring. It's a time when we come together, reconnect with nature, and celebrate the bounty that the earth provides. There's something deeply satisfying about the process, from the first cut into the tree to the final drop of sap collected. It's a reminder of the generosity of the natural world, and of our place within it.

Every year, as we gather our buckets and head into the woods, there's a sense of excitement in the air. We know that we're taking part in something ancient, something that connects us not only to the trees but to all the generations before us who have done the same. And as we sip the cool, clear sap, we're reminded that spring is here, and with it, a new beginning.

The Witch's Botanical Apothecary

Sweet Chestnut

Sweet Chestnut

The Sweet Chestnut tree has woven itself into so many aspects of my life that it's almost impossible to imagine a time when I wasn't aware of its presence. It's not just about the towering trees that surround our village or the fact that we have so many of them on our own property. There's something ancient and comforting about these trees, something that ties us back to our land and its long-forgotten stories. I often think about how these magnificent trees, first made their way here, likely brought by the Romans centuries ago. They brought chestnut trees as they spread across Europe, introducing them for both practical and culinary reasons, and I have a feeling the trees in our village are direct descendants of those early Roman plantings.

The Romans were practical people, and the Sweet Chestnut tree was one of their valuable imports. They didn't just bring chestnuts for their nutty taste or their ability to be ground into flour, although that was certainly part of the appeal. What the Romans really valued was the wood. Chestnut wood has remarkable qualities, rot-resistant, strong, and long-lasting, making it the ideal material for the vineyard poles they needed to support their grapevines. Wine was essential to Roman life, and any tree that could support their vineyards was just as important as the food it produced.

If you've read the book from the beginning you will see that Roman Civilization has been a big influencer to our natural environment and customs. From the plants in the hedgerow, the trees in the forest and even the lavender outside my kitchen door. Of course these were then taken to the new world. Whilst I'm off on a Roman tangent and forgive me, this is probably giving away too much of dithering personality but did you know the ancient Romans were partly responsible for the Space Shuttle design? Probably more for a conversation down the pub, but the story begins with the standard width of Roman chariots. Roman chariots were designed to fit two horses side-by-side, which determined the width of the wheels and the roads they travelled on. This measurement became the basis for the Roman road system, which influenced the design of roads across Europe. Fast forward to the industrial age: when railways were built in England, they used a track gauge (the distance between the rails) of 4 feet, 8.5 inches, which roughly matched the width of the Roman chariots. This gauge became standard and was adopted by the United States and much of the world for train tracks. Now, here's where it ties into the Space Shuttle. The Space Shuttle's solid rocket boosters (SRBs) were manufactured in Utah and had to be transported by rail to the launch site in Florida. Because they had to fit through tunnels and across railways built with the same standard gauge, the width of the boosters was constrained by the size of these railways. Thus, the SRBs were designed to fit the limitations of the rail tracks, which, in turn, were influenced by the width of Roman chariots!

So, in a strange twist of history, the dimensions of the Space Shuttle's SRBs were indirectly influenced by a decision made by the Romans over 2,000 years ago. Ok ill pop my head back out the rabbit hole.

I sometimes wonder if this is why our village has so many Sweet Chestnut trees. There's a whole area in the local woods that's almost entirely made up of chestnuts, their thick trunks reaching skyward, creating a beautiful canopy in the summer and scattering prickly burrs on the forest floor in autumn. The trees have a stately presence, and it's easy to imagine the Roman settlers planting them, knowing that their wood would last generations. Whether or not those chestnut trees were initially planted for food or for wood, they've become an inseparable part of our landscape now, and I love that they connect us to a time so long ago.

Our real love for chestnuts as a food (other than Christmas) began during a family holiday in Corsica a few years ago. Corsica is known for its chestnut groves, and in many ways, the island's relationship with the tree is even deeper than ours. The locals use chestnut flour in everything, from bread to pasta to cakes, and one of the most memorable meals we had was Pulenta, a traditional Corsican dish made with chestnut flour. It's a bit like polenta but with a nutty, earthy flavour that makes it entirely unique. I was fascinated by how chestnuts, once ground into flour, could sustain entire communities during the long winters when other crops were scarce.

I'll never forget sitting in a small, rustic restaurant in Sant'Antonio, wedged between narrow cobbled streets, perched high on a hilltop with stunning views of the countryside and turquoise Mediterranean Sea, surrounded by the warm smell of chestnut dishes cooking over open fires. The Pulenta was served with a rich, gamey stew and a local cheese called Cabrettu, made from goats milk and aged in Chestnut leaves. This was unlike anything we had ever tasted before. Chestnut flour is naturally sweet, and it gave the dish a depth of flavour that was both hearty and comforting. The combination of flavours was so simple yet so perfectly balanced. I remember thinking about how the Romans must have appreciated this versatility in the chestnut, not just as a practical crop but as a food that could sustain them through hard times.

I'll share the Pulenta recipe at the end, or at least my version of it, but ever since that trip, we've made it a point to incorporate chestnuts into more of our meals. Whether we're roasting them on an open fire, grinding them into flour, or using them in soups and stews, there's something deeply satisfying about cooking with chestnuts. It's as though we're carrying on a tradition that's been passed down through the centuries.

Like many of you reading, we too have the tradition of roasting chestnuts on an open fire, especially on Christmas Eve. There's something magical about gathering around the fire with friends and family, the air filled with the smell of roasting chestnuts, and the warmth of the flames flickering on our faces. It's become a yearly tradition that ties us to the land and the season, and it's something we all look forward to.

Roasting chestnuts is a simple process, but there's an art to it as well. First, you have to score the shells, just a small cut, enough to let the steam escape as they roast. If you skip this step, the chestnuts can explode from the pressure as they cook, which can make for an exciting (if somewhat dangerous) situation! Once the chestnuts are scored, we place them in a cast-iron pan or directly on the grill over the fire. There's a certain rhythm to the process, turning them every few minutes, or give the pan a vigorous shake, listening for that telltale crackling sound that lets you know they're almost done.

The smell is irresistible, and as the shells blacken and split open, the chestnuts inside become soft, sweet, and warm. There's nothing quite like peeling away the charred shell to reveal the golden nut inside, perfectly roasted. We always pair them with mugs of mulled wine or hot cider, or hot chocolate for the kids, (or for me with Baileys) and on Christmas Eve, we exchange books and then spend the evening reading by the fire. It's a cozy, peaceful way to end the year, and the chestnuts are always the perfect snack for a night of stories and quiet reflection.

We've lovingly adopted the tradition from Iceland called Jólabókaflóð, or "the Christmas Book Flood." It's a simple, heartfelt way to slow down and enjoy the holiday spirit. After gifting each other carefully chosen books, we settle in with blankets, mugs of hot chocolate for the children and mulled wine for us and spend the evening reading together. The crackle of the fire, candlelight, and the quiet turning of pages create a peaceful atmosphere that we look forward to every year. I secretly wish that one day someone will give my book at Jólabókaflóð.

This tradition has its roots in Iceland during World War II, when imported goods were scarce, but paper was readily available. Icelanders began giving books as gifts, which soon became a cherished part of their Christmas celebrations. Today, books are still one of the most popular gifts in Iceland, and families gather on Christmas Eve to enjoy their new reads in cozy, intimate settings.

We've found that this tradition adds a special touch to our holidays, offering a moment of quiet connection before the excitement of Christmas Day and Father Christmas arriving down the chimney. It's a beautiful reminder that sometimes, the simplest gifts, like a good book and time spent together, are the most meaningful.

There's also a magical element to the Sweet Chestnut tree that I've always been drawn to. In witchcraft and folklore, chestnuts are often associated with protection and fertility. Some traditions say that carrying a chestnut in your pocket can ward off illness or bad luck, and chestnut wood has been used in protective charms for centuries. The tree itself is considered a symbol of endurance and longevity, and its wood, which is resistant to rot, was often used in the construction of homes and tools meant to last a lifetime.

In our family, we've always felt a connection to the natural world, and I think that's part of why the chestnut tree resonates so strongly with us. There's a power in its roots, its wood, and its fruit, a power that goes beyond the physical. It's a tree that has sustained people for generations, not just in body but in spirit as well.

My Pulenta Recipe

Making Pulenta the traditional Corsican way is a beautiful and meditative process, steeped in the island's rustic charm and simplicity. This dish, made from chestnut flour, is deeply connected to Corsica's history, where chestnuts were a staple food for centuries, especially in the mountain villages. The flavour is earthy, slightly sweet, and comforting, and the preparation reflects the slow, mindful pace of life in Corsica.

To begin, you'll need good-quality chestnut flour*, preferably freshly milled, as it retains the rich, nutty essence of the chestnuts. Start by bringing one litre of water to a boil in a large pot, adding a pinch of salt. The water must be at a rolling boil before you slowly sift in the chestnut flour, a little at a time. Traditionally, this is done by hand, and there's a rhythm to it, slowly stirring the flour into the water using a wooden spoon or whisk. This step is crucial; adding the flour too quickly can result in lumps, so the stirring must be continuous and steady.

*In the UK - https://www.naturitas.co.uk/

 In the USA - https://www.wholefoodsmarket.com/

As the flour absorbs the water, the mixture thickens into a smooth, creamy consistency. The key here is patience, keep stirring until the Pulenta begins to pull away from the sides of the pot and forms a soft, dough-like mass. This process can take around 15 to 20 minutes, depending on the freshness of the flour and the heat of your stove. It's a bit like making polenta but with a distinct Corsican touch, as the chestnut flour gives it a unique, rich flavour.

Once the Pulenta reaches the right consistency, it can be spooned into a shallow dish or onto a wooden board, allowing it to cool slightly. Some like to drizzle it with a bit of olive oil or serve it with a pat of butter to enhance the richness of the chestnut flavour. In Corsica, Pulenta is often enjoyed alongside Brocciu*, a fresh sheep's cheese, or with wild boar stew, but it's equally delicious served with any hearty accompaniment, from meats to rich sauces.

*If you can't find Brocciu or Cabrettu cheese, try Marscapone, Cottage Cheese or Queso Fresco

A traditional way to serve Pulenta is to cut it into slices once it has set. These slices can then be grilled or fried, developing a slightly crispy exterior while remaining soft and flavourful inside. It's a dish that carries the essence of the Corsican countryside, simple yet full of depth, much like the island itself.

Chapter 6: Creating a Sacred Space

"Mitä hiljaisemmaksi tulet, sitä kovemmin sisäinen maailmasi puhuu."

"The more still you become, the louder the world within speaks."

Chapter 6: Creating a Sacred Space

Gardening has always been more than just a hobby for me; it's a spiritual journey that started in my childhood. I remember the first time my grandmother encouraged me plant a sunflower seed in her garden. The sheer joy of watching that tiny seed sprout and grow into a towering sunflower was nothing short of magical. This early experience planted the seeds of my lifelong passion for gardening. Today, my garden is not just a place for growing herbs and flowers, it's my sacred sanctuary, a reflection of my personal beliefs and practices, and a space where I connect deeply with nature.

Transforming a garden into a sacred space involves more than just planting. It's about creating a living canvas where every design element resonates with my spirituality and enhances the garden's magical energy. For me, this means incorporating elements like altars, statues, and sacred symbols that hold personal significance and spiritual power. My altar, nestled under the protective branches of an old oak tree, serves as the heart of my garden. It's a place where I meditate, perform rituals, and leave offerings, surrounded by candles, crystals, and seasonal flowers that change with the rhythms of the year.

Adding statues is not just for decoration. Each statue represents a guardian spirit or deity that I feel a connection with. Placing a statue of Artemis, the goddess of nature and the hunt, at the entrance of my garden feels like inviting a protector to watch over this sacred space. The Green Man, symbolizing rebirth and the cycle of growth, watches over my herb garden, reminding me of the interconnectedness of all life.

Sacred symbols are another integral part of my garden. I've carved protective sigils into the wooden fence and painted runes on stones that I scatter throughout the garden. Each symbol is a silent guardian, continuously working to manifest the energies they represent. Creating a labyrinth with stones has been one of my most fulfilling projects, offering a path for meditative walks and moments of reflection.

In this sacred space, every element, from the placement of a stone to the planting of a seed, is done with intention and reverence. My garden is a sanctuary where the physical and spiritual worlds meet, offering solace, inspiration, and a profound connection to nature. Here, I'll share my experiences and tips on incorporating these elements into your garden, helping you create an enchanting and sacred environment of your own.

The Concept of a Sacred Space

Before diving into the specifics, it's important to understand what a sacred space truly means. For me, a sacred space is my personal haven where I can retreat from the chaos of everyday life. It's a place where I can meditate, perform rituals, and connect with the natural world in a profound and intimate way. My garden serves as this sanctuary, where the physical and spiritual worlds intertwine, creating a harmonious environment that nurtures my soul. Every element in this space is imbued with intention and meaning, reflecting my beliefs and enhancing the garden's magical energy.

This is also where I dance. Dancing barefoot under the moonlight in this place is sacred for me, the soft glow of the moon casting shadows among the trees, the gentle rustling of leaves in the night breeze, and the cool earth beneath my feet create an almost otherworldly atmosphere. These moonlit dances are not just a joyful expression of freedom but also a form of moving meditation that deepens my connection to the rhythms of nature and the universe. Some swear by yoga or Pilates, I just dance!

My sacred space is more than a place for quiet contemplation; it is alive with energy and movement. Whether I am tending to the plants, arranging crystals on my altar, or simply sitting in silence, I am always aware of the intricate web of life surrounding me. The statues of deities and spirits that dot my garden serve as guardians and companions, their presence a constant reminder of the spiritual dimensions of the world around us.

In this sacred space, I find peace and inspiration. It is where I can be my truest self, away from the distractions and demands of daily life. Here, I can honour the cycles of the moon and the seasons, celebrate the changing energies of the earth, and immerse myself in the beauty of the natural world. Creating and nurturing this space has been a journey of discovery, and it continues to be a source of joy and solace in my life.

The Heart of the Garden: Creating an Altar

An altar is the focal point of any sacred space. It's where I perform rituals, leave offerings, and meditate. Creating an altar in the garden is a deeply personal process, as it should reflect your beliefs, practices, and the energies you wish to cultivate.

The first step in creating an altar is choosing the right location. For me, it had to be a quiet, secluded spot where I could feel connected to nature yet undisturbed by the outside world. I chose a corner of my garden shaded by an old oak tree, which felt like the perfect place for an altar. The tree itself seemed to emanate ancient wisdom, making it an ideal guardian for my sacred space.

Once the location was chosen, I started designing the altar. I used a sturdy wooden table as the base, which I found at a local flea market. It had a rustic charm that blended beautifully with the natural surroundings. I covered it with a handmade cloth, dyed in shades of green and brown to represent the earth.

On the altar, I placed a variety of objects that hold special meaning to me. There are candles in various colours, each representing different elements and intentions. I also included a bowl of water, a small cauldron for burning incense, and a dish of salt. These items represent the four elements; earth, air, fire, and water, which are central to my spiritual practice.

To personalize my altar, I added objects that resonate deeply with my spiritual journey and personal history. Each item on the altar tells a story and holds a piece of my heart. Crystals for healing and protection gleam in the sunlight, their energies creating a shield of positivity. Feathers I've found during my walks remind me of my connection to the air and the freedom of the spirit. Small statues of deities I work with stand proudly, their presence a comforting reminder of divine guidance.

One of the most cherished additions is my journal, a sacred space within a sacred space, if that makes sense, where I jot down my thoughts, prayers, and experiences. This journal is a living document of my spiritual growth, a place where I can reflect on my journey and plan for the future. This sits in an old tin box. I write with a fountain pen because my handwriting is terrible and the fountain pen slows my writing down to the point that I can read it again.

To truly make the altar a reflection of my entire being, I added items that represent my past, present, and future. Old toys from my childhood, filled with the energy of play and happiness, sit alongside objects collected from my travels, each a token of adventure and discovery. Personal items from my parents, like my mother's locket and my father's old compass all sitting in the tin box, connect me to my roots and family heritage. Small mementos from my children, such as their handmade drawings and little trinkets, represent the love and continuity of life.

Last spring, I decided to incorporate seasonal elements into my altar, making it a living, breathing part of my garden. I gathered fresh flowers from the garden, daffodils and tulips, to celebrate the renewal of life. Their vibrant colours and sweet fragrance filled the space with a sense of hope and rebirth. In autumn, I replaced them with dried leaves and acorns, symbols of harvest and gratitude. This practice of changing the altar with the seasons not only keeps it dynamic but also aligns it with the natural cycles, enhancing its magical energy.

I recall a particularly beautiful autumn day when I was arranging the altar with fallen leaves and acorns. My youngest child joined me, fascinated by the process. We talked about the importance of honouring the seasons and the cycles of life. It was a poignant moment of teaching and bonding, one that reminded me that sharing the things that truly matter to me with others was so important to my happiness.

These elements make my altar more than just a collection of objects; they turn it into a living, evolving representation of my spiritual journey and personal history. Every time I approach the altar, I am reminded of who I am, where I come from, and the spiritual path I am walking. This sacred space is a testament to the richness of life and the enduring power of intention and connection.

Sacred Statues: Guardians of the Garden

Incorporating statues into your garden adds a powerful layer of symbolism and protection. These statues can represent deities, spirits, or archetypal figures that resonate with your spiritual path.

Choosing the right statues is a clearly a highly personal decision, as members of my family have often raised an eyebrow at my choices, just as I know I am guilty of looking at The Gardener's choices with a trained look of disbelief. I try not to but I use the words "you're kidding me!" way too often. For me, I wanted figures that not only resonated with my beliefs but also complemented the natural beauty of the garden. I have always felt a deep connection to the goddess Artemis, the protector of nature and wildlife. Finding a statue of her was a serendipitous moment. I placed her near the entrance of the garden, symbolizing protection and guidance for all who enter.

I also added a statue of the Green Man, an ancient symbol of rebirth and the natural cycle of growth. Placing him near the herb garden felt right, as his energy supports the flourishing of plant life. His watchful presence serves as a reminder of the interconnectedness of all living things.

As soon as I positioned the Green Man, a butterfly landed on his stone face. It felt like a sign that he was pleased with his new home. Since then, I've noticed an increase in pollinators in that part of the garden, which has only benefited my herbs. There may well be a scientific reason for this effect, I did try looking it up, but alas this is still observational science at this time. Others have witnessed it and if you hunt on the internet there are plenty of theories, but science can't explain it so they assume it doesn't exist. I'm sure some clever person in a white lab coat will one day say "aha!" and we'll all look bemused and say "that's great, but we have known this for centuries!"

Sacred Symbols: Embedding Magic into the Garden

Sacred symbols are potent tools for infusing your garden with magical energy. These symbols can be anything from runes and sigils to more complex geometric designs.

Runes and sigils are powerful symbols used in many magical traditions. I decided to carve a protective sigil into the wooden fence that surrounds the garden. The process was meditative, as I focused my intent on protection and harmony. Every time I pass that spot, I'm reminded of the protective energies at work and the annoying splinter I got doing it.

I also painted runes on small stones and placed them strategically around the garden. For example, I used the rune "Algiz" for protection and placed it near the entrance. The rune "Fehu," symbolizing abundance, found its place near the vegetable patch. These symbols serve as silent guardians, continuously working to manifest the energies they represent.

Sacred geometry involves using geometric shapes and patterns that hold spiritual significance. I incorporated a simple mandala design in the centre of my garden using coloured stones and plants. The mandala represents the universe, and each section is dedicated to different aspects of my spiritual practice. Creating this mandala was a really fun and fulfilling project, and every time I sit by it, I feel a profound sense of peace and connection.

In addition to altars, statues, and symbols, creating sections of the garden dedicated to the four elements, earth, air, fire, and water, enhances the overall magical atmosphere.

I have created elemental corners in my garden where each corner is dedicated to one of the four classical elements, earth, air, fire, and water, each representing different aspects of life and spirituality. These corners not only serve as spaces for specific activities but also help me connect more deeply with the elements and their unique energies.

The earth corner of my garden is the epitome of stability and nurturing. This area is rich and lush, brimming with plants that are deeply connected to the earth. I've chosen sturdy, low-maintenance plants like ferns and moss, which thrive in the dappled sunlight filtering through the trees. Their verdant fronds and soft textures create a sense of calm and stability.

One of my favourite rituals involves visiting this corner early in the morning, barefoot, to feel the cool, damp earth beneath my feet. There's something profoundly grounding about this simple act; it reminds me of my roots and the importance of staying connected to the physical world. In the centre of this corner, I've placed a small stone altar. On it rests a bowl of rich, dark soil, a symbol of the earth's nurturing aspect. Sometimes, I sprinkle herbs or seeds into the bowl as offerings to the earth, thanking it for its sustenance and support.

I remember a particularly challenging period in my life when I felt lost and ungrounded. I spent many hours in the earth corner, tending to the plants, rearranging the stones, and simply sitting with my back against the old oak tree that stands sentinel over this space. The act of connecting with the earth, both physically and spiritually, provided a sense of stability and reassurance that helped me navigate through that difficult time.

The air corner of my garden is a haven of movement and sound, filled with tall, swaying plants like grasses and bamboo. These plants catch and dance with the wind, creating a dynamic environment that embodies the element of air. To enhance the air element further, I've hung wind chimes made from seashells and crystals. Their gentle tinkling creates a soothing soundscape that enhances the sense of lightness and freedom in this space.

This corner is perfect for meditation and inspiration. I often bring a cushion and sit among the grasses, allowing the sounds and movements of the wind to clear my mind.

The air corner is where I go when I need to brainstorm new ideas or find creative solutions to problems. There's something about the fresh, clean air and the gentle swaying of the plants that helps unlock my creative potential.

One summer afternoon last year, my friend and I spent hours in the air corner, crafting wind chimes from materials we had collected during our beach trips. As we worked, the breeze played with the chimes, filling the air with a symphony of delicate sounds. It was a magical experience that felt like a personal bonding between us.

The fire corner of my garden is a vibrant, energetic space dedicated to transformation and purification. Here, I planted sun-loving flowers like marigolds and sunflowers, whose bright, fiery colours evoke the essence of this element. In the centre of this corner stands a fire pit, which serves as a focal point for evening gatherings and rituals. We also dance around the fire at Halloween and Christmas Eve.

Lighting a fire and watching the flames dance is one of my favourite ways to connect with the fire element. The warmth and light of the fire create a transformative atmosphere, perfect for letting go of old patterns and inviting new energies into my life. I often gather with friends around the fire pit, sharing stories and performing rituals under the night sky. These gatherings are filled with laughter, song, and a sense of community that is both heartwarming and invigorating.

The evening before my cousin's wedding, we held a fire ceremony to release old fears and set new intentions. We wrote down our fears on pieces of paper and threw them into the flames, watching as they transformed into ash. The act of releasing these fears to the fire felt incredibly liberating, and we left the ceremony feeling lighter and more empowered about our future.

The water corner of my garden is a serene and tranquil space dedicated to emotions and intuition. At the heart of this corner is a small pond filled with water lilies, surrounded by a bubbling fountain that creates a continuous, calming flow. The sound of the water is incredibly soothing, providing a perfect backdrop for reflection and introspection.

This corner is where I go to connect with my inner self and explore my emotions. The water's gentle movement mirrors the ebb and flow of feelings, reminding me of the importance of emotional fluidity and balance. I often sit by the pond, watching the water lilies open and close with the sunlight, reflecting on my thoughts and experiences.

When I lost my grandfather, even though it wasn't unexpected, I was feeling overwhelmed, and as I sat by the pond, tears began to flow. The act of allowing myself to feel and release my emotions in this peaceful space was incredibly healing. The water seemed to absorb my sorrow, and although I can't claim that it left me with joy, as it didn't, the loss was a big one for me, but I left with a sense of calm and acceptance.

Each elemental corner in my garden serves a unique purpose, but together they create a harmonious and balanced environment. The earth corner grounds me, the air corner inspires me, the fire corner transforms me, and the water corner heals me. These spaces are not just physical locations; they are manifestations of my spiritual journey and personal growth.

Creating these elemental corners has been a deeply rewarding process, filled with moments of discovery and connection. Each corner reflects a different aspect of my personality and spirituality, and spending time in these spaces helps me stay balanced and cantered.

During the spring equinox, we started in the earth corner, planting new seeds and honouring the cycle of growth. We moved to the air corner for a meditation session, allowing the wind to carry our intentions for the season. As the sun set, we gathered in the fire corner, lighting a fire and sharing stories of renewal and transformation and playing the guitar. Finally, we ended the evening in the water corner, reflecting on our experiences and setting intentions for emotional balance and finished our wine.

These celebrations not only deepen my connection to the elements but also foster a sense of community and shared purpose. Friends and family who join me in these rituals often remark on the unique energy of the garden and the sense of peace and harmony it provides.

Creating a sacred space in your garden through design elements like altars, statues, and sacred symbols, and dedicating areas to the elements, transforms an ordinary garden into a magical sanctuary. It becomes a place where you can retreat from the chaos of everyday life, meditate, perform rituals, and connect deeply with nature. Whether you are grounding yourself in the earth corner, finding inspiration in the air corner, experiencing transformation in the fire corner, or seeking emotional healing in the water corner, each element brings its unique energy to your spiritual journey.

Ritual Practices: How to Consecrate and Bless Your Garden Space

Creating a sacred space in your garden is more than just arranging plants and decorations. It's about imbuing the space with intention and energy, making it a sanctuary for both the body and spirit. This process involves various rituals to consecrate and bless the garden, ensuring it resonates with your spiritual beliefs and practices. One of the most profound ways to achieve this is through seasonal celebrations and rituals, which honor the changing cycles of nature. These rituals connect us deeply to the earth and its rhythms, enhancing the magical energy of our sacred space. Here's how I consecrate and bless my garden, enriched with personal anecdotes and experiences.

Each season brings its own unique energy and opportunities for rituals and celebrations. By aligning my activities with these natural cycles, I create a harmonious and dynamic sacred space that evolves throughout the year.

Spring Equinox: Renewal and Balance

The Spring Equinox, a time of renewal and balance, is one of my favorite seasonal celebrations. This event marks the moment when day and night are equal in length, symbolizing the balance of light and dark. For me, it represents new beginnings and the reawakening of life after the long winter.

Ritual Practices:

- **Planting New Seeds:** On the day of the equinox, I gather a selection of seeds to plant in the garden. This ritual symbolizes the planting of new intentions and the start of fresh projects. I kneel in the earth corner, feeling the cool soil beneath my fingers as I carefully place each seed into the ground. The act of planting is meditative, a promise of growth and renewal.
- **Decorating the Altar:** I decorate my garden altar with fresh flowers and green leaves, symbolizing new life. Daffodils, tulips, and sprigs of newly budded branches adorn the space, bringing a vibrant burst of colour and energy.
- **Meditation and Affirmations:** I sit quietly at the altar, meditating on my goals and aspirations for the coming year. I write these intentions on small pieces of biodegradable paper and plant them alongside the seeds, believing that as the plants grow, so too will my dreams and ambitions.

Summer Solstice: Abundance and Peak Energy

The Summer Solstice, the longest day of the year, is a time of abundance and peak energy. It's a celebration of the sun at its zenith, a moment to honor the light and the growth it brings.

Ritual Practices:

- **Bonfire Gathering:** I host a bonfire in the fire corner of my garden. Friends and family gather around the fire, sharing food, singing songs, and performing rituals to honor the sun. The warmth and light of the fire mirror the sun's energy, creating a powerful atmosphere of celebration and community.
- **Sun Offerings:** We create sun-shaped offerings using flowers, herbs, and natural materials, which we then place around the fire pit. This act symbolizes our gratitude for the sun's life-giving energy.
- **Fire Torches Procession:** Inspired by rituals such as Guy Fawkes Night, we incorporate a procession with fire torches. We start from the village green and walk through the garden, lighting torches as we go. The procession culminates at the fire corner, where we light the bonfire. This tradition brings a sense of

excitement and reverence, connecting us to both historical and contemporary practices. The locals thought we were a bit weird the first time and more than a few curtains (drapes) were twitching at the windows, but now most of them know us and that we are Green Witches, most of the village is invited.

Autumn Equinox: Harvest and Reflection

The Autumn Equinox marks the harvest and the balance between light and dark. It's a time for introspection, giving thanks for the abundance of the year, and preparing for the coming winter.

Ritual Practices:

- **Harvesting Herbs and Vegetables:** I gather herbs and vegetables from the garden, thanking the earth for its bounty. This harvest is not just a practical task but a ritual of gratitude and connection.
- **Decorating the Altar:** I decorate the altar with harvested produce, dried leaves, and acorns. These symbols of autumn connect me to the cycle of life and death, reminding me of the importance of balance and letting go.
- **Reflection and Journaling:** I spend time in quiet reflection, journaling about the past year's experiences, lessons, and achievements. This practice helps me process my thoughts and set intentions for the winter months.

Winter Solstice: Rest and Renewal

The Winter Solstice, the shortest day and longest night of the year, is a time of rest and reflection. It marks the return of the sun and the promise of new beginnings.

Ritual Practices:

- **Lighting Candles:** I light candles in the garden to honour the return of the sun. Each candle represents a hope or intention for the coming year. The soft glow of the candles creates a serene and contemplative atmosphere.
- **Evergreen Decorations:** I decorate the altar with evergreen branches, holly, and pinecones. These symbols of resilience and hope remind me of the enduring cycles of nature.
- **Releasing the Old:** I write down things I want to release from the past year on small pieces of paper. During a quiet moment, I burn these papers in a fireproof bowl, symbolizing the release of old energies and the welcoming of new possibilities.

Last winter solstice, I decided to hold a small, intimate ceremony with just my immediate family. We gathered around the altar, adorned with evergreen branches and holly. As we lit the candles, we each shared our hopes and intentions for the new year. My oldest daughter, holding her candle, wished for kindness and joy to fill our home.

My son, with his serious expression, hoped for success in his studies, and of Chelsea Football Club. My youngest wishes for happy fairies. As I burned my papers, releasing old fears and regrets, I felt a profound sense of family. This isn't about being a part of a religion, in my eyes anyway, its about love, family, nature and connecting it all together.

Modern Rituals: Blending Tradition with Contemporary Practices

As our children go to school they are part of a community that celebrates all sorts of modern rituals, so incorporating modern rituals into my garden celebrations adds a unique layer of connection to both the past and the present. It brings an element of fun and relevance, reminding me that ancient customs can seamlessly blend with contemporary life to create a vibrant and dynamic sacred space. By embracing festivals like Guy Fawkes Night, Halloween, Christmas, and even quirky events like the Cooper's Hill Cheese-Rolling, I've found ways to enrich my garden rituals, making them more inclusive and engaging for friends and family.

Guy Fawkes Night Inspiration

On Guy Fawkes Night, communities gather around bonfires and participate in torch-lit processions, culminating in a bonfire where an effigy of Guy Fawkes is burned. In past years the effigy was made by local children, placed in a box cart on wheels and drawn around the town asking for "a penny for the Guy" from passersby. Guy Fawkes was a member of a group of English Catholics who tried to blow up the Houses of Parliament in 1605 in the failed "Gunpowder Plot" and the celebration is to celebrate the plots failure and the survival of the king. In Britain we celebrate with lots of fireworks, in a similar way that in the US they celebrate the 4th of July. Drawing from this tradition, I organize a similar event during the summer solstice. We gather at the village green, holding fire torches, and walk through the garden, lighting our way to the fire corner. We don't however burn an effigy of anyone! This procession, accompanied by songs and chants, creates a sense of unity and reverence for the sun's energy.

Halloween: Honouring Ancestors and Embracing the Mystical

Of course, we will talk about Halloween in other areas of this book too, but Halloween, rooted in the ancient Celtic festival of Samhain, is a time to honour ancestors and embrace the mystical aspects of life. In my garden, I transform this night into a celebration that blends traditional customs with modern fun.

Ancestor Altar: I set up an ancestor altar with photos, mementos, and favourite foods of departed loved ones. This altar is placed in a quiet corner of the garden, adorned with candles and autumn leaves, creating a sacred space to honour and remember those who have passed.

Pumpkin Carving and Lanterns: Carving pumpkins and placing them around the garden not only adds a festive touch but also serves as a protective measure, warding off negative spirits. The glow of the lanterns creates an enchanting atmosphere, perfect for the evening's activities.

Mystical Walk: As darkness falls, we take a mystical walk through the garden, guided by the light of our lanterns. Along the way, we share ghost stories, myths, and legends, connecting with the mystical energies of the night.

Christmas: Celebrating Light and Generosity

Christmas, with its roots in pagan winter solstice celebrations, is a time of light, generosity, and warmth. Incorporating Christmas traditions into my garden rituals brings a festive and joyful energy to the cold winter months.

Ritual Practices:

- **Yule Log Ceremony:** We do have some French connections to our family and it must be said the French do understand the importance of the Yue Log more than perhaps the English or American sides of our family. I incorporate a Yule log ceremony into my winter solstice celebrations. We decorate a log with holly, ivy, and ribbons, and then burn it in the fire pit, symbolizing the return of the sun and the warmth of the coming year.
- **Decorating with Evergreens:** The garden is adorned with evergreen branches, holly, and mistletoe, symbols of resilience and eternal life. These decorations not only honour ancient customs but also bring a sense of continuity and hope.
- **Feast and Sharing:** Hosting a feast in the garden, even in the chill of winter, creates a sense of community and generosity. We share food, stories, and gifts, celebrating the spirit of giving and togetherness.

We bundle up in warm coats and jumpers and gather around the fire pit. As we decorate the log and watched it burn, a sense of warmth and camaraderie envelopes us. The crackling fire, combined with the shared laughter and stories, create an unforgettable evening of light and love.

Other Modern Festivals with Ancient Roots

Easter: We celebrate all religions not just one, which confuses many, who question why we would celebrate Easter, but celebrating renewal and rebirth, Easter has deep pagan roots too in the festival of Ostara, honouring the goddess of spring. In my garden, I celebrate by planting new flowers, decorating eggs, and hosting an egg hunt. These activities symbolize the joy of new beginnings and the blossoming of life.

Yes, we even do Easter Egg hunts for the children!

May Day (Beltane): May Day, or Beltane, marks the beginning of summer and is a time of fertility and growth. We celebrate with a maypole dance in the garden, weaving ribbons around the pole as we dance. This ritual symbolizes the intertwining of life and the blossoming of the earth. Last Beltane, we erected a maypole in the centre of the garden. Friends and family gathered, each holding a colourful ribbon. As we danced around the pole, weaving the ribbons into a beautiful pattern, the garden seemed to come alive with energy and joy. It was a celebration of life, love, and the earth's abundance.

Our Own festivals: Cooper's Hill Cheese-Rolling

Incorporating local quirky traditions into garden celebrations adds a playful element that can create memorable moments. The Cooper's Hill Cheese-Rolling is an annual event held on the Spring Bank Holiday in Gloucester, England, which inspired me to host a light-hearted cheese-rolling event in our own garden.

Cheese-Rolling Event: We have a small hill just over the fence from our garden that usually has horses grazing. We use a round cheese wheel for the rolling. Participants chase the cheese down the hill, and the winner is the first to catch it or reach the bottom. The first time we hosted a garden cheese-rolling event, it was an instant hit. Watching friends and family chase a cheese wheel down the hill, stumbling and laughing all the way, was hilarious, spurred I'm afraid by copious amounts of wine and lots of laughter.

Blending ancient traditions with modern practices, such as incorporating elements of Guy Fawkes Night, Halloween, Christmas, Easter, May Day, and even the whimsical cheese-rolling event, adds a dynamic and contemporary layer to these rituals. Through intentional acts of care and reverence, your garden becomes more than just a physical space, it transforms into a living, breathing embodiment of your spiritual journey, a place of solace, inspiration, and profound connection to the earth and its cycles. By embracing both the solemn and the playful, the ancient and the modern, you create a garden that is uniquely yours, a sacred space that evolves with you and offers endless possibilities for celebration, reflection, and joy.

"In Culīnā Sagæ, omnis ingrediēns magicam movet, omnis rēcepta fābulam narrat, et omnis pōtiō cum sapientiā veterum coquitur."

"In the Witch's Kitchen, every ingredient stirs magic, every recipe tells a story, and every potion brews with the wisdom of ages."

Chapter 7: The Witch's Kitchen

As someone who revels in the magic of nature, I find the process of growing, foraging, and baking to be deeply fulfilling. Here are a few of my personal favourites from the recipes shared in the previous chapters, each with a special place in my heart and a story behind it.

Lavender and Honey Bread: The calming properties of lavender and the sweet, floral notes make this bread a staple in my kitchen. It's perfect for those quiet moments when you need a bit of tranquillity. The journey of creating this bread starts in my garden, where the lavender bushes stand tall and fragrant, swaying gently in the breeze. Harvesting lavender at dawn, when the air is crisp and the flowers are at their most potent, is a ritual that brings me immense peace. The process of kneading the dough and smelling the infusion of honey and lavender baking in the oven feels like a meditative practice, grounding me in the present moment.

Thyme and Cheddar Scones: These scones are a go-to for breakfast. The savoury blend of thyme and cheddar offers a delightful start to the day. Thyme, with its robust and earthy flavour, is another herb I cherish. It grows abundantly in my garden, its tiny leaves packed with powerful aroma. Baking these scones reminds me of Sunday mornings in Portland, where I first started experimenting with the guidance of friends from the local coven. The sharp cheddar cheese melting into the scones creates a savoury symphony that pairs perfectly with a cup of tea or coffee.

Wild Garlic and Mushroom Tart: This tart is a celebration of the forest's bounty. The wild garlic and mushrooms create a savoury and satisfying dish that never fails to impress. Foraging for wild garlic and mushrooms is an adventure that takes me deep into the woods, where the air is filled with the scent of earth and leaves. The thrill of finding a patch of wild garlic or a cluster of chanterelles is unmatched. Each ingredient brings a piece of the forest's magic into my kitchen. The tart's flaky crust and rich, flavourful filling make it a beloved dish, especially for gatherings with friends and family.

Rosemary and Honey Panna Cotta: Light, creamy, and infused with the subtle flavour of rosemary, this panna cotta is my favourite way to end a meal on a sweet note. Rosemary, with its piney, slightly peppery flavour, grows in my garden, a testament to resilience and strength. I often think of my mother when I harvest rosemary, as it was her favourite herb. The panna cotta, with its smooth texture and fragrant honey-rosemary combination, is a tribute to her and the legacy she left me.

My connection to these ingredients and recipes runs deep, rooted in the places I've called home. Although I was born in England, I spent much of my formative life in Portland, USA, where I honed my craft as a witch. What can I say except the Americans do love their food! Portland's vibrant, nature-loving community embraced me, and it was there that I learned to appreciate the magic that can be embraced, not so much a ritual but, an everyday indulgence combining every herb, nut, and mushroom into the mundane. Mundane isn't a bad word it's a good word, but maybe I should say placing magic in all aspects of life as perhaps it sounds better.

Returning to England and taking over my mother's garden has been a full-circle moment for me. The garden, once her pride and joy, is now mine to nurture and draw inspiration from. Every plant and herb here holds memories of her teachings and love. My baking, infused with these homegrown and foraged ingredients, is a way of continuing her legacy and creating new magical traditions of my own.

Baking with ingredients from my garden and the woods around me not only connects me to nature but also brings a unique and personal touch to everything I create. Each recipe is a blend of my past and present, a culinary journey that ties together my roots in England and my experiences in Portland. I hope these recipes inspire you to explore the magical potential of your own surroundings and infuse your baking with the natural enchantments of herbs, nuts, and mushrooms. Happy baking, and may your kitchen always be filled with magic!

Lavender and Honey Bread

This aromatic bread combines the soothing properties of lavender with the natural sweetness of honey. Perfect for a relaxing afternoon tea or a leisurely summer picnic, this bread is as delightful to make as it is to eat.

Ingredients:

- 2 cups all-purpose flour
- 1 cup whole wheat flour
- 1 packet active dry yeast
- 1 ½ cups warm water
- 3 tablespoons honey
- 2 tablespoons dried lavender buds
- 1 teaspoon salt
- 2 tablespoons olive oil

Instructions:

1. **Activate the Yeast:** In a small bowl, dissolve the yeast in warm water with a tablespoon of honey. Let it sit for about 5-10 minutes until frothy.
2. **Mix the Dry Ingredients:** In a large mixing bowl, combine the all-purpose flour, whole wheat flour, salt, and dried lavender buds.
3. **Combine Wet and Dry Ingredients:** Create a well in the center of the dry ingredients and pour in the yeast mixture, remaining honey, and olive oil. Stir until a dough forms.

4. **Knead the Dough:** Turn the dough onto a floured surface and knead for about 10 minutes until smooth and elastic.
5. **First Rise:** Place the dough in a greased bowl, cover with a damp cloth, and let it rise in a warm place for about 1-2 hours, or until doubled in size.
6. **Shape the Loaf:** Punch down the dough, shape it into a loaf, and place it in a greased loaf pan.
7. **Second Rise:** Cover and let it rise again for about 30-45 minutes until it has risen above the edge of the pan.
8. **Bake:** Preheat your oven to 375°F (190°C). Bake the bread for 30-35 minutes or until golden brown and sounds hollow when tapped.
9. **Cool and Serve:** Let the bread cool in the pan for a few minutes before transferring it to a wire rack to cool completely. Serve with a drizzle of honey and a sprinkle of lavender buds for extra magic.

A Summer Picnic with Lavender and Honey Bread

Every year, not long after the schools break up for summer we have a mini tradition of going on our family summer picnic. Lavender and Honey Bread is the star of the spread. Picture a warm, sunny afternoon in the English countryside, elegant ancient trees and a gentle breeze. The sky is a brilliant blue, dotted with fluffy white clouds, and the air is filled with the gentle hum of bees and the sweet scent of wildflowers.

We set up our picnic under an ancient Elm tree whose sprawling branches provided ample shade. A checkered blanket was spread out, adorned with a delightful array of homemade treats and foraged goodies. In the centre of it all was the Lavender and Honey Bread, its golden crust glistening in the sunlight and its floral aroma mingling with the fresh scent of the grass.

The crust was perfectly crispy, while the inside was soft and airy, each bite releasing the calming essence of lavender intertwined with the natural sweetness of honey. To complement the bread, we had an assortment of toppings: creamy butter infused with wild herbs, tangy homemade raspberry jam, and a selection of local cheeses, including a sharp cheddar and a creamy brie.

The bread paired beautifully with a chilled bottle of sparkling elderflower cordial, its delicate floral notes enhancing the flavours of the lavender and honey. We also enjoyed a fresh salad made from foraged greens, including dandelion leaves and wild rocket, tossed with a light vinaigrette and sprinkled with edible flowers for a touch of magic.

For dessert, we had wild berry tarts, the berries, still a little hard as not fully ripe, which by the way is a tip in itself, don't wait till the fruit is in full bloom, were picked earlier that morning from the brambles near the woods, a treat that seems to get earlier in the season every year these days. The tartness of the berries provided a perfect contrast to the sweet, floral bread. We finished our meal with a pot of freshly brewed herbal tea, made with mint and chamomile from the garden, its soothing warmth a perfect end to a magical afternoon.

A picnic is more than just a meal; it's an experience that connects us to the land and each other. The Lavender and Honey Bread, with its unique blend of flavours and calming properties, helped make the occasion truly special. It's moments like these that remind me of the simple joys and profound connections that baking with nature's bounty can bring.

Rosemary and Walnut Bread

This rustic bread combines the earthy flavour of walnuts with the aromatic scent of rosemary, making it a perfect companion for hearty soups and stews. The robust flavours of rosemary and walnuts create a comforting, homely loaf that is both nourishing and flavourful. As the bread bakes, the kitchen fills with a rich, inviting aroma that beckons everyone to gather around for a slice.

Ingredients:

- 3 cups bread flour
- 1 cup whole wheat flour
- 1 packet active dry yeast
- 1 ½ cups warm water
- 2 tablespoons honey
- 2 tablespoons olive oil
- 1 tablespoon fresh rosemary, finely chopped
- 1 cup walnuts, coarsely chopped
- 1 teaspoon salt

Instructions:

1. **Activate the Yeast:** In a small bowl, dissolve the yeast in warm water with a tablespoon of honey. Let it sit for about 5-10 minutes until frothy.
2. **Mix the Dry Ingredients:** In a large mixing bowl, combine the bread flour, whole wheat flour, salt, chopped rosemary, and walnuts.
3. **Combine Wet and Dry Ingredients:** Create a well in the centre of the dry ingredients and pour in the yeast mixture, remaining honey, and olive oil. Stir until a dough forms.
4. **Knead the Dough:** Turn the dough onto a floured surface and knead for about 10 minutes until smooth and elastic.
5. **First Rise:** Place the dough in a greased bowl, cover with a damp cloth, and let it rise in a warm place for about 1-2 hours, or until doubled in size.
6. **Shape the Loaf:** Punch down the dough, shape it into a round loaf, and place it on a baking sheet lined with parchment paper.

7. **Second Rise:** Cover and let it rise again for about 30-45 minutes until it has expanded.
8. **Bake:** Preheat your oven to 400°F (200°C). Bake the bread for 35-40 minutes or until golden brown and sounds hollow when tapped.
9. **Cool and Serve:** Let the bread cool on a wire rack before slicing. Enjoy with a spread of butter or a wedge of cheese.

Rosemary and Walnut Bread has become a beloved after-school treat for the kids. When they come running through the door, hungry and eager to unwind from their day, the sight and smell of this freshly baked bread waiting for them is always met with cheers and smiles.

The afternoons at our house are filled with the joyous chaos of school bags dropped at the door, laughter echoing through the halls, and the inevitable chorus of "What's for Tea?" as we still try and adhere to "Afternoon Tea" always around 4 o'clock, more or a little snack. To their delight, this bread, still warm from the oven, is a frequent answer. Its crusty exterior and soft, fragrant interior make it irresistible.

Serving Suggestions: For an after-school treat, I like to serve the Rosemary and Walnut Bread with a few simple yet delicious accompaniments:

- **Herbed Butter:** Softened butter mixed with a sprinkle of sea salt and a dash of finely chopped rosemary enhances the bread's flavours, making each bite creamy and aromatic.
- **Cheese Platter:** A selection of cheeses, including sharp cheddar, creamy brie, and tangy goat cheese, pairs wonderfully with the bread. The kids enjoy experimenting with different combinations, discovering new favourite pairings.
- **Fruit Preserves:** Sweet and tangy fruit preserves, like fig jam or apricot preserves, offer a delightful contrast to the savoury notes of the bread. Spreading a bit of jam over a buttered slice is a simple pleasure that the kids love.
- **Fresh Fruit:** Slices of crisp apples, juicy pears, and a handful of grapes make a refreshing side, adding both colour and nutritional balance to the snack.

Why It's Special: Baking this bread feels like weaving a bit of magic into our daily lives. The process of combining simple ingredients, kneading the dough, and watching it rise and bake is a grounding, almost meditative practice. Each loaf is a labour of love, crafted with care and intention.

Sharing it with the kids creates moments of connection and comfort. We often sit together at the kitchen table, chatting about their day while they savor their slices. Sometimes in the summer, we take it outside to the garden, enjoying the fresh air and the natural beauty that surrounds us, or have it with piping hot soup sitting by the log fire in the kitchen in the dark days of winter. These moments remind me of my own childhood in England and the warmth of home-baked bread waiting for me after a long day.

Incorporating elements from my mother's garden into our daily routine feels like a way of honouring her memory and keeping her spirit alive in our home. The rosemary I use in the bread grows just outside the kitchen window, a constant reminder of her love and care. The walnuts, foraged from nearby woods, bring a taste of the wild into our kitchen, connecting us to the land and the rhythms of nature.

This bread, with its blend of earthy walnuts and aromatic rosemary, is more than just food; it's a symbol of home, family, and the simple joys of life. It's these moments, gathered around the table with my children, that make baking such a magical and fulfilling part of our lives.

Pastries: Magical Morning Treats

Thyme and Cheddar Scones

These savoury scones are perfect for breakfast or an afternoon snack. The thyme adds a subtle herbal note that complements the sharpness of the cheddar. But these scones are more than just a delicious treat; they hold a special place in my heart because they were my dad's absolute favourite.

Ingredients:

- 2 cups all-purpose flour
- 1 tablespoon baking powder
- ½ teaspoon salt
- 1 tablespoon sugar
- 4 tablespoons cold butter, cubed
- 1 cup grated sharp cheddar cheese
- 2 tablespoons fresh thyme leaves
- ¾ cup whole milk

Instructions:

1. **Preheat Oven:** Preheat your oven to 400°F (200°C) and line a baking sheet with parchment paper.
2. **Mix Dry Ingredients:** In a large bowl, whisk together the flour, baking powder, salt, and sugar.
3. **Cut in Butter:** Add the cold butter to the flour mixture and use a pastry cutter or your fingers to cut it in until the mixture resembles coarse crumbs.
4. **Add Cheese and Thyme:** Stir in the grated cheddar and thyme leaves.
5. **Combine Wet and Dry Ingredients:** Pour in the milk and mix just until the dough comes together. Be careful not to overmix.
6. **Shape the Dough:** Turn the dough onto a floured surface and gently knead it a few times. Pat it into a 1-inch-thick circle and cut into 8 wedges.

7. **Bake:** Place the scones on the prepared baking sheet and bake for 15-20 minutes or until golden brown.
8. **Cool and Serve:** Let the scones cool slightly before serving. They are best enjoyed warm with a pat of butter.

Thyme and Cheddar Scones and Dad's Garden Shed

Growing up, my dad's garden shed was his sanctuary. It was a place where he could escape the hustle and bustle of daily life, (and probably his visiting mother-in-law!), surrounded by his tools, jars of seeds, and the comforting smell of earth and wood. I have a vivid memory of finding him there one summer afternoon, a stack of freshly baked Thyme and Cheddar Scones on the tool bench, paired with a bottle of his home-brewed acorn beer.

He had a particular way of enjoying these scones. He'd take a bite, savouring the blend of sharp cheddar and fragrant thyme, then wash it down with a swig of his nutty, slightly bitter acorn beer. The combination of flavours was unique, a true reflection of his love for both gardening and brewing. He often said that the scones reminded him of his school days when he came home from boarding school. I don't think his time away at school was the best for him and was homesick, but when he did come home in the holidays and back to the countryside, obviously this was one treat he looked forward to, having a snack with his dad, gramps, in his shed.

Despite many, many attempts, I've never quite mastered the recipe as well as my mother did. She had an innate ability to blend the ingredients just right, creating scones that were perfectly crumbly yet moist, with the thyme and cheddar harmoniously balanced. Whenever I asked her for her secret, she'd smile and say that she never made them as well as her mother did, adding another layer to the family tradition.

My mother's scones were legendary in our family. She would always make them for special occasions, but also for those simple, everyday moments when a little bit of magic was needed. I remember watching her in the kitchen, her hands moving deftly as she mixed the dough, the scent of fresh thyme filling the air. She'd let me sprinkle the thyme leaves over the mixture, teaching me the importance of each step and the love that went into making them.

Every time I bake these scones, I'm transported back to those cherished afternoons in the kitchen with my mum, and the quiet, cozy moments in my dad's shed. The process of making them is a comforting ritual, a way of connecting with my roots and keeping my parents' memories alive. The smell of thyme and cheddar wafting through the house is like a warm hug, enveloping me in nostalgia and love. It shows that that whether it's a recipe or a potion, there is something more to it than just following the instructions, there is a part of our soul that makes an important ingredient. That said, everyone loves them when I make them, so maybe there is something nostalgic in our taste buds for days long gone by and perhaps my daughter will be saying she can never make them as well as I did!

Serving Suggestions: For an after-school treat, Thyme and Cheddar Scones are served with a few simple yet delightful accompaniments:

- **Herbed Butter:** Softened butter mixed with a sprinkle of sea salt and a dash of finely chopped thyme enhances the scones' flavours, making each bite creamy and aromatic.
- **Cheese Platter:** A selection of cheeses, including sharp cheddar, creamy brie, and tangy goat cheese, pairs wonderfully with the scones. The kids enjoy experimenting with different combinations, discovering new favourite pairings.
- **Fruit Preserves:** Sweet and tangy fruit preserves, like fig jam or apricot preserves, offer a delightful contrast to the savoury notes of the scones. Spreading a bit of jam over a buttered scone is a simple pleasure that the kids love.
- **Fresh Fruit:** Slices of crisp apples, juicy pears, and a handful of grapes make a refreshing side, adding both colour and nutritional balance to the snack.
- **Acorn Beer:** (not for the children) Served at room temperature, definitely not served cold!!! I know this is sacrilege for most Americans, but the cold takes away the flavour, sorry guys!

These scones are not just a treat but a piece of family history, a way of honouring my parents' legacies and bringing a touch of magic to our everyday lives. They remind me of the love and warmth of my childhood home, and I hope they bring the same joy and comfort to my children as they grow up with these cherished family recipes. And I hope that this is true for you too!

Wild Garlic and Mushroom Tart

This savoury tart, featuring foraged wild garlic and mushrooms, is a true celebration of nature's bounty. It's perfect for a light dinner and has become one of my absolute favourites paired with a nice crisp *Piesporter* Michelsberg white wine.

Ingredients:

- 1 sheet of puff pastry, thawed
- 1 cup wild garlic leaves, finely chopped
- 2 cups mixed mushrooms (e.g., chanterelles, porcini), sliced
- 1 tablespoon olive oil
- 2 tablespoons butter
- 2 cloves garlic, minced
- 1 cup grated Gruyère cheese
- 2 eggs
- 1 cup heavy cream
- Salt and pepper to taste

Instructions:

1. **Preheat Oven:** Preheat your oven to 375°F (190°C).
2. **Prepare Pastry:** Roll out the puff pastry on a floured surface and fit it into a tart pan. Prick the bottom with a fork and bake for 10 minutes until lightly golden.
3. **Sauté Vegetables:** In a skillet, heat the olive oil and butter over medium heat. Add the garlic and mushrooms, sautéing until the mushrooms are golden and any liquid has evaporated. Stir in the wild garlic and cook for a minute. Season with salt and pepper.
4. **Make Filling:** Whisk together the eggs and cream. Stir in the grated Gruyère.
5. **Assemble Tart:** Spread the mushroom and wild garlic mixture over the pre-baked crust. Pour the egg and cream mixture over the top.
6. **Bake:** Return the tart to the oven and bake for 25-30 minutes, or until the filling is set and the top is golden.
7. **Cool and Serve:** Allow the tart to cool slightly before slicing. Serve warm or at room temperature.

Foraging for Wild Garlic and Mushrooms

If you haven't already go foraging for wild garlic and mushrooms! It's really not that scary as some people think it is. For me it has become a cherished ritual, especially during the early morning walks with Bunny. Despite her enthusiasm, Bunny has absolutely no nose for finding mushrooms, instead, she often ends up treading on them, so I have to have an eagle eye to spot them first! Still, these walks are a wonderful way to start the day, breathing in the fresh, crisp air and enjoying the quiet beauty of the woods. I start at first light or 5am whichever is the later.

Recognising Wild Garlic: Wild garlic is relatively easy to identify. It grows in dense clusters and has broad, pointed leaves that resemble those of lilies. The most telling sign is its distinctive garlicky smell, which you can detect as you crush the leaves between your fingers. During the blooming season, you might also notice small, white star-shaped flowers.

Mushroom Foraging Tips: When foraging for wild mushrooms, it's important to know how to identify them accurately. Each type has its own unique characteristics, and there's a real joy in recognising these subtle details.

- **Chanterelles**: These are unmistakable once you know what you're looking for. Their bright yellow to orange colour is striking, and they have a funnel shape with a wavy, sometimes uneven cap. What really sets them apart is their false gills, which look like forked wrinkles that run down the stem, rather than true gills. The fruity, apricot-like smell is another good indicator you've found the right ones. They thrive in mossy areas and are often found under hardwood trees like oak or beech.

- **Porcini**: With their large, round brown caps and thick, white stalks, Porcini are an impressive sight. The underside of the cap doesn't have gills; instead, you'll find pores that start off white when the mushroom is young and gradually turn yellow as it matures. Porcini have a wonderfully earthy, nutty aroma, making them a favourite in many kitchens. They tend to grow in symbiosis with certain trees, particularly pines and oaks, so keep an eye out around those when foraging.
- **Hen of the Woods (Maitake)**: Hen of the Woods grows at the base of trees, particularly oaks, in large clusters that can resemble a fluffed-up hen, hence the name. These mushrooms have overlapping, fan-shaped caps with frilly, grey-brown edges. The texture is meaty and tender, making them a fantastic addition to various dishes. They have a rich, earthy flavour and are popular in both traditional and modern recipes. You'll often find them in late summer through autumn.
- **Lion's Mane**: This one looks quite different from other mushrooms. Lion's Mane grows in a white, shaggy mass that resembles a cascading mane of a lion. It lacks gills altogether, and instead, it has long, soft spines that hang down from the mushroom. When young, these spines are firm, but they soften as the mushroom ages. The flavour is mild but distinctly reminiscent of seafood, often compared to crab or lobster, making it a fantastic option for plant-based diets. Lion's Mane is found on hardwood trees like beech and maple in late summer to early fall.
- **Morels**: Morels are prized by many foragers for their unique honeycomb-like appearance and rich, earthy flavour. Their tall, cone-shaped cap has a distinctive pattern of ridges and pits, making them easy to spot once you know what you're looking for. They grow near the base of trees, particularly elms and ashes, and are often found in the spring, making them a sought-after delicacy during that season. The interior of a true Morel is hollow, which helps distinguish it from false morels, which are poisonous.

Always make sure to cross-reference with a reliable field guide and, if in doubt, consult with an experienced forager or mycologist to ensure your finds are safe to eat. And just because a daft bouncy Golden Retriever with half a brain eats one, doesn't mean it's safe!

Last Sunday, it was a crisp spring morning, the ground still damp with dew. Bunny and I set out on our usual foraging adventure, the woods were quiet, save for the occasional rustle of leaves and the morning chorus of birds. We walked along familiar trails, with me scanning the forest floor for the telltale signs of wild garlic and mushrooms.

Despite her best efforts as over the year as she has realised what I'm searching for, Bunny often missed the mushrooms and instead happily runs through the underbrush, her tail wagging furiously. Her enthusiasm is infectious, making these walks even more enjoyable. After a while, we stumbled upon a perfect patch of wild garlic. The scent was unmistakable, and I carefully picked enough leaves for the tart while leaving plenty behind to ensure the plants would continue to thrive.

Finding mushrooms, however, is always a bit more challenging. It requires a keen eye and a lot of patience. On this particular morning, I was thrilled to discover a cluster of chanterelles nestled at the base of an old oak tree. Their vibrant colour stood out against the earthy tones of the forest floor. I gently harvested them, ensuring to leave the base of the stalk intact to promote regrowth.

Preparing the Tart: A Taste of the Forest

Back home, I eagerly set about preparing the Wild Garlic and Mushroom Tart. The combination of freshly foraged wild garlic and chanterelles promised a dish bursting with earthy, savoury flavours. The process of cleaning and preparing the mushrooms and wild garlic, and then watching them sauté in the skillet, filled the kitchen with a deliciously enticing aroma.

The puff pastry provided a perfect, flaky base for the tart, its buttery texture complementing the rich filling. As I poured the egg and cream mixture over the sautéed mushrooms and wild garlic, the anticipation built. The final step was baking the tart until the filling set and the top turned a beautiful golden brown.

Serving the Tart: A Culinary Delight

Allowing the tart to cool slightly, I sliced it into generous portions. The golden crust and creamy filling, dotted with vibrant green wild garlic and tender mushrooms, made for a beautiful presentation. Serving it warm, I paired the tart with a simple side salad of foraged greens and a light vinaigrette. And the Piesporter 😊

This Wild Garlic and Mushroom Tart is more than just a meal; it's a celebration of the natural world and the simple pleasures of foraging. The flavours are a perfect reflection of the forest, with the wild garlic adding a subtle kick and the mushrooms providing a rich, earthy depth. Every bite is a reminder of those peaceful early morning walks with Bunny, the thrill of the hunt, and the joy of bringing nature's bounty into my kitchen.

Baking with ingredients I've foraged myself adds a layer of connection and satisfaction that's hard to describe. It's a way of honouring the land and the traditions passed down through generations. Whether you're an experienced forager or just starting, I hope this recipe inspires you to explore the wonders of wild garlic and mushrooms and to create your own delicious, nature-inspired dishes.

Wyrdwife's Tart: Lavender Marshmallow Root, Mushroom, and Dandelion Greens Tart: A Spellbinding Family Recipe

This recipe is more than just a dish; it's a treasured heirloom passed down through generations of witches in my family. My mother, a wise and gentle witch, learned it from her mother, and so on, tracing back, or so it's said, through the centuries. Each ingredient tells a story of the land and the magic within it. As you prepare this tart, you'll feel the touch of those who've come before, guiding your hands and infusing the food with love and history.

In the heart of medieval England, nestled within the ancient woodlands and rolling hills, lived a community of wise women known as wyrdwives. These women, skilled in the arts of healing and herbcraft, were the keepers of profound natural knowledge. Among their many gifts was this recipe: Wyrdwife's Tart.

A Family Heirloom

This cherished recipe has been preserved in our family for centuries, meticulously handwritten in a book of potions and spells by my great, great grandmother. This book, where I have taken a few extracts and from which one day I'll write the full stories, is a treasured heirloom filled with the wisdom of the ages, passed down through the generations. Each page carries the essence of our ancestors, their knowledge and that magic I think is living on through us.

Ingredients Steeped in Magic

The main ingredients of the Wyrdwife's Herbal Tart included:

- **Mugwort:** Known for its dream-inducing qualities, mugwort was often used in potions and charms.
- **Marshmallow Root:** Valued for its soothing properties, it was a staple in many medieval remedies.
- **Wild Mushrooms:** Harvested from the forest, they added an earthy depth to the tart and were believed to contain magical essences.
- **Dandelion Greens:** A symbol of resilience, these greens were used for their bitter yet healing properties.
- **Lavender:** Known for its calming effects, it added a fragrant note to the tart.

Each of these ingredients was selected not only for their flavour but also for their magical and healing properties, making the tart a blend of nourishment and enchantment.

The Role of Wyrdwives in Society

Wyrdwives occupied a unique place in medieval society. They were both revered and feared, often consulted for their healing abilities but also mistrusted by those who did not understand their ways. The Wyrdwife's Tart has been seen as an important remnant of their knowledge and power. It was often prepared during significant lunar phases, particularly the full moon, when the magical potency of the ingredients was believed to be at its peak.

The tart was served during gatherings and rituals, offering both physical sustenance and spiritual protection to those who partook. It was said that consuming the tart could bring about prophetic dreams, protect against malevolent spirits, and heal various ailments and help remove inhibitions.

Persecution and Preservation

As the medieval period waned and the witch hunts began, many wyrdwives were persecuted for their practices. The Wyrdwife's Tart, along with other elements of their craft, became clandestine, passed down in secret to protect the knowledge from being lost. Despite the danger, some brave wyrdwives continued to prepare the tart, keeping the tradition alive through the darkest times.

Legacy in Modern Times

Today, the Wyrdwife's Tart stands as a testament to the resilience and wisdom of these ancient women. Modern practitioners of herbalism and those who honour the old ways continue to bake this tart, celebrating its rich history and the powerful connection to the natural world it represents. It is a culinary relic, a delicious bridge between past and present, infused with the spirit and lore of the wyrdwives who first brought it to life.

In our family, we never forget that baking itself is a type of potion. The blending of ingredients, the transformation through heat, and the love poured into the process all contribute to the final magical creation. As you prepare this tart, may you feel the presence of my great, great grandmother and all the wyrdwives before her, guiding your hands and infusing your creation with their ancient magic.

Ingredients:

Tart Crust:

- 1 1/2 cups all-purpose flour
- 1/2 cup cold butter, diced
- 1/4 cup ground hazelnuts
- 1/4 tsp salt
- 3-4 tbsp ice water

Filling:

- 1 cup marshmallow root tea (cooled)
- 1/2 cup heavy cream
- 1/4 cup honey
- 2 large eggs
- 1 tsp vanilla extract
- 1 tbsp dried lavender flowers
- 1 small shallot, finely chopped
- 3 cloves garlic, minced
- 2 tbsp olive oil
- 2 cups assorted wild mushrooms (morels, chanterelles, shiitake), sliced
- 1 cup dandelion greens, chopped
- 2 tbsp fresh thyme, chopped
- 1/2 cup feta cheese, crumbled
- Salt and pepper to taste

Directions:

1. **Harvesting the Ingredients:**
   - **Marshmallow Root and Lavender:** These gentle herbs grow abundantly in my garden. I remember helping my mother dig up the marshmallow root and carefully drying the lavender flowers under the summer sun. Their fragrance would fill the air, a promise of the flavours to come.
   - **Wild Mushrooms:** Foraging for mushrooms is a tradition in my family. We'd venture into the ancient forests that surround our home, initially guided by my mother's keen eye although she would always show the mushrooms to my dad for a second opinion if she wasn't sure of a certain mushroom as he was very knowledgeable on fruits from the forest. Morels, chanterelles, and shiitakes were our treasures, each one bringing a piece of the forest's magic into our home.
   - **Dandelion Greens and Thyme:** Dandelions, often overlooked, were celebrated in our family. Their greens were a staple, and we'd pick them fresh from the meadow the other side of our garden fence. Thyme, a symbol of courage, grew in a sunny spot by the kitchen window, always within reach.
2. **Prepare the Crust:**
   - In a large bowl, combine the flour, ground hazelnuts, and salt.
   - Cut in the cold butter using a pastry cutter or your fingertips until the mixture resembles coarse crumbs. I remember my mother teaching me to feel the texture, saying, "The magic is in the touch, close your eyes and feel it." I know when it's ready with me eyes closed.
   - Gradually add ice water, one tablespoon at a time, until the dough begins to come together.

- Shape the dough into a disk, wrap it in clingfilm, and refrigerate for at least 30 minutes.
3. **Prepare the Marshmallow Root Tea:**
    - Steep 1-2 tablespoons of dried marshmallow root in 1 cup of boiling water for 10-15 minutes. Strain and let the tea cool. This tea has been a remedy and a comfort in our family, soothing many a weary soul. It's a delicate flavour in this dish but adds some of the magic. It is partly there to bring out the flavours of the other herbs, and once I tried this dish without the root tea and it was a much poorer reflection on this lovely dish.
4. **Prepare the Filling:**
    - Heat the olive oil in a large skillet over medium heat.
    - Add the shallot and garlic, sautéing until they become translucent and fragrant. Don't you love that smell?
    - Add the sliced mushrooms, cooking until they release their moisture and start to brown. This step requires patience, much like the art of witchcraft itself. Cook slowly and stir in your thoughts of friends, smiles, laughter and love.
    - Add the chopped dandelion greens, cooking until they wilt. Remove from heat and let cool slightly.
5. **Add the Love:**
    - Cook slowly and stir in your thoughts of friends, smiles, laughter and love. Don't get so engrossed in your cooking to forget the most important ingredient. Baking is performed with love, it is a ceremony that brings love and care to others. This is a recipe for family happiness.
6. **Combine the Filling Ingredients:**
    - In a large bowl, whisk together the cooled marshmallow root tea, heavy cream, honey, eggs, vanilla extract, and dried lavender flowers.
    - Stir in the mushroom and dandelion green mixture.
    - Add the fresh thyme and crumbled feta cheese. Season with salt and pepper to taste.
7. **Assemble the Tart:**
    - Preheat your oven to 375°F (190°C).
    - Roll out the chilled dough on a floured surface to fit your tart pan.
    - Press the dough into the pan and trim any excess.
    - Pour the filling into the prepared crust, spreading it evenly.
8. **Bake and Serve:**
    - Bake the tart in the preheated oven for 30-35 minutes, or until the filling is set and the crust is golden brown.
    - Allow the tart to cool slightly before slicing and serving.

This Lavender Marshmallow Root, Mushroom, and Dandelion Greens Tart is a delightful fusion of floral, earthy, and slightly sweet flavours. It's more than a meal; it's a bridge to the past, a taste of the enchantment that has flavoured our family's lore. As you share it with others, may you feel the warmth and magic of generations of witches, guiding your culinary journey.

A Personal Tale of Wyrdwife's Tart

This is an extract from an article I wrote in the local paper last year, some of you may have seen it, if so apologies for repeating!

The festoon lights in the trees cast a warm colourful glow over the beer garden, creating an enchanting almost carnival atmosphere as we celebrated my friend Sam's birthday at our local pub, The Old Bell. Cheery conversations echoed around us, occasional explosive laughs, clinks of glasses and toasts, blending with the murmur of other customers enjoying the evening. The menu caught my eye, especially one dish: "Wyrdwife's Tart." My curiosity piqued, no procrastination, I ordered it immediately, wondering if it could match the version passed down through my family.

As the tart arrived, I felt a mix of excitement and nostalgia. One bite, and I knew, it was good, but slightly crest fallen as it lacked the depth, the essence of a true Wyrdwife's Tart, or at least one as good as my great, great grandmother had detailed in the leathery book of potions and spells we keep in the nook by the pantry. The memory of my mother's kitchen, filled with the aroma of herbs and the magic of my school days, washed over me. This tart, while pleasant, was a shadow of the original. I scowled.

That night, amidst the laughter and memories, a resolve formed. I would make a real Wyrdwife's Tart and bring it to the chef. I told my friends what I was going to do and they all agreed I should and toasted my success. Next morning though I regretted saying it out loud as now I actually had to go through with it and I'm pretty shy really. It's amazing what some liquid courage can do when with friends. Early the following Saturday morning, armed with my tart and a pouch of courage-inducing herbs in my bag, I walked down into the village and into the pub. The barmaid who must have been new glanced up, curious. "Can I see the chef?" I asked, my heart pounding. She hesitated but relented when I smiled and said, "Tell him the local witch is here to talk about his tart." Which of course could have been interpreted quite differently!

After a couple of minutes and still no sign of the chef I almost turned to retreat out the side door, but I stayed. Minutes felt like hours before the chef's head appeared around the kitchen swing door. Relief softened his expression when he saw me, vaguely recognising as our family is quite well known in the village, and no pointy hat or warts in sight. We sat at a small table by the dart board, the barmaid, Sonia, bringing three plates as I peeled of the metal foil and unveiled my tart, still warm from being cooked while the whole house had been asleep. The aroma, a blend of lavender, mushrooms, and earthy greens, filled the still air.

I sliced the tart, sharing it with them. No emotion at first and my heart skipped a beat, but then their eyes smiled. "How did you get these flavours?" the chef asked eyebrows raised, truly interested and I must say a bit surprised I think that this nutter who had just walked into his pub had made this. I shared the story of my great, great grandmother, our ancestors, her handwritten book (although I must admit I didn't say everything we know about the book we call Wren, but I have given more info elsewhere in the book), and the generations of wyrdwives who had perfected this recipe. His curiosity deepened with each word as although he had made his pie from a recipe he had never actually tasted one before then. He clearly loved his trade and was interested in food beyond it being a commercial exploit.

Before I knew it, I was supplying the pub with two Wyrdwife's Tarts a week. The chef's enthusiasm didn't stop there; he attended garden lectures at my house, eager to learn about the magical properties of the herbs. He even joined our fire torch walk, not just observing but really joining in. I can honestly say he has become a good friend. You see the power of good magic!

A casual evening out had turned into a new business venture. It reminded me of how witches, through the ages, have blended tradition with enterprise. My family's recipe, a symbol of resilience and wisdom, now had a new chapter, one that connected the past with the present in a most delicious way.

Each tart I bake carries the whispers of my ancestors, their hands guiding mine, their magic infusing every ingredient. It's more than just a tart; it's a bridge across time, a testament to the enduring power of our craft. Sharing this tart, both at the pub and with those who appreciate its history, brings a joy that is as deep as it is magical.

Puddings: Sweet Enchantments

Rosemary and Honey Panna Cotta

This creamy dessert is infused with the subtle flavours of rosemary and sweetened with honey. It's a light and refreshing way to end a meal, and it also happens to be a favourite of my son, George. Each year for his birthday, he asks and I prepare this dish, adapting the presentation to his current interests. This year, I've found some gargoyle molds that are sure to delight him, especially with a touch of raspberry and blackberry juice for a bit of scary colour. Preparing this panna cotta has become a funny family tradition.

Ingredients:

- 2 cups heavy cream
- 1 cup whole milk
- ½ cup honey
- 2 tablespoons fresh rosemary leaves
- 2 teaspoons gelatine powder
- ¼ cup cold water
- 2 tablespoons raspberry juice (optional, for colour)
- 2 tablespoons blackberry juice (optional, for colour)

Instructions:

1. **Infuse Cream:** In a saucepan, combine the heavy cream, milk, honey, and rosemary. Heat over medium heat until it just starts to simmer. Remove from heat and let the rosemary infuse for 30 minutes.
2. **Soften Gelatine:** In a small bowl, sprinkle the gelatine over the cold water and let it sit for about 5 minutes to soften.
3. **Strain and Reheat:** Strain the rosemary from the cream mixture and return the liquid to the saucepan. Reheat gently until warm.
4. **Dissolve Gelatine:** Add the softened gelatine to the warm cream mixture and stir until completely dissolved.
5. **Add Colour (Optional):** Stir in the very smallest amount of raspberry and blackberry juices, just more than a pinch, if you wish to add a bit of colour to the panna cotta.
6. **Pour into Molds:** Divide the mixture among ramekins or fun molds. For George's birthday, I'm using gargoyle molds. Refrigerate for at least 4 hours, or until set.
7. **Serve:** To unmold, dip the bottom of the molds briefly in hot water, then invert onto plates. Drizzle with additional honey and garnish with a sprig of rosemary.

A Family Tradition: Birthday Panna Cotta

Preparing Rosemary and Honey Panna Cotta for my son George's birthday has become a new tradition in our family. Every year, I spend ages trawling the internet for new and creative molds that will make him laugh or groan. When he was younger, we used Thomas the Tank Engine molds, and they were always a hit at his birthday parties. This year I found some fantastic gargoyle molds that will add a bit of fun and giggles to the dessert.

George's Special Birthday Panna Cotta: To add a special touch for George's birthday, I've decided to incorporate a little raspberry and blackberry juice into the panna cotta mixture this year. This will give the gargoyle shapes a hint of colour, making them look even more magical and appealing. He loves anything that looks a bit mysterious and spooky, and these garnishes will be perfect for his party. One of the gargoyles is picking his nose, so I have a small green round sweet candy to insert in the desired place!

While I have elegant moon and stars molds for dinner parties, birthdays are all about fun and creativity. The gargoyle molds I found this year are particularly exciting, and I can't wait to see George's face when he sees them.

Celebrating with Sweets

A birthday isn't complete without a selection of candies and sweets to complement the panna cotta. Here are some of George's favourites that we'll be serving at his party:

Homemade Honeycomb Toffee: This crunchy, sweet treat pairs wonderfully with the creamy panna cotta. The kids love the bubbly texture and the rich, caramelized flavour.

Fruit Gummies: Made from real fruit juice, these colourful gummies are a healthier alternative to store-bought candies. They come in fun shapes and vibrant colours, making them a hit with the kids.

Chocolate Frogs: Inspired by George's love for mythical creatures and harry potter, these chocolate frogs add a whimsical touch to the dessert table. They're filled with creamy ganache, providing a delightful surprise with each bite.

Candied Citrus Peels: These sweet and tangy treats add a burst of flavour and a pop of colour. They are also a wonderful complement to the panna cotta, balancing its creamy sweetness with their zesty punch.

A Special Birthday Celebration

As I prepare for George's birthday, the kitchen fills with the fragrant aroma of rosemary and honey. Bunnworth (Bunny), our golden retriever, lounges nearby, always hopeful for a dropped morsel. The process of making panna cotta is soothing and meditative, reminding me of the simple joys of life and the magic of creating something special for my loved ones. I always open the windows and listen to the birds in the garden at this time of year.

When the molds are finally set and it's time to unmold the panna cotta, the excitement builds. The gargoyle shapes turn out perfectly, their eerie details accentuated by the subtle hues from the berry juices. Arranged on a platter and drizzled with a touch of honey, they look both delicious and fantastical.

George's face lights up when he sees his birthday panna cotta, and the joy and wonder in his eyes make all the effort worthwhile. Serving the panna cotta alongside his favourite sweets, we gather around to celebrate, sharing stories, giggles, and the delightful flavours of this special dessert.

The magic in cooking isn't really about the food at all it's about making memories and creating new or continuing traditions that connect us to our past and future. Each spoonful of Rosemary and Honey Panna Cotta is a testament to the love and care that goes into making something truly special. For George's birthday, and for every occasion, it's the perfect way to add a touch of enchantment to our celebrations.

Combining Magical Flavours

Creating magic in the kitchen isn't just about individual ingredients; it's about the harmonious combinations that elevate your baking to new heights. Here are a few of my favourite magical flavour pairings:

- **Basil and Lemon:** The bright, peppery notes of basil combined with the citrusy zing of lemon create a refreshing and uplifting flavour, perfect for summer cakes and cookies.
- **Lavender and Honey:** This soothing duo brings a delicate sweetness and floral aroma to scones, shortbread, and even ice creams, offering a calming treat.
- **Almonds and Cherries:** The sweet, nutty flavour of almonds pairs beautifully with the tartness of cherries, creating a classic combination in cakes, cookies, and tarts.
- **Walnuts and Cinnamon:** This warm, comforting blend is perfect for autumnal baking, adding a cozy, nostalgic flavour to breads, muffins, and pies.
- **Chanterelles and Thyme:** The delicate, peppery chanterelles with the earthy, aromatic thyme create a sophisticated and savoury combination, ideal for quiches and savoury pastries.
- **Porcini and Rosemary:** The robust, nutty flavour of porcini mushrooms combined with the piney notes of rosemary makes for a hearty and grounding flavour, perfect for savoury breads and rolls.

Storing Your Magical Ingredients

Proper storage is essential to preserve the magical properties and flavours of your ingredients:

- **Herbs:** Keep dried herbs in airtight containers away from light and heat. Fresh herbs can be stored in the refrigerator, wrapped in a damp paper towel.
- **Nuts:** Store nuts in airtight containers in a cool, dry place. For extended freshness, refrigerate or freeze them.
- **Mushrooms:** Fresh mushrooms should be stored in a paper bag in the refrigerator. Dried mushrooms should be kept in airtight containers in a cool, dark place.

In The Witches Kitchen Bakery, every ingredient tells a story and brings its own magic to our baked goods. By understanding the unique properties and flavours of herbs, nuts, and mushrooms, and combining them with care, you can create enchanting treats that delight the senses and nourish the soul. Happy baking, and may your kitchen be filled with magic and joy!

"Desolata flos flammae cupiditatis, tua essentia susurravit arcana amoris nunc amissi"

"Forlorn blossom of passion's flame, thy essence murmured secrets of love now lost"

Chapter 8: Silphium

Our cottage garden is nestled between rolling hills in a small valley of well-drained, acidic sandy soil with odd patches of loamy soil in trenches. It's a treasure trove of surprises. Each season, it bursts forth with an array of unexpected plants that we never sowed, springing to life and adding to the garden's enchanting diversity. Many of these plants evoke the flavours and aromas of the Mediterranean, far more than one might expect in this little corner of Surrey.

I often ponder the origins of these unexpected guests and feel a deep connection to the history beneath my feet. It is likely that these plants, or wild incarnations of them, were introduced by the Romans themselves, who settled here during the Roman Warm Period in England. This remarkable era, from approximately 250 BC to AD 400, was characterised by a climate much warmer than what we experience today, albeit we may be getting closer to what it was then. Such favourable conditions allowed for the cultivation of a variety of Mediterranean plants, leading to a time of flourishing vineyards and meticulously tended cottage gardens.

Looking out my study window where I'm sitting writing this book, I can almost see the Roman hands that once worked this land, planting seeds and nurturing vines under the warm sun. Our property, which we know sits on what was once part of a Roman estate, offers tangible evidence of its rich past. We have unearthed fragments of pottery and remnants of ancient vineyards while turning over the soil, each piece whispering tales of a bygone era. My daughter has delighted in finding Roman beads and occasionally little stone tiles from mosaics which she uses to make her own little mosaic pictures.

I feel a profound sense of stewardship as I care for this garden, knowing it is steeped in such deep history. The very act of planting, tending, and harvesting connects me to those ancient gardeners, making me a part of a continuous lineage of caretakers of this land. The unexpected plants that emerge are more than just botanical curiosities; they are living legacies of a time when Romans walked these grounds, infusing their practices with both practicality and magic. Sometimes we forget that The Romans had quite the fascination with magic and witches, and their beliefs were woven into the very fabric of their daily lives.

Imagine living in a world where the supernatural was an accepted part of everyday life. The Romans were highly superstitious folks, believing that magic could touch every aspect of existence, from health and success to love and revenge. They saw magic as a double-edged sword, with "white" magic offering protection and healing through amulets and charms, while "black" magic dealt with curses and spells meant to harm others. It was like living with an ancient version of good and bad vibes.

Now, the Romans didn't just leave these beliefs at the door. They had laws specifically targeting magical practices. The Law of the Twelve Tables, which is one of the oldest pieces of Roman legislation, actually banned spells that harmed crops, livestock, or people. If someone was caught practicing harmful magic, it was no small matter and they could be executed, often in gruesome ways like being burned or buried alive.

Roman literature is filled with eerie depictions of witches. These weren't the charming, enchanting types you might find in Greek stories like Circe. Roman witches were portrayed as terrifying old crones with wild hair, long nails, and pale skin, performing dark rituals under the full moon. Take Erichtho from Lucan's "Pharsalia," for instance. She was depicted as so fearsome that she desecrated corpses and even terrorized the dead, quite the horror story character! Unfortunately us witches have been persecuted through every society. People fear what they don't understand, which is one reason I'm writing this book, to help more people understand that being a green witch is about caring for nature, animals and people. Although see me on a Sunday morning after a night out the day before and you might see a scary picture of wild hair, pale skin and bloodshot eyes!

But here's the twist: despite all the fear and legal restrictions, in Roman times magic was everywhere. People from all walks of life sought out magicians and witches for everything from love potions to healing remedies. Women, in particular, would use curse tablets to deal with romantic rivals or other personal grievances.

In essence, the Romans' relationship with magic and witches was complex and deeply rooted in their culture. They feared it, legislated against it, yet also relied on it to navigate the trials of daily life. They were particularly obsessed when it came to matters of the heart and were big believers in the power of love potions and aphrodisiacs. They thought that these magical concoctions could spark desire, reignite passion, or even win over an unrequited love. The ingredients for these potions were often sourced from nature, utilizing herbs, roots, and other natural substances believed to hold magical properties.

Roman love potions were a blend of various ingredients, each believed to possess unique properties that could influence love and desire. For instance, they used herbs like **parsley, fennel, and dill**, which were believed to arouse affection and stimulate love. These potions weren't just haphazard mixes; they were carefully crafted recipes, often passed down through generations or shared among trusted circles.

Imagine this: a Roman woman, desperate to win the heart of a stoic senator, might visit a local wise woman or witch. She'd be given a potion, a mix of fragrant herbs, perhaps a bit of honey for sweetness, and some rare roots, all thought to kindle love. She'd slip it into his wine, hoping that the magical blend would warm his heart and turn his affections towards her.

Aphrodisiacs were another realm of magic the Romans dabbled in, aiming to enhance sexual desire and performance. Honey, garlic, and certain fish like the mullet were commonly used, believed to have properties that would boost libido and enhance pleasure. The idea was that consuming these foods would not only stir physical desire but also create an aura of irresistible allure around the person.

For example, honey was often referred to as "the nectar of the gods" and was used in various love elixirs. Romans believed that its sweet, rich taste could symbolize the sweetness of love and its ability to attract love just like bees to a flower.

Love potions and aphrodisiacs weren't just about personal desire; they played a crucial role in the social and cultural fabric of Roman life. Marriages, alliances, and social standings could all hinge on the affections and desires of individuals. In a world where social connections were paramount, having a little magical assistance in matters of love was seen as a valuable tool and us witches provided that.

Romans often sought out witches and herbalists who were skilled in creating these potions. These practitioners were respected for their knowledge of herbs and the natural world, even though they might be feared for their power. The use of love magic was a blend of both reverence and practicality. For women, especially, who had limited power in a patriarchal society, these potions could be a way to exert influence and control over their romantic and social situations.

These days, where so much is transient and fleeting, for me this old Roman garden remains a constant, a bridge to the past and a testament to the enduring bond between people and the earth. Each plant, each flower, and each leaf is a reminder of the rich history that our cottage garden embodies. It is a sanctuary where the past and present coexist, and where every discovery, from a delicate herb to a shard of ancient pottery, deepens my appreciation for this sacred space.

One of the most intriguing discoveries in our garden's history involves my great-grandmother, a wise woman with a deep connection to the land. She found a herb that bore a striking resemblance to Giant Fennel but had distinct differences that set it apart. Despite extensive research and consultation with botanists and herbalists, we have not been able to identify this plant definitively. Yet, it shares many characteristics with the legendary Silphium, a plant that was once more valuable than gold in the ancient world.

Silphium, was revered for its myriad uses. Pliny the Elder, the renowned Roman author and naturalist, documented Silphium extensively in his encyclopaedic work, *Natural History*. He described it as a plant of great importance, utilised for its medicinal properties and culinary applications. According to Pliny, Silphium was a cure-all, effective in treating ailments ranging from coughs and sore throats to digestive disorders and wounds. Its resin, known as laserpicium, was particularly prized.

Other ancient writers also extolled the virtues of Silphium. The Greek physician Hippocrates mentioned its use in various medical treatments, highlighting its potency and versatility. The poet Catullus praised it in his verses, illustrating its cultural significance and widespread appeal. The plant's distinct appearance, with its thick stalk, large leaves, and golden flowers, made it easily recognizable.

Silphium was famed in the ancient world for its remarkable dual properties as both an aphrodisiac and a contraceptive, cementing its association with sexuality and love. The heart-shaped seeds of Silphium, which became a symbol of romantic and erotic love, were often exchanged by lovers as tokens of affection and desire. The resin extracted from Silphium, was believed to enhance sexual pleasure and increase libido when consumed. Ancient texts, including those by Soranus of Ephesus, a prominent Greek physician, describe how the resin was used to stir passion and desire, making it a sought-after ingredient in love potions and erotic preparations.

In addition to its aphrodisiac properties, Silphium was also renowned for its contraceptive effects, a paradoxical yet complementary aspect of its usage. Women in ancient Rome and Greece considered Silphium a very reliable method of birth control. Historical records suggest that small doses of the resin could prevent pregnancy, providing women with a rare means of controlling their reproductive health in an era with few contraceptive options. The plant's effectiveness in this regard made it invaluable and further entrenched its status as a symbol of both sexual freedom and responsible love.

As I potter around my garden, nurturing the plants and reflecting on their history, I am struck by the personal freedom and empowerment Silphium must have provided women in Roman times. Just as the birth control pill revolutionised women's lives in the swinging 1960s, granting them control over their reproductive health and enabling a more liberated approach to sexuality, Silphium offered similar freedoms to ancient women. Imagine the relief and confidence it must have brought, allowing women to enjoy intimate relationships without the constant fear of unintended pregnancies. This sense of control over their own bodies and choices must have been empowering, enabling them to engage in relationships with a newfound sense of autonomy.

For women in Roman times therefore, Silphium was not just a medicinal herb but a symbol of personal freedom. The ability to use Silphium as both an aphrodisiac and a reliable method of birth control was simply revolutionary.

The heart-shaped seeds of Silphium played a pivotal role in cementing the heart as a universal symbol of love. In ancient times, the exchange of Silphium seeds between lovers was not just a romantic gesture but a profound expression of affection and mutual commitment, and sometimes it seems, simply, lust. These seeds, with their distinctive heart-like shape, naturally came to symbolize the emotions they were meant to convey. As the practice of giving Silphium seeds as tokens of love spread, so did the association of the heart shape with romantic love. This tradition transcended its botanical origins and became embedded in our cultural consciousness, eventually leading to the heart symbol we recognise today.

The enduring association of the heart with love is also immortalized in literature, notably in the 13th-century French poem "Le Roman de la Poire" (The Romance of the Pear) by Thibaut. In this allegorical poem, the author explores themes of courtly love, and it is one of the earliest literary works to depict the heart as a symbol of romantic affection. The poem illustrates a lover presenting his beloved with a heart-shaped pear, mirroring the ancient practice of giving heart-shaped Silphium seeds. This literary work, along with other medieval texts, played a crucial role in popularizing the heart as a symbol of love, weaving together botanical traditions, cultural practices, and artistic expressions into the rich romantic symbolism that has endured through the ages. The legacy of Silphium thus continues to resonate, linking the past with the present in the universal language of love.

Is what we have in our garden Silphium? Is its sap or resin as strong as the ancient version? I can't tell. If I could then I would indeed already be a millionaire. I have researched all I can find on Silphium, as a journalist I love a good story, and this has it all. Love, passion, intrigue, and mystery! As the mystery is that the herb has disappeared, extinct I doubt but lost; definitely.

The extinction of Silphium is one of history's great botanical mysteries, with several theories suggesting why this once-ubiquitous plant disappeared. One of the most widely accepted reasons is overharvesting. Silphium was highly prized in the ancient world for its myriad uses, from medicine and cuisine to its role as an aphrodisiac and contraceptive. The demand for Silphium was so great that it quickly became a valuable commodity, even appearing on coinage in Rome and Greece; so precious that Roman Emperors hoarded it in their treasuries along with jewels, silver and gold. As a result, it was harvested extensively and without sustainable practices, leading to its depletion. Ancient texts, including those by Pliny the Elder, hint at the plant's overexploitation. The intensive harvesting practices likely exhausted the natural populations of Silphium, contributing to its eventual disappearance.

Another possible contributing factor to Silphium's extinction was the difficulties of it being cultivated successfully outside its native habitat in the Cyrenaica region of present-day Libya. Believed to have first appeared at The Gardens of the Hesperides, which in Greek mythology, are the mythical gardens belonging to the Hesperides, nymphs who were the daughters of the night (Nyx) or of the evening (Erebus). The plant thrived in the specific soil conditions and climate of the Cyrenaican plateau, characterized by well-drained sandy loam and very British-esq seasonal rain. Efforts to grow Silphium in other regions, both within and beyond the Roman Empire, had been said to be difficult to maintain without the right soil and weather conditions. The combination of overharvesting and the plant's strict habitat requirements meant that once the natural populations were depleted, there was no viable way to replenish them. Additionally, changing climatic conditions and land use practices over the centuries may have further impacted the delicate balance needed for Silphium to flourish. These factors together likely sealed the fate of this legendary herb, leading to its extinction and leaving only its storied legacy behind.

There is also science, and It's not just those of us who are excited by its powers in witchcraft or herbology, even the botanists at The Royal Botanic Gardens, Kew have been studying this lost herb and the conditions it may have needed to grow. It is possible that the plant was a hybrid between two different species of Giant Fennel, so it may have reproduced asexually, meaning they would have trouble growing from seed, perhaps only spreading by the root system. Some plant species, particularly hybrids, only propagate from their root systems rather than from seeds. This vegetative reproduction ensures genetic consistency, as the offspring are clones of the parent plant. One notable example is the hybrid fennel (*Foeniculum vulgare*), which, like many perennial herbs, spreads primarily through its roots. This method allows the plant to maintain its unique characteristics, which might not be preserved if propagated through seeds.

In contrast, certain plant seeds have remarkable longevity, capable of lying dormant for centuries until the right conditions trigger their germination. This phenomenon, known as seed dormancy, allows plants to survive through adverse conditions, waiting for optimal moisture, temperature, and light. For example, the Judean date palm (*Phoenix dactylifera*), whose seeds have been found to germinate after being dormant for over 2,000 years. These seeds were discovered in archaeological sites and successfully sprouted when provided with suitable conditions. Such longevity demonstrates the incredible resilience and adaptive strategies of plants, allowing them to endure and thrive across millennia.

So, could some roots from the Cyrenaican plateau have found their way here to this old Roman garden? Certainly the combination of well-drained soils and the moderate climate of the Libyan plateau created ideal conditions for growing grapes and was recognised within the Greek and Roman empires as a producer of some of the finest wines, so perhaps a few Silphium roots snuck into the vines transported to this little part of Surrey, or did our Roman friends purposely bring Silphium with them, as certainly many tried (mostly unsuccessfully) to cultivate it in different parts of the Roman Empire. Or have the conditions only become just right for dormant seeds to germinate again? Either way we have a herb here that is rather unique.

My great-grandmother originally thought this plant was an annoying weed, but now it has become a cornerstone of our herbal alchemy practices. Its tall, sturdy stalks and delicate, feathery leaves exude a unique energy that feels both ancient and potent. Though it resembles Giant Fennel, there is something otherworldly about it, something that speaks to the deep history and magic of the land.

In my garden, extracting, drying, and preparing the sap of what we want to believe to be Silphium or derivative of it, has been a journey of experimentation. Inspired by the detailed accounts of Dioscorides, Pliny the Elder, and Theophrastus, I meticulously follow the ancient methods described in their texts to preserve the authenticity and potency of this legendary herb. Their works, "De Materia Medica," "Natural History," and "Enquiry into Plants," respectively, provide invaluable guidance on harvesting and processing Silphium, but modern gardening inevitably introduces new challenges and learning opportunities.

Pliny the Elder says that the juices of this plant were collected in two different ways, either from the root or from the stalk; the consequence of which these two varieties of the juice were known by the distinguishing names of "rhizias" and "caulias." To extract the sap, I start by carefully making an incision in the tuber at the base of the stalk allowing the sap to ooze out naturally. Dioscorides emphasizes the importance of timing and precision, and I have found that this advice is crucial. Firstly I thought, like some plants, that the sap would flow best when the plants were in transition, so I tried just before they began to flower, nada, nothing! I was really struggling to find the right part of the season to extract the sap and getting frustrated. Early attempts in the wrong season resulted in dismal "clumpy" sap production. Then I re-read the text written by Pliny the Elder who may have been suggesting harvesting at the "falling at the rising of the Dog-star, when the south winds begin to prevail" which I thought might be referring to the prospect of falling of leaves indicating the beginning of a plant's senescence, a period when the plant starts to shed its leaves, often due to changes in temperature and daylight, which in some agricultural contexts, particularly before the full understanding of seasons as we do today, the timing of leaf fall or plant senescence could signal the right time for harvesting certain crops. In other crops like Grapes senescence of the leaves was the first indication that the grapes have ripened fully or potatoes which are typically ready to harvest when the vines have died back completely. This indicates that the tubers have reached full maturity and the skins have hardened, which helps in storage. That with trial and error, I harvest around mid-July to early August, coinciding with the heliacal rising of Sirius or the falling at the rising of the Dog-star. I can now get a good mixing bowl full, whereas I started with a teacup!

I wasn't sure why at first, but there were a number of references of Silphium sap being mixed with bran so I tried it. I discovered that this process promotes fermentation, which not only preserves the sap but enhances its medicinal properties. The beneficial microorganisms developed during fermentation modify the sap's flavour and consistency, making it more palatable and I think more effective.

Bran also plays a crucial role in absorbing excess moisture from the sap, stabilizing it. I have found that this absorption ensures the sap remains potent over longer periods. Additionally, bran helps distribute the sap's active compounds evenly and consistently.

Regularly shaking the mixture is another important step. This prevents the sap from settling and separating, maintaining a uniform consistency and ensuring even maturation. It also helps prevent the growth of mould or other unwanted microorganisms on the surface.

I typically use wheat or barley bran as their fibrous and absorbent nature seems to work best. By adopting this method, my Silphium sap remains effective and easy to store.

Pliny the Elder's "Natural History" guides me in the purification and storage of the dried resin. According to Pliny, the resin must be purified by removing any impurities or foreign matter, which can be done by gentle sieving and sorting. Initially, my attempts at purification were labour-intensive and not very effective due to my inexperience. Over time, I developed a more efficient sieving process that ensures a higher quality of purified resin. I admit I use an old pair of tights (panty hose) to sieve the resin. The consistency reminds me of globby paint so after some research how people strain paint, I tried this and it worked so much better than cheesecloth or wire mesh or anything else I tried.

Following Theophrastus' advice in "Enquiry into Plants," I allow the sap mix to air dry. This process is crucial for preserving its medicinal properties. The sap mix or cake is spread thinly on a clean, flat surface and left to dry in a shaded, well-ventilated area. Early in my practice, I made the mistake of drying the sap in direct sunlight (or as much sunlight as we have in England) as I was in too much of a hurry and I had to learn patience, as it caused it to dry too quickly, crack and lose some of its potent qualities. Adjusting to Theophrastus' method of air drying in the shade, under some pine trees in the corner of the garden has made a significant difference. The sap now dries evenly, forming a resin known as laserpicium, which is then carefully scraped off and stored in airtight containers to preserve its potency and prevent it from absorbing moisture.

In my practice, Silphium has proven incredibly versatile, yet not without its challenges. The seeds (some round and some heart shaped) are perfect for adorning protective amulets, to ward off negative energies and bring good fortune. However, germinating these seeds has been difficult. Despite following ancient practices, modern environmental conditions differ, and most seeds have failed to sprout. This challenge has again taught me the importance of patience and accepting failure is a part of learning. By experimenting with different soil compositions and watering schedules, I've begun to see more consistent results. What seems to work best is turning over the soil in the winter so it's really ragged and broken and full of divots and scattering the seeds over this really higgledy-piggledy earth. They seem to like broken earth a bit like poppies, where light and moisture can get into the nooks and crannies.

The golden yellow leaves, known as "maspetum" look very much like Parsley, rich in medicinal properties, are used in healing potions and salves, offering relief from various ailments. One of the most rewarding aspects of using Silphium leaves has been the development of a healing salve that works wonders on minor wounds and skin irritations. Early batches were either too greasy or not potent enough, but through refining the recipe and adjusting the ratio of ingredients and adding some lavender oil, I've created a product that is both effective and pleasant to use. It must be said the smell of Silphium flowers, leaves and sap is definitely not my favourite, so adding some sweeter smelling ingredients really helps. Feedback from family and friends has been invaluable in perfecting this salve and is perfect for those grazed knees when the kids get back from playing football.

The roots, when dried and ground, make a powerful addition to incense blends to enhance psychic abilities and promote spiritual clarity. Initially, drying and grinding the roots was a laborious process, with inconsistent results. I learned that slicing the roots into really thin pieces, like crisps, before drying them ensures a more uniform and quicker drying process. Once properly dried, the roots are easier to grind into a fine powder, making them ideal for use in incense blends.

Of course, the greatest use is the one that made this herb the superstar of its day. Does it work? Oh my....

I had to think long and hard about whether to discuss how I use Silphium as an aphrodisiac, whether in my potions, mixed with wine, or more broadly in my practice. This isn't just a question of health, but also of ethics. It may not be wise to delve into details that could encourage others to rely on it, and that's not something I want to happen. Experiment, yes, but don't depend on it. If I explain my own methods, someone might misinterpret it as a recommendation, which it isn't!

For transparency, I must admit: I'm not entirely certain what's growing in my garden. Just because I want to believe it's Silphium doesn't mean it truly is. What I *do* know is that this herb, whatever it is, is rare and exhibits remarkable properties that may be similar. Therefore, I've chosen to share only what's already available through research or personal experimentation.

Why? Because if any of you happen to come across it, or think you have, it's definitely worth exploring. I don't believe Silphium is truly extinct, more likely it disappeared from one known geographical area, and it was simply overlooked or misidentified elsewhere. It's even possible that someone could sell it to you. I've seen at least two websites claiming to do just that.

However, never use any herb unless you're absolutely sure of its identity. If in doubt, steer clear. And be especially cautious not to confuse it with Giant Fennel, as that's *not* Silphium. I once had a well-meaning neighbour, a knowledgeable gardener, who pointed out what he thought was wild Fennel. It was clearly Hemlock, deadly poisonous.

So, don't just take anyone's word for it. Do your own research, always.

Warning: what I will say is don't use in a bowl of punch at a summer party. I speak from experience.

ἐν Κυρήνῃ δὲ χρῶνται πολὺ τῷ σίλφιον καὶ πρὸς ὄψα καὶ πρὸς τὰς ἄλλας κατασκευάς, καὶ τῷ οἴνῳ παρατίθεται τὴν ἰδιάζουσαν γεῦσιν διδόν.

Athenaeus' "Deipnosophistae":

Book III, Chapter 100: Athenaeus "In Cyrene, they frequently use Silphium in their cooking and as a condiment in their wines, its unique flavour lending a distinctive taste to their meals and drinks."

Ancient Poetry and Literature:

The Roman poet Catullus, in his Carmina (poems), also alludes to the romantic and sensual uses of Silphium. References the herb in the context of love and romance suggesting its association with enhancing sexual desire.

Quaeris quot mihi basiationes tuae, Lesbia, sint satis superque. quam magnus numerus Libyssae harenae lasarpiciferis iacet Cyrenis oraclum Iovis inter aestuosi et Batti veteris sacrum sepulcrum; aut quam sidera multa, cum tacet nox, furtiuos hominum vident amores: tam te basia multa basiare vesano satis et super Catullo est, quae nec pernumerare curiosi possint nec mala fascinare lingua.

You ask how many of your kisses, Lesbia, are enough and more than enough for me. As great a number as the Libyan sands that lie on silphium-bearing Cyrene between the oracle of sweltering Jupiter and the sacred tomb of old Battus; or as many as the stars, when night is silent, that see the secret loves of men: to kiss you so many kisses is enough and more than enough for mad Catullus, kisses which neither the curious can count nor an evil tongue can curse.

One of the greatest lessons I've learned in this journey is the importance of aligning with the natural rhythms of the garden and the plant itself. By observing the life cycle of Silphium and adjusting my practices to match its needs, I've been able to extract and prepare the sap more effectively. Each season brings new insights, and with each passing year, my connection to this ancient herb deepens.

Despite the challenges, the process of cultivating and using Silphium has been incredibly fulfilling. It has taught me the value of patience, adaptation, and respect for the wisdom of the ancients. The mistakes I've made along the way have been valuable learning experiences, guiding me toward better techniques and greater understanding. It also reminds me of the knowledge we have misplaced, maybe lost, but absolutely possible to rediscover. Today if it's not on google then it gets ignored. To the everyday Romans or Cyrenaicans the knowledge of how to extract, purify and use Silphium was a common knowledge that I am having to painfully re-learn. I recently had the privilege to visit the magnificent library at The Royal Botanical Gardens at Kew for a meeting about Silphium. This is truly a modern wonder of the world. So much knowledge on plants and herbs that is nowhere to be found on the internet. I could have camped there for a week! I heard once, and I can't say that it's true, but that the internet has revolutionised "access", but that revolution is to only 2% of the knowledge we have, and then we build our future knowledge or discoveries on that little bit and utilise AI again sits on top of just that little bit to generate new learnings, but it's not based on the breadth of human knowledge. So much knowledge about how plants and herbs can be used to benefit us was in the heads of witches, that if only we had their observations who knows what ill we might cure, or what discovery we might make. There is a strong link between the medicine we today call science and the chemistry or properties of plants and the effect they have on us. Some we can re-learn, but there is also so much to re-discover and with the modern tools around us, take further. Ok that's me jumping off my hobby horse.

I encourage you to explore the ancient plants that might be growing in your own garden or local area. Don't pull up the plants you don't at first recognise. Investigate their histories, their uses, and their magical properties. You may find, as I have, that these plants hold secrets and stories that can enrich your practice and deepen your connection to the earth.

As we delve deeper into the mysteries of Herbal Alchemy, let us honour the past and embrace the wisdom it offers. Whether it's through the discovery of a rare herb like Silphium or the cultivation of common garden plants, there is magic to be found in the natural world. It's up to us, the modern witches, to uncover and harness that magic, weaving it into our daily lives and spiritual practices.

Silphium, with its elusive nature and rich history, serves as a powerful reminder of the magic that surrounds us, waiting to be discovered and revered. So, let us continue our journey with open hearts and curious minds, ever ready to embrace the enchantment of Herbal Alchemy.

I don't know if you have ever tried writing a book, but if your anything like me you'll re-read, rephrase and spot things you have missed a million times. Writing this book hasn't exactly been easy but writing it was easier than trying to edit the blooming thing! Every time I re-read there is a section to add or re-word. So, as I sit here tapping away trying to edit the book, I can see a big splurge in my notes I forgot. Oops! Sheep and Goats!

First off, history tells that sheep and goats munching on Silphium often ended up in a rather comical state. Imagine your flock looking like they've had a bit too much of a herbal nightcap, sleepy and content. The potent compounds in Silphium are documented as having sedative properties, turning these usually active creatures into the animal kingdom's version of sleepyheads or teenagers. Ancient herders must have had their hands full, ensuring their flocks didn't overindulge and end up needing a nap halfway through grazing!

Not only that, but these Silphium-snacking sheep and goats had another quirk, they sneezed a lot. Picture this: a field of sheep, full bellied, dozing where they stood, noses twitching, and sneezing in unison, waking with a start! The aromatic compounds in the plant, while beneficial in moderation, could irritate their respiratory systems. This was a clear sign to herders that their animals had found a Silphium patch and were having a grand old time.

Now, let's get to the meat of the story, literally. Just like today's Wagyu beef is revered for its rich marbling and flavour, Silphium-fed livestock produced meat that was the culinary star of ancient times. The essential oils and aromatic compounds from Silphium were absorbed into the animals' tissues, imparting a unique and highly prized flavour. This wasn't just any meat; it was the ancient equivalent of a gourmet delight and delicacy.

Beyond flavour, the meat was exceptionally tender, much like how Wagyu beef practically melts in your mouth. The plant's compounds likely influenced muscle development and fat distribution in the animals, making their meat not only tastier but also more succulent. No wonder ancient markets had high demand for this luxurious meat!

Balancing the benefits of Silphium with its challenges required ancient herders to be quite the savvy managers. They had to ensure their flocks didn't overconsume this magical plant, which could lead to health issues and, more importantly, deplete the valuable Silphium resources.

The relationship between livestock and Silphium extended far beyond agriculture, weaving into the economic and cultural fabric of ancient societies. The enhanced meat quality from Silphium-fed animals boosted their market value, contributing to the economic prosperity of regions where the plant was abundant. Imagine a marketplace buzzing with excitement over the latest batch of Silphium-fed lamb, a gastronomic event of epic proportions!

Ancient practices like those involving Silphium remind us of the importance of balancing modern advancements with traditional wisdom. It's like rediscovering a lost recipe from a time when culinary and medicinal practices were deeply intertwined.

So why is this bit on Sheep and Goats important, apart from it being another clue to why the Silphium crop was over harvested and over grazed. Observing how wildlife uses your garden as their fridge or pantry can give you clues to the value of plants in the natural world. Animals possess thousands of years of knowledge encoded in their DNA, something we can learn from. So, next time you spot a dozy, sneezy goat, take a moment to see where it's been eating, you might just discover a treasure trove of natural remedies or culinary delights.

"Mihti vastis the phuvvarres, To grimoire jekhto stedi akanas. Te ares kathe, vastem shuden, Nane thovis buter, te katarre distaven. Te djiuva leski mihti feri jekht, Kathe grimoire stedi o domovoj kher"

"By the power of earth and stone, This grimoire's place is here alone. Bound to this house, its spirit tied, Never to be removed, only within destroyed. May its magic flourish and never roam, For this book is bound to home"

Chapter 9: Witchcraft Essentials

Before we dive into the details of making potions, I think it's really important to first get a sense of how everything in witchcraft fits together, spells, potions, smudges, and all that good stuff. Witchcraft is like this vast, beautiful world, full of different practices and terms, each with its own purpose and method. And it helps to know where potions fit into the bigger picture.

In my own journey, I've discovered that enchantments and potions have their own roles, but they're definitely connected. Enchantments, for example, are all about giving objects power, like charging up an amulet, talisman, or even something ordinary to bring luck, protection, or success. It's like you're infusing an object with a magical boost. Potions, though, are different. They're actual liquid mixtures made from herbs, plants, and other ingredients, and you can drink them, apply them to your skin, or use them in baths, depending on what you want to achieve. While enchantments bring magic into objects, potions work through the magic of their ingredients, coming to life when they're used.

Potions and spells also work in harmony. A spell is basically a ritual or a set of words that you say to bring about a certain result. Spells often include candles, herbs, crystals, and specific timings, sometimes based on moon phases. Potions can play a part in a spell, but they stand on their own too. Like, if I'm working on a love spell, I might brew a love potion to give it that extra push. It's like layering magic to really make things happen.

Smudging is another practice that ties into potion-making, but in its own unique way. Smudging is all about burning herbs, like sage, to cleanse a space or person of negative energy. While smudging uses the smoke from burning herbs, potions rely on infusing those herbs into liquid. Both are drawing on the power of herbs, but in different forms, like smoke for smudging, liquid for potions.

And then there's incantations, those magical words or chants that are often woven into spells and rituals. When I'm brewing a potion, I might use an incantation to give it an extra charge. But incantations aren't potions, they're more like a verbal tool that complements the physical magic of potions.

The way these different practices fit together is important as many get confused. Each one, whether it's enchanting something, casting a spell, brewing a potion, smudging, or using an incantation, brings its own kind of magic. They work together, making the whole experience richer and more powerful. It's like putting together a recipe where each ingredient adds its own flavour, but together they create something far greater.

For me, understanding how all these pieces fit together has deepened my connection to witchcraft, making it more holistic, meaningful, and, honestly, even more magical.

The Importance of Incantations in Spells and Potions

Incantations, the carefully chosen words or phrases spoken during spellcasting or potion-making, hold a significant place in the realm of magic. These verbal expressions are more than mere utterances; they channel energy, focus intent, and invoke the desired effects of the spell or potion.

Incantations have been integral to magical practices across cultures and eras. In ancient civilizations, such as Egypt and Mesopotamia, priests and magicians used incantations as part of their rituals to invoke gods, spirits, or natural forces. The "Egyptian Book of the Dead," a collection of spells and incantations, was used to guide the deceased through the afterlife, showcasing the deep-rooted belief in the power of words.

Similarly, in medieval Europe, incantations were a cornerstone of witchcraft and alchemy. Grimoires, books containing magical knowledge, spells, and incantations, were highly prized. The "Key of Solomon," one of the most influential grimoires, includes numerous incantations for summoning spirits and achieving magical results. These historical examples highlight the long-standing tradition of using incantations to amplify the efficacy of spells and potions.

One of the primary reasons incantations are crucial in magic is their role in amplifying the caster's intent. Magic is often about directing one's will and energy towards a specific goal. Incantations serve as a tool to focus and clarify this intent. By verbalizing their desire, the practitioner channels their thoughts and emotions more effectively, making the spell or potion more potent.

For example, in the Harry Potter series by J.K. Rowling, incantations are an essential part of spellcasting. The spell "Expecto Patronum" requires the caster to concentrate on a powerful, positive memory while reciting the incantation to summon a protective Patronus. The combination of mental focus and spoken words creates a stronger magical effect, illustrating how incantations can amplify intent. Sorry folks, that example is to help explain, and Expecto Patronum is only a "literary" spell, but she clearly did some homework on intent.

Magic often relies on structure and discipline to produce consistent results. Incantations contribute to this by providing a set framework for rituals. The repetition of specific words and phrases can create a rhythmic, meditative state that enhances the practitioner's connection to the magical process.

In Wiccan traditions, rituals often involve chanting incantations to invoke the elements or deities. For instance, during a ritual to call the quarters, Wiccans might recite, "Hail to the East, the element of Air. May your winds of wisdom guide us." This structured use of incantations helps practitioners enter a focused, ritualistic mindset, making the magic more effective.

In traditional folk magic, some call "hoodoo" or "rootwork," practitioners often use incantations while preparing herbal remedies and potions. For example, I might recite a specific prayer or incantation over a love potion to imbue it with romantic energy. The spoken words act as a conduit, transferring the practitioner's intent into the physical substance.

The Enchanting World of Grimoires:

As a journalist I spend a lot of time researching stories, and as witch with a focus on herbology, I guess it was only natural that I have explored the knowledge of other witches. Exploring the world of spell books or grimoires has been a super exciting part of my journey as a modern witch. These spell books, with their wealth of knowledge on spells, incantations, rituals, and magical theories, have become invaluable guides. I've spent years delving into both famous and lesser-known texts, and I'm excited to share some of what I've learned about these magical tomes and where you can find them.

One of the first grimoires I encountered was "The Key of Solomon," also known as "Clavicula Salomonis." This legendary medieval text, attributed to King Solomon, is renowned for its comprehensive collection of magical procedures and incantations for summoning and controlling spirits. I found it at the British Library in London, where the detailed instructions on creating magical tools and invoking angelic and demonic entities captivated me. Walking into the British Library, with its grand architecture and vast collection of ancient texts, I felt an almost overwhelming sense of history. Looking down upon the worn pages of "The Key of Solomon," I could feel the weight of centuries of knowledge and the power of those who practiced these ancient arts. The British Library houses several editions of this text, making it accessible for those interested in exploring its mysteries, but the first time there I had to be accompanied.

The Lesser Key of Solomon Also known as the "Lemegeton," "The Lesser Key of Solomon" is a companion to "The Key of Solomon." It's divided into five books, with the "Goetia" being the most famous section, detailing 72 demons and the rituals needed to summon and control them. I discovered this text at the Bodleian Library in Oxford. It took a while to get myself an invite but it was so worth it. The Bodleian Library, with its medieval architecture and hushed, reverent atmosphere, feels like stepping back in time. As I studied the intricate sigils and detailed rituals in the "Lemegeton," I felt an odd connection to the magicians of the past, who meticulously recorded their knowledge and experiences in these pages. The library's collection includes several versions of the "Lemegeton," providing a deep dive into the intricacies of demonology and ritual magic.

"The Picatrix," originally written in Arabic and later translated into Latin in the 12th century, is a guide to astrological magic filled with incantations, astrological correspondences, and recipes for potions and talismans. The British Museum's manuscript department has copies of this ancient text (but shhh, don't tell them I told you so!). I had a scholar with me on this occasion who said he was "fascinated by its blend of Hermeticism, Neoplatonism, and Islamic mysticism, offering a unique perspective on planetary influences in magic." Or words to that affect. Now I don't know about you but that sounded like gobbledygook, I did however write it down, I am a journalist after all! So, after a lot of questions and digging, what I think he meant was this: Hermeticism, Neoplatonism, and Islamic mysticism (Sufism) are different ways of thinking about life and our connection to the universe.

Hermeticism comes from teachings linked to a figure named Hermes Trismegistus. It's all about finding hidden knowledge that helps us understand ourselves and the world. People who study this believe that by thinking deeply and reflecting, we can see how our minds connect with everything around us and something divine.

Neoplatonism is based on ideas from the ancient Greek philosopher Plato. Think of a bright light that represents the ultimate reality, called the One. Everything else, including our souls, comes from this source, like rays of light. The goal is to understand this connection and become better people so we can return to that ultimate source through learning and good actions.

Sufism is about having a personal connection with God in Islam. Sufis focus on love and devotion, believing that truly knowing God goes beyond just following rules. They use poetry, music, and dance to express their feelings and deepen their connection with God. In Sufism, the journey to understanding God is about feeling love and unity with everything around us.

So, I think in nerdy scholarship circles, what he was actually saying was "wow this just great!"

"The Egyptian Book of the Dead," or the "Book of Coming Forth by Day," is a collection of ancient Egyptian funerary texts. These spells and incantations guide the deceased through the afterlife. Again, thank you British Museum who have several papyrus scrolls and translations of this text. It is amazing the power of carrying a Press Card sometimes. Viewing these ancient artifacts provided a tangible connection to the religious and magical practices of ancient Egypt, highlighting the power of words and rituals in guiding the soul. Standing in front of these delicate papyrus scrolls, with their meticulously inscribed hieroglyphs, I definitely felt something, you could say it was reverence for the ancient scribes who crafted these texts to ensure safe passage for the souls of their people, but it was more than that. Read the section on Dittany of Crete and that might give you a clue. I think there was an intention placed on those scrolls that I could feel.

"Arbatel de Magia Veterum" is a Renaissance-era grimoire outlining a system of angelic magic. I found a rare edition at the Wellcome Collection in London. This text's focus on invoking the aid and protection of celestial beings, rather than summoning demons, offers a positive and benevolent approach to magic, distinct from other grimoires of its time. The Wellcome Collection, focusses on the interplay between medicine, life, and art, was the perfect setting to explore this text. Surrounded by exhibits that blend science and mysticism, I felt inspired by the Renaissance scholars who sought to understand and harness the divine forces of the universe. They also do a good cup of tea and a fruit scone.

As fascinating as these texts are, there are more exciting texts that I have had the privilege to study. I think my children see through the location of some holiday locations. "So which book are you looking for this time!"

There are some really interesting books in the UK

"The Black Book of Carmarthen" is one of the oldest surviving manuscripts in Welsh, dating back to the 13th century. I studied this manuscript at the National Library of Wales in Aberystwyth. The library, nestled in the picturesque landscape of the Welsh coast, provided a peaceful and inspiring setting. As I read through the ancient poems, prayers, and spells, I liked the sound of the words as they played in my head. The Welsh language is beautiful yet challenging for me, despite being married to Welshman, so I had to get my husband to translate some of the spells for me. One spell that particularly stood out was:

Gwared fy ngelynion, eu llwyr ddinistrio, Yn enw'r Goleuni, bydded felly.

This translates roughly to:

Banish my enemies, utterly destroy them, In the name of the Light, so it shall be.

The use of local herbs like yarrow and mugwort in its spells showcases the integration of native plants in magical practices. Seeing the spell in its original language and understanding its profound meaning brought the text to life and made me feel quite emotional, not sure exactly why. As I have said in other areas of this book, the dark side of magic generally scares me and I quickly move on, however there is a morbid fascination to understand or study, even if not practice. I guess it's like some people like horror movies or musicals but would never want to actually be in one. I really can't sing.

The Book of St. Cyprian also known as the "Black Book," this grimoire has various versions and is attributed to St. Cyprian of Antioch. I found a version at the Ashmolean Museum in Oxford. As I studied the spells for exorcism, protection, and love, often incorporating local herbs like vervain, St. John's wort, and elderberry, I could sense the blending of Christian and pagan traditions that characterizes much of British folk magic.

The Long Lost Friend Originally published in Pennsylvania, "The Long Lost Friend" became popular in the UK during the 19th century. The British Library has this one too. It contains folk remedies, charms, and prayers, using common everyday herbs.

There is a protection potion using rosemary, thyme, and sage, combined with a pinch of salt and fresh spring water. The rosemary offers protection and purification, the thyme promotes health and strength, and the sage provides powerful cleansing. The potion is created by boiling these herbs together, then straining the mixture into a jar. It can be used to sprinkle around the home, added to bathwater, or carried in a small vial for personal protection.

The Red Dragon (Le Dragon Rouge) While primarily a French grimoire, found its way to the UK and has had a significant influence on British occultists. I bought a copy off Amazon! Although earlier I was fortunate enough to read a friends copy whilst on a visit to the Museum of Witchcraft and Magic in Boscastle, Cornwall. This museum, dedicated to the history of witchcraft and magic, provided an atmospheric backdrop for exploring "The Red Dragon." The text is particularly renowned for its focus on summoning and making pacts with demonic entities to gain wealth and power, using potent herbs like mandrake and belladonna in its rituals. The museum's cozy and magical vibe really made me appreciate the hidden knowledge in this book.

The museum is in the picturesque little village of Boscastle. It's not huge but absolutely enchanting and for its size holds one of the most comprehensive collections of witchcraft-related artifacts in the world. Nestled on the rugged North Cornish coast, not far from Tintagel the home of King Arthur and Merlin, the museum's setting adds to its magical allure. The building itself, a charming, old stone structure, feels like a portal to another time. Inside, the dim lighting and carefully curated displays create an ambiance of mystery and reverence. Walking through you can sense the dedication to preserving the history and practices of witchcraft, from ancient traditions to modern-day Wicca.

One particularly intriguing potion from "The Red Dragon" is known as the "Elixir of Wealth." It seemed gentle enough for even me to try, although there were others in the book I would go nowhere near. This potion is designed to attract wealth and prosperity by invoking the aid of spiritual forces, I hoped friendly ones! I was so captivated by this recipe that I decided to recreate it myself. Whether it works, I guess, depends on how many people buy my book!

To begin with, I carefully gathered all the necessary ingredients: mandrake root, belladonna, gold leaf, spring water, honey, and a pinch of salt. Handling the mandrake root and belladonna required caution due to their potent properties, but I was meticulous in ensuring they were fresh and ready for use. The process started with boiling a cup of spring water and allowing it to cool to room temperature, setting the stage for the creation of the elixir.

In a small cauldron, I combined the cooled spring water with a pinch of salt. This foundational step set the potion's purifying base. Next, I added a small piece of mandrake root and a few leaves of belladonna to the water. As I stirred the mixture gently, I recited the incantation from "The Red Dragon": "*By the power of the dragon's fire, I call forth wealth and gold. Spirits of the nether realm, hear my plea, and grant me fortune untold.*"

With each word, I visualized a golden light emanating from the potion and enveloping me, infusing the elixir with the desired energy.

After covering the cauldron, I let the herbs steep in the water for 15-20 minutes. This infusion process allowed the water to absorb the magical properties of the mandrake and belladonna. Once the time had passed, I strained the mixture into a clean jar, removing the herbs to leave a clear, potent liquid. To this, I added another small piece of gold leaf and a spoonful of honey, stirring until the honey completely dissolved. The gold leaf symbolized the wealth I sought to attract, while the honey added a touch of sweetness and harmony to the potion.

To invoke its wealth-attracting properties, I anoint my wrists and forehead with a few drops. Additionally, I sprinkled a few drops around my home and workspace, creating an environment charged with the energy of abundance.

I carry small vial of the elixir with me in my laptop bag, in the hope it will attract wealth and good fortune. The act of carrying the potion was a symbolic gesture, belief, reinforcing my intent to welcome prosperity into my life.

I think experimenting with potions from the past is important to ensure this knowledge isn't lost. The process connected me to the ancient traditions and knowledge contained within the grimoire. As for its effectiveness, only time and the success of my endeavours will tell, but the journey itself, imbued with history and magic, was profoundly rewarding.

Mandrake, a plant with a long history in magic and folklore, is believed to have powerful protective and transformative qualities. Its roots often resemble a human figure, which has contributed to its mystical reputation. Belladonna, also known as deadly nightshade, is another herb frequently mentioned in "The Red Dragon." Its toxic nature is said to grant visions and enhance spiritual communication when used correctly and with caution.

When discussing spell books, one cannot fail to mention The Grand Grimoire. It has a reputation for being one of the most powerful and dangerous magical texts. Its association with dark magic and demonology has made it a subject of both fascination and fear. I, too, harbour a sense of trepidation towards it and tend to avoid it. Historically, it was banned by the Catholic Church, and possession of the grimoire could lead to severe punishment, reflecting its feared status.

Despite its dark reputation, or perhaps because of it, The Grand Grimoire has had a significant influence on Western occult traditions. It has been referenced in various other magical texts, including The Red Dragon in Wales, and has inspired numerous occultists and magicians. Its detailed instructions and the promise of power have attracted many who seek to delve into the more forbidden aspects of magic.

Today, The Grand Grimoire is often viewed with a mix of curiosity and caution. Modern occultists and historians study it for its historical value and its insights into the practices and beliefs of past witches. While some practitioners still use its rituals, they often do so with a deep understanding of the risks involved. For example, there are ways to summon Lucifuge Rofocale, "he who flees the light," described as the Prime Minister of Hell, serving directly under Lucifer. In the UK, we also have Prime Ministers, and there are one or two recent ones, who I wouldn't be surprised if they were related.

The grimoire is available in various editions and translations, though many are modern interpretations rather than exact replicas of the original. It continues to be a source of inspiration and controversy within the magical community, symbolising the allure and danger of seeking knowledge and power beyond the ordinary.

Our Family Grimoire: A Treasure of the House

Our family grimoire is known as Wren, and we don't know why. (if you think you might know, please do tell me!) While not as exotic or grand as the other books mentioned here, it holds a special place in our lives. I think a good place but not completely sure. This book is steeped in history and mystery, having been passed down through generations of our family. However, it doesn't belong to us. As strange as that may sound. It belongs to the house instead. There is a peculiar spell at the front of the book that explicitly states that Wren should never be removed from this house. It can be destroyed within the grounds, but removal is forbidden. We don't know what would happen if it were taken away, and frankly, we don't want to find out.

The grimoire is a hefty volume, mostly loose leaf pages (unbound) measuring a solid five inches deep, and contains hundreds of spells, potions, incantations written in old English, modern English and a form of Romani (Gypsy)called Kalo which emanates from Romani people in Finland and Sweden. We don't have any links to Finland or Sweden as far as I am aware so that again is a mystery. Despite its age and use, there are still 30 blank pages remaining, which I use sparingly. I don't want to add more pages. Why? I don't know that either, perhaps there is a spell on the book that makes me feel that way.

There are two spells related to the book itself, The binding spell and the spell of final rest. The spell at the front of the book which in fact was added after the Spell of Final Rest is the Binding Spell, which ensures that the grimoire remains within the confines of our home. Surprisingly the original spell or incantation has been written in reasonably modern English which makes us suspect the restrictive spell is from relative recent times, yet someone has tried to translate that spell into Kalo underneath in a very precise handwritten note. Again this is unusual as elsewhere in Wren the spells look like they might be in Kalo, which is a terribly complex language to learn and translate, (I tried and gave up!), however when I tried to translate the Kato back into English, which is an easier approach then trying it the other way around, it didn't look like a good translation at all, but who knows!

"By the power of earth and stone, this grimoire's place is here alone. Bound to this house, its spirit tied, never to be removed, only within destroyed. May its magic flourish and never roam, for this book is bound to home."

Mihti vastis the phuvvarres, To grimoire jekhto stedi akanas. Te ares kathe, vastem shuden, Nane thovis buter, te katarre distaven. Te djiuva leski mihti feri jekht, Kathe grimoire stedi o domovoj kher

We assume this relates to some form of enchantment placed upon the physical book or pages within. (See the section on Dittany of Crete)

This incantation serves as a constant reminder that the book's power and presence are intrinsically linked to the house. The idea that the grimoire belongs more to the house than to us adds a layer of mystique and reverence to our use of it.

In the event that the grimoire must be destroyed, a special spell is written in the back of the book. It is pretty well hidden amongst other writings, but it's there. The inclusion of a spell for destroying our family grimoire might seem perplexing at first, but there are several practical and protective reasons for its existence. Magic, as we know, is a powerful and unpredictable force. Having a controlled way to end Wren's power is a safeguard against unforeseen circumstances that could endanger our family or the integrity of the magical knowledge contained within.

I have a letter from my Grandmother about this spell that sits between the pages of Wren, which my Mum must have put in there. It must have been written from my grandmother to my mum, who had obviously asked the same questions that I have asked. I haven't included everything here as some is personal stuff but here is an abridged version removing the personal items.

"If the book fell into the hands of bad people, the spells and incantations inside could be twisted to hurt us or our friends. By having this spell, we can make sure that its power is limited and its secrets are not exploited by anyone with bad intentions.

Magic, as you know, can sometimes get out of control as you saw at Christmas. Our family's safety is the most important thing, and Wren's protection spell, which binds it to this house, is meant to keep this balance. If you truly believe there could be a situation where Wren's presence becomes a direct threat to our well-being, like an irreversible curse or a destructive enchantment that can't be contained. In such cases, destroying the book might be the only way to keep us safe. The Spell of Final Rest is there to protect us from any harm that might come from Wren. Like you, sometimes I can feel it's presence, when it's happy, sad or mischievous. Also like you, there have been times in my life I haven't trusted it and shows us things it wants to show,

If we ever we needed to sell or transfer the house to someone outside the family (over my dead body). In those cases, we might need to destroy Wren to make sure what power is contained here, but we have a duty to pass on this land with the spirits who live here to someone who will care for them. The binding spell ensures that the book remains within the house, but there just could be a circumstance we can't imagine when it might be impossible to follow this rule without resorting to destruction. The Spell of Final Rest ensures that even if we have to destroy Wren, its power is safely and respectfully laid to rest within our home grounds.

Our magic is a precious gift but it is also a burden for when we are called."

I started writing this bit by saying this was wisdom being passed down by my grandmother, but on reflection this wasn't her sharing wisdom, it was re-assuring my mum from something that must have spooked her. The Spell of Final Rest is not about destroying the grimoire; it's about protecting our family. BTW I never understood the *"when we are called"* bit.

Given these potential scenarios, the Spell of Final Rest was clearly crafted to allow for the grimoire's safe and respectful destruction. Below is the incantation once again, this time written in old English, not modern or Kalo. Your guess why the two are in different languages is as good as mine! We assume the binding spell came later. An after-thought? I confided in a friend of mine who works for Intel out in Hillsboro who was part of my circle when I was in Portland. He comes over every year to see us with his family and over some drinks we got onto this. Don't get me wrong everyone in our family has different views, but his made the most sense at least to me. He thinks that someone was less happy with only having a spell of final rest, and added one to prevent anyone else getting their hands on it who might not want to use that spell and somehow use against us. He used the analogy within his world of IT, that the spell of final rest was our business continuity plan if things went horribly wrong, but like most companies they haven't or find it impossible to test that the recovery plan works until the time you actually have to use it. So how do you limit the risk of your well-conceived plan not working? You have to take other measures to prevent the problem happening in the first place, hence the binding spell that prevents the grimoire being taken, as once taken whoever has it might not want to use the Spell of Final Rest but to use it for their own purposes. The spell doesn't say what will happen or to whom if the book is removed, so that part may be for our protection. Maybe it does nothing sinister, just wiped the magic, who knows?

It reminds me of my visit to the Seed Bank at Wakehurst Place, where they preserve the world's seeds for research and potential future use. Maybe I'm reading too much into it, but I couldn't shake the feeling that if humanity ever did something catastrophically foolish—something that threatened the very survival of life, then this would be one of the places we'd turn to restart the world's biodiversity.

During the tour, they explained why they have massive, bank-style vaults underground, where the seeds are stored at -20°C. The staff, dressed in outfits that looked more suited for a space mission than a botanical facility, emphasized that simply storing the seeds isn't enough. They must also be certain that, if necessary, they can germinate them, ensuring that the freezing process isn't inadvertently killing the seeds.

Different seeds have unique and sometimes bizarre germination triggers. For example, *Banksia* seeds require fire to sprout; *Dogwood* needs prolonged cold; and some species respond to smoke, indicating that a fire has passed and it's safe to grow. Other seeds are activated by light, soaking in water, or a precise sequence of environmental cues. One of the most complex examples is the *Papaver californicum* (Fire Poppy). It needs the heat of a wildfire to crack its seed coat, followed by exposure to the specific compounds in the smoke and charred soil, then winter rains soon after. The fire must also clear the surrounding vegetation to give the poppy the space and nutrients it needs to thrive. When only all these conditions are met then bingo, it begins to germinate.

Without understanding these requirements, you could plant these seeds a thousand years from now and wonder why they won't grow, much like the Romans might have puzzled over their inability to cultivate Silphium. In short, having a plan is one thing, but knowing it will work is another. Hence if you can't test your plan like the Spell of Final rest, you need another plan to prevent the need to test it at all.

There are steps removed as I can not share it all, but here is the first part of the Spell of Final Rest

"Mid ifigesa hlype, æcseleaf, and hnutbeorg, Binde þis boc þær deop ræd bid. Befeoh hit under monan cealdan geseondan, Þrittig nihta, læt his drycræft beon geniped. Wanigende, forswigende mid monan siðe, Oð his miht on heolstor silpeð. Donne forbærn hit hat—hatur on niht. In þisse stowe, þin drycræft byrneð. Reste on sibbe, næfre gebunden, Þin gast wunath binnan þisse eorðan."

"With ivy's sap, oak leaf, and walnut shell, bind this book where secrets dwell. Bury it under the moon's cold gaze, for thirty nights, let its magic be. Waning, fading with lunar flight, until its power dissolves. Then burn it hot, hotter still, through the night. In this place, your magic burns. Rest in peace, no longer bound, Wren lays within the earth"

The thought of ever having to perform this spell is daunting, but knowing it exists provides a sense of safety, ensuring the grimoire's magic will remain where it belongs.

Each time I open the book, I am reminded of the careful stewardship it requires. I use its pages sparingly, aware that there are only 30 blank ones remaining. The handwriting of my mother and grandmother graces five pages each, their spells and wisdom preserved for me and future generations. This continuity of knowledge and magic is something I cherish deeply, thinking my daughter will one day be sitting here with the book open.

When I think about the future and the limited space left, I can't help but wonder what we'll do when the pages run out. Perhaps it's not just the spells within the book that are important, but the respect and care we give to our magical practices. Maybe the blank pages are a reminder to only write down what truly matters, to preserve the essence of our family's magical heritage.

A margin note, whilst I'm doing my hundredth re-edit:! Wren has its own shelf, a nook by the fire place. We always say in the family when the log fire really gets going that Wren becomes restless and the large crack or spits from the fire are him laughing. Oh it's definitely a him. It's a kinda joke, but kinda not, if you know what I mean. The Gardener says he can see that the nook has been walled up many times, to keep the book safe from those persecuting witches? Or was it to protect the people of the house from it?

The Witch's Botanical Apothecary

"Mid ælcum drype astyred, ic wefe beorhnesse and lufu, binde min strengðu to þinum."

"With every drop stirred, I weave protection and love, binding my strength to yours"

CHAPTER 10: POTIONS & BREWS

Welcome to the chapter on Potions & Brews in our journey through the ancient and mystical world of Herbal Alchemy. I have often found that the art of potion-making is one of the most fascinating and rewarding aspects of our craft. This chapter is dedicated to demystifying the world of potions and brews, providing you with the knowledge, techniques, and confidence to create your own magical elixirs.

Basic Potion Making Techniques

Creating potions involves several basic techniques that you will need to master. These techniques are the foundation of your practice and ensure that your potions are both effective and safe.

1. **Infusion**: This technique involves steeping herbs in hot water to extract their properties. Think of it like making tea but with a magical twist.
2. **Decoction**: Similar to infusion but used for tougher plant materials like roots or bark. The ingredients are simmered in water for an extended period.
3. **Maceration**: This is the process of soaking herbs in a liquid, usually alcohol or oil, to extract their properties over a more extended period.
4. **Tinctures**: These are concentrated herbal extracts made by soaking herbs in alcohol or vinegar. They are potent and have a long shelf life.
5. **Salves and Balms**: are ointment-like preparations made by combining herbal infusions or decoctions with beeswax and oils. They are applied to the skin.

Equipment and Methods

The tools of potion-making are simple yet essential. A few items you will need include:

- **Mortar and Pestle**: For grinding herbs.
- **Glass Jars and Bottles**: For storing your creations.
- **Measuring Spoons and Cups**: Accuracy is crucial in potion-making.
- **Strainers and Cheesecloth**: For filtering out solid particles.
- **Double Boiler**: For making salves and balms.
- **Labels and Markers**: Always label your potions with the name and date.

Safety Considerations

Safety in potion-making cannot be overstated. Always ensure that you:

- **Research Your Ingredients**: Some herbs can be toxic or cause allergic reactions.
- **Use Clean Equipment**: Sterilize your tools to prevent contamination.
- **Label Clearly**: Avoid accidental ingestion or misuse.
- **Test in Small Quantities**: Especially with new recipes, test a small amount first.

Healing Potions and Love & Attraction Brews

In this section, we will cover two of the most common and sought-after types of potions: healing potions and love and attraction brews. These potions have been staples in the witch's repertoire for centuries, revered for their effectiveness and the simplicity of their ingredients.

Healing Potions

Healing potions are designed to promote physical, emotional, or spiritual healing. They can range from simple herbal teas to more complex brews. For example, a customer once approached me seeking relief from chronic stress. I recommended a calming potion made with chamomile, lavender, lemon balm, and added a blend of **skullcap, passionflower, holy basil,** and **ashwagandha**. Skullcap and passionflower are excellent for soothing the nervous system, holy basil acts as an adaptogen to help the body cope with stress, and ashwagandha enhances resilience and emotional balance. After a few weeks of incorporating this intricate blend into her routine, she reported feeling significantly more relaxed and able to manage her stress better.

Love and Attraction Brews

These potions aim to enhance attraction, deepen relationships, and invite love into one's life. One memorable client was a young woman looking to rekindle the passion in her marriage. I suggested a love potion made with rose petals, vanilla, and a touch of cinnamon, enriched with a more complex mix of unusual herbs such as **damiana, maca root, mugwort,** and **hibiscus**. Damiana is known for its aphrodisiac properties, maca root enhances stamina and libido, mugwort stimulates dreams and intuition, and hibiscus adds a tart, enchanting flavour while symbolizing passion. She returned to me, glowing, sharing how this potent potion helped reignite the spark with her partner and deepened their emotional connection.

In the following sections, we will delve deeper into the recipes, techniques, and magical properties of the ingredients used in these potions. You'll learn step-by-step how to create your own healing and love potions, each tailored to your unique needs and intentions.

Potion-making is an art that combines knowledge, intuition, and a touch of magic. As you embark on this journey, remember that each potion you create is a manifestation of <u>your</u> will and energy. May this chapter inspire and empower you to weave your own herbal alchemy, creating potions that bring healing, love, and enchantment into your life.

Potion making is a beautiful blend of science and magic, a practice that has been honed and perfected over centuries. As a practicing witch and herbalist, I've spent years crafting potions, learning from both my successes and mistakes. In this chapter, I'll share my personal journey with potion making, covering essential techniques, equipment, methods, and safety considerations, along with some candid examples of things I've done wrong along the way.

The Essentials: Equipment

To start on your potion-making journey, you'll need a few basic pieces of equipment. Having the right tools not only makes the process smoother but also ensures that your potions are safe and effective.

First and foremost, a **mortar and pestle** are essential for grinding and crushing herbs. Mine is made of granite, which is durable and provides a good weight for grinding. Some prefer marble or ceramic, but I find granite gives the best balance of heft and texture. The pestle should feel comfortable in your hand, allowing you to grind with ease.

Then, there are the **glass jars and bottles**. These are crucial for storing your ingredients and finished potions. Glass is my preferred material because it doesn't react with the ingredients, ensuring purity and longevity. Plus, it's easy to sterilize. I once used plastic containers, but they tended to absorb odours and colours, which isn't ideal when you're working with potent herbs.

Wooden bowls are another essential item. These are perfect for mixing dry ingredients or preparing certain types of brews. I have a lovely bowl made from olive wood. The smooth, dense grain of olive wood makes it perfect for this purpose as it's less likely to absorb the ingredients' oils and flavours. Other good choices include maple and walnut, which are also durable and non-reactive.

For accurate measurements, you can't go wrong with good **measuring spoons and cups**. Precision is key in potion making, and these tools ensure that your ratios are spot on. I learned this the hard way when one of my early potions turned out too weak because I eyeballed the measurements.

Strainers and cheesecloth are indispensable for filtering out solid particles from your liquids. Whether you're making an infusion or a tincture, these tools help ensure that your final product is smooth and clear. I have a fine mesh strainer for everyday use and a few squares of cheesecloth for the finer tasks.

A **double boiler** is incredibly useful for heating ingredients gently, especially when making salves and balms. It prevents direct contact with heat, reducing the risk of burning your ingredients. I remember my first attempt at making a balm directly in a pot—it ended up burnt and unusable. The double boiler changed everything.

Lastly, always label your potions with the name, ingredients, and date of creation. Once, I mixed up a love potion with a calming potion because I didn't label them. My customer said they had an absolutely fantastic evening but the opposite to the calming effect which they had expected! Now, I label everything meticulously to avoid any mix-ups.

Basic Techniques

The first technique you'll want to master is **infusion**, which is similar to making tea. You steep herbs in hot water to extract their properties. This method is excellent for delicate plant parts like leaves and flowers. I often make chamomile infusions for relaxation.

Decoction is used for tougher plant materials like roots, bark, and seeds. Ingredients are simmered in water for an extended period, usually 20-40 minutes. Tip set a timer! Especially if you are easily distracted like me.

Maceration involves soaking herbs in a liquid, typically alcohol or oil, for several weeks to extract their properties. I made a calendula oil by macerating the flowers in olive oil. Unfortunately, I didn't strain it properly, and after a few weeks, it started to mould. Proper straining and ensuring the herbs are fully submerged are key to preventing this.

Tinctures are concentrated herbal extracts made by soaking herbs in alcohol or vinegar. They are potent and have a long shelf life. It's important to use a high-proof alcohol and the correct ratio of herb to liquid (usually 1:5 for dried herbs).

Salves and balms are ointment-like preparations made by combining herbal infusions or decoctions with beeswax and oils. They are applied to the skin for healing purposes. Trial and error is the only way as it depends on how think or runny your beeswax is, but it's roughly 1 ounce of natural beeswax to 1 cup of infused oil.

Methods and Safety

When it comes to potion making, safety is absolutely paramount. I'm always about mixing magic with a dash of practicality. Ensuring the safety of the potions I create is my top priority. It protects not only me but also anyone who uses my potions. Let me share some tips and personal stories about how to keep things safe, from sourcing your herbs to recognising those sneaky look-alike plants.

Trusted Sources for Herbs

One of the most important things I've learned is to always source herbs from reputable suppliers. The quality and purity of your ingredients make a huge difference. I've had my fair share of mishaps. Two things I just can't stop myself buying, books and herbs.

The books may sit in a pile waiting to be read, but herbs have all too often, by the time I get them home, smelled off and ended up in the bin.

Now, I really try to only buy from suppliers I trust, ones who offer organic, non-GMO herbs with a transparent sourcing process. And you know, growing your own herbs is even better. You get full control over what goes into your plants. Plus, it's super satisfying to use something you've nurtured from a seed.

The Importance of a Network and Joining a Coven

Having a network of fellow herbalists and witches is invaluable. One of the main reasons I joined my first coven in Portland, Oregon, was to share and learn about different herbs. Through the coven, I got access to herbs that were hard to find and learned about their uses from seasoned practitioners.

Being in a coven is fantastic because you can trade herbs, share your harvests, and get insights on safe practices. It's a communal atmosphere where everyone benefits from each other's knowledge. If you're not part of a coven, try joining herbalist groups or local gardening clubs. They can provide support and resources to enhance your potion-making.

Knowing Your Herbs

Understanding the herbs you use is crucial. This means knowing their beneficial properties and being aware of any potential side effects or interactions. Some herbs can be toxic if used incorrectly, and others might not play well with certain medications.

I always dive deep into researching each herb, as well as the customer. I use reference books, scientific studies, and advice from experienced herbalists.

Identifying Look-Alike Herbs

Foraging for herbs can be tricky because some beneficial plants have poisonous look-alikes. For instance, Queen Anne's lace looks a lot like poison hemlock, which is deadly. When I forage, I always bring a reliable field guide and double-check the plants' distinguishing features.

It's super important to know these differences. For example, poison hemlock has purple blotches on its stem, while Queen Anne's lace does not. If I'm ever unsure, I consult with more experienced foragers or herbalists to avoid any dangerous mix-ups, or don't use it.

Testing and Allergies

Always test new potions in small quantities first. This step is crucial to ensure that no one has an adverse reaction. I always test new potions on myself or a small group before offering them to others.

Cleanliness and Sterilisation

Keeping everything clean is essential in potion making. Sterilise your tools to prevent contamination, especially for potions that will be ingested. Using the dishwasher is not good enough for sterilisation, use proper equipment, I used dish-washer clean jars once, thinking my jars were clean enough, and ended up with a mouldy potion. Now, I make sure to sterilise everything by boiling it or using a disinfectant solution.

Clear Labelling and Storage

Clearly label all your potions with the name, ingredients, and date of creation. This helps avoid accidental ingestion and keeps track of potency and freshness. Store your potions in a cool, dark place to maintain their effectiveness. Keep away from children or annoying family members.

Safety in potion making isn't just about avoiding harm; it's about creating the most effective and powerful potions possible. By sourcing your herbs from trusted suppliers, being part of a supportive network, thoroughly understanding your ingredients, identifying look-alike herbs, testing for allergies, maintaining cleanliness, and properly labelling and storing your potions, you ensure the safety and success of your magical practice.

The Power of Mixing Herbs

Mixing herbs is one of the most fascinating and transformative aspects of potion-making, and it's where the magic truly starts to happen. Over centuries, witches have observed how plants interact, often in ways that make their individual properties stronger. This phenomenon, known as **synergy**, is the real secret ingredient that makes a "good potion great". What's even more exciting is that modern science has caught up, giving us a deeper understanding of these interactions and proving what witches have known all along: when combined thoughtfully, herbs can create effects far greater than the sum of their parts.

The Science Behind Herbal Synergy

When you mix two herbs, their active compounds, like alkaloids, flavonoids, or terpenes, come together to create a broader, more potent therapeutic effect. This combination can enhance healing, protection, or even magical intent. One herb might have anti-inflammatory properties, while another might be antimicrobial. When these herbs are combined, they work together to form a more powerful remedy, targeting multiple pathways in the body or mind.

Let's break it down using **ginger and turmeric** as an example. Ginger is widely known for its ability to ease digestion and reduce nausea, while turmeric is celebrated for its powerful anti-inflammatory properties. But when you combine the two, you don't just get double the benefits, you get a compound effect. Their active ingredients, **gingerol** in ginger and **curcumin** in turmeric, complement each other, creating an enhanced anti-inflammatory and antioxidant potion. Science tells us that this is because their chemical structures allow them to interact at a molecular level, heightening each other's effects. Modern research has even shown that adding **piperine** (from black pepper) to the mix can increase the bioavailability of curcumin, meaning the body absorbs and uses it more effectively.

Chemical Interactions in Potions

One of the most interesting aspects of mixing herbs is the **chemical reactions** that can occur. Herbs contain a range of tannins, enzymes, acids, and other compounds, and when you mix them, they can form new compounds altogether. These reactions can either enhance or change the potency of the mixture. For example, combining herbs with tannins, like those found in oak leaves, with herbs that are rich in enzymes may break down the tannins into smaller molecules, which could make the potion easier for the body to absorb.

This is where the real magic lies: not only do the herbs enhance each other's effects, but they can also **modify how the body processes them**. In potion-making, this means that your mixture can have both immediate and long-lasting effects, depending on how the compounds react with one another. Think of it like making bread: flour and water alone won't rise, but when you add yeast, it ferments and creates something completely new and nourishing.

Bioavailability: Unlocking the Power of Plants

A concept that witches have intuitively understood for centuries is what we now know as **bioavailability**, or how well the body can absorb and use the compounds in herbs. Some herbs can make the compounds in others more bioavailable, meaning that they help the body absorb and process the active ingredients more efficiently. Witches have long known that pairing the right herbs together can unlock hidden potential, and now we have the scientific understanding to explain why.

Modification of Effects: Balancing Magic and Medicine

Another fascinating aspect of herbal synergy is how the combination of herbs can modify each other's effects. For example, chamomile is known for its calming properties, while peppermint is more stimulating. Combine the two, and you get a remedy that's both soothing and invigorating, perfect for relaxation without drowsiness. This is one of the reasons I love experimenting in potion-making: it's like discovering new dimensions of a familiar ingredient. By balancing the effects of herbs, you can create potions that are perfectly tailored to your needs or the needs of others.

The Magic of Unexpected Benefits

Sometimes, the real magic happens when two herbs come together and create something entirely unexpected. This is what we call **new synergistic effects**. For example, ginger and garlic are both known for their individual health benefits, ginger for its digestive and anti-nausea properties, and garlic for its immune-boosting and antimicrobial effects. But when you combine them, their antioxidant and anti-inflammatory powers are amplified in ways that are far more effective than either could achieve alone. It's as if the herbs recognize each other and work together to produce a more powerful result.

My Personal Journey and Lessons Learned

Potion making for me has been a journey of continuous learning and growth, or should I just be honest and say trial and error works best for me! Precision is essential, and let me tell you, early in my practice, I was guilty of being way too casual with measurements. This annoyed my mum to no end. "Potions are a recipe, stick to the recipe!" she'd scold, warning me that the wrong mix might have some unexpected effects. Precision ensures consistency and effectiveness, but come on, we're all human and love to experiment a bit, don't we! I'm definitely guilty of wondering, "I wonder if just a pinch of this or that would add some extra oomph." I guess if you're the type who "wings-it" with making a cake, roughly judging the ingredients rather than weighing them - then you might be a little like me and potions"

Patience is another crucial lesson. I've often been too impatient with maceration, trying to rush the process by heating the mixture. Spoiler alert: this can destroy the beneficial properties of the herbs and cause your mother to roll her eyes. True potion making requires time and patience, which I learned the hard way after several botched batches.

Practice is key. Like any skill, potion making improves with practice. My first few potions were far from perfect, think more "witch's brew" in the comedic sense, but each attempt taught me something new. Now, after countless tries and a few laughable disasters, I feel confident in my ability to create effective and safe potions.

Potion making is a sacred art that connects us to the natural world and our own inner magic. By mastering basic techniques, using the right equipment, and prioritising safety, you can create powerful potions to enhance your life and those of others. Remember, mistakes are part of the learning process. Embrace them, laugh at them, and let them guide you on your journey. After all, even the greatest witches had their off days!

Introduction to Healing Potions

Healing potions have been a staple in the world of herbal alchemy for ages. These magical brews harness the power of nature to mend physical injuries, soothe emotional wounds, and restore balance to the mind and spirit. Here in England, we're lucky to have a climate that supports a wide variety of medicinal herbs. Here are some of my favourite healing potions using these wonderful herbs. We'll dive into why these herbs were chosen, how they work together, and how to prepare and use them. Plus, I'll sprinkle in a few stories from my own potion-making adventures and disasters!

Healing a Broken Heart

Healing a broken heart is something many of us have experienced, and at the time it can feel like an insurmountable challenge. I know because I have been there. I don't often think about it now, but when I do it brings back vividly the heartbreak. It was a time of deep sorrow and confusion, and I felt lost and unsure of how to move forward. In the midst of this emotional turmoil, I turned to the natural world for support and found solace in a potion crafted from lemon balm, rose petals, and hawthorn berries.

Why These Herbs?

Lemon balm, with its calming and uplifting effects, was the first ingredient I chose. This herb is well-known for its ability to soothe the mind and alleviate stress, which is crucial when dealing with the emotional rollercoaster of a broken heart. When I brewed my first cup of this potion, the scent of lemon balm alone started to lift my spirits. It's like a gentle hug for the soul, helping to ease anxiety and promote a sense of peace.

Next, I added rose petals, which symbolize love and help open the heart. Roses have long been associated with love and healing, and their delicate petals contain compounds that can uplift the spirit. As the petals steeped in the hot water, they released their essence, creating a brew that felt like it was infused with the very essence of love. It helped me reconnect with feelings of love and compassion, not just for others, but for myself.

Finally, hawthorn berries were the perfect addition to this blend. Hawthorn is renowned for its ability to strengthen the heart, both physically and emotionally. These berries contain antioxidants and other compounds that support cardiovascular health, but their emotional benefits are equally powerful. They help to mend the heart on a deeper level, fostering resilience and courage. During those difficult days, hawthorn berries provided the strength I needed to keep going.

The Synergistic Effect

When combined, the calming properties of lemon balm, the heart-opening qualities of rose petals, and the strengthening effects of hawthorn berries come together to form a potion that truly soothes emotional pain and fosters emotional healing.

For me, this potion was more than just a comforting drink. Just making the potion gave me focus and little by little more strength. It was a nudge in the right direction, helping me find the courage to move forward. While time, travel, and new adventures ultimately played significant roles in my healing process, this potion provided the initial push I needed to start that journey. It gave me a moment of calm in the storm, a chance to catch my breath and begin to see a way through the pain.

How to Prepare

To prepare this healing potion, steep one teaspoon each of dried lemon balm, dried rose petals, and dried hawthorn berries in one cup of boiling water. Let it steep for 10-15 minutes to allow the herbs to release their beneficial compounds fully. Then, strain the mixture and enjoy. You can drink this potion up to three times a day, especially when you feel the weight of your emotions pressing down on you. Drink it with someone who truly loves you, there is something in the sharing of this drink that soothes. My mum made it with me, didn't interfere and blessed it before we drank it. Thankyou mum, I had forgotten that until I just wrote that.

Personal Journey and Reflection

Traveling became a part of my healing journey as well. The excitement of exploring new places and meeting new people brought a fresh perspective and renewed sense of purpose. I took this potion with me on my travels, not the liquid itself, but the power of it in my veins, or that's how it felt. My travels took me to Portland and then mended was able to stop and settle again, settle in the place and settle my heart.

Healing from Trauma

The effects of trauma can be far-reaching, impacting mental, emotional, and even physical health. While time and professional support are essential components of recovery, the natural world offers powerful allies in the form of herbs. A blend of skullcap, St John's Wort, and lavender can create a potent potion that helps calm the mind, lift the spirit, and address the multifaceted nature of trauma.

Skullcap is an incredible herb for calming the nervous system. Historically, it has been used in traditional medicine to treat anxiety, nervousness, and insomnia. Skullcap is particularly useful for those dealing with the persistent hyperarousal that often accompanies trauma, thanks to its ability to soothe and stabilize the mind. Modern science backs up these traditional uses, with studies showing that skullcap can significantly reduce anxiety and improve mood. It works by influencing the production of gamma-aminobutyric acid (GABA), a neurotransmitter that helps calm the nervous system.

Humans have been observing the effects of herbs on each other for thousands of years, long before modern medicine came into play. We all come from the earth and share many of the same compounds found in plants. As witches, we've been keen observers of nature over the centuries, learning and passing down the wisdom of how these natural remedies can help us heal.

St John's Wort is renowned for its mood-lifting properties. This herb has a long history of use in treating depression and mood disorders. In traditional European medicine, it was often referred to as a natural antidepressant. Contemporary scientific research has validated these claims, demonstrating that St John's Wort can be as effective as conventional antidepressants for mild to moderate depression. It works by increasing the levels of serotonin, dopamine, and norepinephrine in the brain, which are crucial for maintaining a positive mood and emotional balance.

Lavender is widely known for its ability to soothe anxiety and promote relaxation. This fragrant herb has been used for centuries in various traditional medicine systems, including Ayurveda and traditional Chinese medicine. Lavender's calming effects are well-documented in scientific literature. Research has shown that lavender can reduce anxiety levels, improve sleep quality, and promote a general sense of well-being. Its aroma alone can have a profound impact on the nervous system, making it a valuable component of any potion aimed at healing trauma.

When combined, skullcap, St John's Wort, and lavender create a powerful synergistic effect that addresses the different dimensions of trauma. Skullcap calms the mind and reduces anxiety, St John's Wort lifts the mood and combats depression, and lavender soothes the senses and promotes relaxation. This holistic approach helps to calm the mind and uplift the spirit, providing comprehensive support for those recovering from trauma.

Preparation Method: To prepare this healing potion, combine one teaspoon each of dried skullcap, St John's Wort, and lavender in a cup of boiling water. Let it steep for about 15 minutes to allow the herbs to fully release their beneficial compounds. After steeping, strain the mixture and drink a small amount twice daily. Regular consumption of this potion can help to maintain a calm mind and balanced mood, providing ongoing support throughout the healing process.

Traditional Uses and Modern Validation

The use of these herbs in traditional medicine spans various cultures and centuries. Skullcap has been a staple in Native American and European herbal traditions, valued for its calming effects. St John's Wort has been used for centuries in European folk medicine, particularly for treating "melancholy" and other mood disorders. Lavender's use is widespread, with historical records indicating its use in ancient Greece, Rome, and Egypt for its calming and healing properties.

Modern science has validated many of these traditional uses. For instance, a study published in the "Journal of Ethnopharmacology" highlighted the anxiolytic effects of skullcap, confirming its traditional use for anxiety and nervous disorders. Similarly, numerous clinical trials have shown that St John's Wort is effective in treating mild to moderate depression, as documented in the "Cochrane Database of Systematic Reviews." Lavender's benefits are also well-supported, with research in "Phytomedicine" demonstrating its ability to reduce anxiety and improve sleep quality.

Personal Experience and Reflection

In my own practice, I have seen the profound impact this potion can have on individuals recovering from trauma. One particularly memorable case involved a client who had experienced a significant traumatic (and quite horrific) event and was struggling with anxiety and depression. He had tried many things and wanted to heal, but not forget. I recommended this blend of skullcap, St John's Wort, and lavender. Over several weeks of regular use, they reported a noticeable reduction in anxiety levels, improved mood, and better sleep quality. This experience reinforced my belief in the power of these herbs and their synergistic effects.

Healing from trauma is a complex process that can be helped my modern medicine and natural remedies. The combination of skullcap, St John's Wort, and lavender offers a natural, effective way to support this journey. By calming the mind, lifting the spirit, and soothing the senses, this potion provides comprehensive support for those working to overcome the effects of trauma. Whether used alone or alongside other treatments, these herbs can be powerful allies in the path to recovery.

Healing Physical Injuries

I've found that when you mix comfrey, yarrow, and calendula, you get this incredibly effective blend that not only speeds up recovery but also soothes pain and reduces inflammation. It's the kind of potion that connects the old ways of healing with modern science, and for me, that's where the real magic lies.

Let's start with **comfrey**, often called "knitbone", and for good reason. It has this almost magical ability to help regenerate cells and reduce inflammation. I've read that historically, it was used to treat everything from broken bones to sprains, and science has now confirmed what our ancestors already knew. Comfrey contains **allantoin**, which actually stimulates cell growth and repair, and **rosmarinic acid**, which has anti-inflammatory properties. Together, they make comfrey a go-to herb for injuries that need some serious repair.

Yarrow is another herb I love working with. It's been around forever, literally used by soldiers in ancient times to stop bleeding on the battlefield. Nowadays, we know it works because of its **hemostatic** properties, meaning it stops bleeding, and its **antimicrobial** and **anti-inflammatory** effects. I've used yarrow in salves and compresses to help wounds heal faster, and it never disappoints.

And then there's **calendula**, also known as marigold. This little powerhouse herb is fantastic for the skin, with its anti-inflammatory and antiseptic properties. Calendula's compounds, like **flavonoids** and **saponins**, help reduce inflammation and promote collagen production, which is key for skin repair. Whether it's for burns, cuts, or irritations, calendula always comes through.

Now, the real magic happens when you mix these three herbs. Comfrey, yarrow, and calendula together create a synergy that takes each herb's strengths and multiplies them. When I combine these herbs into a potion, it's not just one element working alone—it's a team effort that brings about faster, more effective healing. I like to think of it as nature's version of teamwork.

How I Make This Healing Potion:

Here's how I typically prepare this healing potion for physical injuries:

1. **Simmer**: Take one teaspoon each of dried comfrey root, yarrow, and calendula.
2. **Combine**: Add them to two cups of water in a pot.
3. **Heat**: Let it simmer for about 20 minutes. This allows the herbs to release their healing compounds into the water, creating a powerful decoction.
4. **Cool**: After simmering, I let the mixture cool to a comfortable temperature.

How I Use It:

Once it's cooled, I soak a clean cloth in the potion and apply it as a compress to the injured area. The skin and tissue absorb the healing compounds from the herbs, and it really does work wonders. I usually repeat this a few times a day, depending on how bad the injury is.

A Blend of Tradition and Science:

What I love most about this combination is that it's deeply rooted in tradition, but modern science backs it up. Comfrey has been used in European herbal medicine for centuries, yarrow was a staple for Native American tribes, and calendula has been cherished in both European and Ayurvedic medicine. Today, research in journals like the *Journal of Ethnopharmacology* shows that these herbs do exactly what our ancestors claimed, they reduce pain, fight infection, and speed up healing.

For me, potion-making is more than just mixing ingredients, it's about honouring the wisdom of those who came before us and embracing the scientific knowledge we have today. When I prepare this potion, I feel connected to a long line of healers, all tapping into the same power of nature. And when I see the results, like my friend's speedy recovery, it's a reminder that the old ways still have so much to offer.

So, if you ever find yourself in need of a little natural healing, give this potion a try. It's easy to make, and the results speak for themselves. Plus, there's something incredibly satisfying about knowing you've created something with your own hands that can help a friend, sister, or even your child heal faster and feel better.

Healing Trust Issues

Trust issues can really mess with our relationships and overall happiness. They make it hard to connect with others and feel secure. To heal these deep-seated issues, you need a holistic approach that tackles both emotional and mental well-being. For me, a mix of holy basil, lemon balm, and rosemary works wonders. This combination helps calm the mind and boost emotional resilience, making it easier to rebuild trust.

Holy Basil, or tulsi as it's often called, is a superstar in traditional Ayurvedic medicine. It's known for balancing mood and reducing stress. This adaptogenic herb helps your body cope with stress by regulating cortisol, the hormone that kicks in during stressful times. Holy basil has been used for centuries in India to clear the mind and bring emotional balance. And guess what? Modern science backs this up! Studies show that holy basil can cut down on anxiety and depression, making it a great herb for dealing with trust issues.

Lemon Balm is another fantastic herb with calming and uplifting properties. People have been using it since the Middle Ages to reduce stress, sleep better, and lift their mood. Lemon balm contains rosmarinic acid, which boosts the availability of GABA in the brain, a neurotransmitter that helps you relax. Research has shown that lemon balm can significantly lower anxiety and improve cognitive performance, which is just what you need when working through trust issues.

Rosemary isn't just for cooking, it's great for your mind, too! This herb enhances mental clarity and strengthens memory. It's packed with carnosic acid and rosmarinic acid, which have antioxidant and anti-inflammatory properties. These compounds protect your brain from stress and improve cognitive function. Rosemary has been used in traditional medicine for everything from digestive problems to mental fatigue. Modern studies show that rosemary can boost your mood and mental performance, making it perfect for building emotional resilience and trust.

When you mix holy basil, lemon balm, and rosemary, their individual properties amplify each other. Holy basil's mood-balancing, lemon balm's calming, and rosemary's mind-clarifying effects combine to create a powerful potion for healing trust issues.

This blend helps calm your mind, reduce anxiety, and build emotional resilience—key ingredients for rebuilding trust.

Preparation Method: To make this healing potion, steep one teaspoon each of dried holy basil, lemon balm, and rosemary in a cup of boiling water. Let it sit for 10-15 minutes so the herbs can fully release their goodness. Strain the mixture and drink it once daily. Regularly sipping on this potion can help you maintain a calm mind and balanced mood, giving you the support you need to work through trust issues.

Holy basil, lemon balm, and rosemary have been used in traditional medicine across different cultures for centuries. Holy basil is a cornerstone of Ayurvedic medicine, considered sacred and used to promote overall health. Lemon balm has been a go-to in European herbal traditions for its calming and mood-boosting effects. Rosemary has a rich history in Mediterranean cultures, not just for cooking but also as a remedy for memory and cognitive function.

Modern science has confirmed many of these traditional uses. Studies in the "Journal of Ayurveda and Integrative Medicine" highlight holy basil's stress-reducing and mind-clearing properties. Research in "Phytotherapy Research" shows lemon balm's effectiveness in lowering anxiety and boosting mood and cognitive performance. Rosemary's benefits are well-documented too, with the "Journal of Medicinal Food" showing its positive impact on memory and mood.

Healing from Addiction

Recovering from addiction is a tough journey, and it requires a holistic approach to support both body and mind. One of the best natural ways I've found to aid this process is by using a blend of milk thistle, dandelion root, and burdock root. These herbs work together beautifully to help detoxify the body, making them invaluable allies when trying to break from addiction.

Milk Thistle is fantastic for liver detoxification. This herb has been a go-to in traditional medicine for centuries, particularly for liver and gallbladder issues. The magic ingredient in milk thistle is silymarin, a powerful antioxidant that helps protect and regenerate liver cells. There's plenty of modern science to back this up too. Studies in "Phytotherapy Research" show that silymarin can significantly improve liver function, which is a huge help when your body needs to flush out toxins during addiction recovery.

Dandelion Root is another powerhouse for detoxification. Used in both Western and Eastern herbal medicine, dandelion root is brilliant for cleansing the liver and kidneys. It stimulates bile production, which aids digestion and helps the liver process and eliminate toxins. Scientific research, like that in the "Journal of Ethnopharmacology," confirms that dandelion root supports liver health and renal function, making it essential for any detox plan.

Burdock Root has a long history in traditional medicine, including Ayurveda and traditional Chinese medicine. It's known for purifying the blood and supporting overall detoxification. Burdock root contains active compounds like inulin, volatile oils, and phenolic acids that help remove toxins from the bloodstream. Research in "BMC Complementary and Alternative Medicine" shows that burdock root can enhance detoxification and improve skin health, demonstrating its wide-ranging benefits.

When you combine milk thistle, dandelion root, and burdock root, their effects are amplified. Milk thistle's liver-protecting and regenerating properties, dandelion root's liver and kidney cleansing abilities, and burdock root's blood-purifying effects create a powerful detoxifying potion. This blend is particularly effective for those recovering from addiction, as it helps clear toxins, supports liver health, and promotes overall well-being.

Preparation Method: To whip up this healing potion, follow these steps:

1. **Simmer**: Combine one teaspoon each of dried milk thistle seeds, dandelion root, and burdock root in three cups of water.
2. **Heat**: Bring the mixture to a gentle simmer and let it bubble away for 30 minutes. This simmering process helps extract all the beneficial compounds from the herbs.
3. **Cool**: Once it's done simmering, let the potion cool to a comfortable temperature.
4. **Strain**: Strain the mixture to remove the solid bits.

How to Take It: Drink one cup of this potion in the morning and another in the evening. Regularly sipping on this herbal blend can support your body's detoxification processes and aid your recovery from addiction.

Traditional Uses and Modern Validation

These herbs have been used in traditional medicine across different cultures for centuries. Milk thistle has long been a staple in European herbal traditions for liver health, while dandelion root has been used by Native American and traditional Chinese medicine practitioners to promote liver and kidney function. Burdock root has a rich history in Ayurvedic and traditional Chinese medicine for its blood-purifying properties.

Modern science has confirmed many of these traditional uses. Research published in the "Journal of Hepatology" highlights milk thistle's role in protecting liver cells and promoting their regeneration. Studies in the "Journal of Alternative and Complementary Medicine" have confirmed dandelion root's effectiveness in enhancing liver function and promoting detoxification. Similarly, research in "Phytomedicine" demonstrates burdock root's ability to support overall detoxification and improve skin health.

Personal Experience and Reflection

In my practice, I've seen the transformative effects of this herbal blend on people recovering from addiction. One client, who was struggling with alcohol dependency, found significant relief using this potion. They reported improved liver function, better digestion, and a general sense of well-being. The combined detoxifying effects of milk thistle, dandelion root, and burdock root provided the support they needed to continue their recovery journey.

Healing Self-Esteem

When it comes to boosting self-esteem, a little herbal magic can go a long way. I've found that a blend of nettle, chamomile, and peppermint works wonders. These herbs combine to create a potion that nurtures both body and mind, giving you that extra boost of confidence and well-being.

Nettle is an absolute gem of an herb. It's packed with vitamins and minerals, like iron, calcium, and magnesium, which help boost your energy and vitality. When you're feeling run-down and low, nettle can give you that revitalising kick you need. Traditionally, nettle has been used as a spring tonic to rejuvenate the body after the long winter months. Modern research backs up its benefits too. Studies have shown that nettle can help reduce inflammation and improve overall health, making it a great choice for enhancing your physical and mental well-being.

Chamomile is the go-to herb for calming and soothing the mind. It's been used for centuries to help with anxiety, stress, and insomnia. There's something incredibly comforting about a cup of chamomile tea, and that's not just folklore. Modern science supports its calming effects. Chamomile contains compounds like apigenin, which binds to certain receptors in your brain to help reduce anxiety and promote relaxation. So, when your self-esteem takes a hit and you're feeling anxious, chamomile can help calm those nerves and provide a sense of peace.

Peppermint is another fabulous herb, known for its uplifting and invigorating properties. The refreshing taste and aroma of peppermint can instantly lift your spirits and wake up your mind. It's not just the minty freshness; peppermint has real scientific backing. Research has shown that peppermint can enhance cognitive performance and mood. It helps improve concentration and mental clarity, which can be just what you need to tackle the day with confidence.

When you combine nettle, chamomile, and peppermint, you get a powerful synergistic effect. Nettle's energy-boosting properties, chamomile's calming influence, and peppermint's invigorating lift work together to nurture both body and mind, enhancing your overall well-being and boosting your self-esteem.

Preparation Method: To prepare this self-esteem-boosting potion, simply follow these steps:

1. **Steep**: Take one teaspoon each of dried nettle, chamomile, and peppermint.
2. **Combine**: Add these herbs to a cup of boiling water.
3. **Wait**: Let it steep for about 10 minutes to allow the herbs to infuse their goodness into the water.
4. **Strain**: Strain the mixture to remove the herbs.

How to Take It: Drink this delightful potion once daily, preferably in the morning. Starting your day with this herbal blend can set a positive tone, giving you the boost you need to face whatever comes your way with confidence.

Traditional Uses and Modern Validation

Nettle, chamomile, and peppermint have long histories in traditional medicine. Nettle has been used as a nutrient-rich tonic for centuries. Chamomile is a staple in herbal remedies for relaxation and stress relief, and peppermint has been used to refresh and revitalise the body and mind.

Modern research validates many of these traditional uses. Studies in journals like the "Journal of Herbal Medicine" have highlighted nettle's anti-inflammatory and health-boosting properties. Research published in "Phytomedicine" supports chamomile's calming effects and its ability to reduce anxiety. Peppermint's cognitive benefits are backed by studies in the "International Journal of Neuroscience," showing its positive impact on mood and mental clarity.

Healing Family Relationships

To heal family relationships, a potion of hawthorn, rose, and borage is ideal. Hawthorn strengthens the heart and fosters emotional openness, rose promotes love and harmony, and borage brings courage and joy. These herbs work together to create a potion that encourages open communication and emotional healing within families.

Steep one teaspoon each of dried hawthorn berries, rose petals, and borage in a cup of boiling water for 10-15 minutes. Strain and drink as needed during family gatherings or discussions.

This one is perhaps the most difficult, and I'll put my hands up and say I am definitely not the expert on this one. Creating potions to heal family relationships is challenging because it's not just about the herbs. It's also about the energy and intention you bring to the process. When you're emotionally involved, it can be hard to maintain the focus and clarity needed to infuse the potion with the right energy. If I had nailed this one it would have saved so much heart ache through childhood years. I haven't had to make this potion in a long time. I suspect as my children grow I may need to experiment again, but let's hope not.

Healing Mental Health

For mental health, a blend of lemon balm, skullcap, and valerian root is effective. Lemon balm reduces anxiety and improves mood, skullcap calms the nervous system, and valerian root helps with sleep and relaxation. This combination creates a potion that supports mental health by addressing anxiety, mood, and sleep.

Steep one teaspoon each of dried lemon balm and skullcap, and half a teaspoon of valerian root in a cup of boiling water for 15 minutes. Strain and drink before bedtime.

Healing from Burnout

When my children were much younger, I went through a period of burnout that nearly brought me to my knees. The pressures of being a good mum, coupled with the relentless demands of daily life, left me utterly exhausted. Looking back, it's clear how burnout crept in slowly, like a thief in the night, stealing my energy, joy, and sense of self.

As a mother, I was always on the go, trying to juggle school runs, homework, meals, and endless household chores. I felt an immense pressure to be perfect, to have everything under control, to always be there for my kids, and to never let anything slip through the cracks. But no matter how hard I tried, there never seemed to be enough hours in the day. The exhaustion was overwhelming, and my patience wore thin. Little things that never used to bother me suddenly became insurmountable obstacles.

The symptoms of burnout were subtle at first. I was constantly tired, no matter how much sleep I got. My mood swung from irritable to despondent, and I began to feel disconnected from my family. Simple tasks felt monumental, and I struggled to find joy in the activities I used to love. My self-esteem took a hit as I started to believe I was failing as a mother, unable to meet the high standards I had set for myself.

The impact on my family was profound. My children, sensing my stress, became anxious and withdrawn. The gardener and I started arguing more frequently, as my burnout affected our relationship. I knew something had to change, but I felt trapped in an endless cycle of exhaustion and guilt.

One day, a dear friend noticed how worn out I looked and offered some gentle advice. She suggested I try a blend of herbs known to help with burnout: rhodiola, oat straw, and ashwagandha. Rhodiola, she explained, boosts energy and reduces fatigue. Oat straw nourishes the nervous system, providing a sense of calm and stability. Ashwagandha helps the body cope with stress, enhancing resilience and emotional balance.

Desperate for relief, I decided to give it a try. I prepared a simple infusion: one teaspoon each of dried rhodiola, oat straw, and ashwagandha steeped in a cup of boiling water for about 20 minutes. I began drinking this herbal potion once daily, hoping it would bring some semblance of balance back into my life.

Over the next few weeks, I noticed subtle changes. The constant fatigue began to lift, and I felt a bit more energized. My mood improved, and I started to feel more like myself again. The herbal blend didn't just give me a physical boost; it nurtured my mind and spirit, helping me rebuild my self-esteem and sense of worth.

As I regained my strength, I also started incorporating more self-care practices into my routine. I began meditating for a few minutes each morning, finding peace in the quiet moments before the chaos of the day began. I also made time for gentle exercise, like walking in the woods with Bunny or doing yoga, which further helped to reduce my stress levels.

Seeing the positive impact on my life, I recommended the herbal blend to a friend's husband, who worked in insurance in the City of London. He was experiencing burnout from the high-pressure environment of his job. Alongside regular exercise and meditation, he found that the herbal infusion helped him manage his stress and regain his energy. The combination of physical activity, mindfulness, and herbal support created a holistic approach that brought balance back to his life. For this I created little tea bags full of the mix to take to work. You can find empty tea bags on Amazon, but a better selection on Etsy.

Burnout often goes hand in hand with low self-esteem. When you're constantly exhausted and feeling inadequate, it's easy to lose confidence in yourself and your abilities. This herbal blend, along with the practices of meditation and exercise, helped me, and my friend's husband, rebuild that sense of self-worth.

Looking back on those difficult days, I'm grateful for the journey. It taught me the importance of self-care and the powerful role that nature can play in healing. Today, I'm more balanced and resilient, and I approach life's challenges with a newfound sense of calm and confidence. If you're feeling burnt out, know that there's hope and help out there. Sometimes, a little herbal magic, combined with self-care, can make all the difference.

Healing Grief or Regret

Grief and regret often walk hand in hand, don't they? When someone we love passes away, the pain is often accompanied by a wave of "what if's" and "if only's." We miss their presence deeply, and we can find ourselves wishing we had said something different or taken another path. There's no magic cure for these feelings, but we can find ways to manage and navigate through them.

When my parents passed away, I found myself drowning in a sea of grief and regret. The memories of our time together were bittersweet, tinged with moments I wished I could change. I missed their voices, their laughter, and their comforting presence. At the same time, I regretted the times I didn't visit enough, the arguments we had over trivial matters, and the day I left home, slamming the door behind me, a young woman who thought she knew it all. Grief and regret were constant companions as I flew back to the UK, and I knew I needed something to help me cope.

I tried all the herbs and potions I could find, but there's no cure for deep grief or regret in my view. I'm sorry if that disappoints you. Grief and regret are part of the human experience, and we must learn to live with them. But there is a way to bring back the good memories and feel the warmth of the love that radiated from them, that kept me safe and made me laugh and happy.

Walking in their footsteps. It may sound cheesy, but I've come to believe that people leave their essence or aura where they have been. Time is the issue. Now this may sound mad, but as we go through life, we are in many different places. It's just time that binds them all together. Where my parents walked, planted, worked, laughed, loved, danced, smoked, cooked, carried me, played with me, tended my grazed knee, and pulled kites out of trees, they are all in this place. Just the time, the glue, disappears when you die.

Not every problem has a cure that is within our power to create. I think the earth in which we are made and where we live has some of that power. Power outside my control. All I can say is that even though my parents have gone, even though I will always carry some regret, I feel their love around me every day. In so many ancient cultures, living with your ancestors was important, communities that stayed in the essence of the family that went before them. The transient life we lead these days does not have all the answers.

Like every living thing on this Earth, including every herb you will read about in this book, it passes a part of itself on its DNA through its offspring.

My parents never met their grandchildren, but a part of them both; walks, runs, plays hopscotch, giggles, looks on with pride and holds their hands.

My grief is not fixed, I will always miss them and wish some things had been different, but I am content. I am lucky.

Love & Attraction Spells

Love and attraction are among the most powerful forces in the universe. They shape our relationships, our happiness, and our sense of belonging. Throughout history, witches and herbalists have harnessed the power of nature to create spells, potions, and brews to influence these forces, helping people find love, deepen relationships, and foster connections. Whether you're seeking to ignite new passion, attract a soulmate, or strengthen family bonds, there's a magical brew that can help.

To Find Romantic Love

My dear friend Sarah had just come out of a tough divorce. She was feeling a bit battered, skeptical about love, and convinced she would never find another partner. One warm summer evening, I decided we needed a girls' night in, complete with a little magical help to mend her heart and open it up to new possibilities.

I proposed making a love potion, and Sarah burst into laughter. "You know I don't believe in this crap, right?" she said, still chuckling. But she was game for anything that night, so we decided to have some fun with it.

Potion Ingredients:

- 1 teaspoon dried hawthorn berries
- 1 teaspoon dried meadowsweet flowers
- 1 teaspoon dried lemon verbena
- 1 cup water
- A splash of Cornish Dry Gin

Method:

1. Boil the water and pour it over the dried herbs.
2. Let it steep for 10 minutes.
3. Strain the mixture, add a splash of gin, and drink the potion while visualizing the type of partner you wish to attract. (I promised to visualize the Gardener, which I did)
4. Repeat this ritual daily until you feel a shift in your energy.

Why These Herbs?

Hawthorn Berries: Hawthorn berries are traditionally used to strengthen the heart, both physically and emotionally. They help open the heart to new possibilities. Studies in "Phytotherapy Research" support hawthorn's benefits for heart health and its ability to reduce anxiety.

Meadowsweet Flowers: Meadowsweet flowers have a sweet, calming fragrance and are known for their uplifting properties. They help soothe emotional pain and bring about a sense of peace and happiness. Historically used in love spells, meadowsweet is also mentioned in various herbal texts for its calming effects.

Lemon Verbena: Lemon verbena has a bright, uplifting scent that helps to clear the mind and attract positive energy. It's often used in aromatherapy to boost mood and mental clarity. Research published in the "Journal of Ethnopharmacology" shows its effectiveness in reducing stress and improving overall well-being.

The Magic Night

With our potion ready, we took our glasses and headed out to the garden. The summer air was warm, and the stars were just starting to peep out. We decided to add a bit of fun to our ritual by dancing barefoot on the grass to Matt Bianco, letting the cool earth ground us. We twirled and laughed, the gin in our potion, (3rd glass) making us a bit giddy.

Sarah couldn't stop giggling. "I can't believe I'm doing this!" she said, but I could see her skepticism melting away, being replaced with laughter. We talked about the qualities she wanted in a partner; kindness, a good sense of humor, someone who would appreciate her strength and independence, and err, some physical characteristics.

As we sipped our potion and danced under the stars, we laughed until we cried. The combination of the herbs, yes the gin, and the ritualistic fun seemed to lift a weight off Sarah's shoulders. For the first time in a while, she looked genuinely happy and relaxed.

The magic ingredients to this potion: Fun and grass between the toes! Potions are only a part of the spell!

Over the next few weeks, I told Sarah to continue the ritual. She'd make the potion, sometimes with a splash of gin, sometimes without, and take a few moments to visualize her ideal partner. Slowly but surely, I noticed changes in her. She became more open, her laughter more frequent, and her skepticism about finding love started to fade.

One evening, she called me, excitement in her voice. "You won't believe this, but I met someone," she said. "and...I can't believe he's almost everything I wished for" I was quiet for a moment and then said conspiratorially "everything!" quietly – referring to some of the physical attributes she had asked for. "well, I don't know everything" We laughed together, and she admitted that while she still found the idea of potions and spells amusing, there was something undeniably powerful about setting intentions and opening up to possibilities. Was it the symbolism of taking control over new beginnings or life, or was it the potion? I think it's all one and the same.

She wasn't completely convinced, but whether you believe in witchcraft or not, there's something to be said about taking time for yourself, setting clear intentions, and having a bit of fun along the way. So, if you're looking to attract love, why not try this potion? Gather your herbs, add a splash of your favourite drink, and dance under the stars. You never know what magic might happen!

To Rekindle Passion

Potion Ingredients:

- 1 teaspoon dried damiana
- 1 teaspoon dried cinnamon
- 1 teaspoon dried ginger
- 1 cup water or gin

Method:

1. Boil the water and pour it over the dried herbs.
2. Let it steep for 15 minutes.
3. Strain and share the potion with your partner before a romantic evening.

Why These Herbs: Damiana is known for its aphrodisiac properties, cinnamon stimulates warmth and passion, and ginger enhances circulation and excitement.

To Enhance Commitment

Potion Ingredients:

- 1 teaspoon dried rosemary
- 1 teaspoon dried basil
- 1 teaspoon dried thyme
- 1 cup water

Method:

1. Boil the water and pour it over the dried herbs.
2. Let it steep for 10 minutes.
3. Strain and drink the potion together with your partner while discussing your future.

Why These Herbs: Rosemary symbolizes loyalty, basil enhances love and devotion, and thyme promotes courage and long-term commitment.

To Attract Friendship

Potion Ingredients:

- 1 teaspoon dried chamomile
- 1 teaspoon dried lemon balm
- 1 teaspoon dried fennel
- 1 cup water

Method:

1. Boil the water and pour it over the dried herbs.
2. Let it steep for 10 minutes.
3. Strain and drink the potion while visualizing welcoming new, meaningful friendships into your life.

Why These Herbs: Chamomile promotes relaxation and friendliness, lemon balm attracts positive energy, and fennel enhances communication and understanding.

To Strengthen Family Bonds

Potion Ingredients:

- 1 teaspoon dried hawthorn berries
- 1 teaspoon dried rose petals
- 1 teaspoon dried marigold
- 1 cup water

Method:

1. Boil the water and pour it over the dried herbs.
2. Let it steep for 15 minutes.
3. Strain and share the potion with your family during a gathering, focusing on unity and love.

Why These Herbs: Hawthorn strengthens emotional bonds, rose petals symbolize love, and marigold promotes warmth and affection.

To Invoke Lust

Potion Ingredients:

- 1 teaspoon dried ginseng
- 1 teaspoon dried clove
- 1 teaspoon dried damiana
- 1 cup water

Method:

1. Boil the water and pour it over the dried herbs.
2. Let it steep for 15 minutes.
3. Strain and drink the potion to heighten desire and attraction.

Why These Herbs: Ginseng boosts energy and libido, clove enhances sensory experiences, and damiana stimulates passion.

To Promote Forgiveness

Potion Ingredients:

- 1 teaspoon dried lemon balm
- 1 teaspoon dried sage
- 1 teaspoon dried mint
- 1 cup water

Method:

1. Boil the water and pour it over the dried herbs.
2. Let it steep for 15 minutes.
3. Strain and drink the potion while focusing on letting go of past hurts and fostering forgiveness.

Why These Herbs: Lemon balm soothes emotions, sage cleanses negative energy, and mint promotes peace and forgiveness.

Helping Your Children Find Friendship

Potion Ingredients:

- 1 teaspoon dried chamomile
- 1 teaspoon dried peppermint
- 1 teaspoon dried calendula
- 1 cup water

Method:

1. Boil the water and pour it over the dried herbs.
2. Let it steep for 10 minutes.
3. Strain and share the potion with your child, encouraging them to visualize making new friends.

Why These Herbs: Chamomile fosters relaxation and openness, peppermint attracts positive interactions, and calendula enhances communication and understanding.

By carefully selecting and combining these herbs, you can create potent healing potions tailored to specific needs. Each potion harnesses the unique properties of the herbs, working together to amplify their effects and provide holistic healing. Remember to always source your herbs from trusted suppliers to ensure their purity and potency.

"La magie coule à travers l'air et l'eau, portant les murmures des vies anciennes."

"Magic flows through air and water carrying whispers of ancient lives"

Chapter 11: Introduction to Candles, Smudging, and Bath Oils

Welcome to the enchanting world of candles, smudging, and bath oils! Let's discover how these magical tools can transform your rituals, purify your space, and nurture your spirit. Let's embark on this journey together and explore how the ancient wisdom of herbal alchemy can enhance your daily practice.

The Magic of Candles

Candles have always been a cornerstone of magical practices, and for good reason. They focus energy, symbolize the elements, and bring a warm, inviting light to your rituals. In the world of herbal alchemy, candles do so much more, they become extensions of your will, each colour and scent holding specific meanings and intentions.

Imagine lighting a candle and watching its flame dance. This simple act can transform your space and your mindset. Picture a green candle infused with the fresh scents of basil and mint, perfect for drawing prosperity into your life. Or a purple candle, scented with calming lavender, to enhance your spiritual awareness and psychic abilities. By anointing candles with herb-infused oils and carving symbols or sigils into their wax, you can make each ritual uniquely yours and amplify your magical intentions.

The Sacred Art of Smudging

Smudging is an ancient and powerful practice that cleanses and purifies spaces, objects, and even ourselves using the smoke from sacred herbs. This ritual, deeply rooted in various indigenous traditions, is a beloved method in modern witchcraft for clearing out negative energies and inviting positive vibes.

Think of smudging as a spiritual spring cleaning. Common smudging herbs like sage, cedar, sweetgrass, and lavender each bring their own special energy to your ritual. Sage is the powerhouse of smudging herbs, known for its strong cleansing properties. Cedar is perfect for protection and grounding, sweetgrass brings in positive energies, and lavender promotes peace and relaxation.

To smudge, simply light the end of a smudge stick or loose herbs until it catches flame, then gently blow it out to produce smoke. Waft the smoke around your space or object with a feather or your hand, focusing on your intention of purification and renewal. It's a simple yet profoundly effective way to reset the energy around you.

The Alchemy of Bath Oils

Bathing is more than just a way to get clean, it's a sacred act of renewal. When you add the magic of herbs and essential oils, your bath becomes a ritual of deep healing and transformation. Herbal bath oils harness the therapeutic properties of plants, letting their energies soak into your body and spirit through the soothing embrace of water. Creating your own herbal bath oils is a delightful process. Choose herbs and essential oils that match your desired outcome. Feeling drained? Try a blend of rosemary, eucalyptus, and peppermint oils to invigorate and energize. Need to unwind? A soothing mixture of chamomile, rose, and sandalwood can provide comfort and relaxation, perfect for a tranquil end to your day.

To use your bath oils, simply add a few drops to your bathwater, immerse yourself, and let the fragrant, healing herbs work their magic. As you soak, visualize the water washing away negativity and tension, leaving you feeling refreshed and renewed. Candles, smudging, and bath oils offer unique ways to harness the power of herbal alchemy in your everyday life. By integrating these practices into your rituals, you can create a sanctuary of healing, protection, and spiritual growth. As you explore this chapter, I hope you find joy and magic in these ancient practices, and that they become treasured parts of your modern witchcraft journey. Happy casting!

Crafting Magical Candles

Candles have always held a special place in my heart, not just for their practical uses but for their ability to transform a space with their light. Over the years, I've embraced the art of candle-making, particularly using natural beeswax and herbs, to create tools of intention and magic. Today, I'm excited to share my personal process for making these enchanting candles, along with the types I craft for various purposes like protection, health, love, and more.

The Importance of Pure Beeswax

When it comes to making candles, the quality of the wax is paramount. Pure beeswax is my material of choice for several reasons. Firstly, beeswax burns cleaner than paraffin or soy wax, producing minimal soot and a delightful, natural honey scent. It's also eco-friendly and renewable, as beeswax is a byproduct of honey production. Using pure beeswax ensures that the candles I make are not only effective in magical practices but also beneficial for the environment and health.

The Process of Making Beeswax Candles

Materials Needed:

- Pure beeswax (be sure it's 100% pure, free from additives)
- Cotton wicks (pre-waxed)
- Essential oils (optional, for added scent and magical properties)
- Dried herbs (specific to the candle's intention)
- Candle molds or containers
- Double boiler or a makeshift one (a large pot and a smaller pot)
- Thermometer
- Wooden skewers or chopsticks (for holding the wick in place)
- Heat-resistant gloves

Step-by-Step Process:

1. **Preparing the Wax:**
    - Start by cutting the beeswax into small chunks. This helps it melt more evenly and quickly.
    - Set up your double boiler. Fill the larger pot with water and place the smaller pot inside, ensuring it doesn't touch the bottom. Add the beeswax to the smaller pot.

2. **Melting the Wax:**
    - Heat the water in the larger pot, bringing it to a gentle simmer. Stir the beeswax occasionally as it melts. Using a thermometer, ensure the temperature stays between 145-175°F (63-79°C) to prevent burning the wax.

3. **Preparing the Wick:**
    - While the wax melts, prepare your candle molds or containers. Cut the wick to the desired length, leaving a bit of excess. Attach the wick to the bottom of the mold using a bit of melted wax or a metal wick holder. Use a wooden skewer or chopstick to hold the wick upright at the top of the mold.

4. **Adding Herbs and Essential Oils:**
    - Once the wax is fully melted, remove it from heat and let it cool slightly before adding any essential oils (around 150°F or 65°C is ideal). Stir in your chosen essential oils and dried herbs. Be mindful of the amount—too many herbs can cause the candle to burn improperly.

5. **Pouring the Wax:**
    - Carefully pour the melted wax into your prepared molds or containers, making sure the wick stays centered. Pour slowly to avoid air bubbles and allow the herbs to distribute evenly.

6. **Setting the Candle:**
    - Allow the candles to cool and harden completely, which can take several hours. Once set, trim the wick to about 1/4 inch (0.6 cm).

7. **Removing from Molds:**
    - If using molds, gently remove the candles once they are fully hardened. If they stick, you can place the mold in the refrigerator for a few minutes to help them release.

Types of Magical Candles

Protection Candles
For protection, I craft candles infused with herbs like rosemary, sage, and bay leaves. However, I also love to incorporate smaller amounts mugwort, elderberry leaves, and yarrow. Mugwort is known for its protective and psychic properties, elderberry leaves offer powerful protection against negativity, and yarrow is revered for its ability to shield and heal. I often use black or white beeswax, as these colours are traditionally associated with warding off negative energies and creating a safe space.

Health Candles
Health candles are usually green or blue, symbolizing healing and calm. In addition to eucalyptus, peppermint, and chamomile, I use herbs like comfrey, meadowsweet, and calendula. Comfrey is excellent for physical healing, meadowsweet soothes and relieves pain, and calendula promotes skin health and overall well-being. Eucalyptus and peppermint are known for their refreshing and respiratory benefits, while chamomile promotes relaxation and reduces stress.

Love and Romance Candles
For love and romance, pink or red beeswax is perfect. Besides the classic rose petals, lavender, and cinnamon, I also use hawthorn berries, apple blossom, and borage. Hawthorn berries open the heart to love, apple blossom symbolizes love and fertility, and borage brings courage and joy. Roses are the quintessential symbol of love, lavender promotes calm and emotional balance, and cinnamon adds a spark of passion and warmth. I have been experimenting with seeds and extract from the sap of Silphium more recently. The seeds dried and lightly toasted before crushing into a powder seems to work well. I have also had better than expected results from the Giant Fennel seeds.

Prosperity Candles
Gold or green beeswax is ideal for prosperity candles. Alongside basil, bay leaves, and clover, I incorporate herbs like vervain, cinquefoil, and elderflowers. Vervain is known for attracting wealth and success, cinquefoil is associated with money and good fortune, and elderflowers are used for prosperity and protection. Basil is known for its money-attracting properties, bay leaves for success, and clover for luck.

Unity Candles
For a wedding, a Unity Candle is a beautiful symbol of two lives joining together as one. I often use white beeswax for purity and new beginnings, but sometimes I blend it with gold to symbolize prosperity and abundance in the marriage. To create a Unity Candle, I infuse it with herbs and essential oils that promote love, harmony, and enduring bonds. Rose petals and lavender are staples for their loving and calming properties. I also include rosemary for remembrance and fidelity, myrtle for love and joy, and vanilla for sweetness and warmth. For a touch of magic and protection, I add a few drops of jasmine oil, known for its association with love and spiritual growth. The

Unity Candle can be adorned with carvings or sigils that hold personal significance to the couple, making it a deeply personal and symbolic part of their wedding ceremony.

The Importance of Pure Beeswax

Pure beeswax is essential not only for its clean-burning properties but also for its magical correspondences. Bees have been considered sacred in many cultures, symbolizing hard work, community, and abundance. Using beeswax connects the candle's energy with these powerful symbols, enhancing the overall intention of the candle.

Choosing beeswax crafted by bees that feast on pollen from different plants is akin to experiencing the diverse flavour notes in fine wine. Just as the grape variety influence a wine's taste, the flora that bees visit shapes the beeswax's aroma, colour, and energy. For instance, beeswax from lavender fields may carry a gentle, soothing scent, much like a delicate white wine with floral notes, perfect for candles aimed at relaxation or meditation. Conversely, beeswax from wildflower-rich areas can have a more complex and rich fragrance, similar to a robust red wine with layers of flavour, ideal for creating uplifting and invigorating candles. This natural diversity not only imparts unique characteristics to each candle but also aligns with specific magical or therapeutic intentions, making each batch of beeswax a true reflection of its botanical origin. Selecting beeswax from particular pollen sources allows for a more tailored and enriched candle-making experience, much like choosing a wine to complement a specific meal or occasion.

To colour beeswax, you can use finely ground herbs, spices, and botanical powders. For example, turmeric can be used to create a warm yellow or golden colour, spirulina or chlorella powder can impart a green shade, and beetroot powder can give a lovely pink or red tint. To incorporate these natural colours, add the chosen powder to the melted beeswax and stir thoroughly to ensure even distribution. Strain the wax through a fine mesh to remove any undissolved particles if needed. This method not only adds a touch of colour to your candles but also infuses them with the additional energies and properties of the herbs and botanicals used, enhancing their magical and aesthetic appeal.

Common Pitfalls in Candle-Making

Uneven Burning
One common issue is uneven burning, often caused by using too many herbs or an improperly centred wick. To avoid this, make sure to use a moderate amount of herbs and secure the wick firmly in the centre.

Sinkholes
Sinkholes can form in the centre of the candle as it cools. This can be mitigated by pouring the wax in two stages—first filling the mold partially, allowing it to cool slightly, then topping it off.

Overheating Wax
Overheating the beeswax can lead to a brittle candle or one that doesn't hold its scent well. Always keep an eye on the temperature and avoid letting it exceed 175°F (79°C).

Candles infused with herbs and imbued with magical properties have been referenced throughout literature. For example, in "Practical Magic" by Alice Hoffman, candles play a crucial role in the Owens family's spellwork, embodying intentions of love and protection. Similarly, in J.K. Rowling's "Harry Potter" series, magical candles are used for various purposes, from illuminating dark paths to enhancing spells in potion-making.

Crafting candles from natural beeswax and herbs is a deeply rewarding practice that combines the art of candle-making with the power of herbal alchemy. By carefully selecting pure beeswax and infusing it with specific herbs and essential oils, you can create candles tailored to your magical intentions—whether for protection, health, love, or prosperity. Embrace the process, learn from the pitfalls, and let your creativity and intuition guide you. In doing so, you'll not only enhance your magical practice but also create beautiful, meaningful tools that light up your life and rituals.

Creating and Using Smudging: A Guide to Sacred Smoke Rituals

Smudging is an ancient and powerful practice that I've come to cherish deeply. It's a ritual used to purify and cleanse spaces, objects, and individuals, rooted in indigenous traditions from around the world. The act of burning sacred herbs to produce smoke that carries away negative energy and invites positive vibrations has profound significance. Over the years, I have developed a personal approach to smudging, blending a variety of herbs, including some unusual ones, to create potent and meaningful rituals. Let me share with you how I create my smudge sticks, the best herbs to use, and how to perform a smudging ceremony. I'll also highlight examples of smudging in films to illustrate its cultural significance.

The Basics of Smudging

At its core, smudging involves burning a bundle of dried herbs, known as a smudge stick, or using loose herbs placed in a fireproof bowl or shell. The most common herbs for smudging are sage, cedar, sweetgrass, and lavender, each chosen for their specific energetic properties and their abilities to cleanse, protect, and heal.

Essential Ingredients for Smudging

The most well-known smudging herb is white sage. It's my go-to for clearing negative energy and creating a sacred space. Cedar, with its strong protective and grounding qualities, is another favourite. Sweetgrass, with its sweet, uplifting aroma, is wonderful for bringing in good spirits and positive vibrations, often used after sage. Lavender is added to promote relaxation and reduce stress, its calming scent bringing peace and tranquillity.

But I love experimenting with less common herbs too. Mugwort is one of my top picks for its psychic protection and dream-enhancing properties. It's fantastic for rituals involving intuition and divination. Yarrow is another gem, offering strong protection and healing, ideal for shielding against negative influences and promoting inner strength. Juniper, with its purifying and protective energy, is great for cleansing spaces, while rosemary is perfect for enhancing memory and clarity. Bay leaves, with their protective and prosperity-attracting qualities, round out my list of must-have smudging herbs.

Making Smudge Sticks

Creating smudge sticks is a deeply rewarding process that allows you to customize the herbs to your specific needs and intentions. I usually start by gathering fresh herbs early in the day, once the dew has dried. Choosing healthy stems and leaves is crucial. I lay out the herbs on a clean surface, removing any excess stems or leaves, and then arrange them into small bundles, mixing different types to combine their properties. Holding a bundle together tightly, I begin wrapping it with natural cotton string or twine, starting at the base and tying a knot to secure it. I continue wrapping the string up the length of the bundle in a crisscross pattern, pulling tight as I go. Once I reach the top, I tie another knot to secure it, trim any excess string or uneven herb ends, and hang the smudge sticks in a dry, well-ventilated area away from direct sunlight. Drying takes a few weeks, ensuring the smudge sticks will burn evenly.

Performing a Smudging Ceremony

Performing a smudging ceremony starts with setting an intention. I take a moment to focus on what I want to achieve with the smudging, whether it's clearing negative energy, protecting a space, or promoting healing. Holding the smudge stick at a 45-degree angle, I light the end with a match or lighter, allowing it to catch fire then gently blow out the flame to give smoke.

As I walk around the space I want to cleanse, I waft the smoke into corners, doorways, and other areas where energy can become stagnant, using a feather or my hand to direct the smoke. If I'm cleansing objects, I hold them in the smoke or pass the smudge stick around them. For personal cleansing, I start at my feet and move the smudge stick upward, letting the smoke envelop my body, paying special attention to areas where I feel tension or negativity.

Once finished, I extinguish the smudge stick by pressing the burning end into a fireproof bowl or sand, ensuring it's completely out before storing it for future use.

Smudging in Films

The "Twilight" series includes scenes where the Quileute tribe, who are shapeshifters, use smudging to cleanse and protect their spaces, reflecting real-life Native American traditions. "Smoke Signals," an independent film based on Sherman Alexie's book, features smudging scenes that highlight its role in Native American culture, as characters use it to connect with their heritage and cleanse themselves spiritually. In

"The Last Airbender," Uncle Iroh uses smudging to cleanse negative energies and promote harmony, underscoring its use as a tool for balance and purification.

The Benefits of Smudging

Smudging offers numerous benefits, both practical and spiritual. It purifies the air by releasing negative ions, which neutralize pollutants and allergens, resulting in cleaner, fresher air. It also removes stagnant or negative energy from spaces, objects, and individuals, promoting a positive and harmonious environment. The ritual of smudging can deepen spiritual practices, helping individuals connect with their higher selves, ancestors, and spiritual guides. The process can also clear mental fog and enhance focus, making it valuable before meditation, study, or creative work. Moreover, smudging with certain herbs, like lavender and rose, can promote emotional healing, reduce stress, and encourage a sense of peace and well-being.

Smudging is a powerful and ancient practice that offers numerous benefits for the mind, body, and spirit. By creating your own smudge sticks with a blend of common and unusual herbs, you can tailor your smudging rituals to meet your specific needs and intentions. Whether you're clearing negative energy from your home, preparing for meditation, or seeking protection and healing, smudging can enhance your spiritual practice and promote a harmonious environment. Embrace the art of smudging and discover the transformative power of sacred smoke rituals.

Smudging - an excuse to tell you about my wedding

Like most who get married, marrying "The Gardener" was without doubt one of the most profound and emotionally significant experiences of my life. Our wedding, a beautiful handfasting ceremony held in a woodland clearing, was not just a union of two people but the start of a new life, for us and creating a new family. The day was filled with love, magic, and a sense of connection to nature that I will cherish forever.

The Preparation

We chose to get married on Beltane, a day brimming with the energies of fertility, growth, and the sacred union of the divine masculine and feminine. This date was perfect for us, aligning our union with the powerful rhythms of nature. The woodland clearing where we held our ceremony was in the woods behind the small village of Stoke Row in South Oxfordshire. It felt like a magical sanctuary, surrounded by towering trees and vibrant greenery, a place where the earth itself seemed to bless us.

We began by smudging the area with sage, lavender, and meadowsweet, watching the purifying smoke rise and knowing it was cleansing our space for this sacred event. As we sprinkled a mix of love-in-a-mist, damiana, yarrow, vervain, and meadowsweet in a circle around the clearing, I felt a surge of love, passion, and protection envelop us. These herbs, chosen for their powerful properties, created a boundary of sacred energy, ensuring that our ceremony would be both protected and blessed.

The Ceremony

As our guests gathered, a mix of friends, family, fellow witches, and some of The Gardener's Welsh relatives who are Christian churchgoers, I could see their curiosity and uncertainty. Some must have wondered if we would be summoning demons or cavorting naked, but of course, we did none of those things. Just as I attend Christian weddings and find them wonderful and magical in their own way, we wanted our ceremony to reflect our beliefs and values without alienating anyone.

When the ceremony began with the casting of the sacred circle, I felt a profound shift in energy. Walking around the perimeter, invoking the elements of earth, air, fire, and water, I could sense the protective barrier forming around us. This circle was not just a ritualistic boundary but a tangible space of love and sacredness that enveloped everyone present.

Our officiant, or Priestess, was a dear friend and fellow witch called Elly. She called upon the elements and our chosen deities to bless our union. (Lugh, Aine, Cernunnos and Brigid). As we stood in the centre of the circle, I felt the presence of the earth beneath my feet, the breeze of the air, the warmth of the fire, and the flow of water around us, connecting us deeply to the natural world and to each other.

The handfasting ritual was the heart of our ceremony. Holding hands with The Gardener and feeling the cord wrap around us was incredibly intimate and powerful. Each vow we spoke, each promise of love, loyalty, and support, felt like we were knitting our future together. This binding was not just symbolic; it was a profound commitment to walk this path together, heart to heart and soul to soul. The emotions were filling me up and it was hard not to cry.
Exchanging rings, blessed earlier on our altar, was another deeply emotional moment. These rings, charged with the energies of the elements and our intentions, were more than just symbols of our love. They were talismans of our commitment to a harmonious and prosperous life together.

Celebrating Our Union
As our friends and family offered their blessings, sharing words of encouragement and love, I was overwhelmed with emotion. Their support and the energy they contributed to our circle were all around us. Lighting the unity candle that I had made together symbolized our joined lives, and seeing its flame burn brightly filled me with warmth and joy.

When the circle was opened and we were presented as married, the joy and love in the clearing was really moving. Our celebration continued with a picnic under the trees, filled with laughter, barefoot dancing, and the joyful sounds of nature. Planting a tree together, symbolizing our growth and the roots we were putting down as a couple, capped off our perfect day. It was a European Nettle Tree.

Later in the evening, we all walked from the woodland circle to The Cherry Tree Pub in the little village of Stoke Row to continue the celebration. I am sure the locals wondered about this party of barefooted energized people flowing into their pub. This charming, historic pub and a favourite of mine for many years, provided the perfect setting for extending our wedding reception. It was a cozy and welcoming place where we could all relax and enjoy each other's company. Some friends and family members who hadn't been able to attend the actual handfasting ceremony joined us there, adding to the joy and warmth of the occasion. The pub's rustic ambiance, with its old wooden beams and fireplace full of May blooms, set a lovely backdrop for our festivities. We shared even more delicious food, raised our glasses of beer to love and happiness, and created unforgettable memories.

Personal Touches

Every aspect of our wedding was a reflection of our journey together. I wore a flowing dress adorned with flowers and crystals and a flower ring in my hair, feeling every bit the woodland fairy bride. The Gardener wore a green velvet waistcoat which I had embroidered with darker green vines and hops, reflecting his deep connection to the earth, and wine and beer! We both went barefoot, grounding ourselves in the sacred space we had created, feeling the earth beneath our feet.

I had wanted our ceremony to feel personal, rather than just an event, and it was all I had hoped. From the herbs that formed our protective circle, the smudging stick that prepared the woodland circle and the unity candle, every detail was a testament to our love and our commitment to each other and our spiritual path.

Marrying "The Gardener" in a handfasting ceremony connected us to each other, our community, and the natural world. The rituals we performed, the herbs we used, and the vows we spoke all combined to create a day that was uniquely ours. It was a celebration of love, passion, and the magical journey we are on together, a day that will forever be etched in my heart and soul.

Crafting Magical Bath Oils

Creating bath oils infused with herbs is one of my favourite alchemical practices. There's something incredibly satisfying about transforming simple ingredients into luxurious, aromatic elixirs that nourish the body and soothe the soul. Today, I'd love to share with you my process for making these delightful concoctions. I'll also explore what these bath oils can do and share a few special recipes, including one perfect for sharing with your partner! So, let's dive into the fragrant world of herbal bath oils!

The Basics of Making Bath Oils

Making bath oils is a straightforward process, but like all good magic, it requires intention, patience, and a little bit of creativity. Here's how I do it:

First, you need to choose your base oils. My go-to options are sweet almond oil, jojoba oil, and grapeseed oil. They are light, non-greasy, and excellent for the skin. Next, you'll want to gather your herbs. You can use fresh or dried herbs, depending on what's available. I'll get into my favourite unusual herbs shortly. You'll also need some essential oils to enhance the aroma and therapeutic properties of your bath oils.

I start by selecting the herbs based on the desired effect of the bath oil. For example, I might use lavender for relaxation or rosemary for rejuvenation. Once I've decided, I fill a glass jar about halfway with the chosen herbs and then pour the base oil over them until they are completely submerged, leaving a bit of space at the top to allow for expansion.

Next comes the infusion process. I seal the jar tightly and place it in a warm, sunny spot. I like to leave mine on a windowsill where it can soak up the sun's energy. The infusion process takes about four to six weeks, during which I gently shake the jar every few days to mix the herbs with the oil.

After the infusion period, I strain the oil through a cheesecloth or fine strainer to remove the herbs. Squeezing out as much oil as possible from the herbs ensures I get every last drop of goodness. Then, I add a few drops of essential oils to the strained oil to boost its potency and fragrance. The amount will depend on the volume of your base oil and personal preference, but typically, I add about 10-20 drops per cup of oil.

Finally, I transfer the infused oil to dark glass bottles to protect it from light and store it in a cool, dark place. Properly stored, these oils can last up to a year.

While lavender and rosemary are wonderful, I love experimenting with other herbs to create unique and potent bath oils. One of my favourites is Mugwort as you will have seen from other chapters in this book, known for its ability to enhance dreams and psychic abilities. Just be careful not to fall asleep in the tub! We want vivid dreams, not prune fingers!

Another great herb is Calendula, with its bright orange petals. Calendula is not only visually stunning but also fantastic for skin healing and soothing inflammation. I like to think of calendula as the happy little sunshine flower that banishes all skin woes.

Meadowsweet, traditionally used for its anti-inflammatory and pain-relieving properties, is wonderful for a post-workout soak. Perfect for when you've convinced yourself that running that marathon was a good idea. Damiana is known for its aphrodisiac qualities and Love-in-a-Mist, with its delicate blue flowers, is associated with love and romance. It's like a little sprinkle of fairy dust for your love life.

What Bath Oils Can Do
Bath oils infused with herbs can do wonders for your mind, body, and spirit. They are great for relaxation, especially when using herbs like lavender, chamomile, and lemon balm. These oils can help you wind down and ease stress. For skin care, calendula and

rose petals are excellent for soothing and healing. If you're looking for rejuvenation, rosemary and eucalyptus can invigorate and refresh, making them perfect for a morning bath. For romance, rose petals, damiana, and jasmine can create a sensual and loving atmosphere, ideal for a romantic bath with your partner. Finally, for spiritual cleansing, Mugwort and sage can help cleanse your aura and prepare you for meditation or ritual work.

Recipes for Bath Oils

Let me share a few of my favourite recipes.

For a dream-enhancing bath oil, I start with a base of sweet almond or jojoba oil and infuse it with dried mugwort for four to six weeks. Once strained, I add ten drops each of lavender and frankincense essential oils. This oil is perfect for adding a few tablespoons to your bath before bedtime to enhance dreams and promote restful sleep.

For a skin-soothing bath oil, I use grapeseed or sweet almond oil as the base and infuse it with dried calendula petals. After the infusion period, I strain the oil and add ten drops of chamomile and five drops of tea tree essential oils. This oil is fantastic for soothing and healing irritated skin.

For a romantic evening bath oil, I use sweet almond or grapeseed oil and infuse it with dried rose petals and damiana leaves. After straining, I add fifteen drops of jasmine and ten drops of vanilla essential oils. This oil creates a romantic and sensual atmosphere, perfect for sharing with your partner.

Finally, for a rejuvenating morning bath oil, I use a base of grapeseed oil and infuse it with rosemary and eucalyptus leaves. After the infusion, I strain the oil and add ten drops of peppermint and five drops of lemon essential oils. This oil is invigorating and refreshing, perfect for starting your day with a burst of energy.

Creating bath oils is not only a fun and creative process but also a deeply personal and magical one. Each oil I make is infused with my intentions and the unique properties of the herbs, making them powerful tools for self-care and spiritual practice. Whether you're looking to relax, rejuvenate, heal, or connect with your partner, there's a bath oil for every need. So, why not give it a try and see what magic you can create in your own bath?

Crafting Your Own Essential Oils:

Creating your own essential oils is a deeply satisfying and rewarding process, especially when working with uncommon herbs. While it requires some specialized equipment and patience, the end result is uniquely yours and incredibly potent. Let me share how I make my own essential oils, the equipment I use, and how I store these precious oils.

The Journey of Distillation

To start making your own essential oils, you'll need a few key pieces of equipment. The heart of the process is a distiller. I use a home distillation unit that I purchased online. It usually consists of a boiler, condenser, and collection vessel. Along with that, you'll need some fresh or dried herbs, depending on what's available. Fresh herbs generally yield more oil. You'll also need distilled water to avoid any impurities that might affect the oil, a heat source like a stove or electric burner, dark brown or blue glass bottles for storing the finished oils, and a funnel and cheesecloth for straining and transferring the oils.

The first step is preparing the herbs. I love using fresh herbs when possible, as they contain more volatile oils. Herbs like mugwort, lemon balm, or damiana are my go-to choices for their unique properties. I roughly chop the herbs to increase the surface area, which helps in extracting more oil.

Next, I set up the distiller. I fill the boiler with distilled water and place the chopped herbs in the distillation chamber or basket. It's important not to pack the herbs too tightly, as the steam needs to move through the plant material efficiently.

With the distiller ready, I heat the water in the boiler to produce steam. As the steam rises, it passes through the herbs, extracting the essential oils. This steam, carrying the essential oils, travels through the condenser, where it cools and turns back into liquid. This liquid, a mixture of water and essential oils, is collected in the collection tub. Once the distillation process is complete, you'll notice a layer of oil floating on top of the water in the collection vessel. This is your essential oil. Using a funnel lined with cheesecloth, I strain the mixture into a separation funnel and let it sit so the oil can separate from the water. I carefully drain the water from the bottom, leaving the essential oil behind. After that, I transfer the pure essential oil into dark glass bottles using a small funnel.

Proper storage is essential to maintain the potency and longevity of your essential oils. I always use dark glass bottles to protect the oils from light exposure, which can cause them to oxidize and lose their therapeutic properties. I store my bottles in a draw in the kitchen, away from direct sunlight and heat sources. Ensuring the bottles are sealed tightly prevents air from entering and oxidizing the oils, preserving their quality over time. And when using your oils, avoid contaminating them with other substances. Always use clean droppers or pipettes and avoid touching the inside of the bottle with your hands.

The process of making essential oils is a bit like being a kitchen witch, blending science with magic. I remember the first time I tried distilling mugwort. My kitchen looked like a scene from a mad scientist's lab, complete with bubbling pots and aromatic steam. As I waited for the distillation to finish, my cat, clearly intrigued by the new smells, kept trying to climb onto the counter to investigate. Let's just say it was a battle of wits, and I'm still not sure who won!

And then there was the time I made lemon balm oil. The fresh, citrusy scent filled the house for weeks, making it smell like a summer garden. When my friend Sarah walked in, she took a deep breath, and said, "It smells like happiness in here!" That's when I knew I had found a new favourite. Creating your own essential oils is not just a process; it's an adventure. Each batch is a unique creation and never in my experience are two batches the same. They are infused with your energy and intention as much as they are by the herbs. Whether you're looking to enhance your dreams, calm your mind, or add a touch of magic to your daily routine, these oils offer endless possibilities. So, gather your herbs, set up your distiller, and let the alchemy begin. Who knows? You might just discover your own signature blend that becomes a cherished part of your magical practice. Happy distilling!

Building a Community of Witches

"Y'n unn, can dewines hwilas an gwyns, mes yn kettermyn, ni a gelwyr an donk."

"Alone, a witch can stir the winds, but together, we summon the storm"

Chapter 12 – Building a community of Green Witches

I hesitated joining a coven for a long time, unsure if it was the right path for me. Witchcraft, especially Green Witchcraft, had always been something deeply personal, something I practiced alone in my garden, tending to my herbs and aligning my energy with the rhythms of the earth. The idea of sharing that space with others felt almost too intimate, as if inviting others into my sacred connection with nature might somehow dilute it. However, the concept of being part of a coven wasn't entirely foreign to me. My mother and grandmother had both been part of covens in their time, though their experiences couldn't have been more different.

My grandmother's coven was something of a scandal in our family. To put it bluntly, her coven was a little… well, **racy**. It was a group that embraced the sensual side of magic, exploring the more passionate and uninhibited aspects of witchcraft. They were bold, unafraid to push boundaries, both magical and social. My grandmother always spoke of them with a kind of nostalgic affection, as though those nights spent dancing under the moonlight and indulging in wild rituals were among the best of her life. She would laugh as she recounted tales of the mischief they'd gotten into, the rituals that teetered on the edge of the forbidden, and the sheer thrill of being surrounded by women who embraced their power in such a raw, visceral way.
My mother, on the other hand, disapproved of it entirely. She loved her mother, of course, but she could never get behind what she saw as a coven that crossed too many lines. My mother was far more reserved, focused on the practical and healing aspects of witchcraft. She believed in magic, but to her, it was a tool to be used with restraint and respect. She viewed my grandmother's coven as reckless, even dangerous, in the way they blended magic with sensuality and risk. When I was growing up, she would occasionally make passing comments about "those women" and how they blurred the lines between magic and indulgence.

When my mother eventually joined a coven, it was the polar opposite of my grandmother's. Her group was quieter, more focused on study, healing, and the more traditional aspects of witchcraft. There was no dancing under the moon naked, no flirtations with the forbidden. It was a coven of wise women who valued subtlety and structure. For my mother, the coven was a place of learning and community, but it never quite carried the same spark of adventure that my grandmother's seemed to hold.

Growing up between these two very different influences made me feel unsure about where I would fit, or I suppose like most teenagers wondering if I fitted anywhere at all. On the one hand, I admired my mother's practicality and her deep knowledge of herbalism and healing. On the other, there was something undeniably alluring about the stories my grandmother told, about women who weren't afraid to embrace their power in every sense. But when it came to my own path, I found myself leaning more toward the quieter side of witchcraft, like my mother. I loved the earth, the plants, and the way magic seemed to hum through the natural world.

I loved the solace of being alone with my herbs, the gentle ritual of planting seeds, and the quiet transformation that took place in the cycles of growth and decay.

Yet, as the years passed, I began to feel that something was missing. I had grown confident in my practice, but there was a part of me that longed for connection, both with others and with the deeper mysteries of the craft. I wanted to know if there was more to this path than what I had discovered on my own. I wanted to feel the energy of a circle, to see if it truly amplified the magic as I had read. But I couldn't shake the tension between my mother's cautionary stance and my grandmother's wild stories.

Despite my reservations, I began to search for a coven that might suit me, one that was neither as tame as my mother's nor as wild as my grandmother's. It took time, but I eventually found a Green Witch coven that felt like the perfect balance. The women (and men) in this coven were deeply connected to nature, and their focus was on aligning with the natural world, working with herbs, plants, and the elements. There was a calmness to the group that immediately put me at ease, but there was also a sense of quiet power that I could feel beneath the surface, a recognition that nature, in all its beauty, can also be wild and untameable.

The first time I joined them for a ritual, I was nervous. I wasn't sure what to expect, and I still felt a bit guarded. But as the ritual began, any doubts I had melted away. It wasn't about losing myself in the group or following a rigid structure. It was about coming together, each of us bringing our own energy and intentions, and sharing in the collective power that arose from the earth beneath us. There was no pressure to conform, no one pushing the boundaries in a way that made me uncomfortable. It was exactly what I had been looking for, an opportunity to connect with others while still staying true to my own practice.

Over time, being part of this coven has deepened my relationship with the craft in ways I hadn't expected. One of the most profound experiences has been the **sense of community**. For so long, I had practiced alone, but now I realize how powerful it can be to share your journey with others. The women and men in my coven are almost like family to me now, each bringing their own unique wisdom and energy. We support each other, not just in magical work but in life. When one of us is struggling, the coven is there to offer healing, advice, and strength. When one of us succeeds, we all celebrate together.

The rituals we perform are deeply connected to the earth, reflecting the cycles of the seasons. In the spring, we plant intentions alongside our seedlings, watching them grow both in the garden and in our lives. In the summer, we gather herbs and hold festivals to celebrate abundance. In the autumn, we give thanks for the harvest and reflect on what we've learned throughout the year. And in winter, we turn inward, using the dark months for introspection and quiet magic.
But it's not just about the rituals, it's about the knowledge we share. Each person in the coven has their own area of expertise, whether it's herbalism, tarot, crystal healing, or energy work.

We learn from each other, and in doing so, we expand our own practices. It's a living, breathing community, always growing and evolving, just like nature itself.

There are also many professional skills in the coven, from lawyers, teachers, doctors, IT consultants, plumbers, decorators, event coordinators, you name it, if you need anything the coven will support its own.

The Importance of Community

Before joining this coven, I didn't fully understand the importance of being part of a witchcraft community. I thought my solitary practice was enough, and in many ways, it was. But now that I'm part of this group, I see how much stronger magic becomes when it's shared. There's something powerful about standing in a circle with others who share your values and your connection to the earth. The energy we raise together is palpable, and it amplifies everything we do, whether we're casting a spell, offering healing, or simply sitting in silence together.

Being part of a coven also gives me a sense of belonging that I hadn't realized I was missing, but I was. As witches, we often walk a path that's different from the mainstream, and that can feel isolating at times. But in this coven, I've found a group of people who understand me, who share my love of nature and my belief in the power of magic. We may come from different backgrounds and have different approaches, but we are united by our shared respect for the natural world and the magic that flows through it.

Finding a coven in the UK or the USA, or anywhere else in the world can be an exciting but sometimes daunting process, especially if you're new to witchcraft or looking to move from solitary practice into a more communal setting. Covens can offer incredible support, shared wisdom, and a sense of belonging. Whether you're looking for a traditional coven or something more modern like a Green Witch group, the key is to take your time, trust your instincts, and find the right fit for you.

Before you start your search, it's important to think about the kind of coven you want to join. Covens can vary greatly depending on their traditions, structure, and focus. Some are more formal, following traditional paths like Wicca, where there are specific rituals, hierarchies, and practices. Others may be more relaxed or eclectic, bringing together witches from various backgrounds who share a broader interest in witchcraft. You might be drawn to covens that focus on Green Witchcraft, Hedge Witchery, or Kitchen Witchery, or perhaps you're interested in a more ceremonial or ritual-based group. Knowing what you're looking for will help narrow down your options and guide you to a coven that aligns with your beliefs and practices.

In most countries metaphysical or witchcraft shops are often a great starting point. Many of these stores are community hubs where witches gather, share knowledge, and promote events.

The staff usually have a good sense of the local coven scene and can point you in the right direction. Ask if there are any upcoming events, open rituals, or gatherings where you can meet coven members or other solitary practitioners.

These shops often have bulletin boards with flyers advertising local covens, public circles, and study groups. In the USA, places like The Green Man in Los Angeles or Enchanted in Salem, Massachusetts are well-known hubs for the witchcraft community. In the UK, you might check out Treadwell's Books in London or The Witchcraft Emporium in Glastonbury.

Festivals and public gatherings offer a fantastic opportunity to meet coven members and learn about different traditions. Many covens use festivals as a way to recruit new members or invite interested individuals to attend open rituals. Some well-known events in the USA include Pagan Spirit Gathering, Sirius Rising. In the UK, popular festivals include Witchfest, organized by The Children of Artemis, and Pagan Pride UK events held in various cities. These gatherings provide a welcoming space where you can explore different practices and ask coven members about their groups.

The rise of the internet has made it much easier to find covens, especially in areas where witchcraft might not be openly practiced. Platforms like Meetup and Facebook groups allow covens to organize events and invite potential new members to open gatherings or study sessions. You can search for covens in your local area or specific types of groups, such as Wiccan covens, Green Witch communities, or eclectic groups.

Many covens, especially Wiccan ones, will host **open rituals** or **public circles** where anyone interested in learning more can attend. These gatherings give you a chance to meet the coven, observe their practices, and see if it feels like a good fit for you. In the UK, you might find open Sabbats or Esbats held at historic sites or in local parks, while in the USA, many covens hold events in nature reserves or community centres. Attending these public events is an excellent way to explore covens without the pressure of commitment.

Once you start connecting with covens or attending gatherings, it's important to trust your instincts. If something feels off, or if the group doesn't align with your personal beliefs and practices, it's okay to walk away and keep searching. A coven should feel like a supportive, welcoming community, where you feel safe and encouraged to grow in your craft. Avoid groups that try to pressure you into doing things that make you uncomfortable or that have overly rigid hierarchies.

If you can't find one – start your own.

"Živimos jekh čaximos, živel te dikh buti saste, katar o lav, te o baro."

"Making a living as a witch is like tending a garden, each sale, each spell, and each connection is a seed planted for the future"

Chapter 13 – Making a Living as a Witch

When I first started my journey as a Green Witch, I never imagined that my passion for nature and magic could become a sustainable way to earn money. To be fair, it's not my only job, but then lots of people have side hustles these days! I also write as a journalist on a local paper. So you can either say I'm moonlighting, or I have a "portfolio career" which sounds a bit rubbish. Over the years, I've found various avenues to share my knowledge and skills with others, each one deeply connected to my practice. Here's how I make money from each of these areas:

I began with selling herbs, which felt like a natural starting point for me as a Green Witch. My garden is my sanctuary, filled with a wide range of medicinal and magical herbs that I've carefully nurtured over the years. Growing these plants is more than just gardening; it's a spiritual practice. I connect with the earth and the energies of each herb, ensuring that they are grown with intention and care. This connection is important not just to me, but also to my customers. They know that the herbs I sell have been cultivated with love and respect for the natural world, which gives the products an extra layer of magic.

I sell my herbs both fresh and dried, depending on what the client needs. Some people come to me for herbs to use in their teas and tinctures, focusing on the medicinal qualities of the plants. Others seek herbs for spellwork, using them to craft sachets, incense, or candles. Then there are those who enjoy incorporating herbs into their cooking, especially when they know the ingredients have been grown organically and with a touch of magic. My herbs have a wide range of uses, and the versatility of the plants is one of the things that draws people to them.

As my herb sales grew, it felt like a natural progression to expand into herbal cosmetics, which has since become a thriving part of my business. Using the same herbs from my garden, I began creating natural products like creams, lotions, and bath oils, all infused with botanical magic. Each product is designed not only to nourish the body but to uplift the spirit. I blend my knowledge of herbalism with my magical practice, ensuring that these cosmetics are not just practical but also energetically potent. My customers love that the products are handmade, organic, and created with magical energy. They trust that what they're using on their skin has been crafted with care, both physically and spiritually, and that's what makes this part of my business so special.

The calendula and chamomile healing balm is one of my most popular products. Calendula, with its bright orange flowers, is well-known for its anti-inflammatory and skin-soothing properties. I blend it with chamomile, which is equally powerful as a calming agent for irritated skin. Together, these herbs work wonders on rashes, eczema, or dry patches. I infuse the herbs in olive oil for several weeks, allowing their properties to soak into the oil before blending it with beeswax to create a soft balm that's perfect for healing.

Another favourite is my lavender and rose face cream, which is both a beauty product and a magical tool. Lavender is famous for its calming and purifying properties, helping to balance the skin while also soothing the mind. Rose, on the other hand, is often associated with love and beauty. I combine an infusion of these two herbs with a base of almond oil and shea butter, resulting in a luxurious cream that leaves the skin soft and glowing. Many of my customers use this cream as part of their self-care ritual, applying it with the intention of nurturing not just their skin, but their emotional well-being.

I also craft a rosemary and mint hair lotion, perfect for stimulating the scalp and promoting hair growth. Rosemary has been used for centuries to strengthen hair follicles and enhance shine, while mint adds a refreshing element that awakens the senses and cools the scalp. The lotion is a simple blend of coconut oil infused with rosemary and mint, mixed with a little aloe vera to create a lightweight, refreshing treatment. Many people use it as a leave-in conditioner to nourish their hair while infusing it with the energetic properties of protection and clarity that rosemary and mint provide.

One of the most exciting products I've developed is a Sea Buckthorn hair growth salve, which has become a favourite among my customers looking to improve hair thickness and scalp health. The rich combination of vitamins, antioxidants, and fatty acids found in Sea Buckthorn makes it ideal for nourishing the scalp and stimulating hair follicles. The Omega-7 contents, in particular, is essential for cell regeneration, which promotes hair growth and strengthens the roots.
Over time, they've reported thicker, healthier hair, with many even noting that it has helped slow down hair thinning. The deep orange hue of the Sea Buckthorn oil gives the salve a warm, earthy appearance, but it washes out easily in the morning, leaving the hair soft and refreshed.

Sea Buckthorn also shines in post-tattoo care, thanks to its exceptional ability to reduce inflammation and promote skin healing. After getting a new tattoo, the skin can become inflamed, irritated, and prone to infection. This is where Sea Buckthorn's anti-inflammatory and antioxidant properties come into play, making it an ideal ingredient for a tattoo aftercare ointment.

I combine Sea Buckthorn oil with calendula and lavender, both of which are known for their soothing and healing properties. Calendula helps to calm the skin and prevent irritation, while lavender provides antiseptic benefits, keeping the tattooed area clean and aiding in the healing process. I then mix these oils with shea butter and beeswax to create a thick, protective layer that can be applied to the fresh tattoo. The ointment not only reduces redness and swelling but also helps enhance colour retention, ensuring that the tattoo remains vibrant as it heals.

Many of my customers who've used this ointment have reported that their tattoos healed faster and with less discomfort, and they noticed that the colours stayed brighter and sharper over time. This combination of healing and protective ingredients creates a product that supports both the skin's recovery and the preservation of the artwork itself. I have a healthy regular supply being ordered by tattoo shops around the country who buy little bottles which they sell on as a mark-up.

Finally, my sleep-inducing lavender, hops and mugwort bath oil has garnered a loyal following. Lavender, with its well-known calming properties, is the star of this blend, while mugwort adds a magical element, often used in dream work and intuitive practices. The hops are however the real magic ingredient, so look at the hops section earlier in the book. The combination helps to relax the body and open the mind before sleep, making it a favourite for those who practice lucid dreaming or want to enhance their psychic abilities during rest.

Next, I moved into crafting potions and spells. This allowed me to offer something more custom and unique. I make potions for a variety of purposes, from love and protection to abundance and healing. Additionally, I create spell kits, complete with instructions, crystals, herbs, and candles, for those who prefer to perform their own rituals but need guidance. These kits, along with my custom spells, have been a great way to connect with clients who are just beginning their magical practice.

In addition to physical products, I offer tarot readings and consultations. People come to me for advice not only on their spiritual journeys but also for help with everyday problems like career changes, relationships, or health concerns. These one-on-one sessions have proven to be deeply rewarding, as I can help people connect with their inner selves and provide them with clarity. It's also a great complement to my work crafting potions and spells because many consultations lead to custom magical work.

Teaching has also become an essential part of my practice. I host workshops on various topics like herbalism, spell crafting, and creating smudging sticks. I've also expanded into creating online courses, which allows me to reach a broader audience. Teaching people how to work with plants and magic has been one of the most fulfilling aspects of my career.

I love connecting with people in person as well, which is why I offer gardening tours. Walking clients through my herb garden, I teach them about the medicinal and magical properties of each plant. I've even had clients hire me for custom garden design, helping them create their own magical gardens at home. I find joy in seeing others cultivate a connection with nature.

Writing is another way I share my knowledge. I've published a few pamphlets on Green Witchcraft, herbal magic, and spellwork, which has provided another source of income. Obviously now I'm writing my first book. I've also just started to embrace social media and YouTube, where I intend to share tips, tutorials, and insights about witchcraft and herbalism. Monetizing these platforms through sponsorships, ads, and even Patreon support will hopefully be incredibly helpful in sustaining my work.

I also run a subscription box service, where I curate monthly magical kits filled with herbs, spell ingredients, and tools, and I make wands, smudging sticks, and other handmade magical tools. These items are always in demand, especially during the holidays.

Lastly, I organize retreats and nature walks, guiding groups through forests to teach them about foraging and Green Witchcraft. These events are immersive experiences, where participants can connect deeply with nature. For those who want more personal guidance, I offer Green Witch mentorship, working with individuals to develop their practice.

Chapter 14 The Apothecary Almanac

Magical Properties: Healing, Wound & Burn Healing, Anti-Inflammatory, Hydration

Culinary: Aloe Vera gel can be blended into smoothies, enhancing hydration, digestion, and overall wellness.

Cultivation: Ensure Aloe Vera gets bright, indirect sunlight, well-drained soil, and occasional deep watering

Magical Properties: Love, Peace, Fertility, Happiness, Renewal, Beauty, Healing, Rejuvenation, Heart Health

Culinary: Apple Blossom can be infused in teas, syrups, or smoked for calming effects.

Cultivation: Choose well-drained soil, plant grafted saplings, water regularly, prune annually.

Magical Properties: Protection, Love, Prosperity, Purification, Courage, Anti-inflammatory, Antibacterial

Culinary: Basil leaves can be dried and smoked to promote relaxation and mental clarity.

Cultivation: Plant in well-drained soil, provide full sun, water regularly, prune frequently.

The Witch's Botanical Apothecary

Magical Properties: Protection, Purification, Healing, Strength, Prosperity, Wound Healing, Wisdom.

Culinary: Bay Laurel leaves can be infused in milk for unique, aromatic dessert custards.

Cultivation: Plant in well-drained soil, provide full sun, and regularly prune.

Magical Properties: Healing, Protection, Courage, Love, Antibacterial, Antiviral, Digestive Aid, Calmness.

Culinary: Bee Balm petals can be candied for desserts, adding floral flavor and vibrant colour

Cultivation: Plant in well-drained soil, full sun, water regularly, prune.

Magical Properties: Protection, Healing, Strength, Vitality, Fertility Antioxidant, Blood-Cleansing.

Culinary: Blackberry berries can be infused into balsamic vinegar for a tangy, sweet salad dressing.

Cultivation: Well-drained soil, provide full sun, support with trellises

Magical Properties: Strength, Boundaries, Healing, Endurance, Resilience, Cleansing, Prosperity.

Culinary: Blackthorn leaves blended with mint create a refreshing herbal tea for digestive health.

Cultivation: Blackthorn thrives in well-drained soil, requires full sun, and tolerates neglect.

Magical Properties: Courage, Protection, Healing, Purification, Strength, Hormonal Balance.

Culinary: Borage blended with mint creates a refreshing herbal ice cream, enhancing cooling effects.

Cultivation: Sow seeds directly outdoors in spring, ensuring well-drained soil and sunlight.

Magical Properties: Sweetness, Healing, Love, Purification, Anti-inflammatory, Blood Sugar Balance,

Culinary: Candy Leaf can be infused into vodka, creating a sweet, herbaceous cocktail base.

Cultivation: Grows best in well-drained soil, partial shade, and regular watering.

Magical Properties: Healing, Purification, Sleep, Anti-inflammatory, Soothing, Relaxation, Peace, Balance.

Culinary: Chamomile can be infused into honey for unique candies, promoting relaxation

Cultivation: Sow seeds in well-drained soil, full sun, and regular watering.

Magical Properties: Abundance, Healing, Protection, Nourishment, Immunity, Age Regeneration,

Culinary: Chanterelles add earthy sweetness to savory pies, enhancing flavor with their delicate apricot notes.

Cultivation: Chanterelles thrive in well-drained soil, with shade, moisture, and symbiotic trees

Magical Properties: Love, Protection, Divination, Antioxidant, Skin Soothing, Anti-aging, Fertility.

Culinary: Cherries, when blended with sage and thyme, create a unique savory pie filling.

Cultivation: Plant in well-drained soil, provide full sun, water regularly, and prune annually

Magical Properties: Purification, Clarity, Digestive Aid, Headache Relief, Wound Healing, Balance.

Culinary: Costmary leaves can be used to flavor homemade beers, desserts, and herbal liqueurs.

Cultivation: Thrives in well-drained soil, prefers partial shade, and requires regular watering.

Magical Properties: Healing, Youthfulness, Love, Sleep, Skin-soothing, Pain relief, Respiratory aid,

Culinary: Cowslip flowers can be candied or infused into wine for a delicate flavor.

Cultivation: Prefers well-drained soil, partial shade, and regular moisture.

Magical Properties: Fertility, Purification, Detoxification, Pain Relief, Respiratory Aid, Cleansing.

Culinary: Avoid using in culinary dishes

Cultivation: Prefers moist, shady areas; propagate via rhizomes. (underground stems)

Magical Properties: Obsession, Love, Passion, Lust, Divination, Aphrodisiac, Relaxation, Dreamwork.

Culinary: Damiana leaves can be infused into a lip balm, passing its magical properties upon kissing.

Cultivation: Thrives in well-drained soil, full sunlight, and moderate watering.

Magical Properties: Healing, Strength, Resilience, Detoxification, Abundance, Digestive Aid, Energy

Culinary: Dandelion leaves can be sautéed and used in salads for a unique, nutritious flavor boost

Cultivation: Thrives in well-drained soil, full sun, and regular watering.

Magical Properties: Manifestation, Clairvoyance, Love, Summoning, Manipulation, Divination, Banishing

Culinary: Avoid using in culinary dishes

Cultivation: Thrives in well-drained soil, full sun, and regular watering.

Magical Properties: Healing, Immunity, Protection, Strength, Vitality, Antiviral, Purification, Recovery

Culinary: Echinacea petals can be infused into honey, creating a flavorful remedy for colds

Cultivation: Sow seeds in well-drained soil, full sun, and regular watering.

Magical Properties: Healing, Immunity, Purification, Antiviral, Prosperity, Rejuvenation, Spirituality.

Culinary: Try Elderberry Kombucha, a fermented tea spiced with vanilla and ginger

Cultivation: Thrive in well-drained soil, full sun, and regular watering.

Magical Properties: Headache Relief, Purification, Calm, Migraine Prevention, Spiritual Clarity, Pain Relief

Culinary: Feverfew can be infused into wine, enhancing flavor while easing headaches and inflammation

Cultivation: Needs well-drained soil, full sun, and regular watering.

Magical Properties: Healing, Purification, Repelling, Antiseptic, Wound-Healing, Calming, Cleansing.

Culinary: Avoid using in culinary dishes

Cultivation: Prefers well-drained soil, partial shade, and regular watering

Magical Properties: Purification, Strength, Healing, Cleansing, Anti-Inflammatory, Circulation, Fertility.

Culinary: French parsley can be blended into pestos, enhancing flavor and adding vibrant green colour.

Cultivation: Plant in well-drained soil, provide sunlight, water regularly

Magical Properties: Lust, Energy, Vitality, Cleansing, Strength, Power, Obsession, Entrapment

Culinary: Avoid using in culinary dishes

Cultivation: Thrives in well-drained, sandy soil; prefers sunny locations.

Magical Properties: Lactation, Fertility, Protection, Blood Sugar, Diuretic, Detoxification, Strength

Culinary: Goat's Rue can be used in herbal teas to enhance lactation and promote digestive health

Cultivation: Prefers well-drained, loamy soil with moderate moisture. Cultivate in sunny areas.

Magical Properties: Fertility, Immunity, Anti-inflammatory, Antioxidant, Entrapment

Culinary: Combine tart gooseberries with thyme and rosemary to create a flavourful sauce for steak or lamb.

Cultivation: Gooseberries thrive in well-drained, loamy soil with good sunlight.

Magical Properties: Immunity, Healing, Protection, Grounding, Strength, Anti-Inflammatory, Vitality.

Culinary: Hen of the Woods pairs beautifully with rosemary and lemon for a fragrant pasta dish.

Cultivation: Hen of the Woods prefers moist, rich, well-drained soil with high organic matter.

Hop Vines

Magical Properties: Dreamwork, Hallucination, Sedative, Divination, Past Life Regression, Nightmares

Culinary: Hop flowers add a unique floral bitterness to stews, enhancing flavor and aroma profiles.

Cultivation: Prefer well-drained, loamy soil with good organic matter.

Horseradish

Magical Properties: Revenge, Courage, Strength, Antioxidant, Circulation, Manipulation, Deception

Culinary: Horseradish makes a zesty marinade for meats, enhancing flavor with its bold, spicy kick.

Cultivation: Prefers well-drained, loamy soil and full sunlight for optimal growth.

Hyssop

Magical Properties: Blessing, Antiseptic, Expectorant, Digestive Aid, Detoxification, Truth Forcing

Culinary: Hyssop adds a unique flavor to potato soup, enhancing richness with garlic and cream.

Cultivation: Thrives in well-drained, sandy loam soil with full sunlight.

Magical Properties: Fertility, Love, Purification, Protection, Astringent, Diuretic, Antispasmodic,

Culinary: Leaves can be infused in tea with honey, creating a sweet drink that enhances intimacy.

Cultivation: Thrives in well-drained, sandy loam soil with moderate moisture

Magical Properties: Anti-Septic, Peace, Anti-inflammatory, Relaxation, Sleep Aid, Stress Relief,

Culinary: Lavender can be infused into birch sap or sparkling water for a refreshing tonic

Cultivation: Prefers well-drained, sandy or gravelly soil with full sunlight

Magical Properties: Healing, Calm, Protection, Clarity, Love, Antiviral, Sleep Aid, Stress Relief, Purification.

Culinary: Lemon balm soup, blended with chicken broth, garlic, and cream, offers a refreshing twist.

Cultivation: Grow in well-drained, loamy soil with full sun

Magical Properties: Healing, Clarity, Protection, Antibacterial, Calming, Detoxifying, Energizing,

Culinary: Lemongrass can be infused into rice for a fragrant, zesty flavor and aromatic dish.

Cultivation: Grows in well-drained, loamy soil with full sun.

Magical Properties: Cognitive Boost, Memory, Focus, Spiritual Growth, Nerve Repair, Healing, Clarity

Culinary: Lion's Mane mushrooms sautéed in sherry create a unique, flavorful sauce for pasta dishes.

Cultivation: Thrives in hardwood sawdust, prefers moist, well-drained soil

Magical Properties: Emotional Balance Healing, Clarity, Purification, Fertility, Anti-inflammatory,

Culinary: Avoid using in culinary dishes

Cultivation: Prefers well-drained, sandy soil and full sun.

Magical Properties: Love, Strength, Purification, Anti-inflammatory, Antiseptic, Soothing, Fertility, Courage.

Culinary: Marigold flowers can be infused into butter, enhancing bread with a floral, zesty essence.

Cultivation: thrive in well-drained, loamy soil with full sun exposure, needing 6-8 hours daily.

Magical Properties: Love, Purification, Pain Relief, Fever Reduction, Summoning

Culinary: Mix Meadowsweet flowers into bread dough during the dough preparation. Tastes wonderful.

Cultivation: Meadowsweet thrives in moist, rich, well-drained soil; prefers partial shade.

Magical Properties: Healing, Protection, Clarity, Purification, Energy, Cooling, Soothing, Revitalization.

Culinary: Mint can be infused into oils, adding fresh flavour to dressings and marinades.

Cultivation: Mint thrives in well-drained, rich soil; use containers to prevent spreading

Magical Properties: Protection, Vitality, Immunity, Detoxification, Grounding, Regeneration, Strength.

Culinary: Morels can be used to create a rich, flavourful cream sauce with bourbon for gourmet pasta dishes.

Cultivation: Well-drained, sandy loam with organic matter, near elm, ash, oak and apple trees

Magical Properties: Protection, Healing, Intuition, Dreamwork, Purification, Divination, Relaxant,

Culinary: Mugwort can be infused into semolina for enhancing flavour.

Cultivation: Well-drained, loamy soil with full sun exposure.

Magical Properties: Protection, Courage, Respiratory Aid, Lung Support, Soothing, Exorcism, Grounding.

Culinary: Mullein and Coltsfoot are often smoked to soothe respiratory issues and promote relaxation.

Cultivation: Mullein prefers well-drained, sandy loam; Coltsfoot thrives in moist, rich soil.

Magical Properties: Purification, Prosperity, Antiviral, Digestive, Immune-Boosting, Clarity, Binding

Culinary: Oregano can be infused into oils, enhancing flavour while providing antimicrobial benefits.

Cultivation: Oregano thrives in well-drained, sandy loam soil with full sun exposure.

Magical Properties: Fertility, Abundance, Digestion, Antioxidant, Immune-Boosting, Nourishment.

Culinary: Pumpkin can be blended into smoothies with spices, creating a unique, creamy, autumn-inspired drink.

Cultivation: Pumpkins thrive in well-drained, loamy soil rich in organic matter.

Magical Properties: Protection, Love, Fertility, Cleansing, Antioxidant, Immunity, Rejuvenation.

Culinary: Raspberries marinated in ground steak overnight create a fruity base for Shepherds Pie

Cultivation: Thrive in well-drained, loamy soil, requiring organic matter and consistent moisture.

Magical Properties: Clarity, Detoxification, Immune-Boosting, Calming, Anti-Inflammatory, Vitality.

Culinary: Romanesco can be finely chopped and used as a unique, colourful pizza topping alternative

Cultivation: Prefers well-drained, nutrient-rich soil, with pH around 6.0-7.0

Magical Properties: Memory, Healing, Love, Courage, Antioxidant, Antimicrobial, Circulation, Obsession

Culinary: Rosemary-infused ice cream provides a unique flavour complexity.

Cultivation: Well-drained, sandy soil; prefers slightly alkaline pH; requires moderate nutrients

Magical Properties: Love, Healing, Protection, Beauty, Peace, Attraction, Soothing, Rejuvenation, Hex Breaking

Culinary: Rose petal ice cubes, adds a floral touch to cocktails.

Cultivation: well-drained, loamy soil rich in organic matter. Consider well-rotted cow manure

Magical Properties: Divination, Courage, Strength, Insight, Detoxification, Vitality, Clarity, Purification.

Culinary: Avoid using in culinary dishes unless have experienced guidance. Must be cooked

Cultivation: Thrive in well-drained, acidic soil with regular watering and full sun

Magical Properties: Wisdom, Healing, Clarity, Cleansing, Prosperity, Purification, Protection, Summoning

Culinary: Complements mushroom or chicken risotto, providing earthy undertones.

Cultivation: Prefers well-drained, sandy soil; enrich with coconut coir or composted bark

Magical Properties: Longevity, Regeneration, Protection, Restoration, Immunity, Strength

Culinary: Drizzle Sea Buckthorn sauce over cheesecake for an eye-catching presentation and a zesty contrast.

Cultivation: High tolerance for salt spray, well-drained, sandy or loamy soil, requiring full sun

Magical Properties: Immunity, Cleansing, Rejuvenation, Detoxification, Banishing

Culinary: Use birch sap in marinades for fish or tofu - a light and sweet flavor. Avoid bark and leaves

Cultivation: Thrives in well-drained, sandy or loamy soil; prefers slightly acidic nutrients.

Magical Properties: Pain Relief, Fever Reduction, Detoxification, Stamina, Truth Forcing

Culinary: Avoid using in culinary dishes

Cultivation: Loamy soil with mix of peat, composted bark and well-rotted manure

Magical Properties: Abundance, Fertility, Antioxidant, Digestive, Longevity, Strength, Obsession

Culinary: Serve roasted chestnuts alongside cheeses, dried fruits, and nuts on a cheese board

Cultivation: Well-drained, loamy soil rich in organic matter. Apply a layer of organic mulch around the base

Magical Properties: Courage, Purification, Cleansing, Antiseptic, Antibacterial, Binding.

Culinary: Pair thyme with scrambled eggs, omelets, or frittatas for added flavor.

Cultivation: Thrives in well-drained, sandy soil; prefers full sun and minimal watering

Magical Properties: Protection, Courage, Healing, Purification, Clarity, Inflammation, Wound-Healing

Culinary: Avoid using in culinary dishes unless have experienced guidance

Cultivation: Thrives in well-drained, sandy soil; requires full sun, regular watering. Add magnesium and calcium

Magical Properties: Love, Sleep, Dreams, Calming, Heling, Purification, Innocence

Culinary: Vervain can be used in custards offering a light floral note in desserts like panna cotta or ice cream.

Cultivation: Prefers well-drained, loamy soil enriched with organic matter and regular watering

Magical Properties: Wisdom, Abundance, Healing, Brain Health, Heart Health, Fertility, Endurance

Culinary: Blend walnuts into sauces like romesco or dips like walnut pesto or hummus for a unique twist.

Cultivation: Well-drained, loamy soil; full sun; regular watering; organic matter enriches growth

Magical Properties: Protection, Intuition, Emotional Balance, Pain Relief, Wisdom, Grief Support.

Culinary: Willow bark can be used in **small** quantities to add depth to fruit jams or preserves. Caution.

Cultivation: Thrive in areas with abundant water; roots are adapted to absorb large amounts of moisture

Magical Properties: Astringent, Anti-Inflammatory, Soothing, Antiseptic, Wound-Healing, Clarity.

Culinary: Avoid using in culinary dishes unless have experienced guidance. Caution

Cultivation: Thrives in well-drained, loamy soil; prefers partial shade; requires consistent moisture

www.ingramcontent.com/pod-product-compliance
Lightning Source LLC
Chambersburg PA
CBHW081614100526
44590CB00021B/3429